Lenin and the Logic of Hegemony

Historical Materialism Book Series

The Historical Materialism Book Series is a major publishing initiative of the radical left. The capitalist crisis of the twenty-first century has been met by a resurgence of interest in critical Marxist theory. At the same time, the publishing institutions committed to Marxism have contracted markedly since the high point of the 1970s. The Historical Materialism Book Series is dedicated to addressing this situation by making available important works of Marxist theory. The aim of the series is to publish important theoretical contributions as the basis for vigorous intellectual debate and exchange on the left.

The peer-reviewed series publishes original monographs, translated texts, and reprints of classics across the bounds of academic disciplinary agendas and across the divisions of the left. The series is particularly concerned to encourage the internationalization of Marxist debate and aims to translate significant studies from beyond the English-speaking world.

For a full list of titles in the Historical Materialism Book Series available in paperback from Haymarket Books, visit:
www.haymarketbooks.org/category/hm-series

Lenin and the Logic of Hegemony

Political Practice and Theory in the Class Struggle

By
Alan Shandro

Haymarket Books
Chicago, IL

First published in 2014 by Brill Academic Publishers, The Netherlands
© 2014 Koninklijke Brill NV, Leiden, The Netherlands

Published in paperback in 2015 by
Haymarket Books
P.O. Box 180165
Chicago, IL 60618
773-583-7884
www.haymarketbooks.org

ISBN: 978-1-60846-483-8

Trade distribution:
In the US, Consortium Book Sales, www.cbsd.com
In Canada, Publishers Group Canada, www.pgcbooks.ca
In the UK, Turnaround Publisher Services, www.turnaround-uk.com
In all other countries, Publishers Group Worldwide, www.pgw.com

Cover design by Ragina Johnson.

This book was published with the generous support of
Lannan Foundation and the Wallace Global Fund.

10 9 8 7 6 5 4 3 2 1

Library of Congress Cataloging-in-Publication data is available.

In memory of Charles Nunn

Contents

Acknowledgements   x

1 **A Philosophical Fact: Hegemony in the Class Struggle**   1
   Gramscian Hegemony and Lenin   3
   The Post-Marxist Deconstruction of Hegemony   10
   Lenin as Symbol   17
   Hegemony in the Philosophy of Lenin's Politics   22
   The Thread of the Argument   24

2 **On the Relation of Theory and Practice: Karl Kautsky and the First Post-Marxist**   32
   Orthodoxy and Apostasy   33
   'Critical Marxism' and Orthodoxy   37
   The Agrarian Prelude   44
   The First Post-Marxist   47
   The Rejoinder   53
   Theory and Consciousness   59
   History   62
   Science   64
   Workers and Intellectuals   66
   Politics and Epistemology   69
   Practice and Theory   72
   Political Will and the Party   75
   Theory in a Community of Struggle   77

3 **Situating Marxism in Russia: Ambiguous Coordinates**   80
   Karl Marx and the Russian Commune   81
   Georgii Plekhanov and the Transformation of Russian Society   87
   Forces of Revolution and the Problem of Hegemony   92
   Intellectuals, Consciousness and Hegemony   95
   Lenin and Marxist Orthodoxy   100
   Class Struggle in the Democratic Revolution   103
   Hegemony as Socialist Consciousness   108

4 **Marxism, Lenin and the Logic of Hegemony: Spontaneity and Consciousness in the Class Struggle**   115
   Conventional Wisdom   116
   Historical Questions   124

Political Questions   128
An 'Irreconcilable Antagonism ... to the Whole'   131
A Logic of Political Struggle   135
A Strategic Analysis   138
Some Implications   144

5   **Dogmatism and Criticism: Freedom in the Class Struggle**   149
The Argument About Freedom   150
The Argument About Theory   156

6   **Two Orientations to Hegemony: Mensheviks and Bolsheviks**   164
The *Iskra* Consensus and its Limits   167
The Congress and the Split   173
Menshevism and Hegemony   180
Rosa Luxemburg's Critique   185
Lenin and the Logic of Factional Struggle   187
Two Orientations to Hegemony   193
From Orientation to Revolution   197

7   **The Mechanics of Proletarian Hegemony: Solidarity in the Class Struggle**   201
An Alliance of Workers and Peasants   207
Class Alliance in Theory and Practice   213
Proletarian Hegemony and Historical Materialism   217
Proletarian Hegemony and Peasant Ideology   220
'Permanent Revolution'   225
The Advent of the Soviets   233
Lenin's Intervention   237
The Spontaneous Movement and Hegemony   240
Theory and Practice in the Struggle for Hegemony   246

8   **Imperialism and the Logic of Hegemony: The 'People' in the Class Struggle**   250
The War and the Split in Socialism   250
A Hegelian Epiphany?   252
'Kautskyism' and the Highest Stage of Capitalism   257
Parasitism and Social Decay   263
'Imperialist Economism'   267
The State and the Logic of Revolution   272
The Logic of Revolution and Hegemony   279
A People's Revolution   285

9 The Arm of Criticism and the Criticism of Arms: Courage in the Class Struggle   289
Class Struggle and the Rule of Law   291
Class Power and Political Form   297
Class Struggle and Political Community   301
Community and Class Consciousness   307
Class Consciousness and Courage   311

10 A Modern Prince to Discourses of Resistance ... and Back?   315
From Empire to Commonwealth?   317
The Modern Prince and the 'Discourses'   322
Prince and People   326

Appendices
1 Karl Kautsky, 'The Revision of the Austrian Social Democratic Programme'   330
2 Text and Context in the Argument of Lenin's *What Is to Be Done?*   346
3 Lenin as a Reader of *What Is to Be Done?*   359

Bibliography   363
Index   381

Acknowledgements

For encouragement and/or for insight, for suggestions and/or for criticism, for solidarity and/or for resistance, for an opinion or for an example, written or lived, thanks are due to Ed Andrew, to Etienne Balibar, to Clive Bass, to Julie Bass, to Frances Bernstein, to 'Robert Boarts', to Tibby Brooks, to Jenny Clegg, to Jim Gardiner, to Norman Geras, to Danny Goldstick, to John Herman, to Pepita Herrandiz, to John Paul Himka, to Paul Kelemen, to Kim Krawchenko, to David Laibman, to Robert Linhart, to Ralph Marion, to Dave Mather, to Yassamine Mather, to David McLellan, to Alain Noël, to Charles Nunn, to Tom Pocklington, to James Rees, to Chris Roberts, to Maggie Scammell, to Sukumar, to Geoff Waite, to Michelle Weber, to Kirsty Wright and to the editors of *Science & Society*.

Thanks are due to John Paul Himka for assistance with translation from the German; thanks are due to Craig Brandist, to Aurélie Lacassagne and to Lars Lih for advice on translations from the Russian and to Craig Brandist for advice on transliteration from the Cyrillic.

The comments of two anonymous readers were helpful in identifying ellipses in the line of thought and ambiguities in the text; a conversation and subsequent correspondence with Peter Thomas shed some timely light on how the argument might be more effectively framed; Sarah Grey provided insightful advice, probably too little heeded, as to how the argument might be more clearly and accessibly stated. Thanks to them and thanks to Sébastien Budgen who invited me to consider publishing the project.

I would like to think that the book also owes something to two philosophers whose ways of thinking I have pondered over and tried to ponder with, Louis Althusser and Alasdair MacIntyre.

The book was written alongside Daryl Shandro, who helped me think through the argument. Thanks to her and thanks to Sarah, to Craig, to Stephen, to Anna Lisa and to Ella who taught me much about how to take the measure of it.

Alan Shandro
August 2013
Havre-aux-Maisons, Québec

CHAPTER 1

A Philosophical Fact: Hegemony in the Class Struggle

> Everything is political, even philosophy or philosophies... and the only 'philosophy' is history in action... It is in this sense that one can interpret the thesis of the German proletariat as the heir of German philosophy – and one can affirm that the theorisation and realisation of hegemony carried out by Ilich [Lenin] was also a great '[anti-]metaphysical' event.
> – ANTONIO GRAMSCI[1]

∴

> The proposition... that men acquire consciousness of structural conflicts on the level of ideologies should be considered as an affirmation of epistemological and not simply psychological and moral value. From this, it follows that the theoretical-practical principle of hegemony has also epistemological significance, and it is here that Ilich's greatest theoretical contribution to the philosophy of praxis should be sought. In these terms one could say that Ilich advanced philosophy as philosophy in so far as he advanced political doctrine and practice. The realisation of a hegemonic apparatus, in so far as it creates a new ideological terrain, determines a reform of consciousness and of methods of knowledge: it is a fact of knowledge, a philosophical fact.
> – ANTONIO GRAMSCI[2]

∴

The aim of this book is to trace the contours of the '[anti-]metaphysical event' Gramsci signalled, the emergence of hegemony in Lenin's theory and practice,

---

1 Gramsci 1929–35, p. 357. The interpolation '[anti-]metaphysical' is, to be sure, an interpretation, but it seemed less misleading to insert it in view of a widespread sense among Marxists of a philosophical bent that metaphysics is properly understood as the opposite of dialectics. (See, for example, the statement by Plekhanov that serves as the epigraph for Chapter 3.)
2 Gramsci 1929–35, pp. 365–6.

and thus to throw some light upon the kind of 'philosophical fact' it represents. If the argument of the book is thus inevitably historical, it does not aim to be genealogical. That is, while I don't shy away from the occasional parallel between Leninist insight and Gramscian formulation, I am not trying to rediscover Gramsci in Lenin and so make no attempt at a systematic or even extensive comparison. If the argument is historical, it is not, I hope, a history of ideas but of something like an '[anti-]metaphysical event', something like a shift in the relation between theory and practice that establishes a 'philosophical fact', a practical-conceptual field, open to analysis of the nuances of the relation of leadership and hence of political agency, a field in which consciousness and spontaneity, vanguard(s) and movement(s), play different, potentially complementary but sometimes essentially contradictory parts in the class struggle. The very weight of organised numbers in motion, of the masses, can lead to the emergence of unforeseen political forces, possibilities and positions. But a position staked out today can always be invested and transformed tomorrow in accordance with the strategic calculation of an adversary. So the struggle for hegemony presumes the ability to adapt to the changing conjunctures of political struggle, to combine awareness of the underlying forces that shape the logic of struggle with openness to the ways in which different, and differently situated, actors can innovate in the struggle. Leadership in the class struggle thus demands a consciousness open to the struggles of the masses, yet willing, where necessary, to counterpose its own political analyses to their spontaneous movement. It might be objected that this opposition between leader and led simply provides a sophisticated rationale for minority – Jacobin – dictatorship. But this objection would be persuasive only if the concepts and distinctions that inform Lenin's approach to leadership and to political agency did not afford a superior analysis of the logic of class struggle. The question of the truth of the analysis is, in this sense, unavoidable. And if Lenin's analysis does illuminate the logic and dynamics of class struggles, then the real question is the one posed by Gramsci: 'In the formation of leaders, one premise is fundamental: is it the intention that there should always be rulers and ruled, or is the objective to create the conditions in which this division is no longer necessary?'[3]

The notion of hegemony first gained currency in the English-speaking world in the 1960s and 1970s through the influence of Gramsci's *Prison Notebooks*. This was in large measure because it seemed to represent the possibility of combining clarity of analysis with some explanatory depth – and thus to afford a measure of intellectual discipline – in the study of processes whereby the exploited

---

3   Gramsci 1929–35, p. 144.

are constituted ideologically and politically as subaltern and consequently also those whereby they may come, in turn, to assert their own hegemony, disrupting and even overturning the constitution of domination-and-subordination and the bases of exploitation. The notion of hegemony thus served to designate a terrain where the logic of political strategy and leadership intersects the practical – economic, cultural and pedagogical – organisation of everyday life, a terrain that was then befogged by broad-brush deployments of 'false consciousness' when it was not simply spirited away by the magic of social-scientific positivism. The assumptions that enter into the conduct of social actors are to be understood not as simple givens of experience, but as shaped by a logic of struggle, directly by clashes of ideas, less directly perhaps – but no less importantly – by struggles over the structure of the social relations, institutions and practices that sustain – or fail to sustain – the assumptions of our lived relation to our world. The contradictions of common sense, always an uneven amalgam of practical wisdom and myth, have their roots and their possible resolution in these struggles. Although the terrain of hegemonic struggle has been staked out in a number of works of historical materialist scholarship, a couple of decades of postmodern mischief have done much to throw this work of exploration, and with it the notion of hegemony itself, into clichéd obscurity. And insofar as it comes to inform the actions of those engaged in struggle, the concept of hegemony may itself become an object of and a stake in that struggle.

Gramscian Hegemony and Lenin

That Gramsci himself traced the roots of the notion of hegemony to Lenin is reasonably well known and has informed some useful discussions of Gramsci's conception.[4] The protean influence of this conception in contemporary political and cultural criticism has, however, generated no sustained attempt to track the emergence of the '[anti-]metaphysical event' in Lenin's theory and practice and thereby to clarify the nature of the 'philosophical fact' it represents. Although a cursory check of the reference index to the English translation of Lenin's *Collected Works* turns up half a page of incidences of the term 'hegemony', the editors of *Selections from the Prison Notebooks* express perplexity that Gramsci should have assigned responsibility for the construction of the concept – its theorisation as well as its realisation – to Lenin, since, conflating concepts with words, they opine that 'the word hegemony as such

---

4 See Buci-Glucksmann 1975 and Thomas 2009.

does not figure prominently in Lenin's work'.[5] Apparently, Gramsci's reference point is Lenin's practice, not his theory; Lenin was a practitioner of hegemony, in need of a theorist. Similarly, although in his influential essay on the strategic implications of Gramsci's political thought, Perry Anderson references passages where Lenin asserts the indispensability of the idea of hegemony to the workers' consciousness of themselves as a class, he construes the significance of hegemony in Lenin's thought narrowly, as nothing more than a strategic orientation within the bourgeois-democratic revolution, dispensed with (and hence obviously dispensable) once Bolshevik strategy and practice were reoriented in 1917 towards a socialist revolution: '[f]orged to theorise the role of the working class in a bourgeois revolution, it was rendered inoperative by the advent of a socialist revolution'.[6] Again, although Gramsci did indeed trace the concept of hegemony to Lenin, Ernesto Laclau and Chantal Mouffe, in their *Hegemony and Socialist Strategy*, hardly draw at all upon Lenin himself in explicating the Leninist concept of hegemony that is the foil for their own concept. Although the *Prison Notebooks* sharply contrasts the Bolshevik understanding of hegemony both to Trotsky's approach to permanent revolution and to the orthodox Marxism of the Second International, Laclau and Mouffe see fit to trace the logic of its evolution in Russian Marxism with primary reference not to Lenin, but to Trotsky and Plekhanov, at one time – albeit from very different stances – the two foremost Marxist critics of the Bolshevik strategy of proletarian hegemony in the bourgeois-democratic revolution.[7] There is, finally, to my knowledge, no reflection in the literature on hegemony upon the fact that it could be characterised, during Lenin's lifetime, as the central idea of Leninism by no less prominent a Bolshevik than Grigorii Zinoviev – no longer much esteemed as a theorist, to be sure, and arguably self-serving, but, more significant in the present connection, both intimately familiar with Lenin and his work and head of the Communist International during Gramsci's sojourn in Russia.[8]

Indeed, where Gramsci's reference to Lenin is not simply circumvented, the sense of Gramscian hegemony is oriented, according to the conventional wisdom even of Western Marxist scholars, by means of a contrast with Leninist dictatorship, as consent versus coercion, spontaneity from below versus conscious control from above, democracy versus dictatorship. Here Jeremy Lester's *Dialogue of Negation* may stand in for a broad spectrum of

---

5   Hoare and Nowell-Smith 1971, p. 381n.
6   Anderson 1976, p. 17.
7   See Laclau and Mouffe 1985, pp. 48–54.
8   See Zinoviev 1923, pp. 216–21.

interpretation. Lester identifies the notion of consent as pivotal – 'in its optimal form, hegemony is primarily a means for acquiring the consent of the masses through their self-organisation in a range of activities and institutions situated within civil society' – and the struggle for hegemony as the formation of 'a national-popular will... which binds together a historical bloc of forces'.[9] Relations of power are understood as broadly diffused rather than concentrated in the state apparatuses and the task of mediating these relations as correlatively devolved throughout society as a whole. The state, shaped by responsibilities of a universalising and hence an ethical character, is not merely the organisation of repression but also an organisation of constructive consensus. Thus, in an effective challenge to hegemonic rule, the spontaneous feelings of the masses must be transcended in a more authentic consciousness and new active and expansive forms of consent instantiated in popular forms of participation. This supposes an expansive form of party politics where unity emerges from multiplicity only 'through the friction of the individual members' and action is grounded in the everyday lived experience of the participants; it supposes a broader 'counter-hegemonic historical bloc' where active forms of consent are derived not through co-optation and assimilation, but only through 'a genuine process of interest articulation'.[10]

Once the concept of hegemony is thus interpreted through the notion of consent and the contrast between coercion and consent, it is all too easy to abstract Lenin's deployment of the concept from the context of his own reading of the strategic problems and theoretical debates of Russian Marxism and to read it, as Lester does, as nothing more than a kind of institutional *realpolitik* of revolution that would sanction the crudely instrumental utilisation of allies; indeed, of the workers themselves. This procedure is nicely congruent with the conventional wisdom, according to which Lenin conceived the Marxist vanguard party as an elite of bourgeois intellectuals, and yields a Lenin who fits perfectly into the grid of an opposition between the mechanically coercive statism of the East and the organically consensual civil society of the West. Lester constructs an opposition along these lines between Leninist hegemony – centred on and sometimes reduced to the coercive apparatus of the state – and Gramscian hegemony – suffused along intricately detailed pathways through the whole of civil society.[11]

As Lester readily acknowledges, however, Gramsci's politics were not simply consensual; nor were Lenin's politics, as he concedes rather more reluctantly,

---

9   Lester 2000, p. 69.
10 Lester 2000, p. 74.
11 Lester 2000, pp. 86–7.

simply coercive. Lenin certainly supposed, in light of the threat represented by the repressive apparatuses of the state, that the issue of seizing state power was crucial in formulating revolutionary strategy, but although the exploratory purpose and allusive style of his notebooks engendered a fecund variation of perspective and formulation concerning the operation of the state, there is no evidence that Gramsci disagreed. Thinking through the logic of the process of transition to a classless society, Gramsci demonstrated a thorough appreciation of the need to set about establishing hegemony not only politically, but also culturally; not only from the top down, but also from the bottom up. One encounters a similar awareness of the organic character of the transition process in Lenin, albeit constrained, by the circumstances of civil war and imperialist encirclement, to a work of bricolage. Gramsci's politics were coercive (or instrumental) enough to sanction the use of revolutionary force and Lenin's politics consensual (or organic) enough to encompass a concern with the cultural aspects of a worker-peasant alliance. Of course, the contrast between Leninist and Gramscian hegemony limns a conceptual framework for the strategic choice between democracy and dictatorship in the struggle for socialism; thus Lester can underline affinities between Gramsci and Mikhail Bakhtin's 'dialogism', according to which 'all human history is a perpetual struggle between monologue and dialogue'.[12] But to frame the issues of socialist strategy as a choice between democracy and dictatorship, dialogue and monologue, is to equivocate, because neither dictatorship nor democracy can be understood, in historical materialist terms, in abstraction from the relations of class society and the logic of the class struggle.

A similar equivocation is at work in Lester's explication of the relation between the state and civil society in the *Prison Notebooks*. He seeks to defend the coherence of Gramsci's account against Anderson's contention that, suggestive though the *Notebooks*' exploration of this relation may be, it is nonetheless vitiated by the unresolved tensions between three different and contradictory models.[13] Thus, he reads those formulations in which Gramsci expands the notion of the state to comprise both political society and civil society not as expressions of a distinct model, but as designating the mutation, under fascism and dictatorship, of the normal balance of state and civil society. But this is wrong – Gramsci uses such formulations not only and not even primarily in conjunction with the phenomenon of fascism, but also and more fundamentally with respect to 'the general notion of the State' and even

---

12   Lester 2000, p. 101.
13   See Anderson 1976, pp. 25–34.

to the 'night-watchman state' of bourgeois liberalism.[14] The oscillations of Gramscian terminology cannot be gainsaid but it is not very helpful to regard them – here Lester is right, as against Anderson – as an index of competing theoretical models. They are more usefully understood, in my view, as the product of a dogged attempt to grasp at once both the distinctiveness and the connection of two facets of the civil society/state relation: the functional unity of the superstructures in reproducing the contradictory cohesion of capitalist societies and the variation in the institutional arrangements whereby this function is performed, in particular the historical and political construction and reconstruction of the boundary and the distinction between public and private. While variations in the functional requirements of reproduction exert a formative influence upon institutional arrangements, this influence is neither simple nor unilateral; it is mediated by the complex, uneven and contradictory logic of the class struggle. In Gramsci's concern to evoke this process in its multifaceted complexity, the terminology of the state is sometimes predicated of the function performed by institutions, sometimes of the institutions themselves and sometimes of the process as a whole. But it is not only the exploratory character of his *Notebooks* and the circumstances of their composition that make it difficult to fault Gramsci for the oscillation of his terminology; when Althusser, specifically acknowledging the Gramscian precedent, sought to treat in systematic fashion the role of the superstructures in reproducing the conditions of production, his care to predicate the terminology of the state consistently of the function of reproduction earned him the epithets of 'functionalist' and even 'totalitarian'.[15] In his haste to rescue Gramsci from the accusation of incoherence (and, of course, the obligatory charge of totalitarianism), Lester compresses the various facets of the superstructural process into a narrow model of normality and thereby, in effect, conflates issues concerning the institutional autonomy of civil society from the state (pluralism versus totalitarianism in the organisation of the apparatuses of class rule) with issues concerning the logic of struggles around the function of reproduction (structural and strategic cohesion in the deployment of ruling-class power). The result is persistent equivocation as to the location of struggles over state power and their significance within the process of revolution; the Gramscian war of position figures as a judicious balance between the 'Bolshevik model' and the evolutionary politics of Bernsteinian social democracy,[16] but while such a balance may seem judicious within the limits of 'normality', it is not

---

14 See Gramsci 1929–35, pp. 263, 261–2.
15 See Althusser 1971b.
16 See Lester 2000, p. 67.

clear that it is even coherent, let alone judicious, to assume that the logic of the class struggle must respect those limits.

When Gramsci's Leninist reference is used as context for the notion of 'passive revolution', a similar equivocation may be seen to run through Lester's discussion. Gramsci used this term to designate processes of historical transformation in which the social tensions and upheavals of transition are absorbed, managed, steered and configured into forms that reconsolidate and renew the power of the hitherto dominant groups. He linked the passive character of the revolution with a failure of hegemony on the part of a leading revolutionary group unwilling or unable to unleash an independent movement of the popular masses. While the term figured principally in Gramsci's critical analysis of the Italian *Risorgimento*, the notion of passive revolution served him as a device for examining two distinct, though related, aspects of the struggle for hegemony: first, the problem of seizing the strategic initiative, including considerations such as aligning oneself in relation to allies, enemies, and (potentially) revolutionary or counter-revolutionary forces and identifying (and establishing hegemony over) the key issues and institutions around which the struggle for power will be fought out and alliances formed or broken; second, what might be termed the problem of education, of cultivating among the popular masses the kind of organisational ability and capacity for critical reflection necessary for their emergence as independent actors in the revolutionary process.

Lester reads passive revolution as an expression of the merely passive consent of the popular masses to bourgeois rule, a passivity resting upon the unexamined prejudices of common sense and the contradictions that arise when plebeian experience is grasped only through the categories of the dominant ideology. Challenging the 'passive practices' that convey bourgeois hegemony requires a counter-hegemonic force, embodying 'active consentient ideals in [its] own internal structures', to foster '*anti*-passive practices' and thus prefigure 'a future *state in miniature*'.[17] The requirement is replicated in the broader historical bloc as a practice of expansively articulating a diversity of interests so as to 'promote the full development of *all* interests within the bloc' rather than merely absorbing and neutralising some, thus ensuring their subordination to others.[18] The structural-strategic aspect of the struggle for hegemony is thus read in terms of its cultural-educational aspect and thereby effectively assimilated to the latter.

---

17 Lester 2000, p. 74. Emphasis in all quotations is given as in the original unless otherwise noted.

18 Lester 2000, p. 75.

The issues posed by Gramsci's account of passive revolution parallel those arising in the Russian Marxist debates whence the concept of hegemony emerged and assumed an initial shape. Indeed, the emergence of social democracy in Russia was essentially bound up with the assertion of the hegemony of the proletariat in the impending bourgeois-democratic revolution. Plekhanov initially formulated this assertion as a critique of populist faith in the socialist potential of the peasantry. In the context of this debate, the independent growth of working-class consciousness and organisational capacity and the strategic leadership of social democracy simply presented themselves as two different ways of expressing the same thing. But when a tendency arose, in conjunction with the growth of a liberal opposition, to constrain social-democratic politics within the narrow limits of trade unionism, the reassertion of proletarian hegemony would throw into relief the distinction between the strategic and educational aspects of hegemony. And in the course of the 1905 Revolution this distinction would come to structure the political opposition between the Bolshevik and Menshevik wings of the Russian Social Democratic Labour Party (RSDLP). The Mensheviks, conceiving the hegemony of the proletariat in the bourgeois-democratic revolution as a process of proletarian self-emancipation, subordinated their strategy to a project of organising forums of self-government where, through direct participation, the workers themselves could cultivate the virtues requisite to their future political rule. Regarding such hothouse experiments, conceived in abstraction from the inevitable violence of counterrevolution, as irresponsibly utopian, Lenin conceptualised the political consciousness of the proletariat – and consequently the process of its self-emancipation – in terms of the strategic exigencies of the democratic revolution and, crucially, the struggle over state power. Correlative to this, he reformulated the struggle for hegemony as a struggle between two paths in the bourgeois-democratic revolution, a thoroughgoing demolition of the feudal, patriarchal and absolutist legacy of Tsarism, driven by an alliance of proletariat and peasantry, and a transition – strikingly similar in conception to Gramsci's passive revolution – dominated by a landlord-bourgeois coalition in which the revolutionary energy of the masses, lacking focus, is diverted into half-measures that coexist with and prolong the heritage of oppression. These contrasting approaches to the struggle for hegemony yielded opposing readings of the soviets: both Mensheviks and Bolsheviks knew them as organising committees for a general strike, but where the former conceived of them as the site of a kind of proletarian model parliament, Lenin attributed to them the potential of embodying an alliance of workers and peasants and assuming state power. Thus in 1905, where the Bolsheviks sought to organise insurrection through the soviets, the Mensheviks supposed that a focus on insurrection would undermine the process of working-class self-education.

The dispute between Mensheviks and Bolsheviks over hegemony in the democratic revolution enables us to understand that much is at stake, both politically and theoretically, in just how the concept of hegemony is deconstructed and how its different aspects are articulated. Absent an account and appreciation of this dispute, Lester's discussion of passive revolution equivocates persistently between a Menshevik and a Bolshevik reading of Gramsci: it equivocates, that is, over the relative position in the struggle for hegemony of the strategic leadership of a modern prince and the practical self-education of the subaltern masses. Does the hegemonic complexity Gramsci so richly evoked signify primarily the necessity of a leadership capable of charting a course and drawing an alliance of diverse forces together across a web of social-structural contradictions or the threat to the intricately moving totality of human consciousness posed by the unilateral assertion of vanguard authority? It may be suggested that ambiguity on such issues is already there in the *Prison Notebooks*. But where an author must write circumspectly with one eye to his fascist jailers – never more so, one imagines, than when he must evoke questions of the seizure of power – and yet manages to signal the alignment of his ideas with those of 'Ilich', more than ordinary caution is called for in seeking to draw implications from his ambiguities.

The Post-Marxist Deconstruction of Hegemony

The flagship text of post-Marxism, *Hegemony and Socialist Strategy*, by Ernesto Laclau and Chantal Mouffe, has been subjected to withering criticism from a number of Marxist quarters.[19] But inasmuch as Western Marxist accounts of hegemony – shaped by an opposition between West and East, Gramsci and Lenin – equivocate over issues of democracy and dictatorship, consent and coercion, they leave themselves vulnerable to the hegemony of the social currents that enable the anticommunist clichés of the Cold War, pumped up with postmodern jargon, to be paraded as the worldly wisdom of post-Marxism.

The way humans act on the world to satisfy their material needs is also an expression of their life and 'as individuals express their life, so they are'. Practice – human productive activity – has both a material dimension and an expressive, symbolic, discursive dimension. In the course of transforming the world so as to satisfy their needs, humans produce new needs in themselves;

---

19   See Geras 1990, Lester 2000, Rosenthal 1988, Rustin 1988 and Wood 1986.

thus, productive activity transforms both our material circumstances and our identity, the way we understand ourselves and are understood. The identity of individuals – what they are – corresponds to what they produce and how they produce and hence 'depends upon the material conditions determining their production'[20] – thus, roughly, the Marx of *The German Ideology*. The target of the post-Marxist critique is what Laclau and Mouffe term the 'ontological privilege' accorded the working class by what they take to be the defining logic of Marxism. This privilege turns on the distinction between the economic base and the ideological and political superstructures of society, read in ontological terms as a distinction between orders of being, a material or pre-discursive order and a symbolic or discursive order endowed with meaning. Since the political meaning of a struggle depends upon its articulation with other struggles and is consequently open to change, even in retrospect, discursively constituted identities (subject positions) are in principle negotiable rather than fixed, pluralistic rather than monistic, open rather than closed. To assert the pre-discursive character of the economic base is to construe the identities derived from it as literal, as simply given and hence thing-like, fixed rather than metaphorical, open and always in play. To assert the determination of the superstructure by the base is to impose closure upon – to 'suture', in the Lacanian terminology Laclau and Mouffe prefer – the discursive dimension of human practice. Since the superstructure simply reflects the economic base, the laws of development of the economy – stipulating the collapse of capitalism and the advent of socialism – unfold endogenously and with historical inevitability.

This kind of claim – and the base/superstructure distinction upon which it rests – presupposes the adoption of a subject position outside the discursive dimension, with its assumed capacity for a fully clairvoyant understanding of reality in its totality. This is the subject position from which the working-class political project of socialist revolution is conceived; it clothes in Marxist terminology the notion of a position that is outside the symbolic order of society but from which a re-foundation of society in its totality would be possible, a kind of Archimedean point of social revolution, the pivot of the 'Jacobin imaginary' that has dominated the discourse of the political left since the French Revolution. But, explain Laclau and Mouffe, no such position is possible; there can be no subject that is not embedded within, constituted in and through the play of the infinite field of discursive practices, never beyond some particular perspective but always open to reconstitution. The implication is the inevitable failure of history, amidst the unforeseeable play of contingency, to unfold

---

20   Marx and Engels 1845–6, p. 31.

in line with Marxist expectations; the failure of the logic of capital to eventuate in a homogeneous proletarian majority, plus the failure of the workers to act out the subject position prescribed by Marxist theory, would give rise, through recourse to the expedient of 'hegemony', to a kind of recognition/misrecognition of the essential contingency of political struggle. The history of Marxism is thus, intellectually, a history of increasingly less plausible attempts to square the transcendent imperative of Marxist theory with the empirical world of politics. This translates, politically, into a quest for a figure – party, vanguard, leader – that could come to 'represent' the subject position and consequently to think, decide and act on behalf of the proletariat.

The post-Marxist critique thus recycles a pivotal trope of anti-Marxist ideology, given quintessential expression in an image that circulated freely in the aftermath of the breach in the wall dividing East and West as the props of 'actually existing socialism' crumbled in surprisingly rapid succession. As the icons of Marx and Lenin came tumbling down across Eastern Europe and the former Soviet Union, Western cartoonists vied with each other in producing variants of a single caricature: gangs of workers and peasants, armed with hammers and sickles, angrily chasing after the two startled and bewildered communist thinkers. What transgression should have called forth such retribution? The communists are caught unawares, victims of misguided confidence in the truth of their theory, despite all evidence to the contrary. So overweening was this confidence that not only were they willing to reconstruct entire societies upon the promise of a theory, they would impose their blueprint with massive violence, violating the aspirations and the experience of the very people in whose name the promise had been proffered. The anger of the workers and peasants was directed, then, at the betrayal of a promise, but also, through this, at the theoretical arrogance that stood behind the promise. The offence of Marx, and especially of Lenin, was the original sin of intellectual pride. Something like this tale also runs through the academic literature on Marx and Lenin, evident in the practice of attributing to Lenin a claim to 'absolute knowledge', a 'philosophy of certainty'.[21] It is a story with some rhetorical force; it can appeal to the virtues, grounded in plebeian experience, of modesty and tolerance. Its intellectual power, however, is dubious; in it Marxist and Leninist ideas are criticised only by implication, or rather by insinuation. What matters about those ideas is that they were imposed with arrogant disregard for popular aspiration and experience; from the anger of the workers and peasants we can infer the falsity of the ideas. No need, then, to investigate the ideas themselves; we already know, from the experience of their victims, the truth about

---

21   See Harding 1996, pp. 219–42.

them. And should the contradictions of our own quotidian experience tempt us to test its limits, we already know what might lie beyond and can prudently resist the temptation. Never mind that empathy for the experience of the victims and fear of what lies beyond the familiar confines of our own experience have been mobilised more than once, since the wall came down, on behalf of wars of imperial conquest. The post-Marxist critique of hegemony dovetails nicely with the conventional caricature of Lenin at the same time as it renders superfluous a scrupulous reading of his theorisation of hegemony. This caricature thus occupies a strategic position in contemporary debates over the concept of hegemony. The post-Marxist appropriation of hegemony might be characterised, in Marxist and Leninist terms, as simply another form of subaltern insertion in the deployment of bourgeois hegemony.

In order to escape the conceptual closure they assert is implicit in historical materialism, Laclau and Mouffe insist upon the inescapably symbolic – and hence, in their terminology, discursive – nature of practice, rejecting any attempt to distinguish between discursive and non-discursive practices. The identity of any subject position is constituted in and through discourse and is consequently subject to variation in line with the play of discursive practice; hegemony consists in establishing relations of equivalence between different subject positions such that one subject position comes to signify, to represent, an 'impossible' universality of subject positions. To assign hegemony to any particular subject position or identity prior to the play of discursive practice is to privilege it over other identities. Marxists have responded with the claim that refusal of any distinction between discursive and non-discursive practices effectively reduces the social relations of production to relations between people, society to population, and class to just another contingent form of personal identity, rendering inconceivable the systemic character of capitalist exploitation.[22] For the extraction of surplus value, exploitation in its capitalist form is not simply a relation between persons but an essential feature of the capital relation, which is comprised not only of relations between people (contract, recognition, exchange) but also of relations between people and things (production, consumption, ownership). Further, a demonstrable effect of the class system inherent in the capital relation, a condition of its reproduction, is the requirement that the dominant class exercise effective control over the principal levers of coercion in society: that is, over the state.[23] And this line of argument might be extended as follows: if the reproduction of the capital relation shapes the battlefield upon which the struggle for hegemony is fought

---

22   See Rosenthal 1988.
23   See Lester 2000, pp. 125–31.

and the state is a crucial stake in this struggle, then the logic of hegemony both requires and permits the structural unity necessary and the strategic initiative possible on a battlefield, both totality and openness.

The kind of rejoinder congenial to Laclau and Mouffe – that the 'outside' of the discursive can only be known or discussed in discursive terms and is thereby incorporated into the discursive dimension, and that the 'ontological privilege' accorded the subject position of the working class is therefore baseless – is ineffective, depending upon a conflation of ontological issues concerning the existence of objects of knowledge independently of the process of their cognitive appropriation with scientific issues concerning the generative mechanisms at work in those realities, the kind of conflation of categories Lenin pilloried in his work of philosophy, *Materialism and Empirio-Criticism*.[24] If practice does indeed suppose a symbolic, discursive dimension, the point of a distinction between discursive and non-discursive practices is not to dispute this but to distinguish how material elements function differently (as raw materials, instruments, location, motive power, etc.) within and pose varying kinds of constraint upon (as well as opening up varying kinds of possibility for) different kinds of practice. Thus, the distinction between the discursive and the material aspects of a practice will figure quite differently in the practice of conducting a seminar in political philosophy and in the practice of growing corn or of operating a petroleum refinery or of assembling an automobile or a cell phone, in the practice of addressing Parliament and in the practice of torturing prisoners or kettling protestors, in the practice of voting and the practice of organising a picket line; it may figure quite differently depending upon how the relations of production in which such practices are conducted, the relations of ownership and the distribution of labour, are organised. Absent some such distinction, the non-discursive can be understood only as a constraint upon the proliferation of discourse; the constraints it presents can be understood only as repressive rather than productive; and, absent some such distinction, the post-Marxist analysis of practice and consequently of hegemony reduces itself to a single, narrow dimension. Absent recourse to a structural logic of class, exploitation and oppression, the post-Marxists are unable to provide a grounding for their own delineation of the struggle for radical democratic hegemony along lines of left and right and hence for their critique of neo-liberalism, which also appeals, after all, to freedom, equality and democracy. The 'radical' pretensions of the post-Marxist project of pluralist democracy thus rely implicitly – and parasitically – upon the results of 'essentialist' analyses of exploitation and oppression, notably those produced

---

24   See Lenin 1908.

by historical materialism, while explicitly repudiating the theoretical premises of those results.[25]

The limits of the post-Marxist rejoinder may be further delineated from another angle by trying to clarify just what Laclau and Mouffe take to be a working-class subject position. A 'subject position', it turns out, is simply a postmodern idiom for a form of struggle.[26] But their criteria for identifying forms of struggle are unclear; are they, for example, to be distinguished according to their aim (economic security versus political power), the means employed (strike, work-to-rule, sabotage, negotiation), the institutional context in which they unfold or the identity of the adversary? In any case, subject positions, however identified, are (or at least may be) constitutive of the identity of an actor. From the participation of an actor in a form of struggle that might be termed 'working class', Marxists are driven to jump illogically to the conclusion that the identity of the actor and other forms of struggle in which the actor may engage are to be characterised as 'working class', endowing the agent and the class of people who engage in one or another of the forms of struggle with a spurious unity and homogeneity. Relying upon the assertion that 'rhetorical mechanisms... constitute the anatomy of the social world', Laclau would later argue, apropos of populism but consistently with the argument of *Hegemony and Socialist Strategy*, that 'the unity of the equivalential ensemble, of the irreducibly new collective will... depends entirely on the social productivity of a name[,] ... the operation of the name as a pure signifier'.[27] As depicted by Laclau and Mouffe, Marx's use of the '"working class" label' involves the distinct relations of the sale and purchase of labour power and the labour process itself (which they inaccurately define as necessarily manual in character), but they raise the distinction only in order to decry Marx's purported failure to 'explore the variegated decentring of the diverse positions of the "working class" subject'.[28]

But, as Marx understood very well, the wage relation involves the possibility – and hence the reality of the threat, in the experience of some workers – of failure to sell one's labour power, and the fluidity of the market for labour power involves the practical certainty that some sellers of labour power will move between different capitals producing different commodities, others between surplus-value-producing and other sorts of employment, that others will be able to maintain relative security of employment, and so

---

25 See Rustin 1988 and Lester 2000.
26 Laclau and Mouffe 1985, p. 11.
27 Laclau 2005, pp. 110, 108.
28 Laclau and Mouffe 1985, p. 81.

on and on, together carrying the implication of a diversity of forms of struggle on a number of dimensions. The post-Marxist critique assumes that the unity of all these subject positions must take the form of homogeneity; but does this assume that 'the identity and unity' of the working class, as of other objects, 'result from the very operation of naming'?[29] Does it depend upon an auxiliary hypothesis holding that social and political agency must display the transparency of a transcendental subject? But Laclau, Mouffe and anti-Marxist conventional wisdom to the contrary notwithstanding, the logic of historical materialism does not entail any such auxiliary hypothesis. In several respects, as Althusser and his school in particular sought to point out, it suggests the converse.[30] Indeed, in thinking about the unity of the working class, a metaphor of community, with its suggestion of unity in diversity and of indefinite borders (and consequent openness to hegemonic political practice) may be more useful than, or at least a necessary complement to, the notion of even a decentred subject. The practice of building – rebuilding, transforming – communities (sets of social relations, taken in certain of their aspects) will certainly involve bestowing names, but practices, including political practices, work with a more or less limited selection of instruments, employing certain combinations of skills and motive forces upon certain kinds of raw material in a certain material, political and institutional context against certain material, political and institutional resistance, all of which will both constrain and enable in varying ways and degrees the practice of building the community. There may be not-only-rhetorical reasons to prefer some names – and some political projects – to others.

Post-Marxist 'hegemony' thus represents not a project for reconstructing the bourgeois social order along new lines and under new leadership, but a deconstruction of any hegemonic project as an overweening claim to foreclose the innovative diversity of the process of individual self-definition and thereby 'suture' the social order. Indeed, in place of the Leninist (and Gramscian) term 'proletarian hegemony', it has given currency to the language of 'counter-hegemony', a locution suggesting that the alternative to bourgeois rule is no social order at all but a universe of autonomously self-defining individuals. Marx's sardonic pronouncement in the 'Critique of the Gotha Programme', that the bourgeois have good reason to attribute 'supernatural creative power' to labour[31] suggests, however, that just as one cannot simply produce oneself, neither can one simply define oneself. One always finds oneself already in

---

29 Laclau 2005, p. 104.
30 See Althusser 1970a and 1970b.
31 Marx 1875, p. 81.

context and so one is always-already defined, even if the terms in which one is understood/understands oneself are contested. In class society, the material available for the arduous work of transforming contexts and redefining political projects, aspirations and identities is supplied by the historical movement of the class struggle in all its diversity. In this context the social, political and ideological relations of capital do not represent a mere static backdrop against which workers and revolutionary intellectuals strive to fashion a socialist project: just as the workers spontaneously innovate in the course of their struggles, the ruling class innovates, through its political and ideological representatives, in response to working-class struggles. The process of elaborating the political self-definitions of working-class and popular movements and working out the forms of a classless society is one in which the economic, political and ideological relations of capital, and with them the class adversary, are inevitably and actively present. To reckon without this presence is to take the contours of the political arena as given and thereby to assume, in the very terms of one's counter-hegemonic struggle, the position of the subaltern. It is to make political leadership and hence also political agency, strictly speaking, unthinkable.

Lenin as Symbol

When the figure of Lenin reappears, it is introduced by Slavoj Žižek as a counter to the ersatz politics of Third Way managerial liberalism and, by extension, the pragmatic accommodation of post-Marxist radical democratic pluralism, but only by transposing it into the discursive key of post-Marxism, confirming the discursive terms of the Laclau-Mouffe appropriation of 'hegemony' (though perhaps not in quite the same sort of way in which the advent of a Clinton, a Blair or an Obama in opposition to the Reagan-Thatcher-Bush reaction confirmed the hegemonic status of finance capital) as the shared context of debate. Žižek's call to a 2001 conference on Lenin in Essen, Germany, posited a return to Lenin as a necessary precondition for a politics of truth: that is, neither the enlightened administration of the established fact nor the ineffectually self-absorbed and wistful protest of what Hegel termed a 'beautiful soul', but a politics capable of changing 'the very framework that determines how things work', an 'art of the impossible' that could move 'the very parameters of what is considered "possible" in the existing constellation', in full awareness of the implications of such a project. A return to Lenin was called for precisely in order to reaffirm Marxist politics, since Marx himself had been appropriated by academic fashion and thereby domesticated and depoliticised. The aim of this return would be to repeat, 'in the present world-wide conditions, the Leninist gesture of initiating a political project that would undermine the totality of the liberal-capitalist world order'.[32] Lenin figures in this call as a symbol of transgression; to return to Lenin is to adopt a certain revolutionary aesthetic and ethic, to assume his stance of tough-minded revolutionary intransigence and to shoulder, without illusion, the responsibility of revolutionary power, the burden of dirty hands, of necessary compromise and harsh measures. The construction of Lenin as symbolic bearer of a new epochal truth, of a transvaluation of values, is the obverse of the parable of the original sin of intellectual pride; the assignment of values may be reversed but the story remains the same.

Žižek reads the post-Marxist provocation 'society doesn't exist' (that is, the assertion of the constitutive incompleteness of the symbolic dimension that forms the social structure) as the thesis that 'society is not a positive field, since the gap of the Political is inscribed into its very foundations', adding that 'Marx's name for the political which traverses the entire social body is "class struggle"'.[33] This reading makes more credible the clarification that 'the justified rejection of the fullness of post-revolutionary Society does *not* justify the conclusion that we have to renounce any project of a global social transformation[:] ... the jump from a critique of the "metaphysics of presence" to anti-utopian "reformist" gradualist politics is an illegitimate short circuit'.[34] But Žižek leverages this notion of a constitutive 'gap' into a diagnosis of an idealist strain implicit in the philosophical stance of Lenin's *Materialism and Empirio-Criticism*. The metaphor of reflection upon which Lenin relies to assert the objectivity of human knowledge – 'we come to know the way things exist independently of our minds ... only in the infinite process of approximation' – abstracts from the fact that 'the partiality (distortion) of "subjective reflection" occurs precisely because the subject is included in the process it reflects'; it therefore bears the implication of 'a totally adequate "neutral" knowledge of reality' and, in turn, 'our external status' with regard to the reality we reflect.[35] Contra Lenin's materialist intention, 'only a consciousness observing the world from the outside would see the whole of reality the way it really is'. Žižek parallels the Laclau-Mouffe provocation with his own: '[*T*]*here is no universe as a Whole*: as a Whole, the universe (the world) is Nothing – everything that exists is *within* this Nothing'. Alternatively put: '[t]he very notion of the "whole universe" thus presupposes the position of an external observer,

---

32   Žižek 2000b.
33   Žižek 2002b, p. 182.
34   Žižek 2000a, p. 101.
35   Žižek 2002b, pp. 179, 180.

which is impossible to occupy'. In consequence, a 'distorting partial perspective is inscribed into the very material existence of things'. The barrier that stands in the way of our objective knowledge of reality is not 'layers of illusions and distortions' surmountable only through infinite approximation but rather 'our very ontological inclusion within' reality.[36]

The metaphor of reflection is abstracted in Žižek's argument from the logic of the political context in which Lenin invoked it – where Bolsheviks were divided, in the aftermath of the revolution of 1905, over whether or not an objective judgment could be made as to the balance of forces in the current conjuncture of the class struggle and whether or not a Leninist claim to the requisite knowledge betokened insufficient faith in the revolutionary will of the proletariat. It is also abstracted, consequently, from Lenin's *practice* of philosophy.[37] With something of this context in mind, Žižek's claim that the very notion of the whole implies an observer outside the whole exhibits a striking similarity to the empiricist confusion of concept with percept for which Lenin took Bogdanov and the empirio-criticists to task in 1908.[38] This parallel yields some indication as to why Žižek avoids repeating the obvious move of anti-Marxist/post-Marxist conventional wisdom, of transposing the external subject of the reflection metaphor onto the thesis that consciousness must be introduced from without into the spontaneous movement of the working class to generate a Leninist claim to absolute knowledge. Instead, Žižek reads the Leninist thesis of consciousness from without through an analogy with the (Lacanian) psychoanalyst's supposed knowledge of the secret of the patient's desire (and with the need of the Judeo-Christian religious subject for 'an *external* traumatic encounter' in order to know the 'Truth' of God).[39] Just as it is not that the analyst understands the desire of the patient better than the patient understands herself, 'the authority of the Party is not that of determinate positive knowledge, but that of the form of knowledge, of a new type of knowledge linked to a collective political subject'. Because in each case the subject is decentred, the 'external element does not stand for objective knowledge, that is, its externality is strictly internal: the need for the Party stems from the fact that the working class is never "fully itself"'.[40] The external agent (party, God, analyst) is the form in which we (proletarian, believer, patient) necessarily represent our own activity and knowledge to ourselves. The whole point of

---

36 Žižek 2002b, pp. 181, 180.
37 See Althusser 1971a, Lecourt 1973 and Hillel-Rubin 1977.
38 See Lenin 1908.
39 See Žižek 2002b, pp. 182–7.
40 Žižek 2002b, pp. 188, 189.

the argument about externality and internality, for Žižek, is not to identify a subject of knowledge but to show that the relevant *form* of knowledge is the symbolic self-knowledge of a subject.

The name 'Lenin' serves Žižek in similar fashion as the form whereby our commonplace critical insights into, say, the paradoxes of liberal democracy are transformed into the constituents of 'a subversive theoretical formation'.[41] But the 'Lenin' who can play this role is not the Lenin of historical fact, much less the artificer of theoretical tools capable of illuminating the shape of class struggles and the objective logic of the revolutionary process, but precisely the symbol of revolutionary transgression of conventional wisdom and popular imagination. The point of Žižek's return to Lenin is neither the nostalgic re-enactment of 'the good old revolutionary times' nor the 'opportunistic-pragmatic adjustment of the old programme to the "new conditions"' – either of which would be insufferably *passé* – but to repeat, 'in the present worldwide conditions, the Leninist gesture of reinventing the revolutionary project'. The act of self-reinvention out of crisis is definitive of the symbolic 'Lenin' whom Žižek would have us repeat: the Lenin worth retrieving is 'the Lenin whose fundamental experience was that of being thrown into a catastrophic new constellation in which the old coordinates proved useless, and who was thus compelled to reinvent Marxism'. We are urged to rise out of the ashes of the collapse of 'really existing socialism' (1990) as Lenin rose out of the ashes of the collapse of the Second International (1914). '"Lenin" stands for the compelling freedom to suspend the stale existing (post-) ideological coordinates, the debilitating *Denkverbot* (prohibition on thinking) in which we live – it simply means that we are allowed to think again'.[42] We are not, then, being advised to re-enact the substance of Lenin's political practice or to redeploy his theoretical apparatus; these have become old, useless coordinates. '[T]o repeat Lenin is to accept that "Lenin is dead", that his particular solution failed, even failed monstrously, but that there was a utopian spark in it worth saving ... To repeat Lenin is to repeat not what Lenin *did* but what he *failed to do*, his missed opportunities'.[43]

Žižek's 'Leninist gesture' is thus an act at once of revolutionary self-reinvention and of the reinvention of the context (the ideological coordinates) amidst which one acts. If such an act can be accomplished, it is only insofar as the coordinates that define its context are to be understood in purely ideological (symbolic/discursive) terms. Thus Žižek's articulation of bits and pieces of Leniniana with philosophical analysis, pop-culture criticism and high-culture

---

41 Žižek 2002b, p. 312.
42 Žižek 2002a, p. 11.
43 Žižek 2002b, p. 310.

references, Lacanian psychoanalytic speculation and current-events commentary would seem to be governed, like the farrago of Rameau's nephew,[44] by a tactic of shaking our confidence in the psychic and intellectual coordinates of our contemporary bourgeois existence, making us 'think again' (and so, perhaps, readying us for the 'Leninist' gesture?), rather than by a concern with the conceptual, political or historical logic of Lenin's theory or practice. The Leninist 'gesture', the act of revolution, is conceived, then, in abstraction from its insertion in the objective process of the class struggle; it is not a matter of revolutionising the material process of production but an essentially symbolic act, the recognition of a 'utopian spark', a revolution in identity politics. Although his Lenin is at once 'the ultimate political strategist' and a '"technocrat" dreaming about the scientific reorganisation of production', it is not too surprising that Zizek should find this 'Lenin' unable to think – even if 'aware of the *urgency* of doing so – an impossible yet necessary task' – the articulation of politics and economics, of proletarian revolution and the construction of socialism.[45]

As I will show, in *What Is to Be Done?* Lenin begins by diagnosing a polemical adversary's conflation of the distinction between base and superstructure with a different distinction, one between spontaneity and consciousness, in order to delineate a conceptual space that would allow Marxist political actors to think their own agency within the class struggle.[46] That is to say, the conceptualisation of political agency as internal requires that it be distinguished from concepts appropriate to the objective logic – and the material context – of the social structure; this does not, however, imply that the externality of this 'object' of knowledge is merely 'internal' to the acting/knowing political agent. Alternatively put, there is no implication that impediments to knowledge inhere simply in the knowing subject (in the structure of the political agent's practice) and not also in the objective logic of the practical-material process to be known. Obstacles of either sort may present themselves and there is no need to suppose that a single set of cognitive tools is appropriate to address both; how the appropriate tools are most effectively deployed is a matter for the 'long and wearisome' process of practice, scientific, political and productive.

The terms in which Marxists and their adversaries have understood the movement of the class struggle and debated the appropriate strategies and institutions continue nonetheless to shape debates and divisions in working-class

---

44   See Diderot 1782.
45   Žižek 2002b, p. 272.
46   See Lenin 1902.

and popular movements and thereby enter into the present context of political action. They can enter consciously or unconsciously and where, as in the case of Lenin, they are permitted entry only in forms so highly abstracted and even caricatural as to suppress, in effect, the logic of political debate and action, careful and critical re-examination is particularly called for. Grasping Lenin's political analyses and the concepts worked out across those analyses, linked as these were to a movement of theory and practice – a tradition – requires a form of investigation capable of seizing the present as a specific moment in the movement of a process. Such a form of investigation, inevitably redolent of traditions and histories (we think) we already know, must draw back at least momentarily from the present and the will to transgress it, and so it must evoke the impatience of anyone who expects theory to be a simple recipe for action in the here and now. This kind of impatience merely forestalls a critical reckoning with the political practice and theory that enabled Lenin to forge revolutionary intransigence into an instrument capable of grasping the present and thereby defining the shape of a revolutionary political project. Where Lenin figures simply as a symbol of revolutionary transgression, what is lost from view, just as surely as where he is painted, through pity or fear, as a bearer of the original sin of intellectual pride, is the shape of his thought and his politics. The revolutionary who turns to this (or any other) present moment with nothing but a will to transgression, abstracted from the historical traditions and trajectories that give it shape, would be a naive, if not a very beautiful, soul. Precisely because political actors in the tradition of classical Marxism have had to engage with the difficulties and uncertainties of situating themselves politically and theoretically in determinate moments of the class struggle, one can hope to derive from their example analytical tools that can be brought to bear upon present moments; I claim that Lenin's almost dogged insistence that concrete situations be analysed concretely makes him exemplary in this regard.

Hegemony in the Philosophy of Lenin's Politics

It is assumed in the literature on Lenin's politics, whether scholarly or activist, that his 'theory of the vanguard party' is first and foremost a theory of organisation that yields a justification of a certain democratic-centralist model of organisation as particularly appropriate to the pursuit of the proper aim of the working-class movement. This literature is centrally preoccupied with the issue of who can claim the 'class consciousness' that would justify leadership or membership or lend weight to the policy prescriptions of one orientation or another. Beyond the obvious implication of awareness of the need for workers to struggle for the socialist transcendence of capitalist society, the meaning and the function of this consciousness have not been much investigated in this literature, which is typically more concerned with who – what kind of agent – has or is capable of attaining consciousness than with what it is they would be conscious of. Now, political consciousness, like political agency, is inherently intentional or goal-oriented, so it is not at all unreasonable to construe 'class consciousness' as a consciousness of the need to struggle to realise working-class interests in a classless society beyond capitalism. By itself, this yields an instrumental conception of political agency. But political consciousness is also inherently reflexive, moving – or refusing to move – in response to movements in its context, to the activity of other political actors and to its own initial effects. It is not just an aim or a set of beliefs but an activity and a process. It is, then, a moving target. This is a point that Lenin would come to understand very well and the significance of his political practice cannot be grasped without reckoning with it. Taking Lenin seriously as a philosopher, and not just as a practitioner, of politics dictates that the aim and function of political consciousness and political activity and the cognate processes whereby political agents come to understand themselves in acting in the world – processes that determine the significance of one or another form of organisation – be interrogated rather than simply taken as already given in the basic terms of Marxist theory.

This book's line of argument might be understood as proceeding from another Gramscian insight: 'A man of politics writes about philosophy; it could be that his "true" philosophy should be looked for rather in his writings on politics... in a form that is more often than not implicit and at times even in contradiction with what is professedly expressed'.[47] It is difficult to avoid the impression that Gramsci wrote these words about Lenin, with a view to liberating the dialectic of his political practice from what he regarded as the mechanistic fetters of *Materialism and Empirio-Criticism*.[48] While my estimate of Lenin's book on philosophy is much more positive than Gramsci's, it remains that the practice of interpreting some of Lenin's more striking political theses, often abstracted from their rhetorical function and political context, in terms derived from his expressly philosophical work has contributed not a little to readings that demonstrably obscure the logic of his politics and sustain the conventional caricature. Looking for philosophy in Lenin's political writings, I take it, does not mean singling out philosophical aphorisms interspersed amidst political argument and commentary. Such an approach takes

---

47   Gramsci 1929–35, p. 403.
48   Lenin 1908.

as its object, rather, the patterns and discrepancies, the underlying structures and tensions, of a discourse. While it must reckon with what is explicit in the discourse, it must seek, in addition, to discern a logic which, though more or less implicit, can account for the manifest shifts, the play of a mode of thought that is alive to the movement of political reality. It seeks, then, to trace across Lenin's shifting political interventions the emergence of a logic of political analysis that governs the movement of his thought, so as to understand not just what he thought at a particular point in time but how he thought, how theory and practice were adjusted and re-adjusted to each other across successive conjunctures in a distinctive mode of political action and analysis.

Such an approach requires close attention to the texts, but any reading that would distinguish the substance of a text from its formulation must go beyond the letter of the text. To the extent that the practice of a political actor – such as Lenin – is the realisation of a theory, it cannot be grasped without understanding how that actor theorises his (or her) political reality; conversely, what an author is doing *in* what he (or she) writes, *in* theoretical practice, cannot be discerned without examining what is done *with* what is written, that is, what is done *in* political practice. Going beyond the letter in this way is vulnerable to the illusory certainties of conventional wisdom and hence, as Gramsci cautioned, to the danger of dilettantism, of arbitrariness and superficiality. Conventional wisdom enters spontaneously – we are never conscious of everything we assume – into any project of interpretation, suggesting certain possibilities and obscuring others. So it is necessary to proceed, as Gramsci advised, with care. Care in this matter can only consist in the detailed analysis of the material, situating the text in the movement of its political and intellectual context, confronting the strength of alternative readings and delineating the theoretical and political issues addressed by the text or imposed by the context or by the clash of rival interpretations. In this way the textual and contextual evidence may be assessed in light of the existing field of concepts and problems and so enable us, as Gramsci hoped, to 'generate truth'.[49]

The Thread of the Argument

I begin the second chapter with a defence of Karl Kautsky, the leading exponent of the orthodox Marxism of the Second International, from the charge of undialectically separating theory and practice, outlining some parameters of the intellectual context in which the notion of hegemony arose as an issue in

---

49 Gramsci 1929–35, p. 403.

Marxist theory and practice. The materialist conception of history, as articulated by Kautsky, allows us to grasp the struggle for a classless socialist society as the outcome of the logic of the historical development of the forces of production of human society, enabling Marxists, intellectuals and workers to situate themselves consciously as political actors within the historical process. Through careful textual and contextual analysis of Kautsky's claim that 'consciousness' must be introduced into the working-class movement from outside, the unity of theory and practice is shown to emerge out of a historical logic that underwrites the harmonious, even synchronous, maturation of the objective – productive forces – and subjective – socialist consciousness – conditions of socialism, a unilinear logic according to which the contradictions of the historical process are apparently resolved in the seemingly unstoppable advance of the parliamentary political project of Kautsky's German Social Democratic Party (SPD). Critical analysis of this historical logic yields a series of questions about political agency, about the role of politics in forging the unity of the working class, about the logic and the limits of alliance with other social classes and about the need for leadership and the class character of the workers' political party. These are the kinds of question that would give rise to the notion of hegemony, but they are questions to which Kautsky's Marxist orthodoxy was able to supply merely nominal, theoretically ungrounded responses. It was not a separation of theory from practice but the very conjunction of Kautskyan theory with SPD practice that effectively marginalised and suppressed these critical issues.

The number and variety of the issues that can arise in probing the notion of hegemony as it figures in Marxist discourse – leadership and consciousness, party and class, intellectuals and workers, social structure and political agency, organisation and democracy, strategy and class alliance, and so on – may make it difficult to orient oneself in the investigation. It may be useful to think of the concept of hegemony as emerging from and designating a process by which political actors – specifically, revolutionary Marxist political actors – orient themselves amidst the political realities that confront and challenge and envelop and sweep them along; thus understood, it demands not only theorisation but an understanding of the relation between theory and practice. It calls, therefore, for historical treatment. In the third chapter I trace the genesis of the problem of hegemony in the efforts of the early Russian Marxists to work out an account of the Russian social-democratic project of proletarian hegemony in the bourgeois-democratic revolution. Marx and Engels set the stage for the debates over Marxist strategy that would follow by situating Russia in terms of their materialist conception of history. Although Marx did not directly address the strategic issues that confronted revolutionary political actors in Russia – that is, he did not try to situate Marxism in Russia – the silences of his analysis suggest some of the difficulties involved in framing those issues in terms of the logic of Marxist orthodoxy. The difficulties of situating Marxism, as a theory of political actors, in Russia may be traced in the attempts of Plekhanov and Lenin to deploy the unilinear historical logic of orthodoxy in explicating the social-democratic claim to a leading role for the working class in Russia's democratic revolution. These attempts overstretched such key assumptions of orthodox Marxism as the synchronic development of the material and ideological conditions of socialism, productive forces and class struggle, and thereby generated pervasive equivocation in applying its logic to inescapable issues of revolutionary political practice: political leadership and the unification of the working class, alliances with other classes, the nature of proletarian self-emancipation. The equivocation assumed different forms in Plekhanov and in Lenin, but in each case attempts to clarify the implications of the class analysis for political agency simply translated the equivocation into the terms of class consciousness. The term 'hegemony' served as a verbal resolution, a gesture toward resolution of the problem, at once expressing and obscuring the limits of the logic of orthodoxy.

The latent tensions in the project of proletarian hegemony in the bourgeois-democratic revolution – and in the logic of orthodox Marxism – assumed critical form when the emergence of a narrowly corporate Economist tendency in Russian social democracy coincided not only with the revisionist crisis in international social democracy but with the newly apparent threat of a rival, bourgeois-liberal hegemonic project. The notorious claim in *What Is to Be Done?* that social-democratic consciousness could only be introduced into the spontaneous working-class movement from without needs to be read and explicated in the context of Lenin's response to this crisis. Careful examination of the text and context of the claim in the fourth chapter shows that it functions quite differently than Kautsky's apparently similar claim; indeed, violating the assumption of harmony between Marxist consciousness and the spontaneous working-class movement, it signals a break in the unilinear historical logic of Marxist orthodoxy. Contrary to conventional wisdom, however, it not only does not contradict but is in fact more consistent than the alternatives, with the core Marxist theme of proletarian self-emancipation. Allowing the patient reader to trace the emergence of a meta-strategic logic of political analysis – the politico-strategic logic of the struggle for hegemony – Lenin's thesis does not have to do with the substitution of one political protagonist, the intelligentsia or the party, for another, the working class, but with orienting the position of vanguard – conscious – political actors within the class struggle and the struggle for hegemony and, consequently, with the relation of theory and practice. Since this logic implies an understanding of Marxist theory as a 'guide to action' rather than a 'dogma', and therefore as necessarily incomplete and always in process of development, it needs to be extended by an account of the process that drives theoretical development, an account of the relation of theory and practice. The elements of such an account may be foreshadowed but are not yet worked out. While *What Is to Be Done?* may open a possibility for rethinking the challenges of proletarian hegemony in historical materialist terms, it does not yet meet them.

In the fifth chapter I revisit the status of Marxist theory in *What Is to Be Done?* in the context of Lenin's response to his polemical adversaries' call for freedom of criticism within the social-democratic movement. When Lenin's argument against the appeal to 'freedom of criticism' is read carefully, it can be shown to assume not only the irreconcilability of the class struggle but also the desirability of such constitutional norms as freedom of speech and freedom of association. When read in the context of the meta-strategic logic of the struggle for hegemony, Lenin's argument aims to show that the call for freedom of criticism, when not disciplined by engagement in concrete investigation of new challenges and new circumstances faced by the working-class movement, is itself more dogmatic than its ostensible target and may, in practice, pose a threat to the freedom of working-class association; Marxist theory develops in engagement with the revolutionary political project of the working-class movement.

The Second Congress of the RSDLP at once confirmed the triumph of the political perspective of proletarian hegemony in the bourgeois-democratic revolution and inaugurated a split of historic proportions – between Mensheviks and Bolsheviks – in the ranks of its partisans. The necessary conjunction of these two aspects is analysed in the sixth chapter in terms of the project of proletarian hegemony, demonstrating the emergence of two distinct and opposing orientations toward the struggle for hegemony. Once the perspective of proletarian hegemony was embodied in institutions with some authority, the equivocation that pervaded it was translated into highly charged practical disagreements which in turn generated political antagonism. On the logic of Lenin's political analysis, the Marxist party and disagreements within it were at play in the struggle for hegemony; he could quite matter-of-factly subject internal disagreements to the logic of the struggle for hegemony. To the Mensheviks-to-be, who viewed class and party unity through the optic of orthodoxy, this approach could only appear artificial and unnecessarily divisive. The mere nuances that seemed to distinguish Lenin's formulations of the relation of spontaneity and consciousness from those of his former *Iskra* colleagues might well take on a sharper edge in this new context.

The Menshevik orientation to hegemony invoked a sense of independent working-class agency, self-activity – distinct from the strategic dimension of agency in the Leninist orientation to hegemony – that emerged as pivotal in the critique of the Bolshevik stance. The Menshevik politics of proletarian self-emancipation consisted in orchestrating the self-education of the workers through their self-activity; counterposed to the Leninist logic of the struggle for hegemony, however, their practice could not generate strategic independence. What would count as self-activity, political education or working-class independence in Lenin's optic could be defined, by contrast, only in terms of the politico-strategic logic of the struggle for hegemony and the requirements of the political conjuncture.

The burden of the seventh chapter is that the revolutionary process of 1905–7 saw Lenin bring the politico-strategic logic of the struggle for hegemony to bear in a vastly extended arena of struggle, reflect upon the experience of the spontaneous revolutionary movements of the workers and peasants, and make the practical and theoretical adjustments necessary to fashion a coherent – in historical materialist terms – strategy of proletarian hegemony. The upsurge of a revolutionary movement of the peasantry as a whole led Lenin to reformulate the struggle for hegemony as a struggle between two class alliances, proletarian-peasant and bourgeois-landlord, respectively embodying thoroughgoing democratic transformation of Russian society and liberal compromise with entrenched privilege. Lenin grasped the alliance he sought to consolidate as in essence a combination of heterogeneous forces, seeking to foster the distinctiveness of the peasant movement, encouraging the radical democratic and discouraging the socialist aspects of its populist ideology and later promoting the formation of an independent peasant political party: hegemony consists in the leader encouraging the independent initiative of the led. The scope of the peasant movement led Lenin to rethink the stage and form of the development of capitalism in the countryside, reconceptualising the struggle for hegemony in historical materialist terms as a struggle between two paths of capitalist development, the Prussian and American paths: hegemony is not simply a superstructural phenomenon but is grounded in the socio-economic structure.

The invention of the soviets out of the spontaneous working-class movement provisionally transcends bourgeois hegemony – and thereby expresses the political independence of the proletariat – inasmuch as it constitutes an institutional form of proletarian leadership of the people, an organisational embodiment of the worker-peasant alliance. As such it constitutes a spontaneous contribution to the clarification of the theoretical problem of hegemony: hegemony must be grasped not only in terms of ideas (consent) and instruments (force) but also in terms of forms of social organisation. The very fact, as well as the form, of mass organisation transforms the arena and hence also the terms of political debate, alliance and struggle. In thus contributing to the development of consciousness, the spontaneous movement does not displace Marxist theory but occasions an adjustment in Lenin's orientation to the relation of theory and practice. Since circumstances change independently of the dictates of any political actor, even a hegemonic one, the struggle for hegemony requires the ability to adapt to changing conjunctures and thus some combination of sensitivity to the underlying material constraints upon struggle with openness to likely, and even unlikely, springs of change. This ability calls for a dialectic of practice and theory, played out through the contradictions of vanguard, class and masses.

If the language of hegemony is less central in Lenin's discourse after the imperialist war and the fall of the Tsar established a new context for the struggle for democracy in the process of socialist revolution, this does not betoken the displacement of the meta-strategic logic of the struggle for hegemony; indeed, the argument of the eighth chapter is that Lenin's analysis of imperialism constitutes a rethinking of the dynamics and the nature of the socialist revolution in such a way as to generalise the substance of the notion of hegemony and the distinctive logic of political analysis he worked out in the course of the struggle for hegemony in Russia's democratic revolution. Analysis of the conjuncture of world war and the split in socialism in terms of the logic of imperialism led Lenin to conceive the limits of capitalism as an uneven, complex and contradictory process of revolution. In its most advanced, imperialist phase, capitalism did not simplify but reshuffled the alignment of social forces, engendering a labour aristocracy and thus fracturing the assumption of a united working-class movement while calling forth peasant and nationalist resistance to reaction and petty-bourgeois opposition to monopoly. Indeed, there is some indication in Lenin's critique of 'imperialist Economism' that the function of leadership can be – or even must be – exercised from a variety of distinct and even contradictory positions. The process of socialist revolution is driven by the logic of the struggle for proletarian hegemony waged across diverse movements of resistance to imperialism. The emergence of the soviets as an embryonic proletarian state-in-process-of-dissolution prolongs the politico-strategic logic of this struggle.

At issue in the international debate about the dictatorship of the proletariat that broke out after the Bolshevik seizure of power was the logic of the process of socialist revolution and its implications for practice and theory. Lenin's rejoinder to Kautsky's critique reprises the logic of his deconstruction of the appeal for freedom of criticism in *What Is to Be Done?* The transition to a classless society depends upon knitting together a proletarian-popular community charged with assuming and transforming the functions hitherto performed by the ruling classes; in this context the exercise of the dictatorship of the proletariat can be not only repressive but also constructive. I try to clarify Lenin's attempts to grapple with the difficulties of pulling such a community together under circumstances of revolution and counterrevolution, of incipient civil war, in the ninth chapter, by following through the tension between the two assumptions of his earlier argument, the desirability of constitutional liberties and the irreconcilability of the class struggle, as it plays out in accordance with the politico-strategic logic of the struggle for hegemony. Responsive to the struggles and innovations of the actors engaged in it, the process of transition is, on this logic, open-ended; it is not only the workers and peasants who may innovate but also the former rulers, and so the process may always eventuate in reversals and defeat, especially if its contradictions – and its logic – are not mastered.

A final chapter suggests the pertinence to present-day class and popular struggles of Lenin's politico-strategic logic of the struggle for hegemony. Taking as exemplary the influential *Empire* trilogy of Michael Hardt and Antonio Negri, I show how the practice of framing analyses of the current state of capitalism and the class struggle in terms of opposition to (a typically caricatured image of) Lenin's vanguardism undermines the authors' capacity to engage critically and productively with much of the experience of the proletarian and popular struggles of the past century; thus they deny themselves the footholds in history and tradition from which to reach into the future. The practice effectively occludes issues of revolutionary political leadership and agency addressed by Lenin and introduces an unnecessary layer of confusion into the effort to analyse concretely the current dynamic of capital and the class struggle. I proceed to address questions around the relation between individual and collective revolutionary agency raised by Gramsci's modernisation of Machiavelli's new prince in light of the experience of Lenin's vanguard and suggest that this relation is illuminated by the Leninist logic of hegemony, which, relativising the spontaneous and conscious aspects of political agency, gives us theoretical instruments to think about their interpenetration.

Though not necessary to the argument of the book, three items are appended which may nonetheless help sustain it. First is my translation of Kautsky's 'Die Revision des Programms der sozialdemokratie in Oesterreich', the *locus classicus* of his notorious thesis that socialist consciousness must be introduced into the class struggle from without. The context it provides will support both my reading of Kautsky's thesis and the contrast I draw between it and Lenin's superficially similar thesis. Second is my contribution to a symposium in *Historical Materialism* on Lars Lih's recently influential *Lenin Rediscovered*, wherein Lenin is claimed to share with the principal polemical targets of *What Is to Be Done?* a commitment to enacting in Russia the political perspective of the SPD's Erfurt Programme, thus vindicating his credentials as a practitioner of Marxism at the same time as the argument of the text is reduced to a rationalisation of a bid for factional power and so voided of theoretical significance.[50] I demonstrate that Lih's reading, predicated upon a failure to address the theoretical issues arising from the ambiguities immanent in the project of proletarian hegemony, turns upon a misrepresentation of Lenin's text and thereby even falls into a misunderstanding of its context. The third item included is a brief review of the evidence indicating the failure of the claim, occasionally encountered in the literature, that Lenin would subsequently repudiate the thesis of 'consciousness from without' argued in *What Is to Be Done?*

---

50   Shandro 2010.

CHAPTER 2

On the Relation of Theory and Practice: Karl Kautsky and the First Post-Marxist[1]

> [T]he path of development is the path of struggle. The reconciliation of antagonisms implies the stoppage of development.
> – KARL KAUTSKY[2]

∴

It was Karl Kautsky, more than anyone else, who defined the Marxism of the Second International. He was the editor of the most respected Marxist theoretical review of the period, *Die Neue Zeit*, the theoretical organ of the German Social Democratic Party (SPD) and, with Eduard Bernstein, the literary executor of Marx and Engels. As the quasi-official leading theoretician of what was by far the strongest party in the International, he was from the death of Engels in 1895 until the cataclysm of 1914–18 the authoritative voice of Marxist orthodoxy. First the war, however, and then the October Revolution in Russia pushed to the surface the fissures which lay beneath the official unity of German – and international – Social Democracy and which had seemed, until then, mere superficial cracks. Kautsky's brand of Marxism showed itself incapable of coming to grips with the crisis of war; the polarisation of the SPD between those who supported the Imperial German war effort and those who, like Karl Liebknecht and Rosa Luxemburg, declared their outright opposition, left him profoundly isolated. His call for a 'peace without annexations' could not but seem a pious wish, his ostrich-like refusal to recognise that the acquiescence of the majority of socialist parties in the war efforts of their respective governments was tantamount to the collapse of the International, an admission of political – and perhaps theoretical – bankruptcy.

---

[1] An earlier and somewhat abbreviated version of the argument of this chapter was published in 1997–8 as 'Karl Kautsky: On the Relation of Theory and Practice', *Science & Society*, 61, 4: 474–501.
[2] Kautsky 1906b, p. 66.

Orthodoxy and Apostasy

Kautsky's place as the great renegade in the history of Marxism and the workers' movement has been fixed by Lenin's repeated and virulent denunciations of him during the war and in the aftermath of the October Revolution. Without examining the substance of Lenin's critique, which will be considered later, it is worth pausing a moment over its form. The paradoxical nature of Lenin's approach is strikingly expressed in the following: 'Kautskyism is not fortuitous; it is the social product of the contradictions within the Second International, a blend of loyalty to Marxism in word, and subordination to opportunism in deed'.[3] Lenin is underlining, on the one hand, the importance of considering Kautsky not as an individual, not in terms of his subjective motivations, but as representative of a definite ideological trend, the product of the objective clash of social forces.[4] Yet on the other hand, he characterises Kautskyism precisely in terms of bad faith, hypocrisy, of merely verbal adherence to Marxism, adherence in words and promises but not in practice.[5] The latter claim is often conveyed, Etienne Balibar has noted, in the following fashion: Kautsky 'ignored' or 'forgot' certain aspects of Marxism, exemplified in a whole series of analyses by Marx and Engels of the state and the Paris Commune in particular; this 'forgetfulness', acknowledging the class struggle without the dictatorship of the proletariat, yielded distortions of the Marxist theory of class struggle and the state. Lenin backs up his claims with abundant evidence, extensively citing and explicating the analyses of Marx and Engels and comparing them with Kautsky's works. This whole procedure is problematic, Balibar argues, inasmuch as it presumes the notion of a 'primordial authentic Marxism', existing prior to and standing above the struggle of different tendencies, capable of being recognised or discovered (instead of being ignored or forgotten) so as then to be put into practice.[6] '[E]verything happens,' Balibar comments, 'as if Lenin had been able to criticize Kautsky only by turning *his own* ideological concept of Marxism against him: the concept of "orthodoxy", which carries with it its opposite, that of error, heterodoxy and heresy'.[7]

---

3   Lenin 1915d, p. 312; see also Lenin 1918e, p. 230.
4   See Lenin 1915a, p. 153; Lenin 1915b, pp. 241ff; Lenin 1916a, pp. 112–13.
5   See Lenin 1914, 97; Lenin 1915b, pp. 231–2; Lenin 1916a, 448; Lenin 1918e, pp. 234, 282.
6   See Balibar 1974b, pp. 284–7.
7   Balibar 1974b, 287. Balibar goes on to say that by presenting his critique in these terms, 'Lenin himself prepared certain of the conditions which would later allow Leninism to be presented, in its turn, as an "orthodoxy", that is, as a dogma'.

One of the most striking features of the form of Lenin's critique of Kautsky, and certainly the one most commonly noted by commentators, is the frequent juxtaposition of the opportunist Kautsky of the post-1914 period with Kautsky the revolutionary Marxist of earlier days. To conflate this juxtaposition with the whole of Lenin's understanding of Kautsky's political and theoretical evolution[8] would effectively reduce the latter to the contention that Kautsky was guilty of a kind of *akrasia*, of weakness of the revolutionary will, a charge of personal, but little theoretical, interest. Lenin insists, however, that '[t]he first and most fundamental demand of scientific research in general and of Marxist dialectic in particular is that a writer should examine the *link* between the present struggle of trends in the socialist movement ... and the struggle that preceded it for *whole decades*'.[9] In fact, Lenin traces the roots of Kautsky's abandonment of Marxism back to his vacillation on the question of Millerandism – the issue being the legitimacy of a socialist participating as a minister in a bourgeois government – and to the revisionist controversy, when he entered the lists only hesitantly and criticised Bernstein only in yielding up a concession of principle on the question

---

8 This kind of conflation mars the otherwise useful work of Massimo Salvadori 1979, pp. 9–10, 251–5. Concerned primarily with Lenin's polemic with Kautsky on the question of the state, Salvadori misleadingly asserts that 'Lenin accused Kautsky of having abandoned Marxist positions on the state the moment Kautsky refused to acknowledge the validity of soviets as the foundations of a new type of state' (pp. 254–5). Now, first, Lenin set down this particular criticism of Kautsky no later than August or September 1917, when he wrote *The State and Revolution*, whereas Kautsky repudiated the idea of a soviet-based state only later, after the Bolsheviks dispersed the Constituent Assembly. Secondly, Lenin argues at length in Chapter VI of *The State and Revolution* that Kautsky systematically avoided key aspects of the question of the state and failed to understand 'Marxist positions on the state' from the turn of the century, an assessment with which Salvadori agrees (12). Contrary to Salvadori's clear implication, Lenin never – neither in any of the passages cited by Salvadori nor anywhere else, for that matter – asserts either that Kautsky had held the Marxist conception of the dictatorship of the proletariat or that he abandoned it. What Lenin argues, rather, is that Kautsky's views are a distortion of the Marxist theory of the state and that this amounts in practice to the abandonment of Marxism. Although Lenin is a rather better historian of ideas than Salvadori is willing to credit, his critique of Kautsky moves primarily upon the plane not of ideas but of the relation of ideas to reality, to a reality that changes and in the context of which, consequently, the same idea can take on a dramatically different significance at one time than at another. It is perhaps noteworthy in this regard that Salvadori omits mention of the fact that Lenin denounced Kautsky as a renegade not from 1917 or 1918, but from 1914, despite referencing passages (pp. 200, 252) in which Lenin goes out of his way to make this clear.
9 Lenin 1915b, p. 238.

of the state.[10] It would thus have been the easiest thing in the world for Lenin to conclude, in light of the notion of a primordial authentic Marxism, that Kautsky had never been a Marxist.[11] Yet this is just what he does not do; he continues to regard Kautsky as having been a Marxist at least until *The Road to Power* in 1909.[12]

This is the reflex of Lenin's concern to situate Kautsky in relation to the development of social forces and the evolution of the contradictions of the Second International. When he argues that Kautsky's definition of imperialism 'serves as a basis for a whole system of views which signify a rupture with Marxist theory and Marxist practice all along the line',[13] he takes the measure of Kautsky's position not from the standpoint of an 'original' Marxism but through the optic of his own analysis of imperialism. Not only does imperialism create the basis for an alliance of certain 'aristocratic' strata of the working class with the bourgeoisie, the increased reaction and oppression it engenders give rise to 'a petty-bourgeois democratic opposition to imperialism' whose ideal – reflected in Kautsky's notion of ultra-imperialism – would be a peaceful and democratic expansion of capitalism. It is in relation to these transformations in the constellation of social forces that Lenin seeks to triangulate the site of Kautsky's betrayal: 'Kautsky not only did not trouble to oppose, was not only unable to oppose this petty-bourgeois reformist opposition, which is really reactionary in its economic basis, but became merged with it in practice, and this is precisely where Kautsky and the broad international Kautskyan trend deserted Marxism'.[14] The Marxism for whose abandonment Lenin reproaches Kautsky is 'the theory of the proletarian movement for emancipation'.[15] The conditions in which the struggle for emancipation must be waged have changed, and those changed conditions confront the working-class movement with new problems and tasks – or push to the forefront problems and tasks that have hitherto been of less pressing importance. Marxism must develop in response to the ever-expanding needs of the movement if it is not to decay and become detached from it. It is in this sense that Lenin wrote that 'the greatest

---

10 See Lenin 1914, p. 97; Lenin 1915b, p. 239; Lenin 1917i, pp. 481–95.
11 This is the conclusion reached by Karl Korsch, for whom Kautsky's theoretical itinerary consisted only in 'the passage... from *hidden revisionism to avowed revisionism*'; indeed, the Kautskyan defence of Marxism against such as Eduard Bernstein is characterised not as simply inadequate but as a 'legend' (see Korsch 1929, 11, pp. 149–50).
12 See Lenin 1917i, pp. 486–7; Lenin 1918e, p. 283.
13 Lenin 1916b, p. 270.
14 Lenin 1916b, pp. 287 and 289; Lenin 1915a, p. 147.
15 Lenin 1915b, p. 222.

blunder, the greatest crime' of Kautsky was not to have understood that Marxist 'theory is not a dogma, but a *guide to action*' and not to have treated it as such at decisive moments.[16] Failing to apply Marxism to the current situation – that is, to change it, develop it, advance it – Kautsky is thereby unable to sustain a proletarian class position and passes over to the petty bourgeoisie.

There is, then, as Balibar argues,[17] a contradiction implicit in the form of Lenin's critique of Kautsky: a critique of betrayal in the name of the canons of orthodoxy and at the same time a critique of orthodoxy in the name of the shifting fronts of the class struggle. Inasmuch as the dual reference assumed in this critique – to an 'original' Marxism and to the current tasks of the class struggle as reflected in his own analyses – figures as a single standard, it hides a theoretical problem that inhabits the contradictory form of Lenin's analysis. The filiation Lenin asserts between his own Marxism and the Marxism of Marx and Engels has to do with the role of theory in the practice of the class struggle. Marxism is identified, in each case, with a proletarian class position in politics, but what remains outside the compass of Lenin's analysis, though the contradictory terms of that analysis signal its presence as a problem, is any interrogation of the process whereby Marxism comes to be identified in practice with the class struggle of the proletariat, how Marxist theory is itself constituted and transformed in the practice of the class struggle. The history of Marxism cannot be grasped simply as the application (or misapplication) of a pre-given theory – the relation of theory and practice is more complex and elusive than that. It will become clear later on that some resources can be found in Lenin's *oeuvre* with which to address this sort of problem; for the moment, however, I simply want to signal its existence with respect to the historical role of Kautsky's Marxism. If the notion of orthodoxy came to play an inordinate role in this Marxism, an account of it that merely registers departures from its own scriptures is clearly inadequate. Issues having to do with the basis of ideas in social practice, with the subtle interplay of theory and practice, are perhaps posed even more pointedly in the case of an orthodoxy than they are with other theories. In Kautsky's case, the relation of theory and practice was constituted above all through the political project of the SPD; it is in relation to this project that his Marxism is to be understood. But before tracing the relation of Kautsky's theory and the practice of the SPD, it may be helpful to consider a reading that runs through much of Western Marxist theory and that turns on the claim that the dead end of social-democratic politics derives from a separation of theory and practice in the philosophical underpinnings

---

16   Lenin 1920a, p. 71.
17   See Balibar 1974b, pp. 272–91, upon which the present account draws extensively.

of Second International Marxism, a separation transcended in the reassertion of a 'critical Marxist' philosophical perspective expressing the unity of theory and practice.

'Critical Marxism' and Orthodoxy

This kind of reading has been put forward most influentially in Lucio Colletti's essay 'Bernstein and the Marxism of the Second International'. Colletti claims that 'a gulf of principle' separated Marx's dialectical interweaving of conscious historical practice with material determination from the Marxist orthodoxy of the Socialist International.[18] Kautsky and his orthodox co-thinkers were unable to generate an effective revolutionary response to the revisionist challenge posed by Eduard Bernstein because they shared with him 'a vulgar and naive conception of the "economy"... seen as *one isolated factor*, separated from the other "moments" and thereby emptied of any effective sociohistorical content, representing, on the contrary, an antecedent sphere, prior to any human mediation'.[19] Kautsky's failure to grasp Marx's critical demystification of the reified reality of capitalism, the theory of commodity fetishism, sustains a political practice that is itself reified and consequently opportunistic. This failure was underpinned, in Kautsky's Marxist orthodoxy, by a fatalistic cosmology that compressed 'the historical-social world into the framework of cosmic-natural evolution, to such an extent that they were no longer distinguishable'. Indeed, '[m]oral choice itself was reduced in the process to a mere

---

18 Colletti 1972a, p. 69. This general view is also to be found, though with significant variations, in Leszek Kolakowski 1978, Karl Korsch 1929 and George Lichtheim 1967. Kolakowski, for example, writes that Kautsky never understood 'the true sense of Marx's attempt to transcend the opposition between necessity and freedom, between description and prescription' where 'the consciousness of the working class actually *is* the process of the revolutionary transformation of society' and 'the necessity of socialism realizes itself as the free, conscious activity of the working class' (1978, p. 41).

19 Colletti 1972a, pp. 63, 65; see also Korsch 1929, p. 148. In point of fact Kautsky urged (1902, p. 33) that social science aim for a 'recognition of the social whole as a single organism in which one cannot arbitrarily... change any single part'; he explicitly repudiated (1906b, pp. 164–5) the identification of historical materialism with technological determinism; and he attacked (1909, p. 22; see also pp. 23, 25–6) the notion that 'the human will is a separate element *alongside of* and *above* economics'. Indeed, he took both Bernstein (see Lenin 1899b) and Tugan-Baranovsky (see Panaccione 1976, pp. 53–8) to task for a conception that separates the antagonisms of capitalism from their basis in production so as to hold forth the prospect of a peaceful, planned and rational evolution under capitalism.

instinct and the "ethical law" to a natural impulse equivalent to the instinct of procreation'.[20] In this conceptual context, Marx's portrait of the historical tendency of capitalist accumulation is translated in the SPD's Erfurt Programme, drawn up by Kautsky, into 'the terms of a naturalistic and fatal necessity'.[21]

---

20   Colletti 1972a, p. 72. Kolakowski (1978, p. 37) likewise attributes to Kautsky the notion that 'human beings are in no way different from animals as cognitive, moral agents and producers. There is nothing in specifically human nature that cannot be found also in the non-human universe'. The same point is put even more directly by Karl Korsch (1929, p. 142): 'Kautsky limits himself to repeating in all the domains of knowledge that single fundamental 'Darwinist' equation: man = animal'. In point of fact, however, Kautsky explicitly criticised the notion of reducing 'the laws of society to the laws of biology' (1906b, pp. 117–18; see also 1902, pp. 14–20) and, as Sebastiano Timpanaro has noted (1975, p. 102n), the largest part of his *Ethics and the Materialist Conception of History* is 'designed to show that a naturalistic ethics, while it suffices to bring spiritualism into crisis, is not, however, in a position to explain moral conduct in all of its complexity'.

21   Colletti 1972a, p. 55. Geary writes (1976, p. 254) in a similar vein that 'the scientific approach went together [in Kautsky's thought] with a highly fatalistic conception of natural laws', although he notes elsewhere (1976, p. 243) that Kautsky 'took care to underline the difference between fatalism and determinism'. The distinction is indeed crucial for Kautsky. Kolakowski, who is aware of this point, is more measured in his criticism (1978, pp. 36, 40): 'the foundation of the scientific worldview was, in Kautsky's eyes, strict determinism and a belief in unchanging natural laws'; this naturalistic determinism led Kautsky to 'a purely naturalistic interpretation of human consciousness' and hence to the view that 'the necessity of the downfall of capitalism and the transition to socialism is no different than the necessity whereby technological progress has in the past brought socio-economic systems into existence'. Lichtheim concurs (1967, p. 295): 'Kautsky – in conformity with Engels and under the impulsion of his own lifelong preoccupation with Darwin – conceived history as subject to immutable laws and socialism as the determined goal of this process'. In contrast to the revolutionary materialism of Marx and Engels, writes Korsch (1929, p. 68), 'Kautsky transforms the historical law that has hitherto ruled social development into an "eternal" law which must henceforth assert itself immutably'. The contrast between Kautsky and Marx drawn by any of these claims, however, lacks any sense of proportion. After all, Kautsky was capable of applauding Marx's recognition of capital as not a thing but a relationship between persons and hence a historical category (1883, p. 247) and writing that the 'capitalist may equate men and machines as much as he likes, society remains a society of men and never one of machines; social relations remain always relations of man to man, never the relations of man to machines' (cited in Sweezy 1968, p. 170). Marx himself could characterise his standpoint as that 'from which the evolution of the economic formation of society is viewed as a process of natural history' (1867, p. 10). And he could explain in a letter to his friend Kugelmann (Marx and Engels 1975, p. 196), that 'this *necessity* of the *distribution* of social labour in definite proportions cannot possibly be done away with by a *particular form* of social production but can only change the *mode* of *its appearance*, this is self-evident. Natural laws cannot be abolished

This generated the '"providential" faith in the automatic progress of *economic evolution*' which underlay German Social Democracy's parliamentary road to socialism. Mechanically separated from the economic base, the state and politics could not be grasped as a network of social relations. The class character of the state apparatus is obfuscated, the state is seen in voluntarist terms as an invention of the ruling class in much the same way that Voltaire saw religion as the cunning of the priests, and the political objective of transforming the social roots of the power structure is reduced to 'the rise to power of a particular political personnel'.[22] In this way, Colletti turns against Marx's political progeny the same sort of criticism that Marx himself, in the course of developing his materialist conception of history, levelled at Ludwig Feuerbach. Orthodox Marxism thus reproduces the conceptual vacillation of Enlightenment materialism between mechanism and voluntarism. Here, more interestingly, the separation of theory and practice that is said to vitiate Kautskyan orthodoxy rests upon a reified notion of practice incapable of grasping its human/subjective dynamism.

But Colletti's Kautsky is a man of straw. And to refute a caricature is to risk reproducing the real errors of the position criticised (and the real defeats that stem therefrom). 'Genuine refutation must penetrate the opponent's stronghold and meet him on his own ground: no advantage is gained by attacking him somewhere else and defeating him where he is not'.[23] If there is a pronounced tendency in Bernstein's thought to conceive productive activity in purely technical terms – as an interchange between humans and nature, not as the exploitation of one class by another – Kautsky understood that 'the process of creating value and the labour process ... form two different sides of one and the same process, the capitalist process of production, and consequently the direction of production and the despotic rule of capital over the worker also seem inseparable'. He also praised Marx as 'the first thinker to reveal the fetishistic character of the commodity, who recognized capital not as a thing, but as a relationship between persons, and as a historical category'.[24] Thus was he able, following Marx, to theorise class struggle and politics in organic connection with the material process of production. The power of a ruling class is dependent upon its performance of definite social functions connected with

---

at all. What can change in historically different circumstances is only the *form* in which these laws assert themselves'. Lichtheim cites the passage from which this extract is taken while omitting the reference to natural laws.

22   Colletti 1972a, pp. 105, 106; see also Cerroni 1978, pp. 256–7.
23   Hegel 1832, p. 581.
24   Kautsky 1883, pp. 127–8, 246.

production. As these functions erode, so does the power of the ruling class. In the case of the capitalist mode of production, the growth of the productive forces increases the concentration and complexity of production, removing from the capitalist his function as an organiser of production and assigning it to hired functionaries. The divorce of the capitalist class from production erodes the social justification for its existence just as the centrality of the working class to the productive process makes it the class of the future.[25]

Had Kautsky's analysis remained at this level of generality, there might have been some substance to Colletti's claim that orthodox Marxism rested upon a fatalistic faith in the automatism of economic progress independent of human mediation. But Kautsky's account of the transition to socialism weaves the growth of productive powers together with class struggle, organisation and consciousness. Through the accumulation of wealth, capitalism creates the material conditions of socialism and, through the accumulation of poverty, the resistance of the workers. This resistance gradually takes on organised form as the development of large-scale production levels the craft gradations of the workforce, eliminating divisions among the workers as well as the possibility of their raising themselves as individuals, unifying them as a class and broadening the horizon of their struggles.[26] The growth of working-class consciousness is an evolutionary process marked by a series of stages and goes hand in hand with the rise of organisation as ever-wider sections of workers come to realise their common interests as a class. Organisation simply 'concentrate[s] the way the antagonisms' of capitalist society 'are expressed'; if organised struggle is less frequent, it is by the same token not only more extensive but also more intense: 'Owing to organisation [conflict] is felt less and less as an *accidental* antagonism of single *individuals*, and more and more as a *necessary* antagonism of entire *classes*'.[27] The organised practice of the class struggle is the medium through which the workers become conscious of the strength inherent in their essential position in production.[28] Union organisation and the struggle to defend economic interests prepare the workers for political activity; the growth of their needs leads them to pursue political power through the achievement of a socialist majority in Parliament. The workers train and ready themselves, through their trade-union and political activities, for their role as the organisers of socialism: 'Democracy is to the proletariat what light

---

25 Kautsky 1892, pp. 86–7, 171.
26 See Kautsky 1892, pp. 155–6, 172–3.
27 Kautsky 1909, pp. 16–17.
28 See Kautsky 1909, pp. 28–30.

and air are to the organism; without them it cannot develop its powers'.[29] As the conquest of political power in Parliament is the goal that defines the direction of the proletarian class struggle, the index of working-class power, organisation and consciousness, is the electoral success of the SPD.[30] The mainstay of the process, the development of the forces of production, conditions not only the direction of the struggle but also its contours. It generates the concentration of production and the socialisation of the producers that underlies the proletariat's remarkable capacity for organisation and struggle and shapes the form and tempo of the growth of proletarian organisation and consciousness. The increasing concentration of production that goes along with the growth of the productive forces is essential to Kautsky's Marxism, for it constitutes both the material base and framework of socialism and its spiritual condition, the class struggle of the proletariat. Further, through the intimate connection Kautsky posits between the growth of working-class organisation and class consciousness, a correspondence is established between the maturation of the material and the spiritual conditions of socialism.

The logic of capitalism culminates, according to Kautsky, in its inevitable collapse. But he insists that this inevitability does not preclude human mediation; indeed, it operates through the workers' resistance to capitalist immiseration: 'The moral elevation of the proletariat is identical with the increasing demands it makes upon society... The result of the class struggle can, therefore, be nothing else than increasing discontent among the proletarians'.[31] The breakdown of the capitalist order and its supersession by socialism is

> not necessary in the fatalist sense that a higher power will present [it] to us of itself, but necessary, unavoidable in the sense that inventors improve technique and the capitalists in their desire for profit revolutionize the whole of economic life, as it is also inevitable that the workers aim for shorter hours of labour and higher wages, they organize themselves, that they fight the capitalist class and its state, as it is inevitable that they aim for the conquest of political power and the overthrow of capitalist rule.[32]

Kautsky was quite right to reject the claim that he held a theory of absolute immiseration, as he was right to reject the charge that he envisaged the automatic economic breakdown of capitalism. On his reckoning, capitalist breakdown is

---

29 Kautsky 1902, p. 82; see also Kautsky 1892, pp. 185–8; Salvadori 1979, pp. 65–6.
30 Kautsky 1902, pp. 80–81; see Kautsky 1909, pp. 35–6.
31 Kautsky 1906b, p. 201.
32 Kautsky 1906b, p. 206.

neither automatic nor merely economic. His has been aptly characterised as 'a theory of the political collapse of the capitalist system'.[33] Kautsky read the signs of political collapse in the scandal, decadence, corruption and 'universal uncertainty' that seemed to paralyse Wilhelmine Germany before the war. He did not, however, as Nettl would have it,[34] envisage the posture of the SPD and the working class as the passive expectation of the heir apparent concerned only with avoiding the infection of the deathbed. In the first place, he saw the vacillation and moral decay of the ruling circles as reflecting an organic process of class struggle, the product of despair before the rise of a proletarian power that increasingly constrained bourgeois hopes and possibilities.[35] In the second place, he understood that the working class must go forward if it is not to be pushed back. 'The proletariat,' he wrote, 'cannot be content with warding off as much as possible ... attempts [to limit its political rights]. It will become increasingly hard pressed if it does not succeed in conquering new bases of political life, which permit it to continually make the government serve its class interests'.[36] It may be argued that circumscription of the class struggle within Kautsky's 'strategy of attrition', the patient accumulation of the forces of the working class for the conquest of parliamentary political power, denied or underestimated forms of working-class activity essential for preparing the transition to socialism and thus effectively relegated the workers to a position of political passivity. But this is a very different sort of criticism than the charge of fatalism. In Kautsky's historical and political stance there is no collapse of capitalism apart from the class struggle.

Kautsky is certainly a philosophical determinist: that is, someone for whom there is no breach called 'free will' in the chain of causality that governs what happens, for whom there is no teleology, no purpose, that is not in principle subject to explanation in causal terms. But Colletti and his co-thinkers are quite wrong to suppose that determinism implies fatalism, an attitude or philosophy of inaction, of passive submission to the inevitable. Inaction follows from determinism only on the assumption that one knows that the actions one might take will have no significant or positive effect. It is often the case, however, that there is no way of achieving this kind of knowledge other than by acting. More to the point, Kautsky never claimed to have, and on a number of occasions specifically denied having, any such knowledge.[37] In any case, it is

---

33   Panaccione 1976, p. 63.
34   See Nettl 1966, vol. 1, pp. 408–9; see also Schorske 1955; Geary 1976, p. 227.
35   Kautsky 1909, pp. 84–9.
36   Kautsky 1909, pp. 68.
37   See, for example, Kautsky 1909, pp. 7–15.

one of the central contentions of Kautsky's Marxism that the class-conscious activity of the proletariat, culminating in the political activity of the Marxist party, is an essential aspect of capitalist collapse and socialist construction. It is just not the case that Kautsky has no understanding of specifically human practice; he simply understands it differently than Colletti does. An appropriately focussed investigation of the relation of theory and practice in Kautsky's Marxism cannot, therefore, rest content with matters of social ontology. It must examine his politics and his epistemology, the kind of activity he advocated and the kind of knowledge he thought Marxists engaged in the class struggle needed and could have. These issues arise and are addressed most revealingly in the context of the political project of the SPD, especially in the terms of his response to Bernstein's critique of Marxism.

The SPD was thrown into an uproar when Kautsky's old friend, colleague and co-author of the Erfurt Programme, Eduard Bernstein, published his critical theses on the Party's quasi-official Marxist self-understanding toward the end of the 1890s. Despite the abstract theoretical character of the issues addressed, the ensuing debate was by no means an intellectual tempest in a teacup. It engaged perspectives essential to defining the SPD's political project. Though his criticisms ran the gamut of Marxist theory, from political economy to ethics, from philosophy to methodology to politics, Bernstein claimed no originality for his views and was astonished by the stormy reception accorded their publication, whose point, as he saw it, was merely to urge the SPD to abandon an outmoded rhetoric of revolution and to declare itself to be what it already was in its day-to-day practice, 'a democratic socialist party of reform'.[38] Indeed, neither his specific criticisms nor his tactical advice were strikingly original. But as the very fact of the controversy demonstrates, Bernstein's profession was not simply a description; it was also an intervention in a process. What was new in his thought was less its content than the socio-political function it performed: by an 'ingenious systematization of scattered and hitherto imprecise conceptions', he provided the reformist tendency then in process of formation inside the SPD with 'a body of doctrines establishing an indispensable ideological unity between diverse currents of varying origin'.[39] These currents were bound up both with the SPD taking on the role of a party of reform and with it opening out from its working-class fortress to the non-proletarian classes and strata of society. The political significance of the Bernstein controversy lay in this question of the workers' collaboration with other classes.

---

38 Bernstein 1898, p. 197.
39 Angel 1961, p. 259.

In this respect, a brief look at the debate over the SPD's agrarian policy, which foreshadowed the Bernstein controversy, will provide some context before I turn to consider Bernstein's critical challenge to the Marxist self-image of the SPD. I will then examine the nature of Kautsky's rejoinder, noting in particular the absence of an innovative response to the difficulties Bernstein's critique posed for the Marxist project. Once Kautsky's understanding of the nature of Marxist theory and its function in the context of the SPD political project is spelled out, his defensive posture and the resulting limitations of Kautskyan orthodoxy can be more fruitfully understood as neither a failure of revolutionary will nor the expression of a reified social ontology, but rather the product of a determinate unity of theory and practice in which each term reinforces the limits of the other and whereby the evidence through which those limits might be addressed as problematic, and hence transcended, is effectively marginalised.

The Agrarian Prelude

The agrarian question came to occupy the SPD in the mid-1890s in response to an intensifying crisis of agriculture experienced with much greater acuity in southern Germany, where small-scale peasant agriculture was widespread, than in Prussia, where large landed estates predominated. The perspective of the south German Social Democrats was very much the one Bernstein would later express as follows:

> if Social-Democracy would not...limit itself to being the party of the workers in the sense that it is only the political completion of trade unionism, it must be careful to interest at least a great part of the peasants in the victory of its candidates. In the long run that will only happen if Social-Democracy commits itself to measures that offer an improvement for the small peasants for the immediate future.[40]

The southerners sought to vote for government budgets including measures – such as mortgage relief, loans and aid to cooperatives – that corresponded to the economic interests of the peasants. But the implication, a desire to prop up small and middle peasant holdings, contradicted the historical perspective Kautsky set forth in his commentary on the SPD's Erfurt Programme. The problem, for Kautsky, was not that the south German initiative would slow

---

40 Bernstein 1898, p. 181.

the process of capitalist concentration and class polarisation. This it could not do – the peasant plot was doomed to inexorable extinction. The difficulty was rather that it would put the SPD in the position of fostering illusions about the vitality of archaic forms of production, obscuring consciousness of the historical logic of the proletarian conquest of power.

At the 1895 Breslau Congress of the SPD, Kautsky offered the following as an alternative to the southerners' proposal:

> We must go to the dispersed peasantry and show them that their situation is in no way transitory, but necessarily flows from the capitalist mode of production, and that only the transformation of the present order into a socialist society will be able to help them. It is possible that this is not 'practical', but it corresponds to the truth and is necessary.[41]

This alternative was indeed impractical: to move, through the propaganda efforts of the party, the best elements of the peasantry, as well as independent artisans and small businessmen, to adopt the standpoint of the proletariat in view of their impending transfer into its ranks.[42] Rather than an alliance of different classes or strata, this formulation envisaged a generalisation of the socialist consciousness of the working class. On Kautsky's account, however, socialist consciousness was generated by the concentration and socialisation of production through distinctively working-class forms of organisation and collective practice. He could provide no plausible account of its emergence on a mass scale outside the working class; indeed, while the social isolation and consequent impotence of the intermediate strata could sometimes generate radical-sounding rhetoric, on the whole it tended to cynicism, despair and political bankruptcy.[43] He acknowledged cooperative institutions, like credit associations, as progress for the peasants, but progress in the direction of capitalism; cooperative production, on the other hand, was not a possibility for the individualistic peasants, fanatically attached to their property (nor, for that matter, was it a possibility for independent artisans).[44] Recourse to the present capitalist and Junker state to defend peasant property not only ignored the class character of the state but also threatened to dilute the SPD strategy of working-class conquest of political power in an amorphous soup of democratic reforms. For Kautsky, 'a Social Democratic agrarian programme

---

41 Cited in Salvadori 1979, p. 51.
42 See Kautsky 1892, pp. 210ff; Kautsky 1898, pp. 195–6.
43 Kautsky 1892, p. 187.
44 Kautsky 1898, pp. 192–5.

for the capitalist mode of production is an absurdity'.[45] Holding out no hope for the peasantry, Kautsky looked to the agricultural proletariat of the large estates and the development of rural industry to fuel the SPD's penetration of the countryside.

The debate over agrarian policy pushed Kautsky to a more thorough examination of the development of agriculture in capitalist society in one of his major works, *The Agrarian Question*, hailed by Lenin as 'the most important event in present-day economic literature since the third volume of *Capital*'.[46] Although it yielded no new political perspective, *The Agrarian Question* introduced some notable theoretical innovations; most notably Kautsky theorises the persistence of the small peasant farm in terms that virtually preclude its disappearance under capitalism. Capitalist agriculture sustains itself on the economic degradation of the small-scale cultivator, whom it reduces to a semi-proletarian dependent upon 'outside' employment for subsistence. But capitalist agriculture's tendency to depopulate the countryside jeopardises its own supply of cheap wage labour and thereby sets in motion a counter-tendency based upon big agricultural capital's interest in preserving the peasant in semi-proletarianised conditions: '[T]he large and small holding … mutually assume each other, like the capitalist and the proletarians but the small peasant then more and more takes on the character of a proletarian'.[47] Although inscribed within the global process of the concentration of capital, the form and tempo of the process are specific to agriculture: the degradation/preservation of the peasant plot is distinguished as a form of proletarianisation by the perpetuation of property ties but also, just as significantly, by the producer's continued isolation, his divorce from the progress of culture and civilisation and his consequent incapacity for organisation and struggle. But

> [i]ntroducing cooperation into production is possible only for those who have nothing to lose but their chains, those accustomed by capitalist exploitation to work in common, among whom organized struggle against capitalist exploitation has developed the social virtues, confidence in the community of comrades, devotion to the community and subordination to its law.[48]

---

45   Cited in Salvadori 1979, p. 55.
46   Lenin 1898, p. 94.
47   See Kautsky 1898, pp. 197–249, particularly 249.
48   Kautsky 1898, p. 194.

The emancipation of the peasantry, Kautsky concludes, is not the work of the peasants themselves but of the industrial proletariat. It is in this sense that he interprets the Marxist dictum that the 'industrial proletariat cannot emancipate itself without at the same time emancipating the agricultural population'.[49] Thus, even while conceptualising the distinctiveness of rural development, probably more fully than any Marxist had done, Kautsky could not take the measure of the peasantry as a social and political force. Indeed, precisely those aspects of its situation that distinguish it from the proletariat undermine it as a social force. *The Agrarian Question* illustrates the decisive importance Kautsky attributed to collective organisation and struggle in achieving socialism and to the concentration of production as the mainspring of this process – by demonstrating the converse.

The First Post-Marxist

Eduard Bernstein gave coherent expression, for the first time, to a mood of moderation that was gaining ground in the SPD under the impetus of a growing prosperity in the 1890s and the lifting of the anti-socialist laws. Having absorbed the lessons of Fabian gradualism while in exile in England, Bernstein set out to bring Marxism into conformity with the temper of the times. He understood his task as 'opposing what is left of the utopian mode of thought in socialist theory [in order] to strengthen equally the realistic and the idealistic element in the socialist movement'.[50] By the utopianism of which Marxism had not yet purged itself, Bernstein meant above all the dialectic, the philosophical expression of negation and revolution. Bernstein condemned Marx's dialectic as theoretical scaffolding that had been thrown up without thought as to the detailed construction to follow and that must consequently distort our understanding of the process of historical development.[51] 'I am not of the opinion', he wrote, 'that the struggle of opposites is the basis of all development. The cooperation of related forces is of great significance as well'.[52] Bernstein's notion of development, 'organic evolutionism', envisaged a gradual, even imperceptible, but unilinear accumulation of progress. The prospect of socialism does have material premises but 'the point of economic development attained today leaves ideological, and especially ethical, factors greater

---

49   Kautsky 1898, p. 452.
50   Bernstein 1898, p. xxxii.
51   Bernstein 1898, pp. 210–11.
52   Cited in Gay, p. 137.

space for independent activity than was formerly the case'.[53] If a transition to socialism still assumes the growth of the productive forces, this process is no longer understood as structured according to the movement of the internal contradictions of capitalist society. Insofar as it entered into the progressive evolution of modern society, the struggle of the workers was grasped not as a struggle *between* exploited and exploiting classes, but as a struggle *for* material betterment and the extension of democracy – not so much as a struggle at all as ultimately an aspiration to 'the development ... of a free personality'.[54] As Rosa Luxemburg aptly observed, '[B]y shifting the concept of capitalism from productive relations to property relations and by speaking of individuals instead of entrepreneurs, [Bernstein] shifts the question of socialism from ... the relation between capital and labour to the relation between rich and poor'.[55] He can thus decry the injustice of capitalism and the oppression it breeds and can discern in the accumulation of social wealth the material possibility of a freer and more prosperous, fulfilling and democratic life for everyone. But he is unable to establish any essential connection between the two kinds of issues and thereby loses the possibility of grasping the transition to socialism as a dialectically and materially structured process. In this sense, Luxemburg was quite right when she accused Bernstein of driving a wedge between the movement and its final aim.

The dialectic, Bernstein argued, underwrote a dogmatic insistence upon such empirically worthless articles of faith as the ever-increasing severity of economic crises and the absolute immiseration of the proletariat. He was led, in order to rescue socialist theory from the dialectic, to reject or qualify a whole series of ideas that lent plausibility to class antagonism and impending revolutionary crisis: the labour theory of value, the increasing concentration of capital, the simplification and polarisation of class structure, and so on. But his approach was not to reject Marxist analyses outright; typically, he proceeded by acknowledging some measure of validity: 'The fall of the rate of profit is a fact, the advent of over-production and crises is a fact, ... concentration and centralization of industrial capital is a fact, the increase of the rate of surplus value is a fact'.[56] The picture of capitalism that emerges from Marx's pen is not false, but it is incomplete and hence overdrawn. If the laws of capitalist production enunciated in *Capital* are best understood as laws of tendency, where Kautsky invariably insisted upon their law-like status, Bernstein always

---

53 Bernstein 1898, pp. 15–16.
54 Bernstein 1898, p. 149.
55 Luxemburg 1900, p. 65.
56 Bernstein 1898, p. 42.

stressed (against what he took to be Marx's usage) their tendential character. And he found counter-tendencies everywhere. The labour theory of value is adequate for certain purposes and within certain limits, but so too is the utility theory of Böhm-Bawerk and Jevons; there is a tendency to concentration of capital, but small and medium enterprises multiply nonetheless; the numbers of the proletariat increase, but with no diminution of the bourgeois or the middle strata; capitalism may well bear the seeds of anarchy and crises, but it bears equally, in the shape of cartels and the credit system, the means of regulating and minimising disproportions. Capitalist society presented itself to Bernstein as a myriad of contrary tendencies, without exhibiting any inherent dynamic, any dialectic.

If capitalist society does display any general tendency, it is in Bernstein's eyes a movement in the direction of ever-greater diversity. Social divisions, economic activities and incomes had been 'graduated and differentiated' rather than polarised and simplified.[57] And the process of differentiation is as pervasive within the working class as without:

> [I]t is just in the most advanced of the manufacturing industries that a whole hierarchy of differentiated workmen is to be found between whose groups only a moderate feeling of solidarity exists... [V]ital differences in manner of work and amount of income finally produce different conduct and demands of life. The highly-skilled fine instrument-maker and the collier, the skilled house decorator and the porter, the sculptor or modeller and the stoker, lead as a rule, a very different kind of life and have very different kinds of wants.[58]

Bernstein laid great stress, Peter Gay observes, upon 'the variety of the class struggle'.[59] Class struggle may not disappear in Bernstein's account, but it assumes milder rather than sharper forms; rather than becoming more concentrated, it becomes more diffuse. In any case, it no longer constitutes the form of motion of modern society: the unity of the workers as a class does not derive from class polarisation and the concentration of production. The diversity of the workers, as described by Bernstein's keenly empirical eye, belies any such materialist dialectic of class unity. Rather 'the activity of the workers as a class coincides with their activity as a political party, as Social-Democracy'.[60]

---

57   Bernstein 1898, p. 49.
58   Bernstein 1898, pp. 103, 105.
59   Gay 1952, p. 223.
60   Cited in Gay 1952, pp. 199–200.

The unity of the working class is thus conceived in exclusively political terms and in the final analysis rests upon a moral ideal, 'the development of a free personality' whose political expression is liberal democracy. While Bernstein continues to speak the language of class, the essence of his socialism consists not in a working-class project, but in the progressive realisation of this liberal-democratic ideal.

'Democracy', wrote Bernstein, 'is at the same time means and end. It is the means of the struggle for socialism and it is the form socialism will take once it has been realized'.[61] Liberalism, at once cultivation of a free personality and resistance to the compulsion of the individual, is the animating spirit of Bernstein's conception of democracy. For him, 'democracy is only the political form of liberalism' while socialism, which could be defined as 'organizing liberalism', is portrayed as the 'legitimate heir' of the liberal struggle to shuck off feudal and absolutist fetters on social development.[62] The merely historical connection of liberalism with the bourgeois does not prevent it from 'expressing a very much wider-reaching general principle of society whose completion will be socialism'.[63] The notion of socialism as the heir to liberalism finds both expression and support in Bernstein's tendency to assimilate capitalist authority in industry to absolutism. The trade unions are portrayed as 'the democratic element in industry' whose 'tendency is to destroy the absolutism of capital and to procure for the worker a direct influence in the management of industry'. Trade unions and cooperatives participate in a general movement of social democratisation that raises the wage worker 'from the social position of a proletarian to that of a citizen'.[64] By taking on greater responsibility in running their own organisations, the workers develop the knowledge, skills and culture to participate in running society. Democratic citizenship, Bernstein understood, was more than universal suffrage. It was a multifaceted process of social evolution, ultimately identical with the development of a universe of free personalities and exemplified in the following: 'Whether a trade union or a workmen's store is or is not socialistic does not depend on its form but on its character – on the spirit that permeates it. They are not socialism but as organizations of workmen they bear in themselves enough of the element of socialism to develop into worthy and indispensable levers for the socialist emancipation'.[65] For all the aspersions he cast upon

---

61   Cited in Gay 1952, p. 239.
62   Bernstein 1898, pp. 149–50, 154.
63   Bernstein 1898, p. 153.
64   Bernstein 1898, pp. 139, 148.
65   Bernstein 1898, p. 187.

Hegelian dialectics, there is something in Bernstein of the very Hegelian notion of society as a spiritual totality.

As both means and end of socialism, liberal democracy maps out the contours of a process of social evolution. The advent of democracy did not signal the end of social conflicts but it opened the forum that, in contrast to authoritarian political forms, permitted these conflicts to be engaged consciously. While, under authoritarian rule, the contending forces collide blindly and hence explosively, democracy provides a political mirror in which the strength of the different forces is reflected so that party fervour can be tempered by social knowledge and conflict thereby moderated: 'In a democracy the parties, and the classes standing behind them, soon learn to know the limits of their power and to undertake each time only as much as they can reasonably hope to carry through under existing circumstances'.[66] Liberal democracy is 'in principle the suppression of class government', the very form of compromise between classes: 'The right to vote in a democracy makes its members virtually partners in the community and this virtual partnership must in the end lead to real partnership'.[67] In contrast to the 'unbending organizations and corporations' of feudalism, the 'liberal organizations of modern society' are distinguished by their flexibility – 'they do not need to be destroyed, but only to be further developed'.[68] The right to vote may long appear a hollow sham, but as the workers grow in numbers and in cultural and intellectual force – that is, as the formal universality of citizenship is infused with substance, with 'free personalities' – the ballot becomes 'the implement by which to transform the representatives of the people from masters into real servants of the people'.[69]

Bernstein's synthesis, then, is not amenable to any neat distinction between democracy and socialism. Liberal democracy, one might say, is the official résumé of the social diversity into which the laws of motion of capitalism are dissolved. This is no materialist dialectic, but the universal development of free personalities does correspond to the diversification of society. Liberal democracy, expressing and nurturing this ideal, is the very form of Bernstein's 'organic evolutionism'. Viewed along these lines, his famous dictum, according to which 'the ultimate aim of socialism is nothing but the movement is everything',[70] signifies not a split between the workers' movement and its socialist aim,

---

66 Bernstein 1898, p. 144.
67 Bernstein 1898, pp. 143–4.
68 Bernstein 1898, p. 163.
69 Bernstein 1898, p. 144.
70 Bernstein 1898, p. 202.

but the unification of movement and aim, theory and practice, through the medium of a moral ideal. Bernstein clarifies,

> Whether [an aspiring class] sets out for itself an ideal ultimate aim is of secondary importance if it pursues with energy its proximate aims. The important point is that these aims are inspired by a definite principle which expresses a higher degree of economy and of social life, that they are an embodiment of a social conception which means in the evolution of civilization a higher view of morals and of legal rights.[71]

The revaluation of 'the movement', of day-to-day work in trade unions, cooperatives and other branches of social life, is a concrete political expression of the diversity inherent in Bernstein's ideal. Since the different facets of the movement may variously embody the social progress and liberation whose pursuit gives the movement meaning, there is no need for an ultimate aim over and above the molecular process of improvement.

That the canons of Marxist orthodoxy constrained the development of the day-to-day movement was the burden of Bernstein's critique. In his view the most pernicious of these constraints was the notion of proletarian dictatorship. It was in opposition to this idea that he characterised the struggle for democracy and 'the formation of political and social organs of democracy' as 'the indispensable preliminary condition to the realization of socialism'.[72] The temporal priority of democracy to socialism is a function of the conceptual priority of liberal democracy as the form of motion of modern society whose completion socialism is. The dictatorship of the proletariat was repugnant to Bernstein not so much as a misguided strategic orientation, in which respect it was simply illusory in a civilised democracy, so much as it was a backward-looking derogation from the principles of a higher society, as 'political atavism', less inexpedient than simply unthinkable.[73] But the concept of the dictatorship of the proletariat gains a cutting edge through the related concept of bourgeois dictatorship and the realities of social and political repression that stand behind the latter. Bernstein had at least to address the issue; nowhere in his thought is the primacy of liberal democracy over class struggle more evident. Only through its fear of overheated socialist rhetoric and its desire 'to spare the country the ravages of a violent revolution' does the bourgeoisie constitute

---

71 Bernstein 1898, p. 222.
72 Bernstein 1898, p. 163.
73 Bernstein 1898, pp. 146–7.

a 'united reactionary bloc'.[74] Only the shadowy existence of 'proletarian dictatorship' in the columns of the left-wing press held the workers back from membership in the democratic community of citizens. In essence the capitalist was no more reactionary than he was parasitic; bourgeois and worker might peacefully collaborate in the direction of social progress and, with a supple approach, the liberal bourgeois might even be won for social democracy.[75] While democracy was a decisive means for the advancement of the workers, it was not the simple political expression of working-class power. It represented an irreversible acquisition in the progress of civilisation, more durable even than the Iron Chancellor.[76] It was the end around and the means by which the alliance of social classes could be forged. It was, indeed, class alliance elevated to the substance of the social process.

The Rejoinder

The organic metaphor for social development figured quite differently in Kautsky's argument than it did in Bernstein's. Already, in summing up his theoretical orientation in *The Agrarian Question*, Kautsky had written:

> Human society is an organism, an organism different from the plant or the animal, but nonetheless an organism and not a simple aggregate of individuals and, being an organism, it must be organized in a unitary manner. It would be an absurdity to suppose that one part of a society could develop in one direction and another, just as important, in the opposite direction. Society can only develop in *one single* direction. But there is no need for each component of the organism to rely upon itself for the motive force necessary for its evolution; it is enough that one component generate the force necessary for the whole.[77]

Where Bernstein used the organic metaphor to evoke the complex and many-sided character of society and the naturalness of social evolution, it expressed for Kautsky the notion of a society driven forward by and integrated around a dominant force. The driving force is ultimately the development of the material forces of production manifested in the concentration of production

---

74   Cited in Angel 1961, p. 236.
75   See Angel 1961, pp. 236–8.
76   See Bernstein 1898, pp. 146–7.
77   Kautsky 1898, p. 452.

and the organised class struggle, the very process whose significance is dissipated in the diversity of Bernstein's 'organic evolutionism'. In vindicating the essential function of this dynamic in social development, Kautsky did acknowledge something of the social complexity that captivated Bernstein's imagination. Capitalism, he admitted, was giving rise to a 'new middle class', but Marxism does not have Bernstein to thank for this observation; Kautsky himself was among the first to identify this stratum.[78] While holding that Bernstein minimised class differences and magnified variation among workers, Kautsky did concede the fact of differentiation within the working class. Bernstein, in turn, was quick to signal Kautsky's refusal to recognise that this differentiation must be reflected in the consciousness of the workers.[79] As in the debate on the agrarian question, it is not that Kautsky contested or disregarded the complexity of social reality, but that he proved unable to grasp its political significance, to connect it with the political project of the SPD and with his account of socialist consciousness. Even where the theoretical framework of Marxist orthodoxy was reworked to accommodate the combination of tendency and counter-tendency, each conditioning and modifying the workings of the other, the resulting complication figured in Kautsky's thought only as context in which working-class agency and the political project of the SPD unfolded, not as an interactive dynamic that called for a capacity for reflexive adaptation in the self-understanding of the agents and in their definition of their projects.

His response to Bernstein shapes Kautsky's political writings over the following decade and informs even a scholarly work like *Ethics and the Materialist Conception of History*. The most striking characteristic of his rejoinder is its defensive posture, by which I do not mean his hesitancy in coming out publicly against an old friend but rather a polemical stance – shared even by Bernstein's more eager (Luxemburg) or vituperative (Plekhanov) opponents – that consisted precisely in the reassertion of the orthodox Marxist logic of productive forces and class struggle. Kautsky easily parried Bernstein's unsystematic critical thrusts. On some points, such as the collapse of capitalism and the impoverishment of the workers, he claimed that Bernstein had fabricated his own Marxist man of straw; on others, such as the concentration of capital and the growth of the working class, he took him to task for his methods, disputing his use of statistics and the accuracy of his empirical account. On still others, such as the new middle class and the diversity of the working class, Kautsky admitted Bernstein's observations but sought to minimise them and deny

---

78 See Gay 1952, pp. 203–4.
79 See Angel 1961, p. 276.

their originality, thus blunting their political import by appropriating them for orthodoxy. There is, of course, nothing objectionable in principle about the defence of received ideas; Kautsky was, after all, engaged in an anti-critique. And where the logic of orthodoxy could easily dispel critical illusions – for instance, in its grasp of the class character of the Imperial German state and the German bourgeoisie's resistance to projects for democratic class collaboration – there was nothing wrong with reasserting it. But despite the theoretical and practical weaknesses of the revisionist critique, Bernstein raised crucial issues that define the political core of the controversy and that have bedevilled Marxist parties and working-class movements throughout the past century: the political significance of differentiation within the working class, the possibility of cooperation with other classes and, structured by these, the relation of day-to-day practice to ultimate goals. Bernstein's voice was not a Marxist one, but when Kautsky and the orthodox addressed these issues, they did so in terms that obscured their political significance.

The Achilles' heel of Bernstein's 'organic evolutionism', however, the issue of state power, was just where the logic of Marxist orthodoxy corresponded more closely with the social reality of Imperial Germany. Whereas Bernstein saw power diffused throughout society, the political expression of the integral character of the process of capitalist development in Kautsky's account was the indivisibility of state power. The state was thus the strategic nodal point of class struggle. Where Bernstein saw society gradually suffused with the spirit of socialism through the spread of cooperative institutions, the increasing democratic participation of trade unions in organising production, and the elevation of the general level of culture, the logic of Kautsky's Marxism carried the imperative of a decisive shift of power in the state: 'The idea of the gradual conquest of the various departments of a ministry by the socialists is no less absurd than would be an attempt to divide the act of birth into a number of monthly acts'.[80] Kautsky's 'strategy of attrition' conveys the image of the class struggle as the deployment of two vast armies against each other on the field of battle.[81] The preliminary skirmishes through which socialist forces are built up and bourgeois power sapped – strikes, elections, agitation, propaganda, etc. – do not differ in substance from the molecular movement of day-to-day practice Bernstein celebrated. But the theoretical axis around which this strategy is conceived is the working-class seizure of state power, a Social Democratic majority in a parliament that has become the effective master of the state apparatus. This is what Kautsky meant by the decisive battle,

---

80 Kautsky 1902, p. 19.
81 See Kautsky 1909, pp. 16–19.

the revolution – and it is revolution in this sense which he counterposes to Bernstein's 'organic evolutionism'.[82]

Although Kautsky refused to engage Bernstein on the dictatorship of the proletariat, describing it as a problem whose solution could safely be left to the future,[83] the question of the state shaped the controversy between them. The Kautskyan thesis of the state as the strategic nodal point of the class struggle was the theoretical expression of the SPD's real isolation from state power. Imperial Germany had some of the trappings and reality of a bourgeois democracy: real, if limited, freedoms of expression, publication, assembly and organisation and an elected Reichstag in which the Social Democrats were steadily gaining in numbers, if not influence. But the bourgeoisie and the landed Junker class maintained a stranglehold over the military-bureaucratic state apparatus. Suffrage in the Prussian Landtag was on an unequal, class basis, weighted against the workers, and other democratic rights were similarly laden with restrictions patrolled by the police and judicial watchdogs of the state, above all in the matter of the rights of Social Democrats.[84] Decisively, in the view of Kautsky and the SPD, the only path for Social Democratic access to power, the Reichstag, itself had no power other than the power of public opinion. It was just a talking shop. The Kaiser could, in theory at least, dispatch a platoon of soldiers to break it up at any time.[85] The Social Democrats' exclusion from the locus of power mirrored the social and cultural isolation of the working class amidst the class polarisation that pervaded German society.[86] The liberal bourgeoisie, paralysed between the spectre of red revolution from below and the reality of Bismarckian revolution from above, showed no vocation for national leadership and precious little enthusiasm for democracy. The big bourgeoisie itself took on the imperial and bureaucratic tone of the Wilhelmine state, refusing to negotiate with Social Democratic trade unions while winking at their existence and organising itself into employers' associations to combat,

---

82 This is not, of course, the only sense of revolution known to Kautsky but it is the one operative in his debate with Bernstein. That he also understood socialist transformation as the generalised liberation of human creative potential is evident from *The Social Revolution* (1902), where two senses of revolution are distinguished: '[A] socialist revolution can at a single stroke transfer a factory from capitalist to social property. But it is only gradually, through a slow course of evolution, that one may transform a factory from a place of monotonous, repulsive, forced labour into an attractive spot for the joyful activity of happy human beings' (1902, p. 20; see also pp. 106–88).

83 See Salvadori 1979, p. 66.

84 See Roth 1963, p. 267; Schorske 1955.

85 Russell 1896, p. 98.

86 See Rosenberg 1962; Roth 1963, chapters I and VI; Lidtke 1966, p. 37.

through lockouts, the unions' growing influence.[87] The working class was the overwhelmingly predominant, and certainly the only consistent, proponent of democracy.

Kautsky's theorisation of the SPD project had to synthesise the democratic reorganisation of the Imperial German state with the working-class struggle for socialism. Bernstein, subordinating the goal of socialism to the logic of a liberal-democratic diffusion of power, undermined its class character; in reasserting a distinction between democracy and socialism, Kautsky paradoxically identifies the proletariat as the only agent of democracy, at least in continental Europe. The paradox is unlocked, of course, by the priority Kautsky accords to the logic of the class struggle. Democracy in itself, *contra* Bernstein, did not signify the end of class rule; it was simply 'a form of rule by majority', compatible in the abstract with either bourgeois rule or the rule of the working class. Kautsky believed as strongly as Bernstein in the essential role of democracy, which he saw as the vital medium through which the proletariat develops its powers in beginning to exercise them, '[b]ut neither present practice nor future prospects have yet proven ... that democratic forms in themselves are sufficient to render the class rule of the proletariat superfluous for its emancipation'.[88] If democracy is 'the indispensable precondition for the elimination of class rule', that is just because 'it is the only political form through which the proletariat can accede to class rule'.[89] Socialism, therefore – and this is the pivotal difference between Marxist orthodoxy and revisionism – is not the completion of the logic of democracy but the outcome of the logic of class struggle. For Bernstein, democracy is the vehicle of class cooperation; for Kautsky, class antagonism is the engine for interweaving proletarian with democratic interests. By socialising production, the logic of capital accumulation renders the working class, unlike the intermediate strata in capitalist society, an increasingly potent force. Social struggles can less and less be fought out to a decision except at the level of society as a whole – that is, except as a unified class struggle for state power. But the organic character of capitalist society, whose highest expression is the concentration of ruling-class power in the centralised apparatus of the modern state, narrowly circumscribes the political expression of growing working-class industrial might. Increasingly superfluous in production, no longer fitted for the leadership of society and hence incapable of unifying a majority around 'a great social goal', its position increasingly vulnerable to the ascending forces of socialism, the bourgeoisie

---

87 See Roth 1963, p. 143.
88 Cited in Salvadori 1979, p. 66.
89 Cited in Salvadori 1979, p. 65.

was turning its back on democracy.[90] Thus, concludes Kautsky, 'a progressive democracy in a modern industrial state is henceforth possible only in the form of *proletarian* democracy'.[91] 'Parliamentarism', he writes, 'far from making a revolution ... superfluous, is itself in need of a revolution in order to vivify it'.[92]

The logic of his analysis is only confirmed by the exception that Kautsky, at least initially, was willing to allow. Kautsky and others heartily criticised Bernstein for viewing Germany through English spectacles. But Kautsky himself held out hope that a transition to socialism under English conditions 'might be peaceably accomplished, not through a social revolution but by means of a series of progressive concessions by the ruling class to the proletariat',[93] a possibility consonant with Bernstein's perspective. Kautsky explained the English exception in terms of the deeply-rooted English tradition of parliamentary democracy and the absence of militarism and a bureaucratic state. But key features of English politics – not only the governing aristocracy but also the lesser development of militarism and bureaucracy – displayed a striking resemblance to the Middle Ages. A legacy of feudal particularism made England 'the great modern nation in which the efforts of the oppressed classes are mainly confined to the removal of particular abuses ... [and] the state in which the practice of protection against revolution through compromise is furthest developed'.[94] If this interpretation fits awkwardly into the logic of Kautsky's historical optic, it may be worth recalling that what is essential in the latter is not a specific level of development of the productive forces but their progress insofar as it drives the process of socialisation of production and class polarisation. What is notable about this particular interpretation is that England points not (after the fashion of Bernstein) to the future, but to the past. 'English internal policy', Kautsky goes on, 'now begins to shape itself on its German competitor'.[95] The fullness of England's particularistic social structure and the corresponding fluidity of its politics pass the historical torch to the Teutonic deployment of contending class forces around the centralised power of the modern state.

The contrast between Kautsky's insistence upon the conquest of state power and Bernstein's engagement with the day-to-day movement cannot fail to evoke earlier polemics between Marx and the anarchists. The comparison

---

90   See Kautsky 1902, pp. 75–9.
91   Cited in Salvadori 1979, p. 66.
92   Kautsky 1902, p. 80.
93   Kautsky 1902, p. 64.
94   Kautsky 1902, p. 26.
95   Kautsky 1902, p. 64.

is not only a recurrent theme in Kautsky's writings but also an essential conduit for his argument. It has some textual basis in Bernstein's favourable references to Proudhon.[96] It derives some plausibility from intellectual alignments induced by the debate: Georges Sorel, student of Proudhon and future tribune of syndicalism, took Bernstein's part, praising him for his 'return to the spirit of Marxism' and fearing that 'the triumph of Kautsky would signify the definitive ruination of Marxism'.[97] More importantly, the comparison can rely upon a common 'emphasis on consistency between means and ends' that supersedes serious scrutiny of the strategic problem of state power and underwrites 'a certain structural homology' between anarchism and Bernstein's post-Marxism.[98] To acknowledge that Kautsky's invocation of the earlier debate, settled, he assumed, by Marx and by history, had some basis in reality should not obscure its significance as a concentrated expression of his defensive stance in the later debate. It should suggest, further, that his assumption, in the name of Marxism, of a posture of historical superiority relied not only upon his particular orthodox Marxist historical conception but also upon a particular conception of Marxism.

Theory and Consciousness

The merely defensive character of Kautsky's rejoinder to revisionism can be properly appreciated only through an examination of his conception of the character and political function of the Marxist theory he defended. Kautsky's conduct of the defence has been widely criticised but not adequately understood because, I think, the question of *why* he was engaged in this defence has not been addressed. To address it is to ask about his conception of the role of Marxist theory. A response is suggested by his account of the process whereby the logic of capitalist development brings about the harmonious maturation of the 'objective' and 'subjective' conditions of socialism, the development of the productive forces and the rise of the workers' consciousness of class, and underwrites the harmony of the Marxist party and the working-class movement. Such a response might seem to sit uneasily with the Kautskyan thesis that socialist consciousness must be introduced into the working-class movement from without, with its disjunction between socialist consciousness and the class struggle. Properly understood, however, it is just this thesis that

---

96 See Bernstein 1898, pp. 156–61.
97 Sorel 1900, pp. 148–75.
98 See Geras 1976, p. 154.

demonstrates the underlying harmonies. Although the thesis is developed in various ways in a number of Kautsky's works, including his exposition of the Erfurt Programme and, especially, his historical writings, its *locus classicus* is his 1901 critique of the Austrian Social Democratic Party's draft programme. Made famous – or infamous – by its citation in Lenin's *What Is to Be Done?*, the argument runs as follows:

> The draft states: 'The more the development of capitalism swells the ranks of the proletariat, the more is the proletariat both obliged and able to take up the struggle against it. It becomes conscious' of the possibility and of the necessity for socialism.
>
> In this connection socialist consciousness appears as the necessary and direct result of the proletarian class struggle. But that is incorrect. Socialism, as a doctrine, certainly has its roots in modern economic relationships just like the class struggle of the proletariat, and just like the latter, emerges from the struggle against the poverty and misery of the masses that capitalism creates. But they arise simultaneously, not one out of the other, and on different conditions. Modern socialist consciousness can arise only on the basis of profound scientific knowledge. Indeed, modern economic science is as much a condition of socialist production as, say, modern technology but, with the best will in the world, the proletariat could no sooner create the former than the latter. They both arise out of modern social relations. The bearer of science is not the proletariat but the bourgeois intelligentsia; modern socialism originated with individual members of this stratum, who initially communicated it to intellectually advanced proletarians, who in turn introduce it into the proletarian class struggle where circumstances permit. Socialist consciousness is thus something introduced into the class struggle from without and not something that emerged originally within it.
>
> Accordingly, the old Hainfield programme quite rightly stated that part of the responsibility of Social-Democracy is to imbue the proletariat with the consciousness of its position and its mission. This would not be necessary if this consciousness arose automatically from the class struggle.[99]

The logic of this passage is commanded by the link it asserts between socialist consciousness, scientific knowledge, and the bourgeois intelligentsia and by a distinction between these, on the one hand, and the class struggle of the

---

99 Kautsky 1901–2, pp. 79–80.

proletariat, on the other. The priority of the former over the latter would seem to undercut the basic Marxist thesis that 'the emancipation of the working classes must be conquered by the working classes themselves'.[100] If the political consciousness that is a precondition of emancipation cannot be generated through the experience of the workers in struggle, then emancipation itself must be a gift received from the hands of bourgeois intellectuals. Unable to theorise the social dialectics of real historical change, Kautsky is obliged to introduce the bourgeois intelligentsia as a kind of *deus ex machina*. His failure to proclaim the ascendancy of intellectuals in the working-class movement or to repudiate the idea of proletarian self-emancipation poses a problem for this interpretation, unless it is dismissed as an index of theoretical incoherence[101] or, if the claim is made that the idea of 'consciousness from without' served in any case as the 'theoretical justification of a socialist party transforming itself into a party of professional politicians and manipulators', treated as a shame-faced admission of contradiction between Marxism and the political practice of the SPD.[102] I will show, however, that this difficulty is simply an artefact of defective interpretation, arising from a failure to look carefully at what Kautsky meant by 'socialist consciousness'. Once the term is clarified, the apparent contradictions dissipate and the interpretative contortions to which they give rise prove unnecessary.

What, then, did Kautsky mean by socialist consciousness? His mention of the 'individual members' of the bourgeois intelligentsia in whose minds 'modern socialism originated' is a transparent reference to Marx and Engels. His identification of 'profound scientific knowledge' and 'modern economic science' as preconditions of socialist production seems to equate socialist consciousness with the Marxist science of the intellectuals. But the equation is modified in important respects. First, Kautsky is concerned with socialism 'as a doctrine' that emerges alongside the class struggle out of the 'struggle against the capitalist-created poverty and misery of the masses'. Second, he speaks about 'modern socialist consciousness', 'modern economic science', 'modern socialism'. The adjective 'modern' [*heutige* or *moderne*] occurs no less than six times in this passage. Thus, while Kautsky situates socialist consciousness in relation to the theory of scientific socialism, he does not thereby cast it in terms of an ahistorical polarisation of intellectuals and workers but instead invokes the historical development of the theory in the very concept of socialist consciousness.

---

100   Marx 1864, p. 14.
101   See Geary 1976, pp. 244–5.
102   Kolakowski 1978, p. 43.

History

The historical dimension is illuminated in Kautsky's works on the history of communism. One of the main themes of his *Foundations of Christianity* is a running comparison between the modern socialist movement and the primitive communism of the early Christian congregation. The communist themes of early Christian literature originated, he maintains, not in the influence of Platonic philosophy but in the communist practices of the proletarians of the era, in a proletarian impulse to equality and community. This was a rough-hewn, levelling communism whose ambition to divide up the existing wealth of society reflected both the despair of the often-idle proletarians of the Roman Empire and an ingrained contempt for labour characteristic of a society based upon slavery. It contrasts strikingly with modern socialism which, expressing the growing power, confidence and self-consciousness of the modern labouring proletarians, envisages the utmost expansion of human needs and productive forces. Nonetheless, he writes, '[t]he *struggle* for communism, the *need* for communism today originate from the same source, namely *poverty*, and so long as socialism is only a socialism of the feelings, only an expression of this want, it will occasionally express itself even in the modern workers' movement in tendencies resembling those of the time of primitive Christianity'.[103]

Kautsky traces the dissolution of Christian communism as a significant social force to the sixteenth century. This period also saw the birth of modern socialist theory, in Sir Thomas More's *Utopia*, and practice, in the 'spirit of revolt' of plebeian communist agitation. Both the passing of the old and the advent of the new reflect the birth pangs of capitalist production, the modern proletariat and the modern state.[104] More's historical originality consisted in portraying a mode of production that was superior to capitalism while retaining the achievements of capitalist civilisation. The communism of the lower orders displayed both a spirit of revolt, most evident in Thomas Münzer's leadership in the German Peasants' War and the first faltering steps, taken by the Moravian Hutterites, toward a communism of industrial production.[105] It was, however, still tinged with gloomy asceticism, the 'expression of a tortured, despairing class' in profound contradiction with the 'serene and cultivated' communism of Thomas More. This contradiction, strikingly exhibited in More's denunciation of Münzer's communism as a 'horrid heresy', is of

---

103 Kautsky 1908a, p. 466.
104 Kautsky 1888, pp. 161, 171.
105 Kautsky 1895, pp. 205–15.

the very essence of socialist beginnings. The antagonism between More and Münzer contains the seed of the great antagonism which runs through the entire history of socialism, and which was only resolved by the *Communist Manifesto*, the antagonism between utopianism and the labour movement. The antagonism between More and Münzer, the theorist and the agitator, is essentially the same as that between Owenism and Chartism, between Fourierism and egalitarian communism in France. However much More longed to see his ideal state realised, he shuddered at every attempt to end exploitation from below. From his standpoint, therefore, communism would not develop in the class struggle by the logic of facts; it must be ready-made before one could think of inducing a powerful ruler to impose it on mankind from above.[106]

Kautsky thus distinguishes specifically modern socialism from early Christian communism on two grounds: first, an other-worldly spirit of resignation gives way to a 'this-sided' spirit of revolt; second, the Christian devotion to distributive levelling is transcended in the modern drive to extend the reach of human productive power. To these grounds correspond two aspects of modern socialism, although these arise in opposition to each other: the class revolt of the workers and a theory that relates the expanding productive forces to the requirements of social progress. The core of Marxism, for Kautsky, is its grasp of the contradictory process whereby working-class struggle and the development of productive power are brought into correspondence. As the theory of this process, Marxism is the resolution of the contradictions inherent in earlier socialisms. In this sense Kautsky equates Marxism, in contrast to its predecessors, with 'modern socialism'. 'Modern socialist consciousness', then, is the theory that explains the unity of the dynamic of productive forces and social progress in general with the proletarian class struggle. It is thus, paradoxically, consciousness of the unity of socialism and the working-class movement. The paradox is pointedly expressed in Kautsky's assertion that 'the socialist workers lacked, despite all the genius of some of them, the vast knowledge necessary in order to found a theory of socialism in which socialism would be organically allied to the workers' movement. The socialist workers could only take up the old bourgeois socialism, that is, utopianism and adapt it to their ends'.[107] Kautsky's thesis that socialist consciousness must be introduced into the working class from without does not contradict the notion of proletarian

---

106 Kautsky 1888, pp. 188–90.
107 Kautsky 1908b, p. 27.

self-emancipation but, rather, presupposes it. The paradox is resolved by grasping the essentially historical character of Kautsky's thesis.

As the scientific theory that demonstrates the resolution of the contradiction between the society's general interest in developing the forces of production and the workers' class interest in their emancipation, Marxism represents a certain phase in the contradiction of modern socialism: its resolution. The constitution of this science required conceptual skills and a degree of knowledge accessible only to intellectuals – in particular those (in the event, Marx and Engels) who could transform their sympathy for the oppressed into a 'revolutionary point of view', to 'take up a critical position vis-à-vis bourgeois society or, put in another way, ... [to] place themselves on the terrain of the proletariat'.[108] This identification between the Marxist critique of bourgeois society and the point of view and interests of the proletariat guaranteed that the working-class movement would assimilate the results of Marxist science, especially as the logic of the class struggle renders the socialist utopias bankrupt. In 'The Three Sources of Marxism', Kautsky proclaimed that 'the conditions for the necessary union of the workers' movement and socialism are fulfilled in all respects'.[109] The chapter headings of the same text announced Marxism not only as the union of socialism and the workers' movement but also as the synthesis of natural and social science; of French, German and English thought; and of theory and practice. Kautsky's perfunctory acknowledgement of the infinite progress of knowledge notwithstanding,[110] Marxism is here related to the labour movement as the resolution of all contradictions.

Science

Since Kautsky construes socialist consciousness in terms of Marxist theory, the last word in social-scientific knowledge, it can be further specified by his reflections upon the character of social-scientific understanding. Marxism met the primary criterion of any real science: the search for 'a uniform conception of all phenomena under an indisputable whole. In social science this means the recognition of the social whole as a single organism in which one cannot arbitrarily... change any single part'.[111] In the scientific study of society, recognising the laws of motion of society depends upon a search for uniformity and

---

108   Kautsky 1908b, pp. 10–11.
109   Kautsky 1908b, pp. 10–11, 26.
110   Kautsky 1908b, p. 13.
111   Kautsky 1902, p. 33.

regularity, for the universal, the homogeneous in social struggles: 'the larger the number of similar appearances one observes, the greater the tendency to notice the universal – those indicating a social law – and the more the individual and the accidental disappear, the easier it is to discover the laws of social movements'.[112] This distinction informs another Kautsky draws, between 'the methods and organs' of the class struggle and its 'direction': 'the latter can be theoretically investigated in advance while the former are created in practice and can only be observed afterwards by the logicians, who can then investigate their significance for further evolution'.[113] The distinction between theory and practice coincides here with one between universal and particular, homogeneous and accidental. The universality of the class struggle permits the scientific determination of its law of development, whereas the very particularity of the forms of struggle in varying circumstances poses a limit to scientific knowledge. Discrepancies between the logic of Marxist analysis and the particular courses taken by social struggles are readily reduced to the inescapable discrepancy between the concrete richness of reality and the austere scientific abstraction through which reality may be known – hence to a matter of the form, rather than the content, of knowledge.

There is a positivistic strain in Kautsky's account of science, but it is encompassed by and even incorporated into his Marxist historical logic. The small numbers involved in the struggles of antiquity and the Middle Ages accented the diversity of class struggles in different communities: 'Since no mass movement could appear in the class struggle and the general was concealed in the accidental and the personal, there could be no profound recognition of the social causes and the goals of class movements'. The class struggle is universalised with the development of capitalism, moulding an aggregate of diverse communities into a single social organism and subordinating the personal and the accidental to a uniform social law. Thus, claims Kautsky, 'the mathematical mass observation of phenomena, statistics, and the science of society that rises from political economy and reaches its highest point in the materialist conception of history have only been possible in the capitalist stage of production'. Only then 'could classes come to full consciousness of the social significance of their struggles and ... set themselves great social goals ... as the result of scientific insight into economic possibilities and necessities'.[114] The diverse forms of working-class life and activity to which Bernstein appealed might be interpreted as merely phenomenal expressions of an underlying unity or as

---

112 Kautsky 1902, p. 32.
113 Kautsky 1902, pp. 92–3.
114 Kautsky 1902, pp. 32–3.

historically transient emanations of newly emergent proletarian strata. This, in essence, is what Kautsky did with his claim that Marx and Engels erred only in expecting the revolution too soon.[115] Both the untheorisable particularity of practice and the unexpectedly slow tempo of history functioned to reduce the contradictory complexity of the class struggle to the single contradiction between bourgeoisie and proletariat, capital and labour, and hence to distract attention from the critical issues of class unity and division that haunted the political project of the SPD. Bernstein, by contrast, showed some theoretical perspicacity in claiming that 'if social evolution takes a much greater period of time than was assumed, it must also take upon itself *forms* and lead to forms that were not foreseen'.[116]

Workers and Intellectuals

Kautsky's conception of Marxist theory underwrites a structural ambiguity in his understanding of the relation between workers and intellectuals in the socialist movement. In a sense, the congruence between Marxist theory and the historical logic of working-class struggle depoliticises the function of the intellectual. Kautsky characterises the task of intellectuals, of 'bourgeois elements endowed with scientific training', as the development and diffusion of

> an analysis of the major structures of the social order and a broad social consciousness that rises above the interests of the moment ... What the workers ask of the academics is knowledge of the *goal* ... [T]hey have no need of them for the leadership of their own class movement.[117]

This claim relies upon Kautsky's distinction between the direction of the class struggle, which can be grasped theoretically in advance, and its methods and organs, arising from practice and amenable to theoretical treatment only after the fact.

But scientific knowledge gives the intellectuals no claim to leadership of the movement, for what is involved is the discovery of a goal rather than its invention, making theoretically explicit a goal already implicit in the movement; the correspondence of movement and goal is assured by the historical logic of capital and the class struggle. The function of the intellectual is

---

115   Kautsky 1909, pp. 3–4.
116   Bernstein 1898, p. xxiv.
117   Cited in Salvadori 1979, p. 76.

to elaborate and clarify a theoretical consciousness of this correspondence. Intellectuals, wrote Kautsky, 'have only one task in our party: to defend clarity. Everything else is taken care of by the proletarians alone'.[118] In this light, Kautsky's response to Bernstein can be regarded as a kind of theoretical rearguard action against intellectual unclarity, which might slow down the progress of the movement but could not, in the last analysis, divert it from its goal. Kautsky was scathing about Bernstein's eclectic dabbling in all manner of complicated questions, raising doubts without providing a clear and coherent account of his own views.[119] He would later claim that critics of Marxism 'don't oppose it with other ideas but merely give off doubts about the need for theory in general... In the workers' movement it is opposed only by such expressions as "dogmatism"... and no longer by any new system'.[120] The triumph of Marxism, the resolution in theory of the contradictions of socialism and the workers' movement, serves Kautsky as index and guarantee of the resolution in practice of the contradictions of the working-class movement. Parrying the accusation implicit in the observation that an ecclesiastical aristocracy had grown from the soil of primitive Christian communism, he could maintain in *Foundations of Christianity* 'not only that socialism will not develop any internal contradictions in the period preceding its victory comparable to those attending the last phases of Christianity, but also that no such contradictions will materialize in the period in which the predictable consequences of the victory are developed'.[121]

If we look more closely at the role Kautsky supposed Marxist theory and socialist consciousness to play in the working-class movement, however, another sense will become apparent in which the defence of theoretical clarity is of inestimable political value. In his critique of the draft programme of the Austrian Social Democrats, Kautsky asserts that what distinguishes a socialist programme from any bourgeois programme is its statement of principles, a concentrated expression of Marxist theory which 'contains the ultimate aim and the reasons that inspire our efforts'. Against those who view the statement of Marxist principles as of merely symbolic or ritual significance, he maintains that its import is intensely practical. In particular, it has 'the great practical task of maintaining the unity of the proletarian movement'. First, the more unified the conception of the ultimate aim and the more vitally this understanding is expressed in everyday practice, the more easily the danger is overcome that

---

118   Cited in Salvadori 1979, p. 77.
119   See Lenin 1899b.
120   Kautsky 1908b, p. 36.
121   Kautsky 1908a, pp. 468–9.

friction between different aspects of the working-class movement will undermine its strength. Further, a clear statement of Marxist principles stakes out unity between the different phases of the workers' movement, reining in the temptations that, amidst the fluctuation of social and political conjunctures, might lure it onto the rocks of anarchism or opportunism.[122]

Implicit in the circumstances, interests and struggles of proletarian life, socialist consciousness enabled the worker to seize upon the identity of her or his position with that of other workers and so to realise, and thereby to augment, their potential collective power, their capacity for self-emancipation. Marxist theory, then, as the linchpin of socialist consciousness, was the theoretical expression of proletarian solidarity and of the historical conditions for its emergence and triumph in a dialectical process of struggle and organisation that moves through definite stages: the docile submission of the early wage labourers gives way to sporadic and individual acts of resistance and thence to ever-more comprehensive, disciplined, determined and conscious modes of collective struggle. Every section of the working class goes through this process and as the logic of capital accumulation constantly opens up new reserves of labour power, the process is constantly repeated, though through the example of the more advanced ranks it may be somewhat abridged in those that follow. Thus Kautsky accounts for the recrudescence of anarchistic and 'primitive' socialist modes of thought. But just as '[t]he country that is more developed industrially only shows, to the less developed, the image of its own future',[123] so do the more advanced, organised and conscious ranks of the working-class movement reveal the future of their newer, less experienced cohorts.

The function of theory is to maintain the unity of the working-class movement; only Marxist science, grasping the universality of the proletarian class struggle amidst the jumble of personality and accident encountered in the empirical world of day-to-day practice, provides a coherent account of the basis of this unity. Thus, Marxism is the theoretical expression of the unity of the working class. Indeed, the defence of Marxist theory expresses the virtue of proletarian solidarity and, in so doing, strengthens it. Those to whom the defence of intellectual clarity is consigned perform an indispensable role in the working-class movement. Having probed Kautsky's thought in order to determine the content of socialist consciousness and its function in the working-class movement, we are now in a position to appreciate just how wrong-headed Colletti is in attributing to him a reified and fatalistic social

---

122   Kautsky 1901–2, pp. 69–70.
123   Marx 1867, pp. 8–9.

ontology. Just as mistaken is the more generally held view that Kautsky exemplifies the disjunction of theory and practice. Not only does Kautsky's reassertion of Marxist orthodoxy in the teeth of Bernstein's revisionist challenge not reify human practice into an ahistorical natural order, not only does it rely upon the dialectical logic of the class struggle, it *exemplifies* self-conscious political practice. Specifically, in view of Kautsky's portrait of Marxist theory, it *enacts* proletarian solidarity. The ambiguity just noted in Kautsky's understanding of the role of the intellectual in the working-class movement does not vitiate this point; it simply reflects, I think, the uncertainty inherent in any self-conscious attempt to gauge the effectiveness of one's own practice in the context of a network of interdependent, collective action.

Politics and Epistemology

The logic of orthodox Marxism, as deployed by Kautsky in the agrarian and Bernstein debates, effectively pushed the problem of alliance between subordinate classes on the one hand and issues of diversity in the working class and contradictions in its movement on the other to the margins of his political vision. In one and the same process, the development of capitalism brings about the socialisation and organisation of the working class as a unified political force and relegates the peasants and artisans to the sidelines of social and political struggles. The socialist consciousness in terms of which Kautsky construes the unity of the working class is a consciousness of uniformity, of homogeneity of class position and interest; the intermediate strata can only rally to it. Bernstein's critique displayed a symmetrically opposite limitation: the objective class polarisation of German society and the class character of the imperial state were obscured in an elusive ideal of liberal democracy; the unity of the workers was thereby subordinated and assimilated to the pursuit of class cooperation. The debate between orthodoxy and revisionism assumed the shape of a vicious circle, with each side sustaining itself upon the weakness of the other. The several elements of Kautsky's Marxist orthodoxy held him within this orbit.

The limits of Kautsky's Marxism are not to be explained, however, in purely theoretical terms. Had the theory not encountered an echo in reality, it would doubtless have been subjected to more searching scrutiny. Its echo, and a powerful one it was, came from the apparent growing success of the SPD's parliamentary political project. From the early years of the anti-socialist law until the outbreak of the First World War, the SPD recorded a spectacular and nearly unbroken string of electoral gains. The electoral project functioned as a kind of tent-pole around which was arrayed a richly textured fabric of political and cultural institutions – women's organisations, youth organisations, the Social Democratic press, workers' libraries, lectures and lecture courses – 'vehicles for creating self-confidence and self-respect among the masses of the workers', the framework of what has been termed 'the Social-Democratic sub-culture'.[124] The SPD's seemingly inexorable electoral advance, buttressed by the growth of trade unionism and the extension of this subculture, underwrote the prospect of an indefinite linear progression to power.

Kautsky's identification of Marxism – as the theoretical expression of the unity of the working-class movement – with the socialist consciousness of the proletariat serves to establish a concrete connection between theory and the political practice of the SPD's parliamentary project. Theory provides the rationale for this project by explaining how the logic of capital accumulation and class polarisation progressively generates an electoral majority for the SPD. And as the expression of proletarian unity, it inhabits the rhetoric and the strategic organisation of the electoral campaign. Practice, in turn, generates the evidence by which the theory can be tested: electoral support for the SPD, self-consciously distinguished from all other (bourgeois) parties as the political party of the working class, is plausibly understood as evidence of working-class identification and solidarity, willingness to struggle for the common interests of the class. The abstract character of the ballot is an appropriate expression of Kautsky's understanding of working-class unity. Each ballot cast for the SPD signifies some consciousness of common class position and interests and some willingness to subordinate what is particular, personal or accidental in one's identity to the universal or homogeneous expression of proletarian solidarity. For Kautsky, who held that '[e]lections are a means to count ourselves and the enemy and they grant thereby a clear view of the relative strength of classes and parties, their advance and retreat',[125] the electoral practice of the SPD was of great epistemological significance. Growth in the Social Democratic vote total counts as evidence of class polarisation and the intensification of class antagonisms, offering tangible, indeed striking, confirmation of the essential correctness of Marxist orthodoxy. This inference from electoral statistics could draw further support from the figures for party membership, for membership in unions and other institutions of the 'Social Democratic sub-culture', and for the circulation of Social Democratic periodicals. The unity of all these voters, members and readers was embodied in the leading institutions of the Social Democratic movement.

---

124   See Roth 1963, Chapter 9.
125   Kautsky 1902, p. 80.

Inferring, from these indices of numerical growth, the degree of social and political cohesion and ideological maturity of the working class, depends upon the strength of the connection between these institutions and the broad social movement they represented. It supposes that the formal unity of the SPD and the trade unions, and their professed fidelity to the struggle for socialism, accurately represented a process, vast in scale and molecular in its complexity, of social, political and ideological unification of the working class. Precisely this was Kautsky's great unexamined assumption. The whole architecture of his thought dictated that the relation of Marxism and the working-class movement had to be harmonious and that challenges to this harmony were to be grasped in terms of either particularistic aberration or regression to an earlier stage of development. The orientation of his theoretical-political posture subordinated the concrete struggles through which the substantial unity of the working class and/or the alliance of popular classes would have to be forged – and hence the question of working-class unity seriously posed – to the universality of scientific law, the general direction of the class struggle and the institutional unity of the SPD. The unity of Kautskyan theory and Social Democratic practice forms what might be termed, after Gaston Bachelard, an 'epistemological obstacle': theoretical vision is tested and focused in practice but this very process insensibly delimits the field of vision, occluding appropriate recognition of certain critical problems and constraining the possibility of rectification through self-criticism; theory and practice invest each other in a configuration whose parameters are self-reproducing.[126]

The logic of capital transforms particularistic struggles into a universal class struggle; on Kautsky's account, the advanced strata of the class represent, through their organisation, consciousness and discipline, the universal or general interest of the class. These strata are distinguished in this from the rear echelons of the movement, which are as yet unable to disengage themselves from the particularistic claims and attachments that can diffuse and disorganise the struggle, but the former nonetheless embody the future of the latecomers. It is almost as though the vanguard strata transcend, in consciousness of class homogeneity, their embeddedness in particular circumstances. But, as Hegel understood, particularity is a universal characteristic of practice. The most advanced strata of the Social Democratic proletariat were not simply

---

126 '*It is in terms of obstacles that the problem of scientific knowledge must be posed*. And it is an issue that neither concerns external obstacles, like the complexity or transience of phenomena, nor incriminates the weakness of the senses or the human mind: it is that blockages and difficulties appear by a kind of functional necessity, intimately, in the very act of knowing' (Bachelard 1972, p. 13).

workers. They were, for instance, by and large skilled, not unskilled; urban, not rural; Protestant, not Catholic; German, not Polish; male, not female, and so on. Kautsky's Marxist orthodoxy pulls up short before the challenge of theorising these concrete features and therefore leaves unexamined the possibility that the SPD advance might also represent a coalition of narrow, but growing, interests. The universality of socialist consciousness (and of Marxist theory) dons by default the particular lenses of the advanced workers. Paradoxically, when counterposed, as their own future self-consciousness, to the narrow particularism of the backward strata of the movement, this notion of working-class unity has every possibility of fuelling tensions, ambitions and resentments between workers, abetting bourgeois efforts to divide the workers' movement by separating particular short-term interests from the general interest of the class.

Practice and Theory

The abstract terms in which Kautsky conceives working-class unity and the historical process of its emergence, instantiated in the institutions and electoral practices of the SPD, might serve to reproduce, even exacerbate, divisions within the working class. The subsumption of struggles for particular aims under the umbrella of electoral unity might entail the sacrifice of some concrete interests to others. On the other hand, the same practical-theoretical apparatus functions to depreciate the evidence adduced against the orthodox Marxist theorisation of the SPD project. As Bernstein complained, while Kautsky might have admitted the fact of differentiation in working-class circumstances and lives, this fact led to no revision in his understanding of working-class consciousness.[127] The assumption that the institutional framework and the electoral project of the SPD represented the unity of the working-class movement was thus part and parcel of Kautsky's epistemological apparatus. But this conjunction of theory and practice was not merely a set of conceptual blinders; it was partially constitutive of a certain practical reality, a specific pattern of unity and division of the working class, and at the same time of a certain configuration of theoretical understanding and mystification of this reality.

The sort of process at work may be briefly illustrated by reference to Richard Evans's analysis of the Hamburg suffrage disturbances of 'Red Wednesday', 17 January 1906.[128] The response of the Hamburg ruling class to SPD gains in

---

127   See Angel 1961, p. 276n.
128   Evans 1979.

local elections was an attempt to impose a drastic increase in the property qualification for voters. The local SPD leadership launched a mass campaign in opposition, culminating in a political general strike and a series of popular assemblies on 17 January, the date fixed for the final debate on the suffrage proposal. The strike call drew massive support, in the main from building workers and dock workers, two trades particularly affected by economic crisis and high seasonal unemployment. The excitement of the masses was doubtless also heightened by the example of the Russian Revolution. During the protest meetings the workers pressed for a march on the town hall, an initiative the SPD could not stop but tried to control. Arriving in the town centre, the crowds were hemmed in by police, at whom they directed a barrage of insults, jeers and empty bottles. In face of the tense situation, the best-organised section of the crowd marched off, under SPD leadership, to congratulate the mayor on his supposed opposition to the suffrage restriction. In the meantime, however, confusion and violence spread through the main crowds as the police pushed them toward the Fish Market, a socioeconomically depressed neighbourhood peopled by casually employed dock workers and the structurally unemployed. The second phase of the disturbances, attacks on property and looting, with police attacking and dispersing the crowds, began here, followed by indiscriminate police terror against individuals and small groups in the area, leading to several deaths.

The official SPD line on the events of Red Wednesday was, as Evans points out, a mirror image of the police version. Each side saw the incident as the result of a plot by the other; neither would distinguish between the earlier and later disturbances. While the police wanted to pin responsibility for the later looting on the Social Democratic participants in the earlier demonstrations, the SPD wanted to see the 'lumpen-proletarian' looters of the Fish Market as the authors of the earlier bottle-throwing provocations.[129] The use of the 'lumpen-proletarian' category to write off working-class violence was a stock SPD manoeuvre. There is implicit in this procedure a conception of working-class unity fashioned after the image of the most advanced section of the workers, cosmetically marginalising the anarchic combativeness of the politically unorganised, undisciplined proletarian milieux. This conception reflects reality but also partially constitutes that reality, since it informs a political practice evident in the tactics of the Hamburg SPD that counterposes the advanced workers to the masses. Was the chaotic, marginal, futile character of the violence on Red Wednesday the product solely of the socioeconomic class position of its authors or did it owe something to the failure

---

129 See Evans 1979, p. 21.

of the Social Democrats, instead of simply being more 'advanced' than the masses, to act as their leaders? The significance of this question transcends whatever practical success might have been achieved on Red Wednesday. First, because, as Evans indicates, citing the weeklong Berlin riots of 1910, the Moabit disturbances, Red Wednesday was no isolated incident in the practice of the SPD. Second, because the question was never posed – it was repressed. In this regard, the function performed by the sophistical invocation of the 'lumpen proletariat' was reproduced on a theoretical plane by Kautsky, for whom the most organised, disciplined and class-conscious workers represented the future of the others. Effectively assuming away the question of the unity of the working class and thereby the question of political leadership, Kausky's sophisticated account of the workings of capitalist development and class polarisation had the same effect as the vulgar gendarme theory of the Hamburg SPD leaders.

That the spontaneous enthusiasm of mass struggle that sometimes emerged at the margins of Social Democratic political practice degenerated in this way into riot and chaos could thus be read as confirmation of the essential correctness of that project itself – the more so as the SPD did, after its own fashion, unify the workers who, after all, supported it, voted for it, and hung pictures of its leaders in their homes. More precisely, it represented and, through Kautskyan theory, conceived of itself as the representative of working-class unity. This conception and its practical correlates draw upon real structures of capitalist society. As Rosa Luxemburg noted, 'in the peaceful, "normal" course of bourgeois society, the economic struggle is split into a multitude of struggles in every enterprise ... The political struggle is not directed by the masses themselves in a direct action but in correspondence with the form of the bourgeois state, in a representative fashion, by the presence of legislative representation'.[130]

That a politics of representing the working class reflects the reality of the partitioning of workers' struggles does not preclude its helping to reproduce the partitions, as the events of Red Wednesday illustrate. Luxemburg was too sanguine on this score in supposing that leaders who 'stand aside or endeavour to resist the movement ... will simply be swept aside by the rush of events'.[131] The SPD's political project marked progress in the organisation and political education of the workers, but the chaos at the margins of the project also suggests its internal contradictions: subordinating mass struggles to the requirements of a parliamentary project can, at a certain point, effectively disable

---

130   Luxemburg 1906, pp. 207–8.
131   Luxemburg 1906, p. 207.

them and so undercut the vantage point from which the limits of such a project can be seen. From a form of development of the working-class struggle, the politics of the SPD turned into its fetter.

The real weakness of Kautskyan orthodoxy consists not in a separation, but in a certain conjunction of theory and practice whereby the relation of Marxism and the Marxist party to the working class is constituted as given rather than as something to be established through particular, politically conditioned conjunctures of class struggle. The false obviousness of this 'given' corresponded to the apparent congealment of class relations in pre-war Germany. With the advent of the war, the underlying contradictions of the class struggle, the divisions in the working-class movement and the emergence of a petty-bourgeois reformist opposition to imperialism worked themselves to the surface of political life. The inability of Kautsky's orthodox Marxism to reckon with these new phenomena left the working-class ship bereft of a theoretical rudder.

Political Will and the Party

Kautsky exemplified his own conception of the role of the intellectual in the working-class movement: he was a writer and a clarifier of concepts and issues, not an activist or an organiser. That he produced no commentary upon the events of Red Wednesday is, in this light, unsurprising, although the previous year, pronouncing 'ruinous' any attempt to launch a general strike 'in a situation that cannot become a revolutionary one', he had claimed that 'it would be the greatest piece of folly to declare a general strike in Hamburg in defence of the local electoral law, to employ the mass strike – the ultimate and sharpest weapon of the proletariat, which demands its most complete devotion and its highest spirit of sacrifice – in a single city, merely in order to defend a quite miserable, local suffrage law from further deterioration'.[132] The comparison is further sustained by the position he later formulated in debate with Rosa Luxemburg over the tactic of mass strikes. When, in the midst of the SPD's campaign for Prussian electoral reform in 1910, Luxemburg championed an escalation from street demonstrations to mass strikes combining economic and political objectives, Kautsky demurred, arguing that tactics must be subordinated to strategy and to the impending Social Democratic triumph in the Reichstag elections of 1912. While the mass strike would be an appropriate tactic in certain circumstances, for instance when existing democratic rights were attacked, its imprudent use could lead to defeats that might prejudice the

---

132 Kautsky 1905a, p. 387.

whole strategy. The spontaneous outbreak of mass strike activity, he claimed, was unforeseeable, something over which the Social Democrats could have no influence; the party had 'not only the right but also the duty to utilize its organization to prevent the outbreak of a premature mass strike which would surely fail'.[133] Kautsky's theorisation of the mass strike as appropriate in merely hypothetical circumstances has been criticised as a rationalisation of the Social Democratic status quo, weak-kneed subservience to the organisational conservatism of the SPD hierarchy. But to characterise his position thus is to reduce the difficulties it entails to a simple lack of willpower. The action he counsels, however – holding back premature outbreaks – is hardly passive or fatalistic. On the contrary, anyone who has ever been on a picket line knows that 'holding back' can require great determination and even inventiveness. And the example of the Bolshevik leadership during the 'July Days' of 1917, transforming a spontaneous mass thrust toward premature insurrection into an 'armed demonstration' and thereby averting a certain debacle, attests that 'holding back' is quite compatible with revolutionary activism.

To pose the issues involved in mass strike and extra-parliamentary activity simply in terms of revolutionary will is to obscure the real theoretical difficulties of Kautsky's position. Had the prospect or the reality of a Social Democratic parliamentary majority ever led the Imperial German authorities to, say, disperse the Reichstag, the logic of Kautskyan orthodoxy implies something like mass strikes as a response. There is no need to suggest, as critics do, that he would have manufactured some other theoretical rationale for inaction – for, if I am right, subordinating concrete struggles and particular interests to the quest for the parliamentary legitimation of working-class power reproduces a pattern of unity and division in the working class, plays into ruling-class efforts to fragment the movement through partial concessions, and thus turns the prospect of Social Democratic parliamentary power into a mirage that recedes before every advance. Kautsky's accusation that Luxemburg could not diagnose concrete political conjunctures might well, therefore, be turned against Kautsky himself.

An analogy might be made between orthodox Marxist theory's inability to recognise and adapt to the unprecedented challenges posed by its social environment and the unconscious workings of natural processes, but any similarities do not stem from a broad-brush denial, by Kautsky, of human intentionality or will or the activity of consciousness: the dialectical interplay of struggle, organisation and consciousness takes on a definite content only in terms of the SPD project. It may be helpful, in this context, to distinguish two

---

133 Cited in Schorske 1955, p. 183.

different senses of consciousness – or, perhaps better, aspects of consciousness. If consciousness is construed in the sense of intentionality, consciousness of an end or aim to be achieved and the exercise of agency in pursuit of it, then Kautskyan orthodoxy exaggerates the role of consciousness and will, for although it envisages the gradual accumulation of proletarian forces through the objective workings of the logic of capital, it conceives working-class unity in terms of socialist consciousness and presupposes the political willpower to sustain this consciousness and to generalise it indefinitely. SPD politics were essentially bound up with the educational reformation of the backward working masses in the image of the class-conscious Social Democratic workers. The party, paradoxically, assumes here the role of the 'condescending saviour' against which the words of the 'Internationale' caution the workers. The party occupied a strategic position in Kautsky's thought, expressing the notional resolution of a whole series of contradictions of the working-class movement. However, if consciousness is construed as indicating reflexivity, the process of re-examining one's agency, aims and projects in light of the unexpected or the recalcitrant, the fact that Kautsky did not rework the SPD project in response to the unevenness and complexity of the class struggle suggests a narrow, perhaps one-dimensional, account of consciousness. Inasmuch as he took the relation of the party to the working class and the class struggle as given, Kautsky never really produced a theory of the party.

Where criticism of Kautsky is framed in terms of fatalism, the absence of revolutionary will, or the separation of theory and practice, the risk is that his approach to the logic of class struggle and working-class unity is left essentially intact. There is, in any case, no such thing as a political will independent of theoretical assumptions; practice is always-already theoretically informed. An effective diagnosis of the real impasse of Kautsky's Marxism requires a more fine-grained analysis of political theory and practice. The real critical questions that arise in connection with Kautsky do not have to do with an absence of political will or a hypocritical failure to carry theory into practice, but with the potential and actual dynamics of practice and theory in the class struggle.

Theory in a Community of Struggle

The unity of the working class as an effective political force and a parameter of revolutionary strategy must be conceived not simply as the realisation of a uniformity of position and interest on the part of the workers, but as marked by the unevenness and heterogeneity of the process. The dynamics of the post-war outbreak of a revolutionary mass movement of the working class in the Ruhr were, Moore shows, *essentially* bound up with the confluence of diverse proletarian currents, with the interaction of fiery, unorganised, 'irresponsible' elements with the organised defence of traditional working standards: '[T]his fusion of limited preservation *and* destruction of their collective past ... both helped and forced the miners to create a new collective identity'.[134] Lenin, for whom the 'variegated and discordant, motley and outwardly fragmented' aspect of mass struggles was of the essence of socialist revolution, makes a similar point: 'Capitalism is not so harmoniously built that the various sources of rebellion can immediately merge of their own accord, without reverses and defeats ... [T]he very fact that revolts do break out at different times, in different places, and are of different kinds, guarantees wide scope and depth to the general movement'.[135] A practical orientation toward working-class unity requires not mere willpower, but a dialectic capable of seizing the complex and uneven interplay of heterogeneous forces and the concrete conjunctures defined thereby.

Amidst the Russian upheaval of 1905 to 1907, notably in his article 'The American Worker', where the revolutionary fervour of the Russian workers contrasts with the quiescence of the Americans,[136] Kautsky did try, stretching the logic of Marxist orthodoxy, to reckon with something of the complexity introduced by the unevenness of development. But absent a political actor open to reworking and rethinking its own agency and project in response to the unexpected, to the spontaneous movements of the class struggle, a recognition of complexity could not effectively be brought to bear upon political practice. Part of what is implied by the unevenness, diversity and complexity of the class struggle is that, as Lenin would come to understand, there will always be spontaneous activity beyond anyone's grasp or control, which alters the terms and context of political action. This 'beyond' is incomprehensible as merely 'not-yet-consciousness' – if not because it is in part a reaction to and sometimes a reaction against (the perceived claims of) consciousness, then perhaps because it is shaped in part by the terms of adversarial class projects, themselves reformulated in response to the strategic ambitions of consciousness. If the relation between consciousness and the spontaneous movement is essentially contradictory, then spontaneity must be recognised as a potential site not just of difficulty and danger, but also of criticism, experiment and invention. The point is not that there is something, pure spontaneity or particularity, that is in principle forever beyond the grasp of theory, but rather that

---

134 Moore 1978, p. 257.
135 Lenin 1916c, pp. 356, 358.
136 See Kautsky 1906a.

no one, neither the Marxist activist nor the Marxist party, can hope to grasp everything, politically or cognitively, at once.

Grasping Marxist theory and bringing about the unity of the working class are related, but they are not the same thing. Working-class unity is simply not the sort of thing that could be ordered from just one perspective. Perhaps it is something that is constituted, that comes together, only in being approached from a number of different angles. If this is so, then the unity of the working-class movement is to be sought not in adherence to a common theoretical consciousness, but in the recognition and the conquest, through the political arts of persuasion, compromise and alliance and in the teeth of the political projects of adversarial classes, of an always-tenuous community of struggle. The notion of community, with its connotation of unity in diversity, provides a better metaphor for working-class unity than does the notion of consciousness. Or perhaps it would be better to say that it is necessary, in order to grasp the complexity of working-class unity and hence the situatedness of Marxist politics, to hold these two metaphors in tension. The Marxist position within the working-class movement is paradoxical: a bearer of scientific insight into the logic of capital – the foundation for a form of socio-political unity, a community, along class rather than, say, national lines – the Marxist is required, at the same time, by the constitutive ethos of this community of which he is a member, to treat fellow members as compatriots and to appreciate that in order that all workers might exercise their membership with confidence (whatever the differences of situation, feeling, or insight), the bounds of community may have to extend beyond the bounds of class. To portray the situation of Marxism in the working-class movement in these terms is, I think, to imply a different kind of understanding of the relation between theory and practice. The unity of theory and practice functions in Kautsky's orthodox Marxism, as it sometimes does in the so-called 'critical Marxism' of some of his critics, as an ultimate resolution to the contradictions of history and socialism in a final, though perhaps prolonged, act of consciousness. Once Marxist theory is situated in the context of a working-class movement understood as community, the unity of theory and practice is appropriately viewed not as the culmination of will or consciousness, but as an uneven, necessarily incomplete and possibly reversible process of rectification, subject to criticism on grounds of public accountability as well as to the protocols of scientific verification.

CHAPTER 3

Situating Marxism in Russia: Ambiguous Coordinates

> [N]either motion nor dialectical aphorisms are sufficient to save us from metaphysics in the sphere of systematic thought.
> – GEORGII PLEKHANOV[1]

∴

The previous chapter showed how Kautsky's Marxist orthodoxy enabled workers and socialist intellectuals to situate themselves theoretically and politically and to bring theory to bear upon political practice in terms of a historical logic that turned upon the parallel, even synchronous development of the material and ideological conditions of the working-class struggle for socialism. Critical examination of that logic generated a series of key questions about working-class and Marxist political agency to which Kautskyan orthodoxy could provide no theoretically satisfactory response. These were questions about the role of political leadership and the political party, the unity of the working class, the relation of intellectuals and workers and the significance of class alliances that might have seemed, in light of the apparent successful political trajectory of German Social Democracy, of merely academic interest. But these were inescapable questions for the merely incipient working-class movement – and consequently for Marxists – in Russia. The object of the present chapter is to show how the notion of hegemony arose as part of the initial attempts to situate the social formation of late-nineteenth-century Tsarist Russia in orthodox Marxist terms and, conversely, to situate Marxism, as a theory of political actors confronting pressing political challenges in determinate circumstances, in Russia. The project of situating Marxism in Russia may be traced in the work of Georgii Plekhanov and, somewhat later, of the young Lenin, each of whom set the theoretical logic of orthodox Marxism to work in analysing Russian society.

---

1 Plekhanov 1895, p. 560.

Although the logic of orthodoxy might be stretched to permit some acknowledgement of the unevenness of development, the political and rhetorical context of the controversies that saw the emergence of Russian Marxism tied its first practitioners particularly tightly to the assumption of synchronous development of the material and ideological conditions of socialism. This assumption, however, generated persistent ambiguity in the relation of theory and practice when deployed in the context of Tsarist Russia: the relatively undeveloped state of the productive forces and of capitalist relations of production mandated only a bourgeois-democratic revolution, while the advent of a social-democratic working-class movement carried with it the horizon of socialist revolution. This ambiguity assumed a different shape with Plekhanov than it did with Lenin. For Plekhanov, it centred on the difficulty of giving theoretical expression to the leading, or even independent, role of the working class in the bourgeois-democratic revolution; for Lenin, its focus was the difficulty of theorising how independent working-class political agency could express itself through a bourgeois-democratic rather than a socialist revolution. Attempts at clarification simply translated the ambiguity into the super-structural language of class- or social-democratic consciousness, whence emerged the issue or set of issues associated with hegemony. The notion of proletarian hegemony in the bourgeois-democratic revolution arose as a verbal resolution of the ambiguity in theory and practice, at once expressing it and concealing it.

Although Marx and Engels did not directly address the strategic issues – and the complex of social and political forces – that would confront Marxist political actors in pre-revolutionary Russia (that is, they did not try to situate Marxism in Russia), they did set the stage for the strategic debates that were to follow by situating Russia in terms of their materialist conception of history. Since the very silences of Marx's analysis suggest some of the difficulties that arise when those issues are framed in terms of the logic of Marxist orthodoxy, a brief account of his intervention in Russian discussions may serve as a preface to the strategic debates that follow.

Karl Marx and the Russian Commune

'Today... Russia forms the vanguard of revolutionary action in Europe', wrote Marx and Engels in 1882, prefacing the second Russian edition of the *Communist Manifesto*.[2] Russia's place on their strategic map of class struggles was fixed by

---

2   Marx and Engels 1882, p. 139.

their analysis of the role played by the Tsarist autocracy since the 1848 revolutions as the ultimate guarantor of the stability of a bourgeois Europe haunted by the spectre of proletarian communism. The fall of the autocracy would leave the European stage clear for a set-piece battle between labour and capital and might even sound the signal for it. With this prospect in view, the two old revolutionaries looked with favour upon the campaign of terror with which the Russian revolutionary intelligentsia was then besieging the Tsar.

But what would be the nature of the impending Russian revolution? What social forces would drive it? And what socio-economic forms would emerge out of it? Russia's populist revolutionaries, impressed by critiques of the social dislocation and human devastation wrought by capitalist development, nourished hope for a specifically Russian path of revolutionary progress, one that would bypass capitalism. They appealed to the apparent vitality of the Russian village commune, the *mir*, an institution that combined collective ownership of the soil with some rudimentary elements of self-government. The durability of the *mir* was seen (in contrast to Western Europe, where the remnants of communal social organisation had long since withered away) as an expression of the Russian peasantry's socialist propensities. It thus became the focal point of a perspective in which democratic and socialist aspirations converged. Marxist themes were sometimes invoked to bolster the notion of a non-capitalist path of development for Russia and, in disputes among the populists, to sustain the prospect of a mass peasant uprising against the alternative, conspiratorial action by revolutionary intellectuals. But it is hardly surprising, in light of the fledgling growth of capitalist production in Russia since the Crimean War and the encroachment of capitalist relations upon the *mir* since the Tsar's 1861 edict abolishing serfdom, that concern should have been expressed in populist quarters over the supposed quietist implications of historical materialism for political action.

Marx's reaction was, first, to distance himself from metaphysical and fatalistic readings of his work. Thus, he took the populist social philosopher N.K. Mikhailovskii to task for

> transforming my historical sketch of the genesis of capitalism in Western Europe into an historico-philosophical theory of the general course fatally imposed on all peoples, whatever the historical circumstances in which they find themselves placed, in order to arrive ultimately at this economic formation which assures the greatest expansion of the productive forces of social labour, as well as the most complete development of man.[3]

---

3 Marx 1878, p. 136.

The 'supreme virtue' of such a theory, he wrote, 'consists in being supra-historical'.[4] In more concrete terms, second, Marx left open the possibility that Russia might pioneer a non-capitalist path of development. Vera Zasulich wrote in 1881 on behalf of the populist *Chernyi peredel* [Black Repartition] to solicit Marx's views 'on the possible fate of our rural commune, and on the theory that it is historically necessary for every country in the world to pass through all the phases of capitalist production'. As she posed the terms of the dilemma, the inevitable demise of the *mir* would leave Russian socialists with nothing but 'more or less ill-founded calculations as to how many decades it will take for the Russian peasant's land to pass into the hands of the bourgeoisie, and how many centuries it will take for capitalism in Russia to reach something like the level of development already attained in Western Europe'.[5] Marx's reply cited a passage from the French edition of *Capital* and insisted that whatever historical inevitability might characterise the genesis of capitalist production was '*expressly* limited to *the countries of Western Europe*' where, through the expropriation of the agricultural producers, '*one form of private property is transformed into another form of private property*'. In Russia, by contrast, what would have to be transformed into private property was the communal property of the peasants.[6] Summarising his own study of the subject, Marx averred, 'the commune is the fulcrum for social regeneration in Russia ... [b]ut in order that it might function as such, the harmful influences assailing it on all sides must first be eliminated, and it must then be assured the normal conditions for

---

4   Ibid.
5   Zasulich 1881, p. 98.
6   Marx 1881b, p. 124. Whether the distinction Marx invokes here is in fact at work in his earlier analysis of the genesis of capitalist production is, to say the least, debatable. In order to buttress his own critique of populism, Lenin cited the following passage from Marx's discussion of capitalist ground rent in *Capital* III: '[T]he form of landed property with which the incipient capitalist mode of production is confronted does not suit it. It first creates for itself the form required by subordinating agriculture to capital. It thus transforms feudal landed property, clan property, small peasant property in mark communes – no matter how divergent their juristic forms may be – into the economic form corresponding to the requirements of this mode of production' (Marx 1894, p. 617). Lenin comments, 'Thus, by the very nature of the case, no peculiarities in the system of land tenure can serve as an insurmountable obstacle to capitalism, which assumes different forms in accordance with the different conditions in agriculture, legal relationships and manner of life. One can see from this how wrong is the very *presentation* of the question by our Narodniks, who have created a whole literature on the subject of "village community *or* capitalism?"' (Lenin 1899a, p. 324). Michael Duggett has suggested that Marx indeed treated the capitalist transformation of common property in his account of the enclosure of the commons in England (see Duggett 1975, pp. 173–7).

spontaneous development'. This development assumes the fall of the autocracy: 'To save the Russian commune, there must be a Russian Revolution'.[7]

Marx's letter, together with its preparatory drafts and, in particular, its omission of proletarian revolution in the West as a precondition for the revival of the commune, has been said to underwrite both the tasks and the revolutionary populist perspective of *Narodnaia volia* [the People's Will].[8] Haruki Wada infers that Marx 'emphasize[d] the ability of the peasants to change themselves spontaneously',[9] while Andrzej Walicki attributes Marx's sanguine view of the commune as a potential mainspring of Russia's social regeneration to a 'belief in spontaneous development', a 'nineteenth-century naturalism' that always sought 'a "natural" germ of evolution'.[10] But these inferences are overdrawn and misleading. According to Marx, the vitality of the Russian agricultural or land commune stemmed from a twofold character that distinguished it from more primitive forms of community. No longer based upon the 'strong yet narrow tie' of natural kinship, the agricultural commune was consequently 'more capable of adapting and expanding, and of undergoing contact with strangers'.[11] Second, in the agricultural commune, the house and surrounding yard became private property. Finally, though it remained communal property, the arable land was periodically divided among the members of the agricultural commune, each household cultivating the fields assigned to it and appropriating the fruits. The dualism inherent in the agricultural commune endowed it with a certain stability, 'for communal property and all the resulting social relations provide it with a solid foundation, while the privately owned houses, fragmented tillage of the arable land and private appropriation of its fruits all permit a development of individuality incompatible with conditions in the more primitive communities'.[12] But this same dualism threatened the disintegration of the commune from within; consequently, in Marx's view, it marked a period of transition from communal to private property. Independent labour as a source of private appropriation, the gradual accumulation of moveable property (cattle, agricultural implements, etc.) and the increasing importance of moveable property to agricultural production together serve 'to dissolve the primitive social and economic equality, and to

---

7   Marx 1881b, p. 124.
8   See Walicki 1969, p. 189; Wada 1983, p. 69.
9   Wada 1983, p. 67.
10 Walicki 1969, p. 189.
11 Marx 1881a, p. 108.
12 Marx 1881a, p. 109.

foster at the very heart of the commune a conflict of interests' which saps communal ownership and subordinates it to private property.[13]

Considered in abstraction, the Russian land commune is consistent with two broadly different lines of development: '[E]ither the element of private property which it implies gains the upper hand over the collective element, or the reverse takes place. Everything depends upon the historical context in which it is situated'.[14] The triumph of the collective element depends upon a transition from individual labour to collective labour and for this Marx stipulates two conditions: first, the economic need for such a transition, which will make itself felt when the commune is 'placed under normal conditions' – that is, when the demands of the state and the externally imposed restrictions upon its land-base are removed. Second, the requisite material conditions must be made available to the commune. Here the advantage of the Russian commune over earlier examples of the same type lies in 'its historical context – the contemporaneity of capitalist production – [which] provides it with ready-made material conditions for huge-scale common labour. It is therefore able to incorporate the positive achievements of the capitalist system, without having to pass under its harsh tribute'.[15] It is noteworthy that Marx speaks of the incorporation of the technological achievements of capitalism rather than their independent generation in a social formation of communes. Nor does anything he says indicate that the communal peasantry might act as a revolutionary force, capable itself of establishing 'the normal conditions for spontaneous development'. While capable of adaptation to altered circumstances, 'the peasant is above all hostile to any abrupt change'.[16] With respect both to technology and to politics, the 'historical context' remains decisive. 'If Russia were isolated in the world', wrote Marx,

> it would have to develop on its own account the economic conquests which Western Europe only acquired through a long series of evolutions from its primitive communities to the present situation. There would then be no doubt whatsoever, at least in my mind, that Russia's communities are fated to perish with the development of Russian society.[17]

---

13   Marx 1881a, p. 109n.
14   Marx 1881a, pp. 109–10.
15   Marx 1881a, p. 111.
16   Marx 1881a, p. 110.
17   Marx 1881a, p. 102.

While it is true, strictly speaking, that 'the previous victory of the socialist revolution in the West' did not enter as a necessary condition into the scenario of Russia's 'social regeneration' as sketched by Marx,[18] this omission raises more questions than it answers. Did Marx suppose that European capital would lightly bestow its scientific and technological conquests upon a communistic peasant Russia? Did he envisage the Russian intelligentsia alone in the role of intermediary and organiser of the material conditions of communism?

To raise these questions is to signal the limits of Marx's analysis. There is no account in his writings of the social and political forces that would drive a Russian revolution. So his estimate of the possibilities inherent in the institutional framework of the *mir* remained a fleshless skeleton. Why this silence? Had Marx come to embrace a populist faith in the decisive intervention of the revolutionary intelligentsia in countries, such as Russia, where the people had not yet crystallised into a formation of social classes whose struggle would act as a historical motor force? Perhaps. But it seems more likely that the import of this silence was tactical rather than theoretical, that it was meant to place no intellectual inhibitions in the way of the intelligentsia's assault on the autocracy – an adventure which may not have led, as its protagonists intended, to some form of socialism, but which was nonetheless bound (as a spark that might ignite an impending democratic revolution and then, possibly, the socialist revolution in Europe) to advance historical progress. This was certainly Engels's view. Marx was not writing here as a political actor having to represent such forces in pursuit of such aims threatened by such obstacles, to appeal to such interests and win over such allies while resisting the stratagems of such adversaries. He was writing from outside and could act only by lending elements of analysis to those who had to act – and react – within the field of forces that constituted the concrete political situation in Russia. But historical analysis can serve as a guide to political action only by understanding and incorporating the logic of this field of political forces. Historical materialism, at least as Marx himself applied it, was only a 'guiding thread' to the historical study of social formations, not a substitute for concrete analysis. The task of working out a concrete historical materialist analysis of the social and political forces in process of formation in Tsarist Russia had not yet been undertaken. Marx's analysis may have helped to locate Russia in historical materialist terms, but it could not serve to guide Marxist political action within Russia.

---

18 See Walicki 1969, p. 189.

Georgii Plekhanov and the Transformation of Russian Society

When the assassination of Tsar Alexander II in 1881 triggered the machinery of police repression but not the expected revolutionary onslaught, populism appeared to have reached an impasse as a revolutionary movement. In response the former *Chernye peredeltsi*, Vera Zasulich, P.B. Axelrod, and Georgii Plekhanov formed the first professedly Marxist organisation of Russians, the Group for the Emancipation of Labour. Exiled in Geneva, the members of the Group set about 'spreading socialist ideas in Russia and working out the elements for organising a Russian workers' *socialist party*'.[19] The conjunction of two claims, that the impending revolution could only be a struggle for bourgeois democracy and that the working class engendered by capitalism must nonetheless assume an independent, even leading, revolutionary role, distinguished the Group's stance and established the parameters of Russian Marxism. Plekhanov was the principal architect of the theoretical rationale for this conjunction, which he articulated in terms that reproduced the unilinear historical logic of Kautsky's Marxist orthodoxy. This logic would enable him to initiate Marxist analysis of the historical forces driving the revolutionary process in Russia, but it would preclude him from deriving unambiguous political conclusions.

Plekhanov announced his conversion to Marxism in the 1883 pamphlet *Socialism and Political Struggle* with the following rebuke to his former populist comrades: 'To bind together in one two so fundamentally different matters as the overthrow of absolutism and the socialist revolution, to wage revolutionary struggle in the belief that these elements of social development will *coincide* in the history of our country *means to put off the advent of both*'.[20] The logic of Plekhanov's position is perhaps most clearly spelled out in a materialist dialectic of the content and form of the historical process. With the thesis that 'acting on external [nature], man changes his own nature', Marx shifted the study of society from speculative debate about human nature to concrete investigation of how the process of human productive action on the external world takes place.[21]

---

19   Plekhanov 1884, p. 353.
20   Plekhanov 1883, p. 104. A sense of the impact of Plekhanov's critique of populism may be gleaned from Maxim Gorky's account of a secret meeting of revolutionaries in the final volume of his autobiography, *My Universities* (see Gorky 1923).
21   Plekhanov 1895, pp. 580, 607.

Social man's productive impact upon nature and the growth of the productive forces involved in that impact – such is the *content*; society's economic structure, its property relations provide the *form*, engendered by a given content (the particular degree in the 'development of material production') and rejected in consequence of the *further development of that content*. Once it has arisen, the contradiction between form and content is not 'blunted' but *increases*, thanks to the continuous growth of the content, which far outstrips the ability of the old form to change in keeping with the new needs. Thus a moment arrives sooner or later when the elimination of the *old form* and its replacement by a *new* one becomes necessary.[22]

Although form and content are interwoven, content is assigned priority over form, productive forces over relations of production, the 'economic movement of society' over the context in which it unfolds. In assessing the progressive capacity of social forms, Plekhanov distinguishes dynamic historical forces from mere passive receptivity to change. 'For the philosophy of history, just as for the practical revolutionary, the only forms that have any importance are those that are capable of a greater or lesser quantity of ... *useful historical work*'.[23] The receptivity of a social form to change, suggestive of the possibility of variation in different directions, is subordinated to the internal contradiction of historical forms. Concrete analysis does not aim at the nuances of tradition or variation of circumstance but locates social forms in historical phases periodised in accordance with the degree of development of the productive forces and the class struggle.

Commodity production had already taken root in Russia, Plekhanov claimed, and its unfettered growth was both necessary and progressive. 'Russia will continue to proceed along the path of capitalist development, not because there exists some external force, some mysterious law pushing her along that path, but because there is no effective internal force capable of pushing it from that path'.[24] For Plekhanov, the Russian countryside figures as an empty page upon which capital can inscribe its inexorable logic of class division: '[T]he independent development of the village commune ... consists in disintegrating'.[25] The primitive vitality of the commune, he thought, could not survive the advent of commodity production and the eclipse of the isolated natural economy.

---

22   Plekhanov 1901, p. 512.
23   Plekhanov 1885, p. 137.
24   Plekhanov 1895, pp. 678–81.
25   Plekhanov 1885, p. 309.

Though untouched by the storms of political revolution, it 'turns out to be powerless and defenceless against the logic of economic evolution'.[26] The commune and the peasantry were passive, static, in contrast to capital and the proletariat, which were active, dynamic. The commune is transformed, in the circumstance of commodity production, 'from a means of protecting the producers against capitalist exploitation ... [into] a powerful instrument of [capitalist exploitation]'.[27] The logic of commodity exchange, hastened by the reform edict of 1861, deepened the incipient social divisions in the commune, giving rise to an upstart class of petty rural capitalists and usurers and a mass of semi-proletarians without the means to work their allotments and thus constrained to work for others. In this context, communal obligations and restrictions served only to perpetuate the most primitive and brutal forms of capitalist exploitation and 'the utopian enemies of capitalism', the populist friends of the commune, 'prove in reality to be the accomplices of capitalism in its most coarse, shameful and harmful form'.[28]

Although comprehensively oppressed and exploited under the existing regime, the peasant was no revolutionary protagonist: 'The Russian revolutionary movement, whose victory would be first and foremost profitable to the peasants, finds among them hardly any support, sympathy, or understanding'.[29] Because it ties the interests of the peasants to the land, the commune 'hinders their intellectual and political development by limiting their outlook to the narrow bounds of village traditions'.[30] Parochial in outlook and profoundly unaware of his place in society, the peasant 'remains a mere *cipher* in the sense of some conscious impact upon the blind forces of the economy'.[31]

This reading of the Russian countryside recalls Marx's changeless 'Asiatic mode of production'; Plekhanov did not use the term but he often referred to the

---

26   Plekhanov 1885, p. 241.
27   Plekhanov 1885, p. 240.
28   Plekhanov 1901, p. 686.
29   Plekhanov 1888a, p. 359. Plekhanov did allow that in the event of a revolutionary movement among the peasantry, the orientation of revolutionaries would shift accordingly. But this was nothing more than a rhetorical posture assumed for the purpose of debate with the populists. By treating it as Plekhanov's 'alternative blueprint for the coming revolution' (Frankel 1972, p. 71), Jonathan Frankel misses the forest for the trees. There was simply no room in the theoretical structure of Plekhanov's Marxism for a revolutionary movement of the peasantry. Locked in controversy with the populists for the allegiance of the revolutionary intelligentsia, he could hardly have avoided giving it minimal consideration as a hypothetical possibility, and that is what he did.
30   Plekhanov 1888a, p. 359.
31   Plekhanov 1896, p. 203.

'patriarchal' or 'Asiatic' character of Russian society.[32] This consisted of a myriad of autonomous village communities, the unmoving foundation of a state that embodied and enforced an all-encompassing oppression, a despotism whose cast of characters may change but whose structure endures, feeding on the surplus extracted from the villages and denying the latter the material conditions for progress. Though peasants rebelled from time to time against their exploitation, the very conditions of their existence rendered their revolt scattered, sporadic and ineffectual. Peasant resistance, wrote Plekhanov, was never really political; for redress of their grievances, the peasants did not look to themselves but to a saviour from above. Even where revolts coalesced into an insurrectionary movement, they could do so only in the name of a self-proclaimed 'true' Tsar against a 'usurper'. Such movements were bound to be ephemeral; peasant struggles could never rise above the blind and irrational workings of 'a force of nature'.[33] 'It was upon the peasant', wrote Plekhanov, 'that Oriental despotisms sustained themselves unchanged for thousands of years'.[34]

The peasant was, in this respect, the 'political antipode' of the worker. 'The historical role of the peasant is as conservative as that of the worker is revolutionary', [35] and this conservatism could be shaken only when 'the proletarian, ejected from the countryside as an impoverished member of the village commune, returns as a Social-Democratic agitator'.[36] If Marx's scenario

---

[32] Though present throughout Plekhanov's works, this theme received increasing emphasis after his break with Lenin and provided the intellectual basis for his opposition to Lenin's post-1905 proposal for nationalising the land. It is most prominent in his scholarly *History of Russian Social Thought*, where he writes of Peter the Great's reform programme: 'While promoting a policy of Europeanization, Peter utilized to the utmost the theories of absolutism as practiced among Oriental despots. Through some misunderstanding, this side of Peter's reform has been construed as a sign of democracy ... The prominent characteristics of the newly established order are all in contrast to a democratic order, because in it all were enslaved except one, while in a democracy all are free, at least *de jure*. In the wide gap between these two extremes are all those constitutions which grant freedom to a greater or less number of privileged persons' (Plekhanov 1909, pp. 54, 55). Plekhanov's deployment of this theme is discussed at length in Samuel Baron 1963, pp. 295–305. Elsewhere Baron notes a strong similarity between Plekhanov's reading of Russian history and that of Trotsky, his arch-foe within the Russian revolutionary movement; during the Soviet historiographical debates of the 1920s, Trotsky would defend Plekhanov's historical conceptions while divorcing them from Plekhanov's political views (see Baron 1976, pp. 63, 72; Trotsky 1908, pp. 21–41).

[33] Plekhanov n. d., p. 513.
[34] Cited in Keep 1963, p. 21.
[35] Ibid.
[36] Plekhanov 1888a, p. 361.

required an intermediary to provide the commune with access to the scientific, technological and political achievements of capitalist civilisation, for Plekhanov the intermediary can be none other than the industrial worker. The disintegration of the commune can be halted only through 'a new popular force capable of putting an end to capitalism'. But this force, the working class, itself comes into being only through the logic of capital, from elements thrown off in the very process of communal disintegration.[37] The socialist revolution 'is unthinkable without the presence of the necessary and sufficient historical force born of the contradictions in the present bourgeois system'.[38] And the socialist organisation of production assumes not only the existence of a class of wage labourers but, additionally, that capitalist relations have developed to a point where the socialisation of the productive forces comes into contradiction with private capitalist appropriation and that the workers have become conscious of this contradiction and of the social-revolutionary possibility it creates.[39] Only through the logic of capital do the workers struggle and organise against capital and gradually constitute themselves as an independent political force. The growth of the socialist consciousness of the working class 'generally proceeds parallel to the development of the productive forces and of the [corresponding] organisation of production'.[40] The self-emancipation of the working class is thus the subjective aspect inscribed upon the objectively unfolding logic of history and, as such, it is the unifying theme, at once movement and goal, of Plekhanov's thought.

That traditional Russia, whether patriarchal or communal, could counter capital with nothing more dynamic than the force of inertia enabled Plekhanov to read the alignment of social forces directly from the unilinear logic of capitalism. In such a perspective, engaging in concrete analysis amounts to locating Russian society on the trajectory of capitalist evolution, to estimating the degree of erosion of the patriarchal economy and society under the relentless pressure of capital accumulation. Plekhanov's analysis nonetheless represents an important advance over Marx, who analysed the commune in abstraction from the interplay of social and political forces. Plekhanov's was the first Marxist attempt to come to grips with the difficult question of the social forces driving the Russian revolutionary process. His insistence upon the centrality of this question and his answer to it – whatever its limits – mark the introduction

---

37 See Plekhanov 1888a, p. 361.
38 Plekhanov 1885, p. 137.
39 See Plekhanov 1885, pp. 303–4.
40 Plekhanov 1885, p. 297.

of Marxism as a political trend into Russia. For without an analysis of social forces, there could be no Marxist political strategy.

Forces of Revolution and the Problem of Hegemony

By unfettering the élan of capitalist production and permitting the workers to educate themselves in legal political activity, the impending democratic revolution would foster the growth of the objective and subjective conditions for an eventual proletarian socialist revolution. Defeating absolutism was necessary to remove the patriarchal debris that fettered the development of the productive forces, and the conquest of political liberty was a condition for the growth of working-class political consciousness. It would liberate all classes and strata of society – bourgeois and worker, intellectual and peasant – from the weight of patriarchal exaction and bureaucratic arbitrariness. While confined within the limits of a bourgeois social order, the course of the revolution, as the focal point of diverse and opposing interests, was still to be defined. What social force, by assuming this task, would impress its character upon the course of events?

It would not be the peasantry, whose 'political indifference and intellectual backwardness' were, in Plekhanov's view, the 'main bulwark of absolutism'.[41] Indeed, 'peasant backwardness' also served him as the explanatory context for the 'timidity', 'instability' and resulting inaptitude for revolutionary leadership of the 'educated sections of the higher classes'.[42] But neither could

---

41   Plekhanov 1888a, p. 359. This statement from the 'Draft Programme for Russian Social Democrats' issued by the Group for the Emancipation of Labour was singled out for criticism by Lenin on the grounds that it would preclude the working-class party from assisting any revolutionary struggles of the peasantry against the autocracy (see Lenin 1899d, pp. 245–8).

42   Plekhanov 1888a, p. 360. Plekhanov's theoretical nullification of the peasantry as a social and political force could thus underpin a rather rationalistic treatment of populism. It was not that he mistook the contradictory character of populist ideology, progressive democratic inclinations inhabiting a reactionary romanticisation of the traditional institutions of the people – in fact, Plekhanov was well aware of a petty-bourgeois democratic strain in the populist chorus – but the political passivity of the peasantry left populist ideology hanging in mid-air. Plekhanov was thus unable to conceive of the populists as the more-or-less adequate, more-or-less rational representatives of a definite social force; he could treat them only as utopians and their utopia not as a myth enveloping the struggle of a definite social interest but only as an intellectual expression of peasant incapacity and irrationality.

revolutionary leadership be expected from the bourgeoisie. It was not simply that the Russian bourgeoisie was peculiarly reliant upon government purchases; seen in the light of Western European experience, this was no anomaly but merely an indication of the relatively early phase of its development.[43] It had to do, rather, with the nature of the bourgeoisie as a class which 'do[es] not come into the streets, put up barricades or publish underground leaflets'. Instead, the bourgeois could rely upon a division of labour and enrich himself, 'undermin[ing] the...system little by little' while waiting for the people to fight his enemy's enemy and then reaping the fruits of their victory without having to risk his profits.[44] The Italian *Risorgimento* exemplified this pattern and Plekhanov saw no reason why the Russian bourgeoisie, at its rudimentary stage of development, would act differently.[45] Though the bourgeois may have preferred to operate through constitutional avenues, he was not eager to jeopardise what access he enjoyed to bureaucratic and ministerial backrooms.

> Our bourgeoisie is now undergoing an important metamorphosis: it has developed lungs which require the fresh air of political self-government but its gills have not yet completely atrophied and still permit it to breathe in the troubled waters of decaying absolutism.[46]

The logic of events would drive the bourgeoisie into opposition but could not make it take the initiative.[47]

Responsibility for leadership in Russia's bourgeois-democratic revolution was thus, as if by default, incumbent upon the working class. It was as though the dynamic historical force of capital had come to be concentrated in the workers rather than the bourgeoisie. Addressing the Congress of the Socialist International in 1889, Plekhanov concluded, 'I insist upon this important point: the revolutionary movement in Russia will triumph as a *working-class movement* or else it will never triumph!'[48] Although it would most likely not stand alone in the struggle against the autocracy, 'only the working class is capable of giving that struggle the decisive turn' and in doing so it 'will necessarily drive the whole of our bourgeoisie, i.e. our "society", our world of trade and industry, our landlords, that petty-bourgeois nobility, and finally even the rural

---

43 See Plekhanov 1885, pp. 195–207.
44 Plekhanov 1885, p. 212.
45 See Plekhanov 1885, p. 213.
46 Plekhanov 1885, p. 212.
47 See Plekhanov 1884, p. 355.
48 Plekhanov 1889, p. 400.

"third estate" to a struggle which is *within their power*.⁴⁹ The working class, in the words of Plekhanov's colleague Pavel Axelrod, would act as 'a lever pushing all the enemies of absolutism into an organised attack upon it'.⁵⁰ The phrase 'hegemony of the proletariat in the democratic revolution', coined by Axelrod around the turn of the century, gave pointed expression to this orientation. But the stance itself was essential to the project of situating Marxism in Russia; it was at the heart of the political strategy of Russian Marxism mapped out by Plekhanov since the early 1880s.

The orientation of proletarian hegemony in the democratic revolution, however, was ambiguous, without theoretical foundation in terms of the unilinear historical logic that shaped Plekhanov's Marxism. The difficulty was not that the working class lacked a pressing interest in participating in the democratic revolution. The workers suffered not only from capitalist exploitation but also from absolutism and the police-state fetters on their organised resistance to exploitation; they had a compelling immediate interest in the political freedom and democracy that would allow them to work out the terms and instruments of their economic emancipation. Nor is the difficulty that the workers lacked means for effective participation: socialisation of the productive forces concentrated wage workers in urban centres at the same time as it promoted their mobility, so they were endowed with both the capacity for organisation and the breadth of view necessary for political action. Indeed, the workers were well situated to 'bridge the historical abyss between the "people" and the "educated" section of the population'.⁵¹ Proletarian hegemony, however, did not signify mere encouragement to participate but a claim to political independence, to leadership.

But what this claim amounted to is unclear. Political independence had to have meant something more than the mere existence of a separate Social Democratic organisation, for Axelrod would insist that 'if there is no possibility of assigning to the Russian proletariat an independent, pre-eminent role in the struggle against police Tsarism, autocracy and arbitrariness, then Russian Social Democracy has no historical right to exist'.⁵² But what more? The difficulty is apparent as soon as one asks what in the features of the bourgeois-democratic revolution would count as evidence of proletarian hegemony. Neither the unfolding of the revolution as a mass movement from below nor its initiation by the workers is enough to distinguish it from earlier revolu-

---

49   Plekhanov 1888b, p. 394.
50   Cited in Ascher 1972, p. 135.
51   Plekhanov 1885, p. 345.
52   Cited in Harding 1977, p. 47.

tions in which the 'people' supplied the cannon fodder while their 'betters' seized the fruits of victory. How, indeed, could the working class escape the domination of capital, let alone play a preeminent role, when it is just a *bourgeois* revolution that it is enacting? By spearheading the fight for democracy, Axelrod suggested, the workers would win a position of prestige and influence over all classes and strata of society.[53] But 'prestige' doesn't translate into the kind of class analysis available to Plekhanov's orthodox Marxism. Theorising the political impotence of Russia's traditional social order and especially of the peasantry, Plekhanov effectively compressed the distinctiveness of the Russian social formation into the generic dynamism of the struggle between capital and labour. The logic of this struggle leads to the dominance of the proletariat, but only at the threshold of socialism.

Intellectuals, Consciousness and Hegemony

Plekhanov struggled to resolve the tensions produced by the challenge of theorising proletarian hegemony in terms consistent with Marxist orthodoxy, reformulating the problem in the language of class consciousness. The emergence of a broad working-class movement presumes the conquest of free political institutions, he wrote, but political freedoms cannot be won without the independent intervention of the working class. 'What is the way out? Western European history broke this vicious circle by the gradual political education of the working class'.[54] The capacity of the working class for self-emancipation depends upon 'the clarity of its political consciousness, its cohesion and its degree of organisation'[55] and 'increases in direct proportion to the speed and intensity of the process of [its political] education and assimilation' of socialist ideas.[56] These elements of working-class power were susceptible to the influence of socialist intellectuals, whom Plekhanov charged with accelerating this gradual process, fostering the self-consciousness of the nascent working-class movement. The Russian socialist intelligentsia must

> show the workers their own, working-class banner, give them leaders from their own, working-class ranks, [and] make sure that not bourgeois 'society', but the workers' secret organisations gain dominating influence

---

53   See Ascher 1972, p. 135.
54   Plekhanov 1885, p. 341.
55   Plekhanov 1883, p. 102.
56   Plekhanov 1885, p. 178.

over the workers' minds. This will considerably hasten the growth of the Russian workers' socialist party, which will ... win itself a place of honour among the other parties after having ... promoted the fall of absolutism.[57]

Regarded in this light, might the early beginnings of Russian socialism, while capitalism was still in its early stages, not amount to a distinctive and perhaps decisive circumstance? Translating the problem of proletarian hegemony into the language of class consciousness cannot, however, resolve the equivocation it generates in the logic of Marxist orthodoxy. Indeed, it introduces the additional difficulty of grasping the relation between the intelligentsia and the development of working-class consciousness.

Plekhanov's account of the relation between revolutionary intellectuals and the working-class movement is bound up in complex ways with the theme of proletarian self-emancipation. 'In order ... to contribute to the intellectual and political independence of the Russian working class', wrote Plekhanov,

> our revolutionaries need not resort to any artificial measures or place themselves in any false or ambiguous position. All they need is [to absorb fully] the principles of Social Democracy and ... to impress upon their listeners that 'the economical emancipation of the working classes is the great end to which every political movement ought to be subordinate as a means'. Once it has assimilated this thought, our working class will itself be capable of steering between Scylla and Charybdis, between the political reaction of state socialism and the economic quackery of the liberal bourgeoisie.[58]

Social Democratic intellectuals were to act through the working class – not as through an unconscious instrument, but as a tutor arouses the self-consciousness and self-confidence of the talented learner. Though they constituted a key link in the strategy of proletarian hegemony, they were not an independent force or even, in the long run, indispensable to the proletarian cause. Even when insisting that 'the mere possibility' of a politically conscious movement of the Russian working class 'depends in a large degree upon [the organisational and educational activity] of the intelligentsia among the working class', Plekhanov immediately adds, 'the intelligentsia must as a preliminary step

---

57   Plekhanov 1885, p. 343.
58   Plekhanov 1885, pp. 343–4.

adopt the standpoint of modern scientific socialism'.[59] He held, like Kautsky, that this was tantamount to adopting 'the proletarian standpoint'.[60]

The virtual identification of Marxism with 'the standpoint of the proletariat' is constitutive of Plekhanov's position. There could be no contradiction between Marxism and the working-class movement. In his *Vademecum*, Plekhanov declared of the Group for the Emancipation of Labour, 'in our eyes the worker was never a simple weapon for the attainment of aims foreign to him... Our programme was written in the spirit of Marx. But a programme written in the spirit of that man cannot be a programme of political exploiters'.[61] The same idea is conveyed metaphorically when Plekhanov compares the working-class movement to a company of soldiers on the march:

> [T]he far-sighted distinguish the direction better than the rest and... their judgement of it is therefore closer to reality than that of the near-sighted... Revolutionary Social-Democracy *already* sees what the other proletarians *do not yet* see and, in explaining to the latter the road to be followed in the future, it *achieves a comprehension* of their movement and *accelerates* it.[62]

The road to be travelled by the proletarian army is assumed. The possibility of an alternative line of march, from which Social Democracy might have to dissuade the workers, is not considered. Class consciousness is thus immanent in the class position of the proletariat; the forward march of the labour movement is identified with the diffusion of Marxism through its ranks.

The historical trajectory of the working-class movement is adjusted ever more consciously in line with the logic of the historical process. This process represents, among other things, the resolution of the historical contradiction between science and the producers, between the Enlightenment ideals of the intelligentsia and the needs of the people. In this light, Plekhanov's occasional rhetorical appeal to the ideals of the intelligentsia is not a token of latent elitism. In coming to espouse Marxism, Social Democratic intellectuals forsake any pretensions to intellectual and political autonomy and assume the perspective of the working-class movement, but they do not thereby abandon their ideals. While the proletariat may not be a mere instrument for others to realise these ideals, it is the protagonist in the historical drama of their

---

59 Plekhanov 1884, p. 357.
60 Plekhanov 1883, p. 85.
61 Cited in Frankel 1972, p. 63.
62 Plekhanov 1901, pp. 587, 589.

realisation for everyone. And however much they may expedite this process, intellectuals from the upper classes are not, in the final analysis, indispensable: 'The absence of allies among the "intelligentsia" will not prevent the working class from becoming aware of its interest, understanding its tasks, bringing forward leaders from its own ranks and creating its own *working-class intelligentsia. Such an intelligentsia* will not betray its cause or abandon it to the mercy of fate'.[63]

The identification of Marxist intellectuals with the developed consciousness of the working-class movement knots the circle of Plekhanov's unilinear historical logic. But it does not thereby resolve the equivocation that haunts the strategic perspective of proletarian hegemony. Indeed, equivocation echoes in the difficulty of reconciling the two scales, individual and historical-*cum*-philosophical, he invokes to portray the relationship between intellectuals and the working class. In discussing individual action, he can acknowledge and even insist upon the efficacy of Marxist intellectuals in educating the workers about their class interests. But once the focus expands to encompass the broad sweep of the historical movement, the efficacy of the individual recedes into the dynamism of the class struggle and the forces of production. In his essay 'The Role of the Individual in History', Plekhanov argues that there is no necessary contradiction between determination by universal historical forces and the exertion of individual effort, since the former work through the latter. But here, as elsewhere in his writings, the argument asserting a parallel between the effect of 'general causes' upon the total movement of history and the work of 'individual causes' in modifying the particular features of historical events is pitched abstractly and, beyond the formulaic assertion that it is human beings, after all, who make history, does not do much to explain the relation between the individual and the general.[64]

It does less to clarify the concrete political problems that give point to the philosophical issue. Instead, Plekhanov's emphasis falls here upon the universal logic of capitalist development, there upon individual initiative in educating the working class, as polemical circumstance dictates. This vacillation reflects a failure to conceptualise adequately the political forms and processes that structure the activity of individuals, groups and classes and to translate it into exemplification or determinate variation of the forces driving the total historical movement. The fusion of Marxism and the working-class movement is simply assumed, along with synchrony in the development of the objective and subjective conditions of socialism, rather than being conceived through

---

63 Plekhanov 1888b, p. 394.
64 Plekhanov 1898, pp. 311–15.

the exploration of concrete political issues and the elaboration of concrete forms of political practice, as itself a contradictory process. There is a kind of conceptual slippage at work here that assimilates the political dimension of class struggle either to the growth of class consciousness or to the logic of capital accumulation and thereby effectively elides it.

Plekhanov's recourse to the vocation of the intellectuals as socialist educators of the working class in order to explain the precocious hegemony of the proletariat does not fit easily into a historical logic shaped in accordance with the synchronous development of the material and intellectual conditions of socialism. Like Kautsky, Plekhanov conceives this synchrony by relating the development of consciousness to the proletariat's experience of struggle, which grows roughly in tandem with the maturation of capitalist relations of production and the socialisation of the forces of production. There is no implication that intellectuals need stand aside from the process. The 'portion of the bourgeois ideologists, who have raised themselves to the level of comprehending theoretically the historical movement as a whole', were characterised in the *Communist Manifesto* as bearers of 'fresh elements of enlightenment and progress' for the political education of the proletariat.[65] However, the alignment of these intellectuals with the working-class movement represented for Marx and Engels – and for Kautsky – the expression of a mature capitalism already in the process of dissolution and ripe for socialism. The intelligentsia served Plekhanov, by contrast, as a theoretical bridge spanning the gap between Russia's merely nascent capitalism and the advanced political consciousness that the injunction to hegemony in the democratic revolution required of the working class. The hegemony of the proletariat in the democratic revolution remained an aspiration. The centrepiece of the strategic perspective of Marxism in Russia lacked a basis in theory.

The ambiguities surrounding the aspiration to proletarian hegemony point to the theoretical limitations of the Marxist orthodoxy of the Second International, whose basic assumptions – that the growth of the productive forces determines the direction of history, that the material and the intellectual conditions of socialism develop in parallel, and that Marxist theory and the working-class movement fuse harmoniously – Plekhanov and Kautsky shared. In Germany the apparent growing success of the SPD's parliamentary political project overshadowed and hence helped to obscure these limitations. In his effort to theorise the class struggle in backward Russia, Plekhanov could not rely upon a seemingly authoritative practical resolution of the problems of political leadership and class alliance. Indeed, in calling for working-class

---

65 Marx and Engels 1848, p. 494.

leadership in the impending bourgeois-democratic revolution, he placed on the political agenda problems at the theoretical horizon of Marxist orthodoxy. He was a transitional figure, in this sense, in relation not only to the Russian revolutionary tradition but also to Second International Marxism.

Lenin and Marxist Orthodoxy

By the time the young Lenin took up the cudgels in defence of Marxism against its populist critics in the 1890s, the context of the debate had changed. The intervening decade had seen a dramatic expansion of capitalist production in Russia and revolutionary populism had given way to a 'legal populism' of utopian sentiment but very small deeds. Lenin characterised this development as follows:

> [T]he old Russian peasant socialism split up ... making way for workers' socialism, on the one hand, and degenerating into vulgar petty-bourgeois radicalism, on the other ... From a political programme calculated *to arouse the peasantry* for the socialist revolution *against the foundations of modern society* there has emerged a programme calculated to patch up, to 'improve' the conditions of the peasantry *while preserving the foundations of modern society.*[66]

Disagreement no longer focused on the advent of capitalism in Russia and its implications for revolutionary strategy but on whether the logic of its development must preclude practical proposals to defend the traditional institutions of the people. As a response to this new populist concern, Plekhanov's argument, pitched at a high level of abstraction, that the dynamism of the productive forces might eventuate in a capitalist Russia either directly, through an internal logic of economic development, or indirectly, through international movements of capital and the logic of inter-state competition that led the pre-capitalist tsarist state to foster the growth of capitalism, could hardly be decisive. Indeed, his acknowledgement of Russian capitalism's possible dependence upon the strategy of the Tsarist state might read as an admission that capital was a merely artificial, hothouse growth and that the corresponding decline of traditional 'socialist' institutions could be remedied by persuading the state to pursue more enlightened policies. The analysis Lenin proposed, organised around a concern to undermine the new populism *from within* by

---

66 Lenin 1894a, pp. 264–5.

providing a detailed demonstration of how large-scale production, which the populists identified with capitalism, was growing inevitably out of the very social relations they sought to defend against it, was well designed to address the changed terms of debate. Lenin's analysis was shaped no less thoroughly than was Plekhanov's by the unilinear historical logic of Marxist orthodoxy and, consequently, his theorisation of the strategic aspiration to proletarian hegemony in the bourgeois-democratic revolution produced no less equivocation, though its locus and form were somewhat different. These differences, however, reflect a changed rhetorical and political context rather than any basic theoretical or political divergence.

Lenin anchored his critique of populism in an exposition of the methodological assumptions of historical materialism as the necessary foundation for the scientific study of society: '[O]nly the reduction of social relations to production relations and of the latter to the level of the productive forces provided a firm basis for [viewing]... the development of social formations [as] a process of natural history. And... without such a view there can be no social science'.[67] Though the populists were hardly ignorant of the facts of Russian social development – Lenin's own analysis was largely based on the empirical data they collected – they lacked the conceptual apparatus needed to explain these facts and, consequently, to act effectively upon them: 'As long as people did not know how to set about studying the facts, they always invented *a priori* general theories, which were always sterile'.[68] By identifying the structure of society through its production relations, however, historical materialism enabled the investigator 'to observe recurrence and regularity and to generalise the systems of the various countries in the single fundamental concept: *social formation*' and thereby 'to proceed from the description of social phenomena... to their strictly scientific analysis'.[69] A set of historically determinate social concepts grounded in the development of the material productive forces, historical materialism was indispensable in order 'to set about studying the facts'.[70]

Without grasping the combination of productive forces and relations in historically determinate modes of production, the populists could not conceive the growth of capitalism out of commodity production as a 'process of natural history'. Mistaking the organic connection between the separation of the peasants from their means of production in the countryside ('de-peasantising')

---

67 Lenin 1894a, pp. 140–1.
68 Lenin 1894a, p. 144.
69 Lenin 1894a, p. 140.
70 Lenin 1894a, p. 144.

and the implantation of large-scale capitalist industry in the towns, they could bemoan each of these phenomena but understand neither. The impoverished peasants, no longer able to satisfy their own needs, had to turn to the market; their poverty did not signal the impossibility of Russian capitalism but only one aspect of its development. Bound up with the social division of labour, the market grew in and through the very logic that generated a polarisation of social classes. But the separation of the direct producers from the land and the means of production and their subordination to capital did not result immediately from this logic, which moved through successive phases and even sustained the remnants of the preceding economic order for some time. The development of capitalism

> begins with *merchant's* and *usury capital*, then grows into industrial capitalism, which in its turn is at first technically quite primitive... then organises manufacture – which is still based on hand labour, and on the dominant handicraft industries, without breaking the tie between the wageworker and the land – and completes its development with large-scale industry... [T]his last, highest stage... constitutes the culminating point of the development of capitalism, *it alone* creates the fully expropriated worker who is free as a bird, *it alone* gives rise (both materially and socially) to the 'unifying significance' of capitalism... *it alone* opposes capitalism to its 'own child'.[71]

Concerned exclusively with the formation of the home market, Lenin conceived the growth of capitalism as a radically internal process. Only through the intrinsic relation of capitalist production, the exchange of human labour power as a commodity against capital, could historical sense be made of the transformation of technique and the ramification of the division of labour, but the different forms this relation took on were inextricably bound up with the development of the forces of production. Driven by these forces, the growth of the market was limited only by 'the degree of specialisation of social labour... [which] by its very nature is as infinite as technical developments'.[72] There was no absolute, external barrier to capital's development of the productive forces and corresponding extension of the market. The limits to capital were relative, pertaining to its internal contradictions. Capitalist social relations could be transformed through the play of these internal contradictions, 'but only when such action originates *from the people themselves whose social*

---

71 Lenin 1894b, p. 438.
72 Lenin 1894a, p. 100.

relations are being...changed.⁷³ Lenin characterised Russian Marxists as 'socialists whose point of departure is the view that the reality of our environment is capitalist society and that there is only one way out of it – the class struggle of the proletariat against the bourgeoisie'.⁷⁴

Class Struggle in the Democratic Revolution

Capitalism, unlike earlier modes of production, was consistent with the political freedom of the direct producers, with political democracy. The conquest of democratic liberties could put an end to the institutional bulwarks of personal dependence (absolutism, the social-estate system, bureaucracy and so on) but would not herald the social emancipation of the workers because it could not extirpate the logic of capital accumulation. Indeed, it would give free rein to that logic, Lenin wrote, so that 'political liberty will primarily serve the interests of the bourgeoisie and will not ease the position of the workers, but ... will ease the conditions for their struggle ... *against this very bourgeoisie*'.⁷⁵ Political democracy was not the end of the class struggle but its continuation on a terrain that was more advantageous for the worker, who 'needs the achievement of the general democratic demands only to clear the road to victory over the working people's chief enemy, over an institution that is purely democratic by nature, *capital*'. The pre-capitalist institutions and practices that were the target of the democratic revolution not only encumbered the workers' efforts to build independent organisations and to reflect upon their experience of struggle with capital, they were entwined with the primitive forms of the capital relation – usury and merchant's capital – that prevailed throughout the countryside. '[U]nless these pillars of reaction are overthrown', he wrote, 'the Russian rural proletariat, whose support is an essential condition for the victory of the working class, will never cease to be downtrodden and cowed, capable only of sullen desperation and not of intelligent and persistent protest and struggle'.⁷⁶ Uprooting the institutional bases of pre-capitalist relations of personal dependence, the democratic revolution undermines the most brutal forms of capital; securing the political conditions for capital accumulation and the generalised domination of its developed forms, it affords the rural proletarians a margin of personal independence and dignity and hence the possibility

---

73 Lenin 1894b, p. 372.
74 Lenin 1894a, p. 197.
75 Lenin 1894a, p. 294.
76 Lenin 1894a, p. 291.

of organised resistance to exploitation. In waging a struggle for democracy, the working class of large-scale machine industry acted on behalf of the semi-proletarianised rural masses as yet unable to act for themselves. Acting as the champion of all the oppressed and exploited in the democratic revolution, the proletariat asserted itself as the vanguard of the socialist revolution. The revolutionary struggle against Tsarism 'at the head of all the democratic elements' was thus incumbent upon the working class by virtue of its socialist vocation.

Proletarian hegemony figures in the analysis of the young Lenin alternately in the character of the industrial working class as the vanguard of all the exploited and in the imperative that it assume leadership of 'all the democratic elements'. The persuasiveness of his argument for the Social Democratic project of proletarian hegemony in the bourgeois-democratic revolution depends upon the tacit identification of these two formulations. But if all the democratic elements can really be identified with the exploited, then the distinction between democratic and socialist revolutions, the lynchpin of Social Democratic strategy, would seem rather tenuous. The proletarian claim to leadership of all the exploited was well grounded in Lenin's analysis of the development of capitalism in Russia – if exploitation was everywhere capitalist in nature and if the circumstances of producers everywhere approximated more and more closely those of the industrial working class. But if, perhaps by virtue of common resistance to capitalist exploitation, the rural semi-proletarians could really follow this lead, it is surely a *socialist* revolution that such universal class solidarity would enact. Lenin's own analysis, however, indicates that a democratic revolution is necessary *before* they can follow it. The bourgeois-democratic revolution must therefore reflect a different and more complex alignment of social forces. In this case, the hegemony of the proletariat requires appropriately different analytical foundations; the forms in which hegemony is exercised over non-proletarian allies must be considerably less straightforward. The leadership of 'all the democratic elements' would have to take account of the diversity of class interests involved in the struggle for democracy. But Lenin neither supplies analytical foundations for such an exercise of hegemony nor specifies the forms it might take.

A brief survey of the possible democratic allies of the working class will show that Lenin was no more able than Plekhanov to make historical materialist sense of the notion of proletarian hegemony in the bourgeois-democratic revolution. Indeed, the problem of alliance between different class forces could not even be rigorously posed in terms of the unilinear logic of Marxist orthodoxy.

The emancipation edict of 1861 dealt the social-estate system a decisive blow, according to Lenin, and ushered in a fundamental realignment of social forces in Russia; unity of the whole people against serfdom gave way to struggle between the classes of capitalist society. The struggle of the intelligentsia 'represents "a real social force" *inasmuch as it defends general bourgeois interests*. If, nevertheless, this force was not *able* to create institutions suitable to the interests it defended... the cause lies... chiefly in the position of those classes from which it emerged and from which it drew its strength, in their duality'.[77] The democratic aspirations of the bourgeoisie began to recede before the growing strength of the working class and the spectre of socialist revolution: '[H]ere in Russia [capital] is particularly inclined to sacrifice its democracy and to enter into alliance with the reactionaries in order to suppress the workers, to still further impede the emergence of a working-class movement'.[78] This estimate is echoed in Lenin's equivocal assessment of the Russian state apparatus which figures, on the one hand, as a collection of 'relics of medieval, semi-feudal institutions' while, on the other hand, the bureaucracy that in his view 'de facto rules the Russian state' could be characterised as essentially bourgeois: '[T]he bureaucracy, being made up mainly of middle-class intellectuals, are profoundly bourgeois both in origin and in the purpose and character of their activities; but absolutism and the enormous political privileges of the landed nobility have lent them particularly pernicious qualities'.[79] Here it is almost as though Tsarism were a mere excrescence upon the already-bourgeois body of the state. Like Plekhanov, Lenin attributes the bourgeoisie's inclination toward reaction to the duality of its class position, but the duality is construed very differently. For the former, it was the vestigial ability of the bourgeois 'to breathe in the troubled waters of decaying absolutism' – that is, to amass profit from ministerial favours and bureaucratic corruption – that thwarted the general bourgeois interest in democracy; for the latter, the democracy of the bourgeoisie was contradicted less by its medieval, patriarchal past than by the working-class menace of the future.

---

77   Lenin 1894b, pp. 422, 423.
78   Lenin 1894a, pp. 291–2.
79   Lenin 1894a, p. 291n. This attribution of political parity, verging on primacy to the bourgeoisie, cannot be explained by the facts of the case. As Lenin himself would emphasise at a later date, the Tsarist state, although subject to a process of modification in line with the growth of bourgeois influence, remained essentially pre-capitalist; the bureaucracy, particularly in its upper echelons, was recruited primarily from the landed and office-holding nobility and, while it functioned largely on behalf of the *haute* bourgeoisie, 'the bureaucracy lends its bourgeois activity *a tendency and a form* that is purely and solely feudal' (Lenin 1911, p. 390). Perry Anderson has claimed that, 'after the emancipation of the serfs, the nobility came to rely upon employment in the state apparatus more than ever before' (Anderson 1974, p. 355).

Whereas Plekhanov sees the bourgeois interest in democracy just beginning to creep over the political horizon, Lenin views it as already falling under the shadow of the proletarian class struggle. Since the Social Democratic project of hegemony was conceived in terms of the workers' consciousness of their class antagonism to capital and since this consciousness was thought to grow with the development of capitalism, the resistance of the bourgeoisie would seem to be implicit in the assertion of proletarian hegemony.

But neither could the peasantry be conceived as a revolutionary democratic force. The contention that 'the exploitation of the working people in Russia *is everywhere capitalist in nature*, if we leave out of account the moribund remnants of [the] serf economy'[80] left no theoretical scope for an alliance of the proletariat with the peasantry, that is, with a social force that united the 'petty-bourgeois peasantry' with the nascent peasant bourgeoisie and the masses of semi-proletarianised peasant labourers. Reading the social dynamic of the countryside immediately from the process of capitalist class polarisation, Lenin consigned the revolutionary efficacy of the peasantry to 'the epoch of the fall of serfdom'.[81] All that remained of the peasant estate was the petty-bourgeois residue left by this process, whose vacillation in the struggle for democracy was expressed ideologically in the paradoxes Lenin found in legal populism. Most strikingly, he identified the reactionary side of populism with its defence of communal institutions – that is, with the very aspect of the populist programme that lent it a socialist allure. Populist criticism of land poverty, high payments and bureaucratic tyranny was not socialist, but its democratic thrust could 'facilitate the workers' direct struggle against capital' by helping rid capitalist 'oppression of the medieval rubbish that aggravates it'.[82] But through collective responsibility for taxes and land redemption payments and control over the passports needed for internal migration, the commune already institutionalised the power of the peasant bourgeoisie; as an obstacle to the free movement of the impoverished semi-proletarians, it impeded the rationalisation of capitalist agriculture. The inalienability of allotments merely bound the working peasants more tightly to the local landlord or kulak. Such derogation from democratic freedoms perpetuated the most backward, brutal and stultifying forms of capitalist exploitation.

Lenin's critique of petty-bourgeois democracy was thus at the same time an exposure of the socialist self-deception of populism; indeed, it is reminiscent of the *Communist Manifesto*, which identified petty-bourgeois socialism

---

80   Lenin 1894a, p. 299.
81   Lenin 1894a, p. 279.
82   Lenin 1894a, p. 289.

as 'both reactionary and utopian'. He envisaged with approval the formation of a petty-bourgeois democratic party but 'only when a durable programme of *democratic* demands has been drawn up that will put an end to the prejudices of the old Russian exceptionalism', that is, only when the socialist aspect of petty-bourgeois ideology had been excised. He pledged Social Democratic support for 'any struggle waged by the democrats against reactionary institutions', including, by implication, the commune.[83] However, Lenin does not give the prospect of a forward-looking petty bourgeoisie much weight; it is plausible at all only because, like Plekhanov, he portrays the 'moribund remnants' and 'reactionary institutions' – absolutism, the social-estate system, the commune, etc. – as mere passive obstacles to the logic of capitalist progress. They are not understood as entering into the process whereby the identity of social forces is constituted and their alignment determined. And since this is the case, the alignment of social forces at work in the revolutionary process in Russia effectively becomes an exemplification of the logic of capitalist development. Thereby a dynamic of class struggle characteristic of developed capitalism and appropriate to socialist revolution is transposed onto the process of democratic revolution. In this context, neither the bourgeois nor the peasant is a revolutionary actor; in this context, petty-bourgeois social strata are neither an effective force nor, according to Marx and Engels,

> revolutionary, but conservative. Nay more, they are reactionary, for they try to roll back the wheel of history. If by chance they are revolutionary,

---

[83] Lenin 1894a, pp. 292, 293. Instructive in this regard is Lenin's response to the formation in 1893 of the short-lived *Narodnoe pravo* party [Party of the People's Right]. Subordinating the theme of Russian exceptionalism to the struggle against the autocracy, the *Narodopravtsi* managed to avoid the direct departures from democracy characteristic of legal populism; though retaining a social-revolutionary idiom, they were critical of populist apoliticism and accorded primacy to the struggle for political reforms and liberties. While greeting their manifesto, Lenin held that the advance it represented underscored the inherent inconsistency of all populist democracy. The ideological insistence of the *Narodopravtsi* upon the participation of the masses of the people themselves in the struggle for democracy was defused and contradicted by their abstract notion of the 'people', unrelated to definite social relations of production. In Lenin's view, their desire for a fusion of all revolutionary elements in the common struggle for political rights could draw force from nothing but such abstractions, in naïve disregard of the material conditions and interests from which alone the political engagement of the masses could proceed. The combination of real revolutionary forces is 'much better achieved by the separate organisation of the representatives of the different interests and by the joint action of the two parties in particular cases' (1894a, pp. 330–1).

they are so only in view of their impending transfer into the proletariat, they thus defend not their present, but their future interests, they desert their own standpoint to place themselves at that of the proletariat.[84]

Non-proletarian participation in the revolution was thus accidental rather than essential, a matter of individual volition rather than social force; as such, its effect upon the revolutionary process could not be grasped theoretically. If the proletariat is pre-eminent in the democratic revolution, it is not because it exercises hegemony over other democratic forces but because it is the only effective revolutionary force. In this case, however, the distinction between democratic and socialist revolutions is reduced to a strategic calculation of the instrumentalities available to the workers for achieving socialism, unsupported by historical materialist analysis of the shifting alignment of social forces at each stage of the process. Hegemony in the democratic revolution thus becomes an issue of socialist consciousness.

Hegemony as Socialist Consciousness

For Lenin, as for Plekhanov, the hegemony of the proletariat implied the effective political presence, in the bourgeois-democratic revolution itself, of the perspective of the socialist revolution:

> There are two ways of arriving at the conclusion that the worker must be aroused to fight absolutism: either by regarding the worker as the sole fighter for the socialist system, and therefore seeing political liberty as one of the conditions facilitating his struggle; that is the view of the Social-Democrats; or by appealing to him simply as one who suffers most from the present system, who has nothing more to lose and who can display the greatest determination in fighting absolutism. But that would mean compelling the worker to drag in the wake of the bourgeois radicals, who refuse to see the antagonism between the bourgeoisie and the proletariat behind the solidarity of the whole 'people' against absolutism.[85]

Working-class leadership in the struggle for political democracy is thus cast as proletarian consciousness of the class antagonism with capital and of the resulting need for socialism. And proletarian class consciousness is

---

84   Marx and Engels 1848, p. 494.
85   Lenin 1894a, p. 294n.

conceived as a reflection of the circumstance that the universality of capitalist exploitation – and of resistance to it – is immanent in the particular life situation and experience of the factory worker. The young Lenin expresses the idea with a matter-of-fact didacticism characteristic of Second International Marxism, but it is palpably the same idea as the dialectic of the universal class, 'which lays claim to no *particular right* because the wrong it suffers is not a *particular wrong* but *wrong in general*', that the young Marx discerned in the proletariat.[86]

Lenin's 'Draft and Explanation of a Programme for the Social-Democratic Party', written in 1895–96 and reflecting the initial experience of the Russian Marxist intelligentsia's agitation among factory workers as well as the beginnings of a much broader wave of strike activity, traces a kind of historical phenomenology of proletarian experience. In terms reminiscent of Kautsky, Lenin explicates the process whereby the common experience of exploitation in the modern capitalist factory system leads the workers from resistance through organised struggle to class consciousness. Initially, isolated acts of rebellion, machine-smashing and attacks upon managers express 'a hazy hatred of the capitalist'. This phase was transcended in the current strike wave, demonstrating a more sophisticated understanding of the forms and means of capitalist oppression and a capacity for organised and sustained struggle in defence of vital economic interests. In the course of this struggle the workers come to recognise the various methods and stratagems of capitalist exploitation, analyse them and grasp 'the essence of exploitation as a whole ... [and hence] the social system based on the exploitation of labour by capital'. The struggle is at once a test of strength and a school of organisation: '[T]he increasing frequency of clashes inevitably lead[s] to a further extension of the struggle, to the development of a sense of unity, a sense of solidarity – at first among the workers of a particular locality, then among the workers of the entire country'.[87] Finally the industrial struggle sparks political consciousness. Every clash on the factory floor 'brings the workers into conflict with ... representatives of state authority'. State intervention merely expresses the universality of the class struggle under industrial capitalism where '[a]ll the methods of exploitation ... are concentrated, intensified, made the regular rule ... and spread to all aspects of the worker's labour and life'. Exploitation thus systematised and the organised resistance it provokes engender coordinated action by the employing class and the legal codification of industrial relations, wherein the interests of the employers are endowed with the authority of the

---

86   Marx 1843–4, p. 186.
87   Lenin 1895–6, pp. 113–15.

state: 'The injustice of individual officials is replaced by the injustice of the law itself'.[88] The workers' struggle to satisfy their vital needs is transformed into a class war; they come 'to understand not only the specific interests of the working class, but also the specific place occupied by the working class in the state'.[89]

Only with the rise of capital in its fully developed form of large-scale industry does exploitation emerge from the narrow trappings and relations of personal dependence and appear as an objective, impersonal, class relation: in the factory 'exploitation is fully developed and emerges in its pure form, without any confusing details. The worker cannot fail to see that he is oppressed by *capital*, that his struggle has to be waged against the bourgeoisie as a *class*'.[90] By contrast, the semi-proletarianised masses of the countryside, subordinated to capital in its merely embryonic forms, cannot recognise the *system* that exploits them; isolated by the narrow scope of production, perhaps struggling to maintain a tenuous connection with a petty allotment, the impoverished peasant is unable to distinguish the essential relation of exploitation from the local and personal circumstances with which it is bound up. The divorce of the direct producers from the land and the disintegration of the narrow web of their traditional social relations are definitively accomplished only with the rise of large-scale capitalist industry: in one and the same movement, the workers are thrown together in large-scale capitalist production and finally alienated from bourgeois society, and the growth of consciousness reflects this movement of the fundamental contradiction between the socialisation of the productive forces and the bourgeois relations of production. But the relation of exploitation that appears in fully developed form in the factory is the *same* relation that emerges embryonically in the countryside: '[T]he very antagonism existing in the countryside is fully expressed in the factory; here the split is complete ... *Here* dreams are not possible'.[91] And in this sense the class consciousness immanent in the very situation of the factory worker *thereby* illuminates the essential situation of the not-yet-fully-proletarianised majority of the working population. Thus, it is the very struggle of the industrial workers to emancipate themselves that makes them the vanguard of the exploited masses. And thus, as in the young Marx, it was the very assertion of proletarian self-emancipation that made the industrial worker the

---

88   Lenin 1895–6, pp. 105–6.
89   Lenin 1895–6, p. 116.
90   Lenin 1894a, p. 299.
91   Lenin 1894b, p. 380.

representative of suffering humanity, a class 'which cannot emancipate itself without emancipating... all the other classes of society'.[92]

But this account does nothing to explain how the more advanced social circumstances and consciousness of the industrial proletariat translate into a political practice of leadership in the democratic revolution. It would be misleading to claim that the factory workers are conceived as leading by virtue of what they are rather than of what they do. Their social being, the structure of social relations that constitutes them as a class, is not something apart from their struggles but is expressed in and through their practice of the class struggle. But where practice and consciousness are not simply conceived as developing in close correspondence with the phases of the evolution of capital, their spread is presented as a matter of proselytisation by individual activists – what one commentator has termed 'a chain-letter tactic for the generation of socialist consciousness'[93] – and this provides no rationale for the efficacy of the proselytiser where the social relations of the audience were not yet ripe for the message. As was the case with Plekhanov's, the oscillation of Lenin's argument between the unilinear logic of history and the efficacy of individual agency yields no purchase upon the problem of political leadership.

The problem of political leadership was at stake in the populist philosopher N.K. Mikhailovskii's claim that historical materialism neglects or misconstrues 'the question of heroes and the crowd'. Seeking to explain the wave of anti-Semitic pogroms that swept Russia in the 1880s, Mikhailovskii blamed the arousal of the masses to irrationally imitate 'heroes' upon the routinisation of social life by capitalism and the resulting erosion of the critically thinking, rounded individual. Lenin's response obscures the problem, countering Mikhailovskii's concern with heroes and the crowd in general, regardless of its class composition, with the allegedly more concrete question of the economic structure and class composition of Russian society. The issue of leaders and followers is thereby decontextualised and effectively equated with another of Mikhailovskii's criticisms of Marxism, the alleged 'conflict between the idea of historical necessity and the significance of individual activity'.[94] To this Lenin retorts,

> The real question that arises in appraising the social activity of an individual is: what conditions ensure the success of his actions, what guarantee is there that these actions will not remain an isolated act lost in a

---

92   Marx 1843–4, p. 186.
93   Harding 1977, p. 75.
94   Cited in Lenin 1894a, p. 159.

welter of contrary acts?... [H]ow must actions aimed at bringing about the socialist system attract the masses in order to yield serious fruits? Obviously, the answer to this question depends directly... on the way in which the grouping of social forces in Russia and the class struggle... are understood.[95]

The definition of the issue shifts in the course of the argument. The question of the historical determination of individual action first becomes the problem of individual political efficacy. Political efficacy is then itself conceived abstractly as the alignment of the Russian socialists with the masses, the coincidence of their programme with the interests of one social class or another; if historical determination is thereby reintroduced, it is only in overshadowing the significance of individual action. The real problem the populist critique raises for Marxists, the question of Marxist political leadership in the working-class movement, is thus juggled away.

With its assumption of an essential harmony between Marxist theory and the working-class movement, the unilinear historical logic of orthodoxy precluded posing the problem of leadership critically. This assumption is implicit in Lenin's assertion that '[t]here can be no dogmatism where the... criterion of a doctrine is its conformity to the actual process of social and economic development; there can be no sectarianism when the task is [to promote] the organisation of the proletariat, and... the role of the "intelligentsia" is to make special leaders from among the intelligentsia unnecessary'.[96] The 'irresistible attraction' of Marxist theory, according to Lenin, lies in combining science and revolution, not just by accident but 'intrinsically and inseparably'. The task of science consists in formulating 'a true slogan of struggle', grasping the class struggle 'objectively as the product of a definite system of production relations' and understanding 'the necessity of this struggle, its content, course and conditions of development'.[97] And as these requirements of science are satisfied, 'every awakening of the protesting thought of the proletariat will inevitably guide this thought into the channels of Social-Democracy'.[98] Despite its congenial scientific egalitarianism, Lenin's argument replaces political analysis of the contradictions facing Marxist leadership in the working-class movement with an imaginary guarantee of their supersession.

---

95 Lenin 1894a, pp. 159–60.
96 Lenin 1894a, p. 298.
97 Lenin 1894a, pp. 327–8.
98 Lenin 1894a, p. 297.

Lenin's understanding of the Social Democratic project's mode of insertion into the class struggle moved within the assumptions of the unilinear historical logic of Marxist orthodoxy. The union of Marxism and the working-class movement would, evidently, be constructed in the course of practice, but there was as yet no recognition that this political practice, this process of political construction, was subject to its own logic. No more than Plekhanov could Lenin formulate a coherent conception of the Russian Marxist political project of proletarian hegemony in the bourgeois-democratic revolution. An adequate historical materialist analysis would only emerge out of a crisis in the Russian Social Democratic movement. The political crisis that haunted the project of proletarian hegemony would, in the event, also be a crisis of Marxist orthodoxy. Its resolution would call for the analytical equipment of Marxist theory to be reworked. But an appropriate reworking would not emerge at once. Indeed, Lenin's initial response to the crisis was couched as a strikingly clear reiteration of the logic of orthodoxy.

The crisis arose with the very impetuous development of the Russian working-class movement. As broader and less experienced strata of workers were drawn into the movement, the most prominent leaders and the most experienced revolutionaries were swept up by the political police. Able to draw sustenance from Bernstein's exaltation of the everyday movement, perhaps disoriented before the seemingly immense demands imposed by the political project of proletarian hegemony in the democratic revolution, young Social Democrats saw in the workers' struggles for economic improvement an ambitious enough aim for the Russian working-class movement, leaving the political struggle against the autocracy to the liberal intelligentsia. Similar themes echoed from working-class ranks through the journal *Rabochaia mysl'* [Workers' Thought]. In *What Is to Be Done?* Lenin would analyse this tendency to 'Economism' as a line of engagement – within the spontaneous working-class movement – in a politico-strategic struggle over hegemony in the bourgeois-democratic revolution, that is, in terms of a politico-strategic logic of struggle. Initially, however, he situated the new phenomena in the terms of an historical narrative of the harmonious fusion of Marxism and the working-class movement:

> The separation of socialism and the working-class movement gave rise to weakness and underdevelopment in each: the theories of the socialists, unfused with the workers' struggle, remained nothing more than utopias ... the working-class movement remained petty, fragmented, and did not acquire political significance, was not enlightened by the advanced science of its time. For this reason we see in all European countries a

constantly growing urge to *fuse* socialism with the working-class movement in a single *Social-Democratic* movement. When this fusion takes place the class struggle of the workers becomes *the conscious struggle of the proletariat* to emancipate itself from exploitation by the propertied classes... By directing socialism towards a fusion with the working-class movement, Karl Marx and Frederick Engels did their greatest service; they created a revolutionary theory that explained the necessity for this fusion and gave socialists the task of organizing the class struggle of the proletariat.[99]

In this optic the Economist temptation appears as 'ideological vacillations' occasioned by such transient phenomena as the police decimation of Social Democratic ranks and the fragmentation and demoralisation that took hold as less politically experienced cohorts were drawn into the movement.[100] Its disproportionate fascination with the narrow economic aspect of Social Democracy made *Rabochaia mysl'* the mouthpiece for the hopes and grievances of only the most backward echelons of the workers, thereby braking the progressive influence of the 'working-class intelligentsia', the politically self-educated workers drawn primarily from the 'better-situated strata', the leading edge of the working-class movement whose task it was, in assimilating the theoretical outlook of Social Democracy, to 'take the cause of the Russian workers and, *consequently*, the cause of the Russian revolution, into its own hands'.[101] Economism thus figured in terms of Marxist orthodoxy as a discordant note in the harmonious fusion of Marxism and the working-class movement. Indeed, Lenin's portrait of this process of fusion, its shape and its inner logic bore a striking resemblance to Kautsky's original.

---

99   Lenin 1899d, pp. 257–8.
100   See Lenin 1899c, p. 180; Lenin 1899e, pp. 279–80.
101   Lenin 1899d, p. 281.

CHAPTER 4

Marxism, Lenin and the Logic of Hegemony: Spontaneity and Consciousness in the Class Struggle[1]

> Party struggles lend a party strength and vitality; the greatest proof of a party's weakness is its diffuseness and the blurring of clear demarcations; a party becomes stronger by purging itself.
> – FERDINAND LASSALLE[2]

∴

Reviewing the brief history of the Russian working-class movement in *What Is to Be Done?*, Lenin saluted 'the spontaneous awakening of the working masses' but cautioned that 'the workers were not, and could not be, conscious of the irreconcilable antagonism of their interests to the whole of the modern political and social system, i.e., theirs was not yet Social-Democratic consciousness'.[3] This consciousness was the product of theoretical work by intellectuals and 'would have to be brought to [the workers] from without'. Indeed, he would generalise, 'the spontaneous development of the working-class movement leads to its subordination to bourgeois ideology'. It was incumbent upon Social Democrats, therefore, 'to combat spontaneity, to divert the working-class movement from this spontaneous, trade-unionist striving to come under the wing of the bourgeoisie, and to bring it under the wing of revolutionary Social-Democracy'.[4]

---

1   An earlier and somewhat abbreviated version of the argument of this chapter was published in 1995 as '"Consciousness from Without": Marxism, Lenin and the Proletariat', *Science & Society*, 59, 3: 268–97.
2   Epigraph to Lenin 1902, p. 347.
3   Lenin 1902, p. 375.
4   Lenin 1902, pp. 384–5.

Conventional Wisdom

Ever since *What Is to Be Done?* was published in 1902, Lenin's critics have counterposed its account of the development of working-class consciousness to one of Marx's central tenets, the thesis that 'the emancipation of the working classes must be conquered by the working classes themselves'.[5] This thesis involves two claims: first, that the working class, unlike previous exploited classes, is capable of autonomous revolutionary activity – autonomous in the sense that its struggles need not be subordinated to the ends of others. It need not serve as mere cannon fodder in the battles of rival exploiters. Its own class struggle will eventuate not in the domination of a new exploiting class, but in the transcendence of classes and exploitation. Second, that not only does the working class come, in the course of its struggle, to realise that its emancipation entails the supersession of capitalism and the construction of a socialist society, but that this end can be accomplished only through the independent activity of the working class, through proletarian class struggle. It cannot be accomplished by reformers enacting philanthropic schemes on behalf of the working class. These two claims, which together constitute the idea of proletarian self-emancipation, are at the core of Marx's revolutionary thought. From this perspective it may well seem that, in setting up an opposition between the spontaneous movement of the workers and the socialist theory of the intellectuals, Lenin had abandoned Marxist historical materialism, the method of seeking the groundwork of ideas in the social relations of production, and had fashioned in its stead a theoretical rationale for the ascendancy of revolutionary intellectuals over the proletariat. The notion that socialist consciousness must be imported into the working-class movement from without would thus be subject to the same criticism that Marx had levelled at Ludwig Feuerbach:

> The materialist doctrine concerning the changing of circumstances and upbringing forgets that circumstances are changed by men and that the educator must himself be educated. This doctrine must, therefore, divide society into two parts, one of which is superior to society.
>
> The coincidence of the changing of circumstances and of human activity or self-change can be conceived and rationally understood only as *revolutionary practice*.[6]

The mechanistic Enlightenment account of human action that Marx criticises here involves two claims: first, that an observer can, in principle, know

---

5 Marx 1864, p. 14.
6 Marx 1845, p. 4.

the laws governing human behaviour in such a way as to predict the behavioural outcome of given antecedent conditions; second, that an agent can, armed with this knowledge, contrive to bring about the antecedent conditions and so secure the desired outcome. Marx's thesis suggests two points of criticism. First, to imagine such an enlightened agent contriving the appropriate antecedent conditions to cause others to desire what he desires himself is to suppose these antecedent conditions to be already, at least to some extent, in existence. The mechanistic account cannot, therefore, explain radical social change.[7] Second, such an agent must see his own actions in a very different light than the behaviour of those he takes as his object. At least during the course of his manipulations, he will not experience his own activity merely as the outcome of antecedent conditions but as the expression of his own reasons and purposes, of his rational autonomy. Whether this experience is genuine or illusory, it betokens a schizoid element in the mechanistic account.[8] The political thrust of Marx's critique is that, when a project of radical change is construed in mechanistic terms, this schizophrenia translates into an authoritarian division of society into enlightened reformers and an unenlightened mass to be moulded: hence the *philosophes'* search for the enlightened despot; hence Robert Owen's search for enlightened manufacturers. Political authoritarianism is the logical complement of an idealistic understanding of historical change. In Lenin's case, his critics argue, the demiurge was to be the revolutionary intelligentsia and its subject matter, the proletariat.

This critique was first applied to the claims about spontaneity and consciousness advanced in *What Is to Be Done?* by Vladimir Akimov and Alexander Martynov, adherents of the 'Economist' current that was the principal polemical target of Lenin's book.[9] After the Russian Social Democrats split into Menshevik and Bolshevik wings, Lenin's erstwhile colleagues, the leaders of Menshevism, took over and elaborated the terms of this critique.[10] Their interpretation has since passed into general currency and its logic structures almost all Western accounts of Lenin's political thought, Marxist and non-Marxist alike.[11] The project of presenting *What Is to Be Done?* as the rebellion of Lenin's

---

7   See Goldman 1970, pp. 175–81; Rotenstreich 1965, pp. 54–60.
8   See MacIntyre 1984, pp. 84–5; Sloterdijk 1987, pp. 76–82.
9   See Frankel (ed.) 1969, especially pp. 112–25 and 316–29; Russian Social-Democratic Labour Party 1904, pp. 140–53.
10 See Axelrod 1904; Baron 1963, pp. 248–51; Trotsky 1904a, pp. 45–65; Dan 1970, pp. 236–63.
11 See, for example, Claudin-Urondo 1975, pp. 61–81; Corrigan, Ramsay and Sayer 1978, pp. 29–37; Liebman 1975, pp. 25–42; Marcuse 1961, pp. 15–27; Mattick 1983, pp. 273–80; Pannekoek 1975, *passim*; Besançon 1981, pp. 212–42; Conquest 1972, pp. 34–42; Haimson 1955, pp. 132–8; Keep 1963; Kolakowski 1978; Meyer 1962, pp. 19–103; Polan 1984, pp. 136–44; Service 1985, pp. 88–93; Ulam 1969, pp. 228–51; Wilson 1972, pp. 448–71; Wolfe 1964, pp. 155–66.

voluntaristic impatience against the straitjacket of historical materialism and seeking its intellectual antecedents in Russian populism, especially in the novel of the same name by the revolutionary democrat Nikolai Chernyshevskii, coheres with this interpretation.[12] Chernyshevskii's *What is to be Done?*, which is alleged to have exerted a formative influence upon the young Lenin's mind, picks up the theoretical threads of the mechanistic account dissected by Marx.[13] The novel portrays cooperative institutions as the application of reason and science to human affairs and the emancipation of the downtrodden Russian masses as the product of the benevolence of enlightened upper-class intellectuals. What is missing in Chernyshevskii, as in the Lenin of this interpretation, is any sense of socialism as the outcome of the struggles and aspirations of the people themselves.[14]

The occasion of Lenin's retreat into revolutionary idealism is sometimes held to be his supposed disappointment at the meagre results of the spontaneous struggle of the Russian workers. Sometimes a gnawing fear of the truth of Eduard Bernstein's recent revision of Marxism is diagnosed. But whatever the genesis of *What Is to Be Done?*, on this interpretation it marks Lenin's effective abandonment of historical materialism. If he had subscribed to the central tenets of Marxism, he no longer did so: if the working class was not equal to its revolutionary vocation, the socialist intelligentsia must be made to do its work; if the workers' struggles would not generate socialist consciousness,

---

12   See Valentinov 1969, pp. 111–282 and Valentinov 1968, pp. 23–6 and 63–76; Besançon 1981; Haimson 1955; Ulam 1969; Wilson 1972; and Wolfe 1964.

13   Chernyshevskii 1961.

14   Neil Harding's failure to take cognisance of the theoretical issues surrounding the notion of proletarian self-emancipation and reflected, however inadequately, in the conventional wisdom, leads him sometimes – in his concern to vindicate the Marxist orthodoxy of Lenin's *What Is to Be Done?* – to trivialise the arguments of its proponents. In rebutting the claim of Lenin's 'Jacobin' debt to Chernyshevskii's *What Is to Be Done?*, he concerns himself only with Valentinov's dubious speculations about a hidden code to the novel, known only to initiates, among whom Lenin was supposedly numbered (Harding 1975, pp. 446–7; see Valentinov 1968, pp. 70f). But it does not require a particularly painstaking reading of Chernyshevskii's work to discern in it some of the key themes of pre-Marxist utopian socialism, and it was the repetition of these themes, with the implied denial of proletarian self-emancipation, that Lenin's Economist, and later Menshevik, adversaries thought they recognised in the pages of *What Is to Be Done?* I have shown that the conceptual status of proletarian self-emancipation in Marxist orthodoxy is somewhat more complex than has often been supposed. It is only in evacuating Lenin's Marxist context of this complexity – and of the theoretical issues that arise from it – that Harding is able to dispose so easily of the legacy of Chernyshevskii. Although it is not concerned with Chernyshevskii in particular, the same general point applies to Lih 2006.

they must be subordinated to the revolutionary project of this intellectual elite. Though a conspiratorial vanguard of professional revolutionaries is the initial institutional embodiment of this authoritarian and idealist philosophy, Lenin's undialectical counterposition of spontaneity and consciousness, theory and practice, generates a logic of 'substitutionism' whereby 'the party organisation substitutes itself for the party, the Central Committee substitutes itself for the party organisation, and finally a dictator substitutes himself for the Central Committee'.[15] On this interpretation, Lenin becomes the intellectual progenitor of Soviet totalitarianism: Stalin would be the logical culmination of the Leninist thesis that consciousness must be brought to the working class from without. This thesis thus becomes the intellectual axis on which turns the predominant account of the development and degeneration of the Bolshevik revolution.

The terms in which this interpretation is cast, however, are too abstract to permit an adequate positive account of working-class consciousness and its development. Understood in these terms, the idea of proletarian self-emancipation echoes the dichotomy of autonomy and heteronomy in classical German philosophy. The alternatives are reduced, at this level of abstraction, to just two: either the workers spontaneously develop consciousness of themselves as a class with a socialist vocation (autonomy) or this consciousness must be imposed upon them by others (heteronomy). The dichotomy commands a whole series of conceptual distinctions: consciousness and spontaneity, theory and practice, idealism and materialism, intellectuals and workers, authoritarianism and democracy. But the addition of the qualification 'proletarian' to the act of 'self-emancipation' raises questions as to the circumstances in which this act unfolds, questions that elicit no response – or an inadequate one – from the perspective considered here. For example, in the act of self-emancipation, do all workers come to consciousness at once or are some of them, the leaders, in advance of the others? If, as seems likely, the latter must be the case, what are relations to be like among the workers and between the leaders and the others in order that one may properly speak of the class becoming or being conscious? The circumstances of the class struggle are surely as relevant as its goal in formulating a reply to this question. Alternatively put, is self-emancipation to be understood as a single act of enlightenment or as a process in which increasingly higher levels of consciousness are attained? If, as seems likely, the latter must be the case here as well, in what terms are the different levels of consciousness to be specified? Again, there is no reason to suppose that the circumstances of the process are any less relevant to this question than is its

---

15   Trotsky 1904a, p. 121.

goal. The point is simply this: in order to assign concrete meaning to the notion of proletarian self-emancipation, one cannot just read the abstract concept of self-emancipation into the proletariat; the significance of the idea is bound up with the concrete circumstances of the proletarian class struggle. Once this point is understood, there seems to be no reason to restrict the relevant circumstances to global facts about the capitalist mode of production and its development; such circumstances as whether or not the proletarians are confronted by a democratic republic or an absolute monarchy and whether or not they find themselves in the company of an educated urban petty bourgeoisie or an illiterate peasantry are also relevant. The perspective considered here allows little or no recognition of such circumstances.

The gist of Lenin's rejoinder to his critics, and a constant refrain throughout his political writings, is an insistence upon analysing class struggle in the context of its concrete circumstances: 'The ABC of dialectics', he wrote, 'tells us that there is no such thing as abstract truth, truth is always concrete'.[16] His emphasis upon concrete analysis suggests that the 'self-emancipation' critique of *What Is to Be Done?* not only fails, due to its abstract terms, to provide a grip on the development of class consciousness, but may also, for the same reason, miss its target. Something like this view seems to inform those readings of Lenin that present his treatment of spontaneity and consciousness in a sympathetic light, seeing both theoretical sophistication and political realism in its concrete analysis of the concrete conditions.[17] But this 'social-scientific' concern with concreteness and complexity is not, by itself, an adequate reply to the critique, because it stops short of demonstrating the consistency of Lenin's 'concrete' account with the Marxist thesis of proletarian self-emancipation. While those who stress this concern have been able to point out errors and omissions in the 'self-emancipation' critics' reading of *What Is to Be Done?*, they have either shied away from such a demonstration or carried it out only in disregarding or downplaying Lenin's more radical formulations.[18] The result of this procedure, because it sacrifices both the letter of Lenin's text and the

---

16   Lenin 1904b, p. 478.
17   See, for example, Althusser 1970b, pp. 168–9; Balibar 1974b, pp. 272–9; Cliff 1975, pp. 79–98; Gruppi 1978; and Harding 1977, pp. 161–96.
18   While aware that these formulations pose a problem for his reading of *What Is to Be Done?* as a simple exemplification of 'Erfurtian' – Kautskyan – Marxism, Lih professes himself unable to supply a reading consistent with them and dismisses them as the product of some combination of polemical distortion and editorial haste; his interpretation thus labours under a similar limitation (see Lih 2006). Lih's treatment of the text and the context of *What Is to Be Done?* as well as some cognate hermeneutical issues are considered in Appendix 2.

distinctiveness of the theoretical position that underpins it, is little improvement either in exegesis or in concrete analysis.

Lenin's discussion of spontaneity and consciousness, to which I will refer as 'the thesis of consciousness from without', repays careful textual and contextual analysis.[19] Taking care with this thesis means recognising that it is not a single simple assertion but a complex of several, sometimes apparently contradictory, claims. These claims, which are often interlaced in the text, must be disentangled from each other and the meaning of their terms clarified. Proceeding in this way will turn up indications of an underlying logic of political analysis; by spelling out the implications of this logic, it will prove possible to make coherent sense of the paradoxes of Lenin's argument. This procedure, while starting from close attention to what Lenin actually wrote, necessarily goes beyond the letter of the text, but it is justified if it can indeed unlock a coherent reading of the text where alternative interpretations fail to do so.

The thesis of consciousness from without can only be understood as the expression of an underlying logic of political analysis requiring that concrete political analyses be undertaken before the forms of political activity and organisation appropriate to the existing circumstances of the working-class movement can be determined. For this reason, Lenin's thesis is compatible with various forms of organisation, including democratic forms. If it is the conditions of Tsarist Russia and not Lenin's thesis that require undemocratic forms of organisation, then the thesis may well be compatible with proletarian self-emancipation. But the latter involves more than democratic forms of organisation; it entails conscious and independent working-class political activity. It is in just this respect, however, that the logic of Lenin's thesis proves

---

19   A passage in Benjamin Constant's 1797 'Des effets de la Terreur' is particularly pertinent to the analysis of Lenin's thesis of 'consciousness from without'. It sounds a note of caution with its reminder that the import of an idea may turn out, in consequence of slight differences in the meaning of terms, in its place in an argument, or in cognate ideas, to be quite the opposite of its seemingly obvious significance: 'The most elementary experience of men and of the way in which ideas come together teaches us that the consequences that seem to us to follow evidently from a principle are sometimes absolutely unknown to its most zealous partisans. A slight difference in one of the links in the chain, in the meaning of an expression, in a transitional idea, or in a concurrent opinion can lead to quite a different line of argument and to directly opposing conclusions. Nothing is more contrary to the progress of enlightenment than to cast upon a writer the odium or the absurdity of alleged consequences that he has not drawn from his principles and that we draw without his knowledge: they must be explained so that he may compare them with those he draws; but it is only with the most culpable injustice that such explanation could degenerate into accusation' (Constant 1797, p. 165).

to be not only consistent, but more consistent than the stance of his critics, with the idea of proletarian self-emancipation. The argument behind this claim may be condensed as follows: 'consciousness' is defined by all parties in the controversy by reference to Marxist theory, but the logic of Lenin's position implies a distinctive understanding of Marxist theory as necessarily subject to development (theoretical reorganisation) as a result of its application in concrete analyses. This not only means that individual workers may take part directly, when they become Marxist theorists, in the creative elaboration of proletarian self-consciousness and impart this self-consciousness to the spontaneous working-class movement; it also means that if the thesis of consciousness from without is consistent with the transformation of Marxist theory in response to spontaneous revolutionary innovations of the class, the working class can be understood as taking part indirectly, but nonetheless actively and creatively, in the formation of consciousness. If, as I suggest, Lenin's critics must rely upon an understanding of Marxist theory as, in essence, a doctrine whose tenets have been elaborated once and for all, then proletarian self-emancipation becomes little more than the assimilation of this doctrine and its implication of creativity effectively, if 'unconsciously', denied. If I am right, Lenin's thesis of consciousness from without not only offers a more concrete mode of analysis of working-class consciousness, it also allows a more concrete and richer understanding of proletarian self-emancipation than any that the optic of its critics would permit.

If Lenin's thesis of consciousness from without does not amount to a break with core Marxist tenets, its assertion of a struggle between socialist consciousness and the spontaneous working-class movement, which carries very different implications than the Kautskyan formulation with which it is sometimes wrongly identified, does stretch the logic of orthodox Marxism beyond its breaking point. Once it is situated in the context of the turn-of-the-century crisis of Russian Social Democracy, its bearing upon the struggle for proletarian hegemony in the democratic revolution is evident. The upsurge of working-class industrial action that swept Russia in the mid-1890s was countered by waves of police repression that decimated the ranks of Social Democratic activists. Within weeks of the first congress of the Russian Social Democratic Labour Party in 1898, for example, the members of the Central Committee it elected were under Tsarist lock and key. The role of hardened activists would have to be taken on by eager but inexperienced newcomers. Some would come to despair of the possibility of working-class participation in revolutionary politics; others, despite the best intentions, would stagnate in the isolation of merely local initiatives. Getting beyond this period of disorientation called upon the Social Democrats to rearticulate their political project in terms that addressed these practical obstacles. Differences over just how to reconstruct the broken party organisation and pursue its revolutionary political project would come to be bound up with contending factional claims to leadership.

As this struggle unfolded within Social Democratic ranks, new challenges emerged to the Russian Marxist claim to the hegemony of the proletariat in the democratic revolution. The workers' struggles spurred a resurgence of revolutionary populism while the first hints surfaced – from former Social Democrats – of a project for bourgeois hegemony over the democratic forces. Hegemony in the revolutionary movement could no longer simply be asserted; it would have to be earned, and this would have repercussions for the controversies in the working-class movement. This is the context in which Lenin wrote *What Is to Be Done?* His account of spontaneity and consciousness is shaped in part by the effort to grasp and intervene in the struggle for hegemony. In this light, the strategic logic that informs his thesis of consciousness from without might well be termed a politico-strategic logic of the struggle for hegemony or, more concisely, the logic of hegemony.

As one of Lenin's more careful readers has noted, the conventional wisdom begins with 'an hypostatised version of the "essence" of Marxism to which an equally abstracted Leninism is counterposed'.[20] In the preceding chapters I analysed the limits of the orthodox Marxism of the Second International and mapped some of the ambiguities, even contradictions, to which its logic gives rise when applied to problems – of political leadership, unification of the working class, class alliance, and hegemony – that challenge those limits. The crisis in Russian Social Democracy and in its project of hegemony was thus a crisis of Marxist orthodoxy; the point is reinforced by its coincidence with the international crisis induced by Bernstein's revisionist critique of Marxist theory. In this context, Lenin's thesis of consciousness from without, by disrupting conceptual harmonies that functioned as an illusory guarantee of the unfailing insight of Marxism in theory and the irresistible forward march of the socialist working class in practice and that thereby served as a prophylactic against critical investigation of sensitive issues, may be understood as introducing a breach into the logic of orthodox Marxism. It thereby created an opening in which the movement of the political struggle could be more effectively explored in practice and subjected to critical theoretical analysis. This is not to claim that the politico-strategic logic that subtended Lenin's thesis provides an alternative logic of history that resolves the equivocation besetting orthodox Marxist attempts to theorise the political project of proletarian

---

20 Harding 1977, p. 29.

hegemony in the bourgeois-democratic revolution. As a Marxist, Lenin would always hold to historical materialism; what shifted was the way he held it, the way it informed and was informed by his practice.

Historical Questions

To understand just what Lenin's thesis entails, two different kinds of claims put forward in his discussion of spontaneity and consciousness must be distinguished. There are, first, historical claims made in response to the following questions: who first formulated the theory that defines the contours of socialist consciousness? How, and in what context, was the theory elaborated? Second, there are claims that address the pressing concerns of political practice: how should adherents of socialist theory, would-be leaders of the working class, orient themselves in relation to the spontaneous movement of the workers? Both kinds of claim must be examined because each plays a different part in shaping the terms of Lenin's thesis. Lenin begins his chapter on spontaneity and consciousness by posing the political problem, but he proceeds immediately to set it in historical context. I begin with the historical questions before turning to the politics.

Lenin locates the 'spontaneous element', in the first place, in the broad wave of strikes that spread through Russia in the wake of 'the famous St. Petersburg industrial conflict of 1896'. Before situating consciousness with respect to spontaneity, however, he indicates that the relation between these terms is not a simple one – for, he writes, 'there is spontaneity and spontaneity'. He goes on to suggest that, compared to the spontaneous machine-smashing characteristic of the workers' 'revolts' of the earlier nineteenth century, the strikes of the nineties could be considered conscious. From this he draws the conclusion that

> the 'spontaneous element', in essence, represents nothing more than consciousness in an *embryonic form*. And even the primitive revolts expressed the awakening of consciousness to a certain extent. The workers were losing their age-long belief in the unshakeability of the system which oppressed them and began ... to sense the necessity for collective resistance, definitely abandoning their slavish submission to the authorities. But this was nevertheless more an expression of desperation and vengeance than a *struggle*. The strikes of the 1890s revealed far greater flashes of consciousness: definite demands were advanced, the strike was carefully timed, known cases and instances in other places were discussed, etc. The revolts were simply the resistance of the oppressed,

whereas the systematic strikes represented the class struggle in embryo. Taken by themselves, these strikes were trade-union struggles, not yet Social-Democratic struggles.[21]

Lenin's account of the history of the Russian working-class movement thus describes a dialectic of resistance, consciousness, struggle and organisation. This spontaneous dialectic is identified as embryonic consciousness but runs up against a limitation it cannot surmount by itself. Lenin defines this limitation in two ways: first negatively, in terms of socialist consciousness – the striking workers of the 1890s 'were not, and could not be, conscious of the irreconcilable antagonism of their interests to the whole of the modern political and social system' – and then positively, in terms of the workers' own consciousness – '[t]he history of all countries shows that the working class exclusively by its own effort is able to develop only trade-union consciousness'.[22] This characterisation of the limit to the spontaneous dialectic of working-class consciousness is by no means as straightforward as it may appear, a point to which I will return at some length.

The important point, for the moment, is the fact of Lenin's assertion of this limit rather than the details of his account of it. It is worth noting, however, that he understands the constraint upon the development of working-class socialist consciousness not as a problem specific to the situation of the Russian workers but as a general limit upon the spontaneous dialectic of working-class struggle. The terms of the problem imply that the solution must be brought to the working class from without. The theory of socialism, upon which socialist consciousness depends,

> grew out of the philosophic, historical, and economic theories elaborated by educated representatives of the propertied classes, by the intelligentsia. By their social status, the founders of modern scientific socialism, Marx and Engels, themselves belonged to the bourgeois intelligentsia. In the very same way, in Russia, the theoretical doctrine of social-democracy arose altogether independently of the spontaneous growth of the working-class movement; it arose as a natural and inevitable outcome of the development of thought among the revolutionary socialist intelligentsia.[23]

---

21 Lenin 1902, pp. 374–5.
22 Lenin 1902, p. 375.
23 Lenin 1902, pp. 375–6.

What Lenin says here may be reduced to the following assertions: first, the intellectual raw materials from which socialist theory was first fashioned were the products of bourgeois intellectuals; second, the first artisans of modern socialist theory were themselves bourgeois intellectuals; third, Marx and Engels originally worked out this theory and Plekhanov later adapted it to Russian conditions 'altogether independently' of the spontaneous working-class movement. The advent of socialist theory is thus understood as an intellectual process, a process of ideas whose bearers were intellectuals. That this should have been so is seen as a historical necessity; so, consequently, is the importation of socialist consciousness into the working-class movement from without.

What is important for the purpose at hand is not the accuracy of Lenin's historical account but rather its implications for the development of working-class consciousness – and these depend less upon what Lenin asserts as fact than upon his reasons for construing the facts as necessary. But neither in logic nor in Lenin's argument does the historical thesis of consciousness from without imply the workers' inaptitude for socialist consciousness or the subjection of their movement to the tutelage of a socialist intelligentsia. Even as Lenin dismisses 'talk of an independent ideology formulated by the masses themselves in the process of their movement', he notes that the workers do play a part in working out such an ideology: 'They take part, however, not as workers but as socialist theoreticians, as Proudhons and Weitlings ... they take part only when they are able, more or less, to acquire the knowledge of their age and develop that knowledge'.[24] This throws a new light on the idea of the bourgeois intellectual origins of socialist theory: it suggests that the more fundamental distinction, at least in this context, is not that between bourgeois and worker but that between individual theoretician and the masses 'in the process of their movement'. Perhaps, in describing Marx and Engels as bourgeois intellectuals, Lenin means to suggest that the limitations of a working-class education prevented even the most gifted worker-theoreticians from gaining the breadth and depth of knowledge necessary to found as sophisticated and encompassing a theory as the materialist conception of history. Or perhaps his thought is that, in the process of acquiring this knowledge, a worker-theoretician would have had to ascend to bourgeois social circumstances (note that he characterises Marx and Engels as bourgeois intellectuals by 'social status', not by birth). Either of these views may be contested but neither can be interpreted as attributing an innate theoretical incapacity to workers, as denying a place for worker-theoreticians either in the prehistory of Marxist theory or, more importantly, in its subsequent development. Indeed, an important part of the rationale for the political

---

24   Lenin 1902, p. 384n.

project of *What Is to Be Done?* was to encourage and foster the development of socialist theoreticians (and organisers, agitators and practical activists) from the working class. In order that workers '*may succeed in this* [contributing to socialist theory] *more often*, every effort must be made to raise the level of the consciousness of the workers in general'.[25]

But what of the workers in general, the non-theoretical masses? In this respect, too, the limits of proletarian spontaneity are not such as to prevent Lenin from agreeing that 'the working class *spontaneously* gravitates towards socialism... in the sense that socialist theory reveals the causes of the misery of the working class more profoundly and more correctly than any other theory, and for that reason the workers are able to assimilate it so easily'.[26] In other words, although the spontaneous working-class movement could not generate Marxist theory by itself, once it exists and is made available to the workers, they grasp it easily; they can do so not because they are naive and easily manipulable dupes for the sophisticated intellectual salesmen of some exotic nostrum, but precisely because, in a sense, the theory is not alien to them, because it constitutes a mirror in which they can see their reality and their aspirations more clearly. This, surely, is at least part of what Lenin means in referring to spontaneity as 'consciousness in embryonic form'. Only in this context can one understand the prediction in Lenin's chapter on organisation that the spontaneous movement of the working-class masses would throw up increasing numbers of leaders 'boundlessly devoted to the revolution', who would learn to combine their 'knowledge of the working-class environment and the freshness of socialist convictions' with the professional skills of the revolutionary and who would 'enjoy the boundless confidence of the widest masses of the workers'.[27]

Considered as a historical claim, then, the thesis of consciousness from without does not imply a working class bridled to a superior will or one that shies away from those who would assist its self-emancipation. To claim otherwise would be to make the truth of proletarian self-emancipation dependent upon, for example, the contingency of the social status of the author of *Capital*. But this would be tantamount to the claim that one could liberate oneself only if one had never had a teacher or mentor and had never read a book one could not have written oneself. Of course, the thesis of consciousness from without cannot be considered only as a historical claim, for Lenin's historical discussion raises questions whose answers must be sought in the nature

---

25   Ibid.
26   Lenin 1902, p. 386n.
27   Lenin 1902, pp. 472–3.

of his political project. In particular, this discussion has assumed throughout that socialist consciousness is dependent upon a theory without explaining why. This question, it will be seen, is bound up with the one raised earlier as to Lenin's characterisation of the limit of the dialectic of proletarian spontaneity.

Political Questions

The terms in which Lenin spells out his political project, the organisation of a revolutionary vanguard of the proletarian class struggle, are a function of his treatment of the constraints upon the spontaneous course of the working-class movement. In one formulation, as previously mentioned, these constraints restrict the working class to 'trade-union consciousness, i.e., the conviction that it is necessary to combine in unions, fight the employers, and strive to compel the government to pass necessary labour legislation, etc'.[28] It is customary to read Lenin, proceeding from this definition, as though he were proclaiming Samuel Gompers-style 'trade unionism pure and simple' as the natural *telos* of proletarian consciousness.[29] Indeed, non-Marxist sociologists and historians of industrial relations have even applauded the realism of Lenin's supposed insight, while deploring his failure to draw its reformist conclusions.[30] This interpretation can appeal to Lenin's characterisation of the object of his criticism as 'Economism'. It relies upon passages such as the following one, in which Lenin seems to equate the distinction between spontaneity and consciousness with that between economic and political struggle, and construes the thesis of consciousness from without in terms of the latter:

> Class political consciousness can be brought to the workers *only from without*, that is, only from outside the economic struggle, from outside the sphere of relations between workers and employers. The sphere from which alone it is possible to obtain this knowledge is the sphere of relationships of *all* classes and strata to the state and the government, the sphere of the interrelations among *all* classes.[31]

---

28 Lenin 1902, p. 375.
29 See, for example, Hammond 1957, pp. 15–33; Hyman 1971, pp. 11–14; and Wildman 1967, p. 59.
30 See, for example, Crouch 1982, pp. 32–3; and Pipes 1963, pp. 124–5.
31 Lenin 1902, p. 422.

While this statement is not contentious in itself, if Lenin is to be understood as circumscribing the limits of proletarian spontaneity by the dichotomy between economic and political struggle, his position must appear not only arbitrary (for why should the spontaneous logic of economic struggle not spill over into politics?) but also, unless one is to ransack the back rooms of working-class history for the hidden hand of consciousness (an operation that smacks more of a police mentality than of historical scholarship), historically false. Furthermore, such a perspective invites the equally false conclusion that, once the confines of economic struggle have been transcended, the politics of the working class must be those of the socialist revolution.

In the first place, however, the idea that Lenin mistook narrow-minded business unionism for the essence of the spontaneous proletarian movement sits uneasily with his claim, noted earlier, that even primitive revolts antedating the strike movement of his own time saw the workers begin to question the stability of the system and to overcome their attitude of servility toward the authorities. It is belied by his repeated assertions that 'the strength of the present-day movement lies in the awakening of the masses', that the would-be revolutionary leaders lagged behind the masses, that not he but his opponents, both Economists and terrorists, '*underestimate* the revolutionary activity of the masses'.[32]

Secondly, Lenin acknowledged that the term 'Economism', although entrenched by usage, did not adequately convey the nature of the political trend it designated. Economism, he argued, 'does not so much deny the political struggle as it bows to its *spontaneity*, to its unconsciousness'.[33] The distinction

---

[32] Lenin 1902, pp. 373, 420.

[33] Lenin 1902, p. 387. These statements would seem to be reasonably clear. Neither they nor the extensive discussion they encapsulate have been enough, however, to preclude the unfortunate interpretive procedure of first attributing to Lenin an 'ordinary language' understanding of the term 'Economism' and then, after a facile demonstration that such an understanding amounts to a caricature of his opponents' views, convicting him of an intellectual and political fraud. Perhaps the first practitioner of this 'hermeneutic' was the Economist Vladimir Akimov, who claimed that 'the first economists, and indeed the only real economists, were none other than the members of the Union of Struggle of 1895 – the subsequent founders of *Iskra*' (Frankel (ed.) 1969, p. 247; see also pp. 322, 352). Jonathan Frankel repeats this practice in his 'Introduction' (1969b) to Akimov's work and in Frankel 1963; it vitiates otherwise useful historical accounts in Lih 2006 and Wildman 1967.

Wildman accepts Akimov's claim on the ground that the agitational leaflets Lenin and his colleagues produced in the League of Struggle were concerned almost exclusively with petty economic as opposed to broader political demands. Accordingly, he dismisses Lenin's retrospective account in *What Is to Be Done?*: '[A]lthough the *early*

between spontaneity and consciousness would seem to be more fundamental in Lenin's argument than that between economic and political struggle and should not, therefore, be defined in terms of the latter. Finally, the 'etc.' with which Lenin concludes his initial definition of trade-union consciousness indicates the incomplete, open-ended character of this definition. He immediately goes on to note that trade unions have always engaged in political struggles and refers his readers to a lengthy chapter on the difference between trade-unionist politics and socialist politics. There one finds the following argument:

> The spontaneous working-class movement is by itself able to create (and inevitably does create) only trade-unionism, and working-class trade-unionist politics is precisely working-class bourgeois politics. The fact that the working class participates in the political struggle, and even in the political revolution, does not in itself make its politics social-democratic politics... [T]he revolutionary path of the working-class movement might not be a social-democratic path. When absolutism reigned, the entire West-European bourgeoisie... impelled the workers on to the path of revolution... And if we... degrade social-democratic politics to the level of spontaneous trade-unionist politics, we thereby play into the hands of bourgeois democracy.[34]

The constraints upon the spontaneous working-class movement, the limits upon trade-union consciousness, are thus compatible not only with political struggle but even with revolutionary struggle. Lenin's distinction between

---

Social-Democrats... *zealously carried on economic agitation*... they did not regard this as their sole task. On the contrary, *from the very beginning* they set for Russian Social-Democracy the most far-reaching historical tasks, in general, and the task of overthrowing the autocracy, in particular' (Lenin 1902, p. 376). But Wildman simply misrepresents Lenin's historical claim. Lenin does not assert that the Social Democrats had conducted political agitation in 1895; he claims, rather, that they had conducted economic agitation within the perspective of the political struggle for proletarian hegemony in the democratic revolution and that attempts, however unsuccessful, had already been made to give this perspective practical expression. To substantiate his claim, he referred to the first (December 1895) issue of *Rabochee delo*, produced by the St. Petersburg League of Struggle but immediately confiscated by the police, containing articles and correspondence dealing with political subjects and a leading article in which pride of place was given to the workers' struggle for political liberty. On this evidence – passed over by Wildman – Lenin's account does not go beyond the historical truth.

34 Lenin 1902, pp. 437, 438n.

spontaneity and consciousness is not to be grasped as a fixed line of demarcation between economics and politics or even between reform and revolution.

An 'Irreconcilable Antagonism ... to the Whole'

Lenin offers another formulation of the limits of the spontaneous working-class movement, examination of which will help to pin down this elusive concept. As noted above, he maintains that the workers are unable, through their spontaneous movement, to generate a consciousness of 'the irreconcilable antagonism of their interests to the whole of the modern political and social system'. Now, Lenin does not claim that the workers must be, or even that they are, unaware of their interests or of the antagonism of their interests to those of their employers. What distinguishes his claim, rather, is the extension of this antagonism to the whole 'modern political and social system', the idea of its irreconcilability. What Lenin asserts, then, is that the spontaneous workers' movement cannot but remain unconscious of the total, irreconcilable nature of this antagonism of interests. To make sense of this assertion, one must grasp the significance, for Lenin's conception of consciousness, of the political and social system considered as a whole and of the irreconcilable antagonism of the social totality.

Some sense of the breadth of Lenin's notion of consciousness is conveyed by the following prescription for aspiring socialist workers:

> In order to become a social-democrat, the worker must have a clear picture in his mind of the economic nature and the social and political features of the landlord and the priest, the high state official and the peasant, the student and the vagabond; he must know their strong and weak points; he must grasp the meaning of catchwords and all manner of sophisms by which each class and each stratum *camouflages* its selfish strivings and its real 'inner workings'; he must understand what interests are reflected by certain institutions and certain laws and how they are reflected.[35]

The same theme is given more general expression in the following:

> Working-class consciousness cannot be genuine political consciousness unless the workers are trained to respond to *all* cases of tyranny,

---

35   Lenin 1902, p. 413.

oppression, violence, and abuse, no matter *what class* is affected ... Those who concentrate the attention, observation, and consciousness of the working class exclusively, or even mainly, upon itself alone are not social-democrats; for the self-knowledge of the working class is bound up not solely with a fully clear theoretical understanding – it would be even truer to say, not so much with a theoretical as with a practical understanding – of the relationships between *all* the various classes of modern society, acquired through the experience of political life.[36]

Although it acquires a new significance in the context of *What Is to Be Done?*, the characterisation of proletarian self-consciousness as essentially universal is not new. It may be traced back to the young Marx's portrait of the proletariat as the class 'which has a universal character because of its universal suffering and which lays claim to no *particular right* because the wrong it suffers is not a *particular wrong* but *wrong in general*'.[37] In the course of working out a Marxist orthodoxy for the Second International, Karl Kautsky translated this philosophical vision into more prosaic sociological terms: the development of working-class organisation and consciousness parallels and reflects the growth of the productive forces; this process socialises production and places the workers in ever more homogeneous circumstances; the class struggle is polarised between wage labour and capital as hitherto particularistic antagonisms take on a universal character; the universality of proletarian self-consciousness is, increasingly, immanent in the very situation of the industrial worker.[38] Lenin himself, in his earlier discussions of the development of capitalism in Russia, used this Kautskyan schema to connect the strategic idea of the industrial working class as the political vanguard of the labouring masses with the universalistic tendency of large-scale capitalist industry.[39] The universality of proletarian self-consciousness is here equated with the emergence of the developed class relation of capitalist exploitation in large-scale industry. Since this analysis construes the dialectic of the proletarian class situation as a kind of cognitive essence of the social totality, it is compatible with a thesis of consciousness from without only if the latter asserts simply that the prerequisites for formulating working-class self-consciousness as a socialist theory are irreducible to the immediate experience of proletarian struggle.

---

36 Lenin 1902, pp. 412–13.
37 Marx 1843–4, p. 186.
38 See, for example, Kautsky 1892, pp. 42, 86–7, 155–6, 171–3, 182, 187–8, 201; Kautsky 1902, pp. 80–82.
39 See, for example, Lenin 1895–6, pp. 104, 107, 113–16.

The distinction between socialist theory and proletarian experience would, in a sense, be purely formal; ultimately, there could be no contradiction between them. If this were the case, as Kautsky's example shows, the idea of consciousness from without would effectively underwrite the harmony of Marxist theory and working-class practice.[40]

The notion of the social totality and its relation to working-class consciousness just outlined is not, however, the one that informs the argument of *What Is to Be Done?* The emphasis there is upon the diversity of social and political relations: the position of the poor peasant cannot be assimilated to that of the industrial wage labourer, the political face of the landlord or the state official is not that of the capitalist, and so on. The difference, however, is more than emphasis, for Lenin's political thesis of consciousness from without is far more radical than the common-sense claim that the sheer complexity of the socio-political system considered as a whole stands as a barrier to generating a socialist consciousness of this whole from the workers' economic struggle alone. He asserts not merely a distinction between the conditions of the class struggle and those of socialist theory, but a contradiction between the spontaneous working-class movement and its conscious vanguard:

> the *spontaneous* development of the working-class movement leads to its subordination to bourgeois ideology, *to its development along the lines of the Credo programme*; for the spontaneous working-class movement is trade-unionism, is *Nur-Gewerkschaftlerei*, and trade-unionism means the ideological enslavement of the workers to the bourgeoisie. Hence, our task, the task of social-democracy, is *to combat spontaneity, to divert* the working-class movement from this spontaneous, trade-unionist striving to come under the wing of the bourgeoisie, and to bring it under the wing of revolutionary social-democracy.[41]

It may be suggested that Lenin's emphasis upon the diversity of social and political relations reflects the nascent state of capitalist development in Russia and the corresponding prominence of pre-capitalist (feudal or 'Asiatic') relations. It might be thought that his injunction 'to combat spontaneity' is thus meant to apply only in Russian conditions, only to the immaturity of the working-class movement. But the general terms in which Lenin casts his claims as to both the diversity of social relations and the struggle against spontaneity belie this suggestion. And his recourse to the experience of German socialism directly

---

40 See Kautsky 1901–2.
41 Lenin 1902, pp. 384–5.

contradicts it. He accords to Ferdinand Lassalle, from whom he borrowed the epigraph of *What Is to Be Done?*, the historical merit of having successfully challenged the orientation of the German working-class movement toward reformist trade unionism. The ideological and organisational predominance of socialism in the working class could only have been accomplished through a 'fierce struggle against spontaneity... extending over many years', a struggle that would have to continue. For, despite the advanced development of capitalism in Germany, the working class was still divided along ideological lines. The dominant influence of socialist ideology within the working-class movement could be maintained and extended 'only in an unswerving struggle against all other ideologies'.[42] The socialist struggle against spontaneity appears, then, as a permanent requisite of the class struggle.

In the course of Lenin's argument, the appropriate socialist stance toward spontaneity takes on two apparently contradictory guises. The conscious vanguard is called upon to foster and guide the spontaneous working-class movement and, at the same time, to combat it. This ambivalence, which I will argue is merely apparent, has its roots in a contradictory assessment of spontaneity itself: the latter is adjudged both the embryo of socialist consciousness and the repository of bourgeois ideology. This contradiction is succinctly and pointedly stated as follows: 'The working class spontaneously gravitates towards socialism; but the most widespread (and continuously and diversely revived) bourgeois ideology none the less spontaneously imposes itself upon the worker to a still greater degree'.[43] To make sense of this claim, we must grasp not only the reasons for the dominance of bourgeois ideology but also the dialectical process of its struggle with the spontaneous socialist tendencies of the working class. Lenin's immediate, formulaic and, therefore, most accessible explanation of bourgeois ideological domination, 'that bourgeois ideology is far older in origin than socialist ideology, that it is more fully developed, and that it has at its disposal immeasurably more means of dissemination',[44] is clearly inadequate. Taken by itself, it suggests a mechanistic account of proletarian consciousness as a simple receptacle for ideas produced by bourgeois or socialist intellectuals and an idealistic agenda for change through the conquest of socialist dominance in the means of ideological dissemination. But it cannot be taken by itself, for if, as Lenin claims, spontaneous proletarian struggle is the embryo of socialist consciousness, further explanation is required as to

---

42   Lenin 1902, pp. 385–6.
43   Lenin 1902, p. 386n.
44   Lenin 1902, p. 386.

how bourgeois ideology can gain traction in the consciousness of workers. A full explanation must therefore reference a dynamic of struggle and must situate the terms of the problem (spontaneity/consciousness; bourgeois spontaneity/socialist spontaneity) within this dynamic and thereby relativise them.

A Logic of Political Struggle

The theoretical groundwork for such an explanation can be found in Lenin's text, although it is not spelled out in so many words. It consists in a particular way of analysing the logic of political struggle and in the way each successive analysis relates to and modifies the previous one; it is a meta-strategic conception of the whole social and political system as a complex web of interconnected struggles, as a kind of battlefield. It is not fully spelled out because Lenin wrote as a participant in battle for other participants, assuming in his readers some familiarity with the outcome of previous engagements, less concerned with compiling a history of the war than with discerning the alignment in the current battle. But it is a feature of the battlefield of political struggle that its shape is subject to change with each engagement, so that a picture of the field as a whole must emerge from the conjunction of successive analyses. I will proceed by first drawing on an indication in Lenin's text to suggest a way of situating bourgeois and socialist spontaneity with respect to such a meta-strategic conception, then fleshing out this conception with reference to his analyses of successive phases of the struggle with Economism and finally drawing out the theoretical implications of this conception.

To grasp the distinction between bourgeois and socialist spontaneity in the context of a complex socio-political totality of interconnected struggles requires that two levels of analysis be distinguished: at an initial level, the analysis abstracts entirely from 'consciousness', from the influence of ideology upon the spontaneous struggle of social forces, which is grasped as a function of the social relations of production. Here the interests of the class of wage labourers are determined to be in irreconcilable conflict with the fundamental social relations of the capitalist mode of production. The workers may be expected, by virtue of these social relations, to gravitate spontaneously toward socialist theory in order to explain their situation and orient their struggle to realise their interests. But analysis of the socio-economic basis of the class struggle does not exhaust the determinants of the spontaneous movement. This is perhaps most clearly expressed in 'A Talk with Defenders of Economism', an article Lenin described as a 'synopsis' of *What is to be Done?*:

> To say ... that ideologists (i.e. politically conscious leaders) cannot divert the movement from the path determined by the interaction of environment and elements is to ignore the simple truth that the conscious element *participates* in this interaction and in the determination of the path. Catholic and monarchist labour unions in Europe are also an inevitable result of the interaction of environment and elements, but it was the consciousness of priests and Zubatovs and not that of socialists that participated in this direction.[45]

Lenin is concerned here with disentangling a confusion in his opponents' thinking between two kinds of distinction: that between socioeconomic base and ideological superstructure and that between socialist consciousness and spontaneity. While the former may serve the political analyst in grasping the process of development of the social totality 'from the outside', as it were, the latter is the appropriate tool for the political strategist who, confronted with a determinate alignment of forces, must act upon it from within the totality. Conflating these two distinctions spirits away the space for one's own political action.

Once the functions of these pairs of terms are distinguished, the spontaneous movement is to be understood as that which confronts the socialist consciousness of the would-be vanguard of the proletariat, within its field of action but beyond its control; it therefore encompasses the working-class movement not simply as determined by the relations of production but also as subjected to the influence of the ideological apparatuses of the bourgeoisie (and of the monarchy and so on). It is only at this second, more concrete level of analysis that Lenin locates the dominance of bourgeois ideology in the spontaneous working-class movement: his calls for struggle against spontaneity are invariably coupled with references to the impact of bourgeois ideologists upon the workers' movement. However, what is subject to this domination, if Lenin's twofold distinction is to be taken seriously, is not the working class as such, but the spontaneous unfolding of its movement, that is, its movement considered in abstraction from the socialist vanguard that is informed by Marxist theory and therefore conscious. I have already shown that the vanguard cannot be equated theoretically with the intelligentsia: to the extent that workers assimilate Marxist theory (and, in view of the spontaneous socialist tendency of the working class, it is to be expected that this will happen to some extent), they are here considered part of the conscious vanguard and, while still part of the working class, are distinguished from the spontaneous movement.

---

45   Lenin 1901c, p. 316.

Once spontaneity is understood in strategic terms, the import of Lenin's claim that the spontaneous movement leads to the dominance of bourgeois ideology may be grasped by means of a thought experiment in which the dialectical interplay of the elements of the spontaneous movement is examined. I assume that Marxist workers and intellectuals abstract themselves from the unfolding logic of the class struggle and that the remaining actors in the drama, workers and bourgeois, are capable of strategic reflection and action in pursuit of their interests, though the workers are not, and the bourgeois may not be, cognisant of the *irreconcilable* nature of their interests. The workers' struggles to improve their conditions at some point meet resistance from the bourgeoisie; though some improvement may have been achieved, the resistance implies that the purer forms of bourgeois ideology, which assert an underlying harmony of interests, will at best maintain a very precarious purchase upon proletarian experience. The spontaneous struggle can easily undermine the foundations of this form of ideological domination, but there are a number of ways in which the workers can conceive their experience of opposing interests. How they will do so depends in part upon the response of bourgeois ideologists. The latter, if they are intelligent and sensitive, will adapt their ideas to the reality of working-class experience, perhaps by suggesting more pressing or fundamental common interests in the face of an external threat (to the nation, the family, the faith, traditional culture and values, the natural order of things, and so on), perhaps by proposing new means (a fresh voice in high places for labour's point of view, belated recognition of labour's responsibility or indispensability or moral virtue, a new spirit of compromise or trust or understanding) of reconciling the antagonism of interests. Such themes may strike chords, sometimes very basic chords, in workers' experience; indeed, there is no reason to suppose there is any specific aspect of proletarian experience upon which they cannot play. Ideological struggle is thus a struggle over the terms in which the actors in the class struggle are to construe their experience of it. The institutions and practices of the working-class movement, which are generated in a history of victories, defeats and compromises and which in turn structure proletarian experience, will bear the marks of ideological struggle.

In this way, the process of struggle takes on a dialectical character whereby bourgeois ideology and proletarian experience come to be partially constitutive of each other. But this dialectic can be only partial, for it is founded on and conditioned by antagonistic relations of production; on the assumption that the class struggle is irreconcilable, bourgeois ideology cannot fully capture proletarian experience. Hence there can be no necessity for workers to rest content with the forms of struggle sanctioned by bourgeois ideology at any given time; like the bourgeois, they can innovate with the ideological and experiential materials at their disposal, so the ideological limits to their struggle cannot be specified in absolute terms but only in terms of the dialectic of struggle. It is possible, therefore, that some workers could come to a Marxist understanding of the irreconcilability of class antagonism – but just here the force of the assumptions I attribute to Lenin's account of spontaneity really begins to kick in, for these workers, as bearers of consciousness, can no longer be considered part of the spontaneous movement and thus become subject to the same self-denying ordinance that applied to the original Marxists.

Once the logic of spontaneity is spelled out in these strategic terms, Lenin's claim that the spontaneous working-class movement is necessarily subordinate to bourgeois ideology may be rephrased as the following two claims. First, that the working-class movement cannot establish a position of strategic independence vis-à-vis its adversaries without recognising the irreconcilability of its interests with the whole politico-social system organised around the dominance of bourgeois interests; second, that such recognition cannot be effectively brought to bear upon the class struggle in the absence of an organised leadership informed by Marxist theory. These claims raise further questions as to what is entailed in recognising the irreconcilability of class interests, the meaning of the strategic independence of the working class, the reasons for the necessity of Marxist theory, and the appropriate forms of organisation of the proletarian vanguard. These questions can be addressed in terms of the kind of strategic analysis I attribute to Lenin once the logic of this analysis is extended from spontaneity to consciousness. This can be done, and the activity of this logic in Lenin's text verified, by considering his analysis of the political conjunctures out of which the Economist controversy emerged.

A Strategic Analysis

The terms of this thought experiment, with their implication of a fatalistic passivity, were approximated in political reality with the appearance in 1899 of E.D. Kuskova's *Credo*, an essay in the adaptation of Bernsteinian revisionism to Russian conditions. Although not the direct target of Lenin's polemic, this document would assume a pivotal significance in his argument, for the logic of spontaneity, Lenin warned, would drag the working-class movement 'along the lines of the *Credo* programme'.[46] Kuskova discerned in the history of the working-class movement a fundamental tendency to develop 'along the line of least resistance' and in Russia the weight of cultural backwardness and

---

46   Lenin 1902, p. 384.

the intensity of political oppression pressed the workers' movement into the narrow mould of economic struggle. With the rudimentary tasks of constructing a labour movement just under way, pretentions to revolutionary leadership, even to an independent workers' political party, were merely a waking dream. Russian Marxists, realistically, could undertake nothing more than 'assistance to the economic struggle of the proletariat and participation in liberal opposition activity'.[47] The *Credo* thus envisages a division of labour between the economic struggles of the politically incompetent working masses and the oppositional politics of the liberal intelligentsia and thereby straightforwardly cedes political hegemony over the working class to the liberal bourgeoisie.

Kuskova was a peripheral and a transitory figure in the Russian Social Democratic movement; by the time Lenin wrote *What Is to Be Done?*, the *Credo* programme no longer found any partisans in the movement.[48] Yet Lenin now came to see it as the political crux of a broader, more amorphous tendency (Economism) toward the subordination of the politics of proletarian hegemony in the Russian democratic revolution to narrower corporate concerns. Thus, for example, he taxed with Economism not only the preoccupation of the journal *Rabochaia mysl'* [Workers' Thought] with the practical minutiae of economic struggle, but even the tactics of *Rabochee delo* [Workers' Cause], which championed the political struggle for rights as an outgrowth of the workers' economic struggles. This is not to say that Lenin identified these positions with that of the *Credo*; he acknowledged that their leading proponents thought of themselves as revolutionary Marxists. But what, then, is the nature of the connection he established between them? I want to show that this connection must be founded upon, and the identity of Economism as a tendency defined in terms of, the situation of these different positions in relation to a strategic logic of political struggle; similarities in content between Kuskova's views and those of *Rabochee delo* (or between either of these and other possible variants of Economism) are of secondary importance in Lenin's analysis and can, in any case, only be identified once the strategic framework of the analysis is in place. To put the same point in a different form, the impact upon working-class consciousness of both sides of the Credo's division of labour, of 'liberal opposition activity' as well as of the workers' economic struggles, must be examined through Lenin's strategic optic. The inadequacy of much of the discussion of Lenin's thesis of consciousness from without stems from a perspective that narrows its focus to the dichotomy of workers and socialist intellectuals and thereby disregards both the breadth of the terrain upon which Lenin situates

---

47 See Kuskova 1899; for Lenin's initial analysis, see Lenin 1899c.
48 See Galai 1973, pp. 255–70; Wildman 1967, pp. 143–4.

the formation of proletarian consciousness and the problem, central for him, of the nature and modalities of the ideological influence of the bourgeoisie. It disregards, therefore, the struggle for hegemony. I turn, therefore, to Lenin's analysis of the liberal opposition.

When former Social Democratic fellow travellers like Peter Struve began to gravitate toward liberalism around the turn of the century, attempts failed to reach a *modus vivendi* between the liberal opposition, crystallised around Struve's journal *Osvobozhdenie* [Liberation], and the revolutionary Marxists. When Struve issued a plea to the government to reform itself or risk strengthening the revolutionary movement, Lenin retorted, in his long article 'The Persecutors of the *Zemstvo* and the Hannibals of Liberalism', with a critique of the tactics of Russian liberalism. Lenin situates Struve's liberal constitutionalism, like the corporate concerns of the Economists, in a field of opposing political strategies whose principal line of demarcation is defined by the struggle between the autocratic Tsarist state and the Social Democratic strategy of proletarian hegemony in the revolution. He conceives the *zemstvos*, elected institutions of the propertied classes whose constitutional rights the liberals sought to extend, as one small corner of this strategic force field, through which was refracted a dialectical logic of the struggle of political forces around the state power. Through the influence of public opinion, the *zemstvos* could function as an 'auxiliary factor' in the struggle for revolution 'by causing the government to waver in its measure of repression at critical moments' – but, incapable of more than 'liberal petitions and...benevolent neutrality', they could not operate as 'an independent factor'.[49] For this reason, appeals for the extension of *zemstvo* rights, when counterposed to the struggle for revolution, would serve 'as an instrument for strengthening the autocracy through half-concessions, as a means of bringing over a certain section of the liberals' to the side of the government.[50] When the revolutionary movement assumed threatening proportions, the Tsarist authorities, acting in accordance with 'the time-honoured police method of...divide and rule, yield the unimportant to preserve the essential, give with one hand and take back with the other',[51] would use appeals just like Struve's 'Rights and an Authoritative *Zemstvo*' in an effort to isolate and defeat the revolutionaries, conceding 'something in the nature of an advisory and aristocratic constitution' and deceiving even liberal hopes once again.[52] There is a certain symmetry between this dissection

---

49 Lenin 1901b, p. 73.
50 Lenin 1901b, p. 74.
51 Lenin 1901b, p. 70.
52 Lenin 1901b, p. 75.

of liberal tactics and Lenin's analysis of Economism: in each case, he evinces some sympathy with the concerns of his opponent, whether these be remedying workers' grievances or restricting arbitrary rule, *on the condition that these are not counterposed to the struggle for revolution*. In each case, however, he diagnoses blindness to the logic of the struggle for state power on the part of opponents bedazzled by narrower preoccupations.[53]

But against the background of the strategic logic of this process, Lenin discerned something more than mere illusion in Struve's assertion that 'a moderate party always stands to gain from an accentuated struggle between extreme political elements';[54] Struve's attempt to extract concessions from Tsarism by invoking the threat of revolution constituted the embryo of a liberal strategy that risked delivering a stillborn revolution. This liberal game was not simply a constitutional charade to be played out by bourgeois politicians and the Tsar behind closed doors; it required that the revolutionary force of the masses be treated as a kind of stage army, capable merely of frightening the Tsar and then retreating to the wings when the serious business of negotiating the redistribution of power got under way. Its logic had, therefore, to extend beyond the parlours of the propertied classes; it required that ideas, attitudes, institutions and modes of political understanding that would enable the masses to play their assigned role be encouraged and fostered among them. But if liberal strategy were to receive an 'echo' among the workers, it had best sound a distinctively proletarian note. Lenin thought he heard just such an echo in, for example, *Rabochee delo*'s call for workers to fight for political rights as a means to achieve their economic demands. The similarity between this call and Struve's appeal for rights is apparent, but what is crucial to Lenin's analysis is not this formal similarity but the strategic complementarity of the two within the logic of political struggle. The strategic complementarity envisaged in Kuskova's *Credo* had been wrecked in theory by Marxist criticism and in practice by the workers' spontaneous movement beyond purely economic struggle; re-establishing it would require adapting it to the new circumstances, with adjustments to take into account the intervening moves of other political actors. The Economist tendency within the working-class movement changes its form, moving beyond the *Credo*'s strict (economics-for-workers,

---

53   In a note to Plekhanov and Axelrod, who had persuaded him to soften the acerbic tone of the article, Lenin wrote, 'To me the centre of gravity of the whole article lay in settling the question of the constitutionality of the *zemstvo*. "*Zemstvo*" liberalism represents in terms of its effect on society an equivalent of what "Economism" represents in terms of its effect on labour. We must persecute both of these minimisations' (cited in Pipes 1970, p. 277).

54   Cited in Lenin 1901b, p. 78.

politics-for-intellectuals) division of labour. But inasmuch as such change of form would still exclude any aspect of the socio-political totality from the strategic purview of the working-class movement, it amounts merely to a call to revise this division of labour rather than to eradicate it root and branch. It would therefore concede the strategic initiative to the political adversaries of the working-class movement. Lenin recognises that proletarian struggles may spontaneously challenge this political division of labour and force further revision of its terms. His critique of Economism only involves his critique of spontaneity indirectly; directly it is a critique of 'spontaneism', that is, of the failure of consciousness theoretically and practically to master the logic of the spontaneous process. The ultimate target of his critique is not the errors and omissions of specific Economist pronouncements but the tendency to define the political project of the working class in restrictive terms, for this tendency betokens a failure to recognise that the class struggle is refracted through a strategic logic of political struggle and hence an inability to anticipate possible moves of adversaries or react independently to their innovations.

To grasp Economism not as a particular set of ideas (economics versus politics) but as a tendency (spontaneism) within the strategic logic of political struggle is to understand it as an accommodation to the spontaneous movement. That it is to be understood in this context means that the link Lenin asserts between Economism and the dominance of bourgeois ideology in the working-class movement carries no implication of conspiracy (although neither does it exclude conspiracies). Lenin's account of the spontaneous movement rests upon a distinction between its two aspects: the logic of the class struggle understood in terms of social relations, which generates a tendency toward socialism, and the ideological influence of the bourgeoisie upon this tendency. The relation between these two aspects is conceived dynamically, as a process of struggle that constantly generates itself anew while periodically adjusting its form and terms. As I have already suggested, Lenin saw this process as unfolding in the context of a history of victories and defeats, accommodations and compromises; the ideas, attitudes and traditions generated through this history are embodied in institutions and practices that structure the experiences and perceptions of the participants. If this is so, the working class is never an ideological *tabula rasa*; there is no zero point at which an ideologically virgin proletariat is simply seduced by unscrupulous bourgeois ideologues. Consequently, the precise ideational content to be attributed to each of the two aspects of the spontaneous process cannot be determined in the abstract. Depending upon the historical and political context, the same idea may arise more or less directly from proletarian experience or find its way to the workers through the propaganda engines of the bourgeoisie or the state.

The substance of Lenin's critique of the Economists has therefore to do with the implications of their ideas for the logic of the political struggle, not with the provenance of these ideas.

Once the class struggle is conceived as intersected and refracted by the strategic logic of political struggle, the crucial importance in Lenin's definition of socialist consciousness, of the recognition of the total and irreconcilable nature of the antagonism of class interests, may be better understood. First, it is part of the logic of political struggle that the actors make their 'moves' in the context of the social and political whole: that there can be no sphere, no aspect, no element of the social totality excluded in principle from this struggle. Thus, the working-class movement must be seen, strategically, as 'within the sights' of its political adversaries. But this means not simply that it is an actor in a drama that is political as well as economic, but also that its character as a political actor is subject to definition through this process. Any restriction of the strategic perspective of the working-class movement may concede to its adversaries not only crucial political objectives, but also raw materials necessary for the arduous work of political self-definition. Any limitation upon the scope of proletarian political concern allows strategic adversaries the scope for political and ideological activity that could refract the dynamics of class antagonism so as to effect a more or less provisional, more or less temporary, more or less unstable reconciliation of the 'irreconcilable antagonism' of proletarian interests to 'the whole of the modern political and social system'. This does not mean that a theoretical formulation that avoided any restriction of the scope of working-class strategy would thereby guarantee the workers against the influence of bourgeois ideology – indeed, Lenin's point is that in capitalist society this influence is inescapable; such a theoretical formulation would be a necessary, not a sufficient, condition for an effective struggle against it.

Second, while the logic of Lenin's analysis implies that the class struggle is structured by its history, this logic also implies that it proceeds indefinitely into the future, its direction, rhythm and contours conditioned by the development of capitalist relations of production but their precise determination always subject to inflection and refraction through the strategic logic of political and ideological struggles. Since the spontaneous process that presents itself to the Marxist political analyst does not reflect the logic of the economic class struggle in any simple way, the limitations of this process cannot be defined simply in terms of this logic; they are also relative to the logic of political struggle, or perhaps it would be better to say that they are relativised by the latter: while there is no absolute threshold beyond which the spontaneous movement cannot proceed, neither can there be any fixed point beyond which the working-class movement can be said to have definitively transcended spontaneity. The process of struggle is thus open-ended: since any new move may significantly alter the socio-political context of an adversary's response, it may supply material for innovation; since the antagonism of class interests is the underlying principle of the game, the players may have no reason to obey the existing rules; and since they are capable of innovation, there is no reason to assume that the next move will be made subject to the same rules as the last move. As Alasdair MacIntyre put a similar point in a very different context, 'moving one's knight to QB3 may always be replied to with a lob across the net'.[55] Since, whatever the current rules and practices may be through which the class struggle is structured and channelled, nothing in the socio-political totality can be ruled definitively out of play, the field of play cannot be restricted to the spontaneous process but must include consciousness itself, the theoretical understanding deployed in the formulation of revolutionary strategy. That is, the political bearing (and consequently, the class orientation) of Marxist theory is also an object of the political struggle.

Some Implications

Lenin's thesis of consciousness from without may now be summed up by considering its implications for questions raised earlier. In the first place, the apparent ambivalence of Lenin's attitude toward spontaneity is to be understood, through his distinction between the two components of the spontaneous movement, as the product of a coherent but complex theoretical position. His appeal to the conscious vanguard both to foster and to combat the spontaneous working-class movement is not a sign of incoherence but of the assumption of a sophisticated strategic stance within the unfolding political and ideological struggle. This stance may be described as follows: part of what the vanguard does when it fosters the revolutionary socialist aspects of the spontaneous proletarian struggle is to combat the influence of bourgeois ideology within the movement by bringing to consciousness the 'irreconcilable antagonism' of class interests that underlies the struggle.

Second, the association of consciousness with theory, and in particular with Marxist theory, may be understood as follows. If consciousness must encompass recognition of the irreconcilability of proletarian class interests to the whole of the modern (bourgeois) social and political order, it must take a theoretical form. It must do so not just because workers typically have little experiential access to many of the higher reaches of this whole, but also because

---

55   MacIntyre 1984, p. 98.

working-class experience will always reflect various attempts to reconcile workers' interests to the prevailing order, and the failure of such attempts (or their merely partial, provisional and temporary success) may always be attributed to ephemeral aspects of the political struggle (or to a fatality of human nature). The fact that the spontaneous movement is shaped in part by a logic of political struggle that prescribes strategic, tactical and ideological innovation implies that new and unforeseen conjunctures will be generated and, in the face of constantly renewed and occasionally innovative attempts to establish a reconciliation, an understanding of the irreconcilable (and not simply as-yet-unreconciled) nature of class antagonism must necessarily rely upon theory. It is, of course, Lenin's belief that the core of Marxist theory consists precisely of the conceptual tools necessary to forge such an understanding; only when informed by this theory can the experience of the working-class movement be brought to bear independently upon the ever-changing political conjuncture.

Third, the implications of Lenin's thesis for the idea of proletarian independence can now be more fully drawn out. If it is true, as Lenin the Marxist thought, that the antagonism of class interests is irreconcilable within capitalist society, then any attempt to reconcile class interests – indeed, any institution, practice or idea that promotes reconciliation – must be construed strategically as a form of subordination of the working class to heteronomous forces. Understanding the irreconcilability of class antagonism, including the ability to sharpen and deepen this understanding through analysis of renewed forms of reconciliation, is therefore a prerequisite of proletarian independence. Proletarian independence is realised to the extent that this understanding informs the direction of the working-class movement. This implies, of course, that Marxist theory be embodied in the leading institutions of the movement, but it implies nothing about the nature of these institutions. The extent and social composition of the membership and the relations among members and between members and non-members will depend upon workers' receptiveness to the Marxist project. This in turn will depend upon both the concrete history of the class struggles and the capacity of Marxists to elaborate analyses which illuminate the situation and the aspirations of the workers in light of this history. The vanguard organisations may be more or less broad, more or less open, more or less democratic in accordance with the circumstances of the struggle: as noted above, in presenting his thesis of consciousness from without, Lenin invoked the German Social Democratic Party as an example and, whatever reservations must now be entered, the SDP was then almost universally regarded as being in the vanguard of democratic organisation. If Lenin at one time advocated a narrow, conspiratorial and hierarchical party of professional revolutionaries, this must flow from his analysis of the context of the struggle in Russia and not from his thesis of consciousness from without.

Fourth, Lenin's thesis bears important implications for the conceptual status of Marxist theory. His insistence in *What Is to Be Done?* upon a theoretical foundation for political struggle did not express a desire to encase the socialist movement in a narrow theoretical mould, but rather a recognition of the unprecedented situation that confronted it. The call for theory is a call for 'the ability to treat these experiences [of other countries] critically and to test them independently'.[56] Marxist theory must be understood, as Lenin would later write, not as 'a dogma', not as a given set of axioms, propositions and predictions, but as 'a guide to action' – that is, as a theoretical matrix to be applied to ever new and changing conjunctures of the class struggle and in the course of this application concretised and modified.[57] That it must be so understood is both a theoretical and a political necessity. It is a theoretical necessity because Marxist theory is the comprehension of the irreconcilable antagonism of proletarian interests to the whole of the capitalist socio-political order; it must grasp this whole theoretically and must therefore be open to modification so as to grasp the process by which the innovative logic of political struggle can refract the lines of demarcation of the class struggle and so constantly, and sometimes significantly, modify the contours of the whole. It is a political necessity because Marxist theory is also an object in the political struggle; failure to develop, concretise and modify it invites its revision and appropriation by forces that would disarm the working-class movement. In this fashion Lenin portrays the significance of Bernsteinian revisionism and of Economism; in this fashion he would later criticise Kautsky and the Mensheviks as abstract, dogmatic Marxists – that is, as no longer Marxists. The politico-strategic logic of the struggle for hegemony could not constitute by itself a coherent historical materialist account of proletarian hegemony in the bourgeois-democratic revolution, but it did break through the conceptual harmonies that fettered orthodox Marxist efforts to produce such an account.

If the conceptual and political status of Marxist theory requires that it be developed, concretised and modified, one further question must be addressed: just what forces propel its development? In *What Is to Be Done?* Lenin does not pursue this question beyond his reference to the need to train worker-theoreticians. It might be suggested that the process of theoretical development is restricted, by implication, to the theoretical cloister of 'consciously' Marxist workers and intellectuals. But if the reading presented here is accurate,

---

56 Lenin 1902, p. 370.
57 Lenin 1920a, p. 71.

it simply does not follow from Lenin's thesis of consciousness from without that proletarian spontaneity plays no important role in the development of Marxist theory. Indeed, properly understood, his thesis suggests the contrary, for the logic of political analysis that informs it implies that the workers are capable of 'spontaneous' innovations; since the constraints upon the spontaneous movement are to be grasped in relative rather than absolute terms, there is no reason why its innovations could not sometimes be seeds capable of bearing revolutionary, even theoretically revolutionary, fruit. Now, what Lenin's thesis does imply is that such innovations can play no more than an episodic part in the drama of proletarian self-emancipation (the seeds will be unable to take root) unless they are absorbed and their practical and theoretical implications drawn out and clarified by Marxist theory. But if the theoretical absorption of spontaneous proletarian innovations leads to significant modifications in Marxist theory, it will be true, in an important sense, that the masses of workers and not just the theoreticians take an active, independent and creative part in elaborating socialist consciousness.

'Marxism *learns*...from mass practice', Lenin would later write, 'and makes no claim whatever to *teach* the masses forms of struggle invented by "systematisers" in the seclusion of their studies'.[58] As I will show in subsequent chapters, Lenin would learn from mass practice, notably from the spontaneous proletarian initiative in establishing the soviets, and he would significantly modify the structure of Marxist theory in consequence of this learning. He could do so, if the interpretation put forward here is correct, not in spite of the thesis of consciousness from without, but because of it. The thesis that consciousness must be imported into the spontaneous working-class movement from without is a necessary precondition for the importation of proletarian spontaneity into consciousness, into Marxist theory, and consequently for a concrete, and not merely rhetorical, appreciation of the Marxist thesis of proletarian self-emancipation. This struggle of consciousness with spontaneity that was at the same time an opening to spontaneity was not in itself the realisation of proletarian hegemony, but it was a necessary condition for its future realisation.

Consider the alternative: to deny Lenin's thesis is to assert that socialist consciousness is immanent in proletarian spontaneity, that Marxist theory and the spontaneous proletarian experience of the class struggle are, or will come to be, in harmony. But not only would it be exceedingly difficult to explain the existing consciousness of most of the working class consistently with this claim, it would be just as difficult to understand what Marxist theory could

---

58   Lenin 1906f, pp. 213–14.

possibly learn from mass practice. Thus, it should come as no surprise that Rosa Luxemburg, apostle of proletarian spontaneity and critic of Lenin, could write,

> Marx, in his scientific creation, has outstripped us as a party of practical fighters. It is not true that Marx no longer suffices for our needs. On the contrary, *our needs are not yet adequate for the utilisation of Marx's ideas*... Though that theory is an incomparable instrument of intellectual culture, it remains unused because, while it is inapplicable to bourgeois class culture, it greatly transcends the needs of the working class in the matter of weapons for the daily struggle.[59]

For those who maintain such a view, it must always be possible to attribute divergences between Marxist theory and the working-class movement to the failure of the latter, as yet, to embody the consciousness represented by the former. Whether this failure is ascribed to the immaturity of historical conditions (the 'right' or Kautsky variant) or to the machinations of an opportunistic leadership (the 'left' or Luxemburg variant) is less important than the common assumption of an underlying harmony between Marxist theory and the working class. It is difficult to see what could possibly count as evidence, in the eyes of those who hold this assumption, against this dogmatic view of Marxism; not to question this assumption is to fail to grasp the theoretical and political necessity for Marxist theory to learn from the masses. When sung to this tune, paeans to proletarian self-emancipation must take on a subtly, but distinctly, paternalistic air: the independent activity of the working-class hero will generate anew a consciousness whose design was prefigured by the Marxist intellectuals. This is not the paternalism of the cop or the drill sergeant but that of the 'enlightened' teacher or social worker. It is paternalism nonetheless because it does not, ultimately, take seriously the independence of the 'student'. So, to return at last to Marx's critique of Feuerbach, who indeed will educate the educator, if not the student? Paradoxically, it is none other than his thesis of consciousness from without that enables Lenin to situate himself, as a Marxist theorist, *within* the class struggle and so to learn from the proletariat – that is, to change, while his critics elevate Marx's historical theory of society above history and society and thereby make of it a changeless and consequently an incipiently authoritarian dogma.

---

59   Luxemburg 1903, p. 111.

CHAPTER 5

Dogmatism and Criticism: Freedom in the Class Struggle

[T]he most beautiful of all doubts
Is when the downtrodden and despondent raise their heads
    and
Stop believing in the strength
Of their oppressors.

Therefore, if you praise doubt
Do not praise
The doubt that is a form of despair.
— BERTOLT BRECHT[1]

∴

'[T]he perplexity of the Economists over the practical application of our views in *Iskra* clearly revealed that we often speak literally in different tongues'; whence the need to begin '*ab ovo*' in an attempt '*systematically to "clarify" all our basic points of difference with all the Economists*'. Thus did Lenin derive his recourse to theory from the very logic of the debate over practical proposals; thus the rationale he presented in the preface to *What Is to Be Done?* for devoting a chapter to the 'fundamental question of the role of Social Democrats in relation to the spontaneous mass movement'.[2] But the prior question, the first question 'of a general nature' to be addressed in order to frame the controversy between the two tendencies in Russian social democracy properly, concerned 'why such an "innocent" and "natural" slogan as "freedom of criticism" should be for us a veritable war-cry'.[3] Lenin's response cannot be understood without realising that professing oneself 'critical' was recognised in Social Democratic circles as a mark of sympathy for Bernstein's critique of Marxist dogmatism

---

1 Brecht 1987a, pp. 334 and 336.
2 Lenin 1902, pp. 350–1.
3 Lenin 1902, p. 350.

and 'freedom of criticism' as a Bernsteinian standard. So the title Lenin gives his first chapter, 'Dogmatism and "Freedom of Criticism"', presents the issue, with some irony, in the terms in which his adversaries understood it.

Missing the irony – and the substance of Lenin's argument – might facilitate reading the chapter as a simple exercise in dogmatics, a reaction against anyone with the independence to question Marxist theory. Indeed, to the very small extent that the chapter is dealt with in the secondary literature, this impression reigns almost unchallenged. Thus, Bertram Wolfe can claim the whole chapter is 'one long attack on the very phrase "freedom of criticism"',[4] while it represents little more, for Robert Service, than an announcement, 'without quite saying it in so many words', of Lenin's 'pride in being considered dogmatic'.[5] Even Lars Lih, who recognises that Lenin's position is not illiberal, characterises the debate as one between tolerance and 'ideological purity'.[6] But read with some care, Lenin's argument can be grasped as one long deconstruction of the terms of the debate. Read in the context of the politico-strategic logic of the struggle for hegemony, it can be shown to be consistent with and even to depend upon a qualified defence of freedom of criticism and to require an account of theory as a guide to action rather than a dogma.

The Argument About Freedom

Lenin sets the scene for his argument by evoking the perplexity that someone might experience when initially confronted by the strange spectacle of one of the parties to 'controversies between socialists and democrats' making 'solemn appeals' to this principle. He invites the reader to imagine the reaction of an 'onlooker who has heard this fashionable slogan repeated at every turn but has not yet penetrated the essence of the disagreement' and who is driven to the conclusion that the slogan has been reduced to a mere 'conventional phrase' invoked ritualistically, like a nickname, until its specific sense is lost. He poses the question: 'Have voices been raised in the *advanced* parties against the constitutional law of the majority of European countries which guarantees freedom to science and scientific investigation?'[7] Now, the question is rhetorical, serving to underscore the puzzlement Lenin seeks to evoke. This rhetorical gambit allows Lenin to frame the problem as he understands it: the puzzle is

---

4 Wolfe 1963, p. 158.
5 Service 1988, p. 22.
6 Lih 2006, p. 474.
7 Lenin 1902, p. 352.

not that the principle of freedom of criticism should be a matter of concern but what the significance could be of invoking it in the current controversy.

The notion of freedom is abstract and therefore protean; its invocation can only be assessed when it is understood in its context. What Lenin does, in effect, is to pose an alternative for his readers: either the slogan is advanced in response to a challenge to the very principle of freedom of criticism, or it is invoked in tandem with and in defence of some specific criticism which, it is alleged, is being suppressed. If the former were the case, one would assume the existence of an identifiable challenge, but this possibility is ruled out by the rhetorical character of Lenin's question and by his acknowledgement, in the implied response, of a consensus among the advanced – democratic, socialist, perhaps also liberal – parties as to the desirability of a constitutional norm underwriting freedom of criticism. The appropriateness of a constitutional limitation upon the capacity of the state to set the legal parameters for political debate was not, in Lenin's view, at issue. Nor, for that matter, was the appropriateness of freedom of criticism as a norm governing debate among the advanced parties. The issue, rather, was the appropriateness of the appeal to this norm by one party in the context of a controversy against the other. The issue concerned how the norm of freedom of criticism pertained to the broader controversy. Any judgement on this issue presumes familiarity with the particulars of the debate, its circumstances and its course; Lenin's argument is developed by an explication of this context. This appeal to context does not imply that the abstract principle of freedom of criticism is irrelevant to his argument, for its acceptance by the parties is one of the defining features of the context. This is to say that Lenin's argument assumes freedom of criticism as a norm governing political debate. And, as we will see, it is not simply assumed as background but positively deployed.

There follows a brief polemical survey of Bernstein's challenge to Marxism, the widespread support it could count on among 'the educated classes' and its first practical fruit in Millerand's acceptance of a ministerial position in a reactionary bourgeois government. If people are to be judged 'by their actions and by what they actually advocate' rather than appearance and self-description, Lenin concludes, then 'freedom of criticism' amounts to 'freedom to convert Social-Democracy into a democratic party of reform, freedom to introduce bourgeois ideas and bourgeois elements into socialism'.[8] 'The current [*sovremennyi*] use of the term "freedom of criticism"', Lenin asserts, is plagued by 'the same inherent falsehood' that informs other appeals to 'freedom' in the context of capitalism: '[U]nder the banner of freedom for industry the most predatory wars were waged; under the banner of freedom of labour,

---

8 Lenin 1902, p. 355.

the working people were robbed'.⁹ The falsehood inherent in the appeal to freedom is apparent in the latter two cases. Freedom of industry allows the most powerful capitalist concerns to subdue their competitors and the most expansive capitalist countries to bring the others under their competitive sway. The competitive free-for-all is a means whereby one subordinates another to its will; compelled to compete, the latter is forced to be free. Freedom of labour pits workers against each other in competition to sell their labour power. The freedom of each worker individually to sell his or her labour power does not subject one to another; rather, it subjects all workers to the blind workings of their own social relations and thereby to the class of owners of capital. The promise of universality implicit in appeals to freedom is subverted by their insertion in the context of capitalist society; the falsehood of the appeal is inherent in these cases in that the freedoms invoked are constitutive of the social relations of capital and so are self-subverting.

In what respect might falsehood in an appeal to freedom of criticism be similarly inherent? One might suppose that implicit in Lenin's analogy is a 'marketplace of ideas' metaphor – along with the suggestion that a competition of ideas is the best way of discovering the truth – and that the falsehood of the appeal lies in the necessarily unequal distribution of the resources requisite to the effective communication of ideas in a marketplace structured by capitalist social relations. But freedom of criticism, unlike freedom of labour, is not constitutive of capitalist social relations and so it is difficult, especially in terms of the 'marketplace' metaphor, to see how appealing to it could be similarly self-subverting. If the contrast between word and deed invoked by Lenin involves a falsehood, it is unclear what grounds there might be for thinking the falsehood inherent. Lenin does point to a peculiar feature, anomalous in terms of the 'marketplace of ideas' metaphor, in the posture of the critics: 'Those who are really convinced that they have made progress in science would demand not freedom for the new ideas to continue side by side with the old, but the substitution of the new views for the old'.¹⁰ The anomaly rests upon the assumption that progress in a marketplace of ideas depends upon the willingness of the competing schools of thought to assert and to defend their ideas as true. It consists in appealing to freedom of criticism while refusing to defend the truth of one's ideas. It consists, that is, in the incongruity of appealing for means – freedom of criticism – justified by reference to an end – pursuit of truth – in apparent disregard of the end. While this may be anomalous, it is

---

9   Ibid.
10 Ibid.

unclear that the anomaly is inherent, and neither is it clear what it tells us about the appeal to freedom of criticism.

To make sense of the claim that the appeal to freedom of criticism was vitiated by an inherent falsehood, it should be borne in mind that the claim is not made of any or every use of the slogan but of its 'current [*sovremennyi*] use', that is, its use in the revisionist controversy in the Social Democratic movement.[11] Once this qualification is recognised, Lenin's claim can be fleshed out in terms of the contention whose truth was, on his account, centrally at issue in the controversy: that the antagonism of class interests between bourgeois and worker was irreconcilable, that it could not be moderated to permit their collaboration in a broader social movement in pursuit of democracy and freedom and that the political independence of the working-class movement was consequently imperative. In appealing for freedom of criticism, the Bernsteinians were claiming political space for debate and hence unity with the Marxists. To appeal to freedom of criticism was thus to raise, implicitly, the issue of freedom of association. The Bernsteinians thus placed themselves on a false political footing, for they could not seek to demonstrate the truth of their own analysis (and hence the falsity of Marxist analysis) without having to confront openly the depth of the differences between them and thus the tenuousness of their claim to political and organisational unity. That this falsehood is indeed inherent in their appeal to freedom of criticism can be shown by examining the relation between freedom of criticism and freedom of association in the context of the class struggle. This Lenin proceeds to do by means of an extended metaphor:

> We are marching in a compact group along a precipitous and difficult path, firmly holding each other by the hand. We are surrounded on all sides by enemies, and we have to advance almost constantly under their fire. We have combined, by a freely adopted decision, for the purpose of fighting the enemy, and not of retreating into the neighbouring marsh, the inhabitants of which, from the very outset, have reproached us with having separated ourselves into an exclusive group and with having chosen the path of struggle instead of the path of conciliation. And now some among us begin to cry out: Let us go into the marsh! And when we begin to shame them, they retort: What backward people you are!

---

11 Although the context of Lenin's claim makes it clear that this is indeed the object of his criticism, this point may be obscured by the Fineberg-Hanna translation of *sovremennyi* as 'modern' rather than 'current' as I have it here. Thanks to Lars Lih for advice on the translation.

Are you not ashamed to deny us the liberty to invite you to take a better road! Oh, yes, gentlemen! You are free not only to invite us, but to go yourselves wherever you will, even into the marsh. In fact, we think that the marsh is your proper place, and we are prepared to render *you* every assistance to get there. Only let go of our hands, don't clutch at us and don't besmirch the great word 'freedom', for we too are 'free' to go where we please, free to fight not only against the marsh, but also against those who are turning towards the marsh![12]

The metaphor translates straightforwardly into the language of class struggle. At issue is the cohesion of the 'compact group' – call it the party of struggle – whose adherents have come together freely to prosecute the war against the class enemy. The 'precipitous and difficult path' of struggle leads some of the group to vacillate and to yearn for a haven in 'the marsh', to join the party of peace and conciliation. And when their invitation 'to take a better road' is rejected by the more steadfast partisans of struggle, the latter are burdened with the additional charge of stifling their critics' freedom to seek to persuade them. Lenin's retort, interestingly, is *not* to invoke the circumstances of war to dismiss the appeal to freedom but rather to turn the criticism against the critics. They *were* free, he insists, to seek to persuade, to adopt any political position they wished; but so too were the partisans of struggle free to counter the criticisms and, indeed, free to dissociate themselves from those who would thus importune them. He invokes freedom of association by citing the 'freely adopted decision' that binds the party of struggle and by insisting that the vacillators 'let go of our hands, don't clutch at us'. This appeal to freedom of association is not mere tit-for-tat. Lenin's point is not that appeals to freedom are vacuous, since either party to a dispute could always make them, for in the same phrase he accuses his critics of 'besmirching the great word "freedom"'. Recourse to freedom of association allows him not only to undercut the rhetorical force of the critics' appeal to freedom but also to shift the debate to another level of analysis. Implicit in his rhetorical stance is an argument that might be spelled out as follows:

An appeal made to the principle of 'freedom of criticism' not by an individual or group against the state, but by one individual or group against another, assumes sufficient unity of purpose between these parties to make debate between them productive (a unity of purpose that is typically more closely knit than the unity supposed by common citizenship). But the possibility, existence and durability of any such measure of unity are matters about which

---

12   Lenin 1902, p. 355.

the interested parties may well disagree. Indeed, the nature or the depth of disagreement on any controversial issue may lead one or other of the parties to call into question an established consensus as to the necessary unity of purpose. But where sufficient unity of purpose is itself in question, the appeal to 'freedom of criticism' merely begs the question, for it implicitly asserts a proposition whose truth is (part of) what is at issue.

The argument is preliminary; it is an argument about how (and how not) to proceed with the argument. It does not suppose agreement with Lenin's position on the substance of the issues at controversy. If one party to a dispute believes that the existence of sufficient unity of purpose to sustain a fruitful debate is questionable, then it *is* questionable, while recourse to 'freedom of criticism' presumes it is not. In this context, appeal to 'freedom of criticism' can only be a kind of special pleading, whether through confusion or through demagogy, a distraction from the real issues, mere noise. What is more, inasmuch as it insinuates authoritarian ambitions – hence the reaction of Lenin and his *Iskra* colleagues to it as a veritable 'war cry' – it can serve only to inflame and obscure the debate. Political debate may be restricted by the weight of the law or by lack of access to the means of communication, but also by demagogy, by sheer noise. That this is the thrust of Lenin's argument is confirmed by his comparison of the uncritical paeans to 'freedom of criticism' with Krylov's fable of the two barrels:

> There go two barrels, one full of wine, the other empty.
> How quietly the first pulls itself along at a steady pace,
> While the other just bounces along the road,
> Making a thunderous noise and raising clouds of dust.
> Hearing it from afar, passers-by scurry aside in alarm.
>
> But as loud as that barrel may be, unlike the first,
> It is of little use to anyone.
>
> A man who never stops boasting about his own doings
> Likely holds little sense.
> The one who really does something is usually sparing of grand phrases.
> A great man makes noise only in his accomplishments,
> Steadily shaping his deliberations in silence.[13]

---

13   The translation is based on Ralston 1883. I have taken the liberty of modifying the translation for style and readability, relying upon suggestions provided by Lars Lih.

The Bernsteinian appeal to freedom of criticism does contain an 'inherent falsehood', but is it analogous to the others Lenin cites? In the case of freedom of industry or freedom of labour, the invocation of freedom is constitutively attached to capitalist social relations that simultaneously embody and restrict such freedom. If Lenin's analysis of the appeal to freedom of criticism is construed in terms of the politico-strategic logic of the struggle for hegemony, then the analogy does hold. It may be so construed if we approach it as follows: whereas the appeal to freedom of criticism invites us to think of political discourse as a conversation between independent individuals, political discourse in capitalist society is structured by the division of society into classes and by the logic of the struggle between them. Individual members of the dominant classes can take the political space, the resources and the connections necessary to articulate an independent perspective on public affairs as a given. This kind of political space is available to members of the subordinate classes only through forms of association that can serve as a workshop in which independent political perspectives can be hammered out. These forms of association can themselves be constructed only in the teeth of the unrelenting opposition of the dominant classes. This opposition to the independent organisation of the working class is a constitutive condition of the social relations of capitalist society. It may assume a multiplicity of forms, but where the appeal to freedom of criticism serves to spirit away the question of the independent organisation of the working class and, by implication, the reality of class domination, it operates as one of them: this use of 'freedom of criticism' imposes upon the workers the discursive context and standards of the propertied classes. Thus understood, Lenin's analysis of the appeal to 'freedom of criticism' takes the form of an immanent critique: it assumes a moral consensus on the desirability of norms underwriting freedom of criticism but seeks to show that, in the context of the politico-strategic logic of the struggle for hegemony, the very recourse to 'freedom of criticism' may undermine the conditions of effective political voice.

The Argument About Theory

The preceding argument sets the stage for Lenin's response to his polemical adversaries' invocation of the theme of freedom of criticism as a condition for organisational unity, 'not as a theoretical postulate but as a political demand'.[14] Criticising as a shallow analogy *Iskra*'s comparison of the then-current controversy between Marxists and revisionists with the struggle between Jacobins

---

14   Lenin 1902, p. 356.

and Girondins during the French Revolution, Boris Krishevskii, the editor of *Rabochee delo* and at one time a friend and colleague of Rosa Luxemburg,[15] sought to downplay the division within the socialist movement: '[T]he socialist movement in its entirety, in *all* of its diverse forms, including the most pronounced Bernsteinians, stands on the basis of the class interests of the proletariat and its class struggle for political and economic emancipation'.[16] Lenin uses this statement as context for Krichevskii's proclamation that '[f]or a durable unity, there must be freedom of criticism'.[17] His response to Krichevskii demonstrates that the logic of his dissection of the appeal to freedom of criticism on the international stage applies *a fortiori* in the Russian context. But it also brings in more prominently the other aspect of the problem posed by the chapter, the treatment of (Marxist) theory as dogma, deconstructing it and turning it around against its proponents.

Where, instead of elaborating and defending the inescapably controversial assertion that even 'the most pronounced Bernsteinians' base their position on the proletarian class struggle, Krichevskii frames the question of party unity in terms of a contrast between the tolerant Germans and the intolerant French, Lenin is able to return the accusation of shallowness. He does suggest, since the Millerand ministry was the first independent venture of the Bernsteinian orientation into practice, that the French experience is of particular importance; he also cites German party resolutions to show that while 'opinions may differ as to the expediency of any one of the *methods* employed to reject Bernsteinism... that the German party *did reject* Bernsteinism on two occasions is a fact no one can fail to see'.[18] Lenin's concern, however, is neither to exculpate the French for their intolerance nor to stiffen the laxity of the Germans, but to reframe the terms in which the question is posed. He uses the occasion to instruct Krichevskii on the necessity of a comparative account of national historical experiences to explain and assess German unity and French disunity: the social and political substance of the very same tendency 'reveals itself in a variety of ways according to national peculiarities'.[19] The thrust of Lenin's point is to stress not only the ability to discern the underlying identity of a tendency amidst varying particulars but also the importance of identifying its varying forms of appearance so as to be able to deal with it appropriately in accordance with its form and context. It sets up his claim that

---

15   See Nettl 1966, vol. 1, pp. 84–5.
16   Cited in Lenin 1902, p. 356.
17   Ibid.
18   Lenin 1902, p. 359.
19   Lenin 1902, p. 360.

discussing freedom of criticism as a condition for social-democratic unity in Russia presupposes an analysis of the particular form and context of Russian Bernsteinism; thus it leads into his own analysis of this phenomenon. Further, it enables him to take *Rabochee delo* to task for copying the most recent German resolution on revisionism and, foreshadowing a move that will emerge in more general form in the sequel, to turn the accusation of dogmatism against its authors: 'Instead of freedom of criticism – slavish (worse: ape-like) imitation!'[20]

That '*the very beginning* of the spontaneous working-class movement ... and of the turn of progressive public opinion towards Marxism' was marked by the peculiar phenomenon of 'legal Marxism' was what, in Lenin's telling, principally distinguished *Russian* Bernsteinism.[21] The Tsarist censors' exclusive preoccupation with the dated threat of revolutionary populism allowed Marxist ideas to find expression, albeit in judiciously 'Aesopian' language, in legally available publications. Legal Marxism was a 'combination of manifestly heterogeneous elements under a common flag to fight ... an obsolete social and political world-view': revolutionary Marxist analyses of the class contradictions of capitalist development, together with liberal modernisers dressing in Marxist garb an essentially bourgeois critique of populist nostalgia.[22] This alliance permitted a rapid victory over populism in progressive public opinion and the spread of Marxist ideas even if in vulgarised form. The alliance was broken not because the legal Marxists turned out to be bourgeois democrats, but because their turn toward Bernsteinism, by obscuring the difference between bourgeois and socialist orientations, effectively denied a necessary condition for the alliance: the opportunity for Marxists to unveil the antagonism of class interests. While Bernstein's work circulated freely, recommended to workers by the police head of the state-sponsored monarchist union movement, and these post-Marxist critics could count on a near-monopoly in the legal literature to dispute, *in the name of socialism*, the irreconcilable antagonism of class contradictions, any Marxist riposte could be delivered only within the confines of the underground.[23] The confusion was compounded by the 'absence of public party ties and party traditions' and by a national political culture lacking any conception of party honour, exemplified in the critics' unwillingness to acknowledge a party connection as well as by the lack of a 'generally recognised party body that could "restrict" freedom of criticism, if only by counsel'.[24]

---

20   Ibid.
21   Lenin 1902, p. 361.
22   Ibid.
23   Lenin 1902, p. 363.
24   Lenin 1902, pp. 366–7.

The legal Marxists' breach of the alliance was tantamount, in Lenin's view, 'to bourgeois democracy's denial of socialism's right to independence and, consequently, of its right to existence; in practice it meant a striving to convert the nascent working-class movement into an appendage of the liberals'.[25]

The critical trend was mirrored and complemented by the Economist turn among social-democratic activists, marked by an inability to grasp a connection between 'the invention of doctrinaires' and the practical business of the working-class movement and consequently by genuine impatience with 'all theoretical controversies, factional disagreements, broad political questions'.[26] Thus Lenin contextualises Krichevskii's claim that all the diverse forms of the socialist movement rest upon the proletarian class struggle. The postulate of an underlying unity of purpose amongst all those who claim affiliation with socialism underwrites the view that openness to this diversity is a necessary condition for the movement to flourish and for its unity to endure amidst the widely varying circumstances of political practice. The real danger to the unity of the movement is represented by the imposition of a theoretical straitjacket upon the diversity of socialist forms and experiences. The appeal to freedom of criticism amounted not to a call for debate between contending views but to something like a shot in a guerrilla war against theoretical dogma. In this sense the Russian advocates of freedom of criticism display a paradoxical fear of criticism. Lenin's analysis of their appeal thus converges with his critique of spontaneism and morphs into a defence of the role of theory in revolutionary practice.

Before turning to Lenin's discussion of theory, however, it will be helpful to recall just what was at stake in his sketch of the context of the controversy in Russia. The issue was not the terms of unity of the Russian social democrats but the preliminary or second-order question of the appropriate parameters of debate over unity, in particular the significance of the appeal to freedom of criticism in that debate and of Krichevskii's claim that it was a necessary condition for unity. Lenin concludes his sketch with the claim that it shows a 'glaring contradiction' between the call for 'freedom of criticism' and the specific character of Russian criticism and Economism. The sketch illustrates, first, the fact of disagreement as to the existence of sufficient commonality of purpose to sustain associational unity and thereby, by the argument previously advanced, that the appeal to freedom of criticism is at best irrelevant and perhaps counterproductive to the professed aims of the discussion. It underscores, second, the peculiar irony of an appeal to freedom of criticism directed

---

25   Lenin 1902, p. 363.
26   Lenin 1902, p. 365.

against revolutionary Marxists in circumstances that place them at a particular disadvantage in the debate. It allows Lenin, third, to frame *Rabochee delo*'s replication of a German party resolution as indicating an inability to discern a course of action adapted to the particular context of action, suggesting that the accusation of dogmatism might more appropriately be addressed to those who can't grasp theory as a guide to action.

Thus, when Lenin reiterates the call of the *Iskra* editorial board – 'before we can unite, and in order that we may unite, we must first of all draw firm and definite lines of demarcation'[27] – it is not to be understood as a declaration that the criteria of unity are already given and that to question them is to invite exclusion. Part and parcel of Lenin's argument was the contention that determining whether unity is possible and what forms it might take requires not only a clarification of the aims of unity but also analysis of the particular circumstances; he finds the German position, rejecting revisionism without excluding the revisionists, plausible in context if not compelling. The call to draw lines of demarcation was initially issued as an invitation to 'an open and all-embracing discussion of the fundamental questions of principle and tactics' without which 'our unity will be purely fictitious ... [and] will conceal the prevailing confusion and hinder its radical elimination'.[28] Ideological unity around the political project of proletarian hegemony could not simply reflect the descriptions political actors give themselves. The political orientation of an actor, an organisation, a policy, an argument is always subject to an objective logic of social relations and to a strategic logic of the struggle for hegemony. To draw lines of political demarcation is thus to analyse the circumstances of the struggle theoretically and to impose the categories of the resulting analysis upon other actors. But on the assumption, shared by the participants to the controversy, of the desirability of a constitutional norm guaranteeing freedom of criticism, the act of drawing lines of demarcation poses no threat to those who take a stand outside the lines, for they can criticise from where they are. As an assertion of theoretical underpinnings for the exercise of freedom of association, it precludes debate neither within the association nor between its members and others. Indeed, by setting parameters of debate that contribute to the purposes of the association, it may clarify the nature and implications of its purposes for those outside the lines and thereby shift the terms of broader political debates.

Beneath *Rabochee delo*'s protests against 'ossification of thought' and the reign of 'dogmatism' in the name of 'freedom of criticism', Lenin diagnosed

---

27   Lenin 1902, p. 367.
28   Lenin 1902, p. 354.

'unconcern and helplessness with regard to the development of theoretical thought'.[29] *Rabochee delo*'s inability to orient itself theoretically amidst changed circumstances and new problems did not indicate adherence to an alternative theory but its 'freedom from all integral and pondered theory'.[30] Enacting a political project across changing circumstances requires an ability to evaluate and respond to the changes independently; the theory this calls for is not one applied by rote or seized upon piecemeal in an emergency, but one understood thoroughly enough to be adapted comfortably to the shifting requirements of practice. The importance of theory for revolutionary politics was enhanced for the Russian Marxists by three circumstances: first, the party was still in the process of formation and had yet to define its identity with respect to competing revolutionary tendencies; second, to assimilate the experiences of more established working-class movements in other countries, the young party required the theoretical and political capacity to 'treat these experiences critically and to test them independently'; third, the tasks imposed by the struggle against the Tsarist autocracy were unprecedented for a socialist party and 'the *role of vanguard fighter can be fulfilled only by a party that is guided by the most advanced theory*'.[31]

With the emergence of the politico-strategic logic of the struggle for hegemony, the status – the place and function – of the materialist conception of history in Lenin's thought shifts; it comes to function increasingly as a research programme rather than an accomplished theory, as a 'guiding thread' rather than a 'general historico-philosophical theory'. By taking some distance from the temptation of premature theoretical and practical 'synthesis' (or closure) – by 'tarrying with the negative', as Hegel might say – in examining the experience of the struggle for hegemony in the bourgeois-democratic revolution through the optic of Marxist theory, the optic itself can be opened up to that experience and reoriented where necessary in its light, extended and transformed. The emergence of the logic of hegemony can be thought of as opening up a practical and conceptual space for exploring the antinomies of the struggle for hegemony in Marxist theory. It signals a shift in the relation of theory and practice.

The requisite theory can serve as a guide to action and is consequently capable of being developed in the course of the struggle for hegemony, taking cues from practical experience and from the disputes over principle, tactics, organisation and so on that arise inevitably in the course of practical activity.

---

29   Lenin 1902, pp. 368–9.
30   Lenin 1902, p. 369.
31   Lenin 1902, p. 370.

Factional polemics are, or at least can be, a means of theoretical development; as Lenin would later write, 'one cannot develop new views other than through polemics'.[32] The distinction between what is theoretically significant and what is of merely occasional interest becomes, accordingly, relative to the logic of the class struggle and the struggle for hegemony. Theory may be understood, following Kautsky and some of Lenin's own earlier formulations, as implying a search for uniformity and regularity, for the universal and the homogeneous amidst diverse particulars. If practical activity, inasmuch as it always has a particular aim, is thought to stand in contrast to theory thus understood, Hegel can serve to remind us that this very particularity is a universal aspect of activity. In this sense, an orientation to the particularity of the situation may, if it drives an effort to synthesise diverse determinations of the situation, take on theoretical significance. In this sense, the concrete analysis of the concrete situation is an aspect of practical wisdom.

It is a feature of every conjuncture of the class struggle that there will be a next conjuncture, shaped by the logic of the struggle as it emerges from the current one. The accumulated experience of the working-class movement requires critical assessment and independent testing in light of newly encountered circumstances and tasks; indeed, one's own course of action may so transform the conjuncture as to call, in virtue of either its failure or its success, for critical reassessment of its guiding assumptions. On the logic of Lenin's argument, it cannot be excluded that such reassessment may involve reconceptualising the commonality of purpose that underlies the appropriate terms of political unity in the class struggle. Thus the logic of the development of Marxist theory itself calls for a critical posture, a posture of openness to criticism, while at the same time it implies that the parameters of criticism appropriate to the political project of the vanguard of the proletariat are subject to change in accordance with the conjuncture.

Conversely, where commonality of political purpose is simply assumed and the parameters of political identity are thereby taken as given, the openness of the political project to critical reassessment and its potential fecundity as a research programme are correspondingly limited. With Marxist orthodoxy, the self-understanding of Marxist theory as the resolution of the contradictions of socialism and the class struggle and the implication of an underlying harmony between the Marxist party and the working-class movement constitute the assumption of givenness. Kautsky, of course, was no less insistent than Lenin that Marxism be developed in the light of new circumstances and of the emerging experience of the working-class movement. But inasmuch

---

32 Lenin 1912a, p. 297.

as the givenness of Kautsky's political optic, the political project of the SPD, constrained and inhibited accurate recognition of potential challenges to its parameters and consequently an accurate assessment of the potential impact of new circumstances or emergent experience, the implications of experience were implicitly filtered according to its assumptions. Only when coupled with recognition of a contradiction between Marxist theory and the spontaneous working-class movement – hence of Marxist theory as itself an *object of and in* the class struggle – could practical political attempts to grapple with the contradictory unity of popular alliance and struggle and the phenomena of working-class unity and division begin to be integrated, slowly and unevenly, with the theory of historical materialism, and an account of the struggle for proletarian hegemony that coheres with the tenets of historical materialism begin to be worked out. Because Lenin construes consciousness both in terms of Marxist theory and with reference not only to intentionality – the socialist aim of the struggle – but also to its reflexivity, hence as responsive to its changing context and consequently reflective of the whole process whereby the aim is concretised and transformed, the reflection of these contradictions in 'consciousness' is decisive.

The terms of the issue as posed at the beginning of Lenin's chapter – dogmatism and 'freedom of criticism' – emerge from his polemic thoroughly transformed. What is really at issue, if Lenin is read attentively, is the relation of theory and practice: the deployment of Marxist theory as a guide to action for the political project of the working-class movement and the further development of theory through criticism engaged with the project and through the practical experience of struggle.

CHAPTER 6

Two Orientations to Hegemony: Mensheviks and Bolsheviks

> Our struggle cannot be understood at all unless the concrete circumstances of each battle are studied. But once that is done, we see clearly that development does indeed proceed dialectically, by way of contradictions ... Genuine dialectics does not justify the errors of individuals, but studies the inevitable turns, proving that they were inevitable by a detailed study of the process of development in all its concreteness. One of the basic principles of dialectics is that there is no such thing as abstract truth, truth is always concrete.
> – VLADIMIR LENIN[1]

⋯

> ... the very gist, the living soul of Marxism – a concrete analysis of a concrete situation.
> – VLADIMIR LENIN[2]

⋰

The first Congress of the RSDLP, held in Minsk in March 1898, gave the movement a programme that reflected the aspiration to hegemony in the democratic revolution, but after political police apprehended the Congress participants, it was left without an authoritative organisational embodiment of this aspiration. There followed a period of impetuous but chaotic growth of the social-democratic movement. Local circles of intellectuals and workers formed spontaneously, in isolation from one another and from the historical experience and theoretical development of the movement as a whole, flourishing briefly before the political police broke them up. The prevalent amateurish or handicraft [*kustarnyi*] methods of political work characteristic of these circles formed the

---

1 Lenin 1904a, pp. 411, 412.
2 Lenin 1920b, p. 166.

practical context for the emergence of the Economist tendency. The campaign against Economism waged by Lenin, Plekhanov and their colleagues on the editorial board of *Iskra* [*The Spark*] culminated in the Second Congress of the RSDLP, held in Brussels and London in July–August, 1903. As a result of this campaign, the majority of delegates identified themselves with the *Iskra* organisation. The RSDLP was to be organised, accordingly, as a Marxist vanguard party aiming to lead the working class in the struggle for hegemony.

But just as the Congress marked the triumph of *Iskra* – that is, of the strategic orientation of proletarian hegemony in the bourgeois-democratic revolution – a split of historic significance opened in its ranks. The divergence between Bolsheviks and Mensheviks arose suddenly and unexpectedly in the midst of the Congress. None of the participants was fully clear as to its genesis or its import; even the principal actors saw it unfold hazily amidst the uncertainties and confusion of political struggle. Apparently turning upon minutiae of the party rules and issues of personnel, its genesis might seem to consist of nothing more than a clash of personal loyalties and antipathies in the struggle for power and position. This sort of explanation does not, however, fit the character of the antagonists and is out of all proportion with what ensued from their antagonism. The split sparked charges from each camp that the other had abdicated basic principles of Marxism, but identifying the principles involved without doing an injustice to the adverse position is not a straightforward business.

In this chapter I will argue that the split between Bolsheviks and Mensheviks cannot be understood apart from the unresolved problems of the struggle for proletarian hegemony and the tensions that beset orthodox Marxists' attempts to reckon with them. If the account of the situation of Marxism in Russia proposed above is accurate, it follows that once the strategic orientation of proletarian hegemony was to be embodied in authoritative institutions and practices, the equivocation at its core would translate into political conflict. The two aspects of the Congress, organisational consolidation and political division, thus need to be understood in conjunction. In line with the politico-strategic logic at work in *What Is to Be Done?*, Lenin oriented himself toward the Congress and the party organisation that was to emerge from it as a prolongation of the struggle against Economism. The future Mensheviks reacted to this stance and to the proposals in which it was expressed as a series of uncomradely provocations; their reaction was expressed, at first gropingly, but more reflectively as the factional struggle continued, in their own distinctive stance toward political agency. In retrospect, what had earlier seemed mere differences of nuance between Lenin's formulations and those of his erstwhile colleagues on the editorial board of *Iskra* would take on a new and ominous significance.

Through the course of these factional struggles, two distinct stances on working-class political agency and, consequently, two distinct orientations toward the struggle for proletarian hegemony would emerge in opposition to each other. The Mensheviks would come to emphasise the expressive aspect of proletarian political agency; for them, the self-emancipation of the proletariat consisted essentially of forms of political activity in which workers asserted their class character in practical confrontation with bourgeois political actors. Thus expressing their independence in practical forms, the workers would grow in self-confidence and political self-consciousness; indeed, the identification of appropriate forms of activity was constrained, independently of the exigencies of the politico-strategic conjuncture, by this imperative to proletarian education through self-activity. Self-activity and such cognate notions as consciousness and hegemony were implicitly construed by reference to an ideal of individual autonomy and self-emancipation. If proletarian agency was expressive, the politics of the struggle for proletarian hegemony might well be characterised as a kind of enlightened pedagogy. The sense of agency at work in Lenin's interventions was, by contrast, essentially strategic, centred on the struggle over state power in accordance with the politico-strategic logic of the struggle for hegemony that subtended the thesis of consciousness from without in *What Is to Be Done?* Framed in these terms, proletarian agency is appropriately assessed through its effect upon the strategic context and proletarian independence figures as organised (hence essentially collective) class struggle in this strategic context. What counts as proletarian self-activity, self-emancipation, self-education and self-consciousness is, accordingly, to be construed in terms of class struggle, refracted through the strategic logic of the political struggle for hegemony and modified by the requirements of successive political conjunctures.

These two orientations took on definition as contending ways to make sense of the growing divergence (and to justify one or the other side in it) only in the course of a series of disagreements over practical measures to organise the nascent party and implement the agreed direction of proletarian hegemony in Russia's bourgeois-democratic revolution. To understand the two sides and their opposition, it is necessary to trace their emergence through some of the practical minutiae of the factional struggle. The argument of this chapter begins by acknowledging the *Iskra* consensus on the organisational proposals of *What Is to Be Done?* while noting the concurrent recognition of differences in the formulation of their rationale. The advent and intensification of disagreement among the principals of *Iskra* is followed through the

Congress and its aftermath, with attention to Lenin's 'strategic' stance. The Menshevik orientation to proletarian political agency and, consequently, to proletarian hegemony was articulated by Axelrod and the young Trotsky as a way of understanding – and intervening in – the factional struggle; it also shaped Rosa Luxemburg's critique of Lenin. When Lenin's rebuttal is read in terms of the politico-strategic logic of the struggle for hegemony, it becomes possible to contrast the two stances on hegemony, to trace them to the equivocations in the strategic orientation of proletarian hegemony and to clarify their mutual misunderstandings. Conversely, the controversy and split between Mensheviks and Bolsheviks demonstrates in concrete fashion the implication of the politico-strategic logic of Lenin's analysis that nothing, not even the inner sanctum of the Marxist party, is out of play in the struggle for hegemony.

The *Iskra* Consensus and Its Limits

When leading figures from the Social Democratic underground in Russia concluded an agreement with the Group for the Emancipation of Labour to publish and distribute an illegal revolutionary newspaper, *Iskra* [*The Spark*], it was with a view to overcoming the disarray of the Social Democratic movement and rebuilding the RSDLP around the project of proletarian hegemony in the bourgeois-democratic revolution. To this end, the editorial board's inaugural declaration carried an announcement of ideological war against Economism: 'Before we can unite, and in order that we may unite, we must first of all draw firm and definite lines of demarcation... Open polemics, conducted in full view of all Russian Social-Democrats and class-conscious workers, are necessary and desirable in order to clarify the depth of existing differences'.[3] The following statement from Martov's pen exemplifies the *Iskra* standpoint:

> The struggle between the 'critics' and 'orthodox' Marxists is really the first chapter of a struggle for political hegemony between the proletariat and bourgeois democracy. In the uprising of the bourgeois intelligentsia against proletarian hegemony we see, hidden under an ideological mask, the class struggle of the advanced section of bourgeois society against the revolutionary proletariat... The Economists are attempting to turn the proletariat into an instrument of the bourgeoisie. By restricting it to the immediate economic struggle, they are preventing it from developing its own political program, from becoming an

---

3 Lenin 1900, pp. 354, 355.

independent political force, and consequently from entering into conflicts with the liberals.[4]

Understanding the challenge presented by Economism in this way, Martov was drawn to the same organisational conclusion as Lenin: that it was incumbent upon *Iskra* to 'organise the movement from the top down so as to insure the careful selection and training of its members'.[5]

'[W]hen we speak of organisation, we literally speak in different tongues'.[6] Thus, with more prescience than he could have imagined, did Lenin introduce the organisational recommendations of *What Is to Be Done?* Economists might agree with revolutionary Marxists about the importance of organisation, but the appropriate form of organisation would essentially depend upon 'the content of its activity'.[7] If social-democratic politics were equated with 'the economic struggle against the employers and the government', it would assume the form of a trade-union organisation, 'as broad as possible' and 'as public as conditions will allow'. But if it encompassed the struggle for proletarian leadership of all the popular and democratic forces in overthrowing the autocracy, it would call for the arts of the professional revolutionary in combating the political police and, consequently, for an organisation of revolutionaries, 'not very extensive and...as secret as possible', in which distinctions between workers and intellectuals are of no account.[8] In a country where even trade-union

---

4 Cited in Haimson 1955, p. 131.
5 Ibid.
6 Lenin 1902, p. 452.
7 Lenin 1902, p. 440.
8 Lenin 1902, pp. 452–3. Workers are able to take part, as socialist theoreticians, in the production of socialist ideology 'only when they are able, and to the extent that they are able, more or less, to acquire the knowledge of their age and develop that knowledge. But in order that working men *may succeed in this more often*, every effort must be made to raise the level of the consciousness of the workers in general; it is necessary that the workers do not confine themselves to the artificially restricted limits of *"literature for workers"* but that they learn to an increasing degree to master *general literature*. It would be even truer to say "are not confined"... because the workers themselves wish to read and do read all that is written for the intelligentsia, and only a few (bad) intellectuals believe that it is enough "for workers" to be told a few things about factory conditions and to have repeated to them over and over again what has long been known' (1902, p. 384n). Socialist ideology, as it figures in Lenin's argument, reflects Kautsky's conception of Marxist science as a knowledge of universal laws, but also the struggle for proletarian hegemony against the narrow limits of Economism, the struggle of Social Democratic intellectuals and workers against bourgeois intellectuals and the domination of the working-class movement by bourgeois ideology. It may be recalled that in Kautsky's thought, the harmony of the universalising Marxist science with

activities are illegal, Lenin asserted, a durable organisation of revolutionaries would constitute the foundation necessary to 'ensure the stability of the movement as a whole' through turbulent conditions and to 'carry out the aims both of social-democracy and of trade unions proper'. Secretly connected through the organisation of revolutionaries, nuclei of the most reliable and experienced workers could, without formal organisation, elections or even a list of members, secure 'the widest support of the masses and perform *all* the functions of a trade-union organisation; and [could] do so, moreover, in a manner desirable to social-democracy'.[9] The opposite contention, he maintained, rested upon a confusion of 'the philosophical and social-historical question of the "depth" of the "roots" of the movement with the technical and organisational question of the best method of combating the gendarmes'.[10]

Under autocratic rule, '[s]ecrecy is such a necessary condition' for an organisation of revolutionaries 'that all the other conditions (number and selection of members, functions, etc.) must be made to conform to it'.[11] However, a distinction must be drawn between the secret organisation and the movement:

> Centralisation of the most secret functions in an organisation of revolutionaries will not diminish, but rather increase the extent and enhance the quality of the activity of a large number of other organisations that are intended for a broad public and are therefore as loose and non-secret as possible, such as workers' trade unions, workers' self-education circles, and circles among *all* other sections of the population, etc., etc.[12]

The movement suffered from a dearth of activists in the midst of an abundance of potential recruits. By parcelling out the various 'detailed functions' (for example, reading, supplying information and writing for, and even distributing the illegal press) and distributing them among different 'detail workers', much of the work of the movement could be rendered relatively innocuous

---

the concrete particularity of proletarian struggles served to underwrite a kind of division of labour between theory and practice, intellectuals and workers. Perhaps it was in consequence of the contradiction he identified between consciousness and spontaneity, Marxism and the spontaneous working-class movement, that Lenin was able to assert that '*all distinctions between workers and intellectuals,* not to speak of distinctions of trade and profession, in both categories, *must be effaced*' in the organisation of the Social Democratic vanguard (1902, p. 452).

9   Lenin 1902, p. 460.
10 Lenin 1902, p. 461.
11 Lenin 1902, pp. 475–6.
12 Lenin 1902, p. 466.

and 'almost cease to be secret work', thus dramatically reducing the danger involved and facilitating the participation of the many who would never become professional revolutionaries. But specialisation of function implies centralisation: '[I]n order not to break up the movement while breaking up its functions and in order to imbue the people who carry out the detailed functions with the conviction that their work is necessary and important (without which they will never do the work), it is necessary to have a strong organisation of tried revolutionaries'.[13] The division of labour figures here as part and parcel of an argument from the conditions of autocratic rule to the need for secrecy in order to promote widespread participation in the revolutionary movement, not as a separate argument for the efficiency of organisational centralism.

Iskra was to be the vehicle of revolutionary organisation: '[T]*here is no other way of training* strong political organisations except through the medium of an all-Russian newspaper'.[14] This 'training' consisted of more than the editors impressing upon their readers the need to construct the kind of organisation capable of leading the proletarian struggle for hegemony in the democratic revolution. The organisational significance of the newspaper was far more integral. Not only would it propagate Marxist analysis and argument on the struggle in Russia, forging ideological unity among revolutionaries; not only would it agitate in support of 'every protest and every outbreak' against the autocracy, drawing new forces to the social-democratic cause; the very work of researching, writing, publishing and distributing the newspaper would organise those who carried it out:

> A newspaper is not only a collective propagandist and a collective agitator but also a collective organiser. In this respect *it may be compared to the scaffolding* erected around a building under construction; it marks the contours of the structure and facilitates communication between builders, permitting them to distribute the work and to view the common results achieved by their organised labour.[15]

The practice of revolutionary journalism is no 'bookish' occupation that might isolate its practitioners from the masses but an exclusive engagement in 'all-sided and all-embracing political agitation, i.e., precisely in work that *brings closer and merges into a single whole* the elemental destructive

---

13   Lenin 1902, pp. 465, 469.
14   Lenin 1902, p. 499.
15   Lenin 1902, pp. 502–3.

force of the masses and the conscious destructive force of the organisation of revolutionaries'.[16] Whereas Blanquism restricted political struggle to the dimensions of a conspiracy, in *What Is to Be Done?* conspiratorial organisation is organically connected in its very conception to the working-class movement and to mass political struggle.

The need for an organisation of professional revolutionaries to lead the Russian working-class movement was the brunt of Lenin's argument, but he did not specify how the distinction between party and movement, consciousness and spontaneity, was to be drawn in organisational practice. The contemporary import of *What Is to Be Done?* did not lie in an organisational blueprint but in the effort it represented to work out the organisational implications of the *Iskra* project of proletarian hegemony. As such it was well received, despite some reservations, by Lenin's fellow editors. Potresov wrote to Lenin, 'I've read your little book twice running and straight through and I can only congratulate its author. The general impression ... is superlative';[17] according to the Menshevik historian Theodore Dan, this 'expressed the general attitude to Lenin's work of all members of the editorial board and the closest contributors to *Iskra*'.[18] What reservations there were pertained to his handling of spontaneity and consciousness. Potresov tempered his enthusiasm with the concern that '[s]omewhere in the struggle against "spontaneity", the author has overshot the mark in the direction of "consciousness"'.[19]

Russian Marxists since Plekhanov had relied upon socialist consciousness to resolve the paradoxes of the social-democratic strategy of proletarian hegemony in the bourgeois-democratic revolution. The idea that objective and subjective aspects of the class struggle developed unevenly was thus no innovation in Russian Marxist circles; it was acknowledged even by Economists.[20] And while uneven development may have stretched the logic of Marxist orthodoxy, it did not break the essential harmony postulated by orthodoxy between objective and subjective aspects of the socialist movement, between the working class and Marxism. In *What Is to Be Done?*, however, this harmony was relegated from premise to (potential) conclusion; it figured only as an object of political struggle. What distinguished Lenin's formulations from those of his fellow editors was just this – dialectical – subordination of harmony to struggle and contradiction. The insistence of Plekhanov, Axelrod,

---

16 Lenin 1902, p. 512.
17 Cited in Dan 1970, p. 238.
18 Dan 1970, p. 237.
19 Cited in Dan 1970, pp. 239–40.
20 See, for example, Martynov's speech at the Second Congress (RSDLP 1904, pp. 140–52).

Martov, et al., upon the conscious leadership of the 'revolutionary bacillum' always relied upon the assumption of an implicit harmony with the spontaneous working-class movement.[21] Potresov complained to Lenin, 'You stress too much the *outside influence*, which undoubtedly exists in the history of socialism, but which comes to meet the general negation of the social structure that already exists *within* the working class'.[22] Axelrod and Plekhanov expressed similar reservations in correspondence with each other and it seems that Axelrod also raised them obliquely with Lenin himself,[23] but none of the *Iskra* editors pressed the point. Perhaps because the difference could easily be read as one of emphasis, without obvious practical implications, when Economist delegates to the Second Congress tried to counterpose Lenin and his fellow editors on just this point, the *Iskra* team closed ranks. But later, after his political break with the nascent Bolshevik trend, Plekhanov asserted with characteristic heavy-handedness his opposition to *What Is to Be Done?* on these very grounds.[24]

In light of the urgent practical imperative to rebuild the RSDLP, what seemed mere differences of emphasis or formulation were overridden by the programmatic agreement forged by *Iskra* around the strategic project of proletarian hegemony in the democratic revolution. These differences, especially different formulations of the relation between spontaneity and consciousness, assume a more compelling significance when they are grasped in the context of the ambiguities that plagued attempts by Russian Marxists to theorise this hegemonic project; and it is only by examining the debate over the organisation

---

21   This emerges, for instance, from the injunction in Plekhanov's *Vademecum* (1900) that 'the revolutionary bacillum (whether it originates among the intelligentsia or among the workers) should aid the consciousness of the workers to lag as little as possible behind the real conditions of a given society' and that Social Democratic intellectuals should 'attempt to speed up the adjustment of the workers' consciousness to the conditions of their lives' (cited in Haimson 1955, p. 125). And the following statement from Axelrod's 'The Present Tasks and Tactics of the Russian Social-Democrats' (1898), cited by Harding (1977, p. 154) to illustrate the identity between Axelrod's perspective and Lenin's, manifestly shows the contrary: 'The proletariat, according to the consciousness of the Social-Democrats themselves, does not possess a ready-made, historically-elaborated social ideal. The "economic struggle" with its employers remains the path whereby it slowly formulates such an "ideal" in its consciousness – to speak more plainly – it prepares the workers' understanding for the definitive goals of socialism' (a slightly different translation may be found in Axelrod 1898, p. 239).

22   Cited in Frankel 1969b, p. 68.

23   See Ascher 1972, p. 178.

24   See Baron 1963, pp. 248–51; see also Larsson 1970, pp. 235–6; Haimson 1955, p. 193.

The Congress and the Split

The unity of the *Iskra* camp held, despite some wavering, through the first half of the Congress; the *Iskra* draft programme escaped intact from skirmishes with representatives of the Jewish Workers' Bund and with the handful of Economist delegates. Dissension surfaced during the 22nd session in the debate over the first article of the party rules, the definition of membership. The Rules Commission was so divided over the formulation of this article that it submitted the difference to the Congress. According to Lenin's original draft, 'A member of the RSDLP is one who accepts its programme and supports the Party by personal participation in one of the party organisations'.[25] Unhappy with what he saw as the narrowness and inflexibility of this formulation, Martov submitted an alternative version, defining a member as 'one who accepts the Party's programme, supports the Party financially, and renders it regular personal assistance under the direction of one of its organisations'.[26] The difference between the two versions, whether a member must belong to a party organisation or simply work under its supervision, may not appear to be of great consequence, but this debate occupied the Congress for two sessions and takes up 20 pages in the minutes.[27]

Axelrod opened the case for Martov's formulation by proposing a distinction between the concepts of party and organisation. Invoking revolutionary tradition, he claimed that both *Zemlia i volia* and *Narodnaia volia* recognised as members of the party people who, without belonging to the organisation, assisted the cause. Martov set the distinction in the context of the class struggle: 'The Party organisation is the flywheel that sets in motion the work of the Party in our sense of the word... For me a conspiratorial organisation only has meaning when it is enveloped by a broad Social-Democratic working-class party'.[28] Lenin denied that party organisations had to consist exclusively of professional revolutionaries but insisted upon a strict demarcation between party and class: '[T]he Party must be only the vanguard, the leader of the vast mass of the working class, the whole of which (or nearly the whole) works

---

25 RSDLP 1904, p. 311.
26 RSDLP 1904, p. 10.
27 RSDLP 1904, pp. 310–30.
28 RSDLP 1904, pp. 311–12.

"under the direction" of the Party organisations, but the whole of which does not and should not belong to the Party'.[29] It might appear that the issue was merely terminological, but underlying the incongruity between these distinctions was a tension, as yet unfocussed but already palpable, between two ways of construing political agency and, consequently, two ways of rendering the interaction between vanguard and masses in the process of class struggle.

Implicit in Martov's argument was the assumption that once the conscious vanguard had been organised, the very logic of the workers' class position would align them with it. 'We are those who give conscious expression to an unconscious process... We could only rejoice if every striker, every demonstrator, answering for his actions, could proclaim himself a Party member'.[30] Martov and his supporters urged on behalf of his formulation its adaptability to the demands of 'life'. Any rigid distinction between party and class would be bureaucratic, formalistic, simply unworkable: '[L]ife will assert itself... and the Central Committee, in order not to leave a multitude of organisations outside the Party, will have to legitimise them despite their not quite reliable character'.[31]

The alleged adaptability of Martov's formulation, Lenin charged, was simply camouflage for a lack of clarity that created the potential for confusion. 'Pavlovich' (P.A. Krasikov) put the same point more sharply when he accused Martov of an 'anarchistic conception' that would permit '*irresponsible* persons', individuals who could not effectively be held accountable because they did not belong to a party organisation, to '*enrol themselves* in the Party'.[32] Only his own formulation, Lenin claimed, 'defines at all exactly the conception of a *member* of the Party'.[33] And this clarity of definition gave the Economist 'Brouckère' (Lydia Makhnovets), who championed the widespread adoption of the elective principle in party affairs, a paradoxical reason to prefer Lenin's draft, for ambiguity as to the eligibility of voters would render authoritative elections untenable and democratic accountability impossible. Lenin's centralism was not (yet) democratic but neither was democracy its antithesis, for both centralism and democracy require the effective exercise of authority. Though opponents would later construe this debate as counterposing democracy and bureaucracy, Lenin read it as pitting centralism (or the effective exercise of authority) against adaptability or – Martov's word – 'elasticity'.

---

29   RSDLP 1904, p. 327.
30   RSDLP 1904, pp. 311, 312.
31   RSDLP 1904, p. 320.
32   RSDLP 1904, p. 324.
33   RSDLP 1904, p. 326.

The object of Lenin's formulation was precisely to assign control over membership to the Central Committee: 'We need the most diverse organisations of all types, ranks and shades... [but e]ndorsement by the Central Committee [is] an essential condition for a Party organisation to be considered such'.[34] Centralised control over the admission of organisations would render membership unambiguous or at least indisputable. The point of a clear definition of organisational relations of authority and accountability was to permit effective control over the activity of the vanguard party and thus enable the conscious vanguard to act coherently and effectively upon the spontaneous movement of the class struggle. Seen in this light, the 'elasticity' of Martov's version was a source not only of confusion, but of potential political weakness: 'in the period of the Party's life which we are now passing through', the restoration of party unity with the prospect of growing numbers of new recruits of uncertain commitment, 'it is just this "elasticity" that... opens the door to all the elements of confusion, vacillation and opportunism'.[35] A similar point was made by Plekhanov, who regarded Lenin's draft as a 'bulwark' against opportunism and would throw in his lot with the Mensheviks only some months later; but while he located the source of the problem among the intellectuals whose 'bourgeois individualism' he contrasted with the discipline of the workers,[36] Lenin indicated that the danger was more pervasive, found not only in the intelligentsia but 'in the working class too'.[37] This line of argument appeared to adherents of Martov's draft as a misguided obsession with rules to the detriment of reality: 'Akimov' (Vladimir Makhnovets) professed himself 'confident that the realities of life will, nevertheless, force their way into our Party organisation';[38] 'Kostrov' (Noah Zhordania) noted that '[t]he rules exist for life, life does not exist for the rules';[39] Trotsky 'did not know that one could exorcise opportunism by means of rules. I think that opportunism is produced by more complex causes'.[40] But whatever force this rebuttal possessed was dependent upon the assumption of eventual harmony between working-class reality and Social Democratic consciousness, an assumption that Lenin was ready to question. Since the terrain of working-class reality was traversed and shaped by the politico-strategic logic of the struggle for hegemony, Lenin's concern was – by whatever means

---

34   RSDLP 1904, p. 314.
35   RSDLP 1904, pp. 326–7.
36   RSDLP 1904, pp. 321–2.
37   RSDLP 1904, p. 327.
38   RSDLP 1904, p. 330.
39   RSDLP 1904, p. 329.
40   RSDLP 1904, p. 324.

necessary, including party rules – to secure the most advantageous position possible for one political tendency, revolutionary Marxism, to conduct this struggle against other tendencies, the shape and focus of whose contrary efforts could be anticipated only in part.

In the event, 'life' did assert itself and, with the voting support of the majority of *Iskra*'s opponents, Martov's article was approved by the Congress, 28 to 22. This voting pattern reinforced Lenin's concern about a drift toward opportunism in the party, but the balance of forces shifted when the Economist delegates Akimov and Martynov and the representatives of the Jewish Social Democratic Bund, all of whom had sided with Martov, withdrew from the Congress. It was not the debate over the membership clause, but the elections to the central institutions of the party, that precipitated the split in the ranks of the *Iskra* organisation. With a view to transforming the status of the *Iskra* editorial board from literary circle to official party institution and enhancing the effective administration of the newspaper, Lenin had already, prior to the Congress, circulated a plan for reconstituting the board by electing 'two trios', a three-member Central Committee and three editors for the Central Organ. In the context of the newly emergent tensions within the *Iskra* camp, this plan assumed a new and politically explosive significance: its adoption by the Congress marked the RSDLP's division into Bolsheviks (the majority) and Mensheviks (the minority). Martov and his adherents saw in Lenin's plan, and in the accompanying nomination of an editorial board comprised of Lenin, Plekhanov and Martov (and dispensing with Axelrod, Potresov and Zasulich), not a recipe for efficient administration 'but a struggle for influence on the Central Committee'. Rather than establishing 'normal conditions' for political work, with the election of the new editorial board the Congress 'continued and even stepped up ... the state of siege [in the party], with its exceptional laws against particular groups' that had been created in the course of the struggle against Economism.[41] Lenin's rejoinder indicates that the context and terms of the disagreement had shifted since the debate over the membership clause:

> All the activity of *Iskra* has up to now been a *struggle* for influence, as a separate group, but now it is something more, a matter of *organisational consolidation* of this influence ... Comrade Martov is absolutely right: the step we have taken is undoubtedly a *major political step*, testifying that one of the trends which have now taken shape has been chosen for the future work of our Party ... We not only can but must create a 'state of siege' in relation to unstable and vacillating elements and ... the whole

---

41   RSDLP 1904, p. 432.

system of centralism which the congress has now approved [is] nothing but a 'state of siege' with regard to the so numerous sources of *political diffuseness*.[42]

Refusing to acknowledge the chosen trend, Martov and the other Mensheviks would not cooperate in the work of the central party institutions and launched a campaign to overturn the Bolshevik decisions of the Congress. The Menshevik boycott signified to Lenin the recrudescence of *kustarnichestvo*, the narrow 'circle spirit' that sustained Economism. Thus, although each side acknowledged from the beginning the political importance of the split, at the same time each hurled accusations of personal interest – grasping for power or place hunting – at the other.[43]

A cacophony of personal ambition, fear and sensitivity, jealousy and loyalty was intertwined with the sense that fundamental differences of political principle were somehow at work in the split, making it difficult to formulate an account of the split in terms that do not beg the questions at issue. An account that turns on accusations of betrayal – of an originally agreed-upon position – is of little use when the position originally agreed upon, the strategic orientation of proletarian hegemony, is riven with ambiguity; a plausible account must be able to make sense of the stance of each side without dismissing or demonising either.

Georg Lukács locates the political root of the split in the dispute over the definition of a party member, whether or not

> it was essential for members... to devote themselves wholeheartedly to party work and to submit to the most rigorous party discipline... The Bolshevik concept of party organisation involved the selection of a group of single-minded revolutionaries, prepared to make any sacrifice, from the more or less chaotic mass of the class as a whole.[44]

---

42   RSDLP 1904, pp. 434–5.
43   The history of Lenin's plan and of Martov's prior knowledge of it became the subject of bitter recriminations. Divergent accounts may be found in Getzler 1967, pp. 80–2, and Lenin, 1903b, pp. 86–90. It is possible to understand the recriminations without having to attribute bad faith to one version or the other only by bearing in mind the transformation in the political context of Lenin's plan since the debate on party membership – the political significance of what Martov had been party to had changed.
44   Lukács 1924, p. 25.

The fact that the Fourth (Unity) Congress of the RSDLP, held in 1906 and dominated by the Mensheviks, voted to adopt Lenin's original definition is difficult to reconcile with a literal reading of Lukács's claim. The emphasis he places upon the single-minded devotion of revolutionaries suggests the real thrust of his argument, that Lenin's definition was the juridical expression and the Bolshevik organisation the institutional embodiment of revolutionary will and activity. Thus, the dispute over the definition of party membership can 'only be understood in relation to the conflict between the two different basic attitudes to the possibility, probable course and character of the revolution ... *Lenin's concept of party organisation presupposes the fact – the actuality – of the revolution*'.[45] But if Bolshevism is identified with revolutionary will and Menshevism, correspondingly, with the reification of that will, it is difficult to explain the solidarity of such future allies of Lenin as Luxemburg and Trotsky with Martov and Axelrod. Indeed, what is really at issue is not strength of revolutionary will or devotion to revolutionary activity but how revolutionary activity is to be understood. The former cannot even be defined without first stipulating the latter.

The revolution whose 'actuality' Lukács has in mind here, the socialist revolution, was not the revolution that was next anticipated by any of the principals to the split, including Lenin. All save the Economists were determined that the autonomy of the working class would take the form of its hegemony in the bourgeois-democratic revolution. And it is arguable that Lukács's own conception of the revolutionary process has greater affinity with the distinctive themes of Menshevism than with Lenin. Lukács saw the proletariat as the identical subject-object of history, the solution to the philosophical problem of knowledge. Since the exploitation of the wage labourer is the essence of the social-historical totality, proletarian revolutionary practice is key to knowledge of the totality. The historical process is thus essentially identified with the coming to self-consciousness of the proletariat-subject. The party, as the vanguard of the proletariat, is an '*autonomous form* of proletarian class consciousness' whose emergence 'always remains the conscious, free action of the conscious vanguard itself'.[46] As the highest form of proletarian consciousness and practice, the party is a kind of prefiguration of communist society, an embryo of emancipated humanity. In identifying wholly with the revolution, the individual party member forges a link with the process of total historical

---

45   Lukács 1924, pp. 25–6.
46   Lukács 1922, p. 330.

transformation and so becomes a moral agent and symbol. Thus, Lukács could read the party as 'the concrete mediation between man and history'.[47]

As argued earlier, the notion of the exploitation of wage labour as the essence of the social totality is fundamentally at variance with the conception of social totality that was at work in Lenin's account of consciousness in *What Is to Be Done?* But it is what renders plausible Lukács's identification of the revolutionary-historical process with the emergence of proletarian self-consciousness. And this identification is consonant with a tendency, for which Lenin would repeatedly criticise his Economist and later Menshevik opponents, to assimilate the politics of the working-class struggle to a process of education. It is also what underwrites Lukács's ascription of moral significance to party membership, which he shared, for good or ill, with Martov but not with Lenin. Lukács was no Menshevik, but these conceptual affinities point not only to the inadequacy of his diagnostic, but also to the delicacy of the analysis required to make sense of the symptoms in the split.

This analysis is a task that cannot be accomplished properly without an appreciation of the unresolved tensions in the Marxist project of proletarian hegemony. Even Neil Harding, who does place the controversy over organisation in the context of the Russian Social Democratic strategy of proletarian hegemony in the bourgeois-democratic revolution, cannot vindicate Lenin as the consistent defender of orthodoxy without reducing the motivation of Martov, Axelrod and their colleagues to considerations of injured pride and personal loyalty and so rendering the political stance of the Mensheviks opaque, because he does not critically examine the coherence of the orthodox Marxist account of hegemony.[48] The need to endow the strategic perspective of proletarian hegemony with authoritative institutional embodiment engaged two distinct stances toward political agency: one reflecting the influence of Lenin's emergent strategic logic of political struggle, the other unable to get beyond the unilinear historical logic of Marxist orthodoxy. The clash between the practical implications of these two stances sparked the split between Bolsheviks and Mensheviks and generated two distinct, indeed contradictory, orientations toward the struggle for hegemony and, consequently, the class struggle and the relation between the Marxist vanguard and the working class.

47   Lukács 1922, p. 318.
48   See Harding 1977, pp. 189–96.

Menshevism and Hegemony

The emergent orientations to hegemony were deeply marked by the fact of the factional struggle. At the forefront in working out the theoretical perspective of Menshevism was Axelrod, whose seminal article of December 1903–January 1904, 'The Unification of Russian Social-Democracy and Its Tasks', conceptualised the struggle for hegemony in terms of an opposition between the formal and bureaucratic centralism of the Bolsheviks and the independent participation of the working masses in all aspects of society and politics, the process whereby class and party would be substantively unified. 'The influence of the proletarian or Social-Democratic element on the contemporary revolutionary movement in Russia', he wrote, 'can only be felt inasmuch as the preparation for the bourgeois revolution is at the same time a process of political education and the unification of the working masses in a revolutionary socialist party'.[49] The purpose of the Social Democrats was to further this process so that the destruction of the autocratic regime thereby becomes 'a direct prologue to the class struggle of the proletariat ... [and thus to] the political expropriation of the bourgeoisie as a prelude to socialist revolution'. The progress the Second Congress made in this direction was, however, merely formal, programmatic, but in the substance of its practical activity 'our movement has progressed in a general revolutionary sense but not in a purely Social-Democratic one'.[50] The cultural and political backwardness of the Russian working class determined the uneven advance of social democracy: its activity in the revolutionary struggle against Tsarism predominated over the specifically socialist task of stimulating the class consciousness and political self-reliance of the proletariat. The workers had been aroused from their 'immemorial slumbers' only by their subjection to the intellectual and political influence of the radical intelligentsia; in the process the end, the proletarian struggle for socialism, had been subordinated to the means, the democratic struggle against autocracy.[51] Bolshevism was the expression of this process: the Leninist 'fetishists of centralisation', reducing the task of organising the proletarian party to the mere introduction of 'technical improvements of an organisational character', had erected a hierarchical division of labour which transformed party members into 'so many cog-wheels, nuts and bolts, all functioning exactly as the centre decides'. Such a purely formal or technical notion of centralism, so far from unifying the party and the class in practice, inevitably eroded the 'conscious

---

49 Axelrod 1903–4, p. 49.
50 Ibid.
51 Axelrod 1903–4, pp. 51–2.

initiative' and 'collective effort' inherent in the organisation of 'political work in the socialist-proletarian sense'.[52] Because it brings the working masses

> face to face with...their direct exploiters...and [with] those members of the upper class who set themselves up as representatives...of public opinion and the 'national interest' but [who] are in fact the ideologists, leaders, advisors and plain political agents of the exploiting classes...active participation in social and political life is the best, if not the only school in which to develop the class-consciousness of the proletariat.[53]

Only in fostering the political self-reliance of the workers would the RSDLP constitute itself in substance, and not merely in form, as the socialist party of the proletariat and, throwing off the tutelage of the radical intelligentsia, emerge as an independent and influential force in Russia's democratic revolution. Axelrod thus made a particular reading of the self-activity of the workers the alpha and the omega of Menshevism, presenting the workers' direct engagement in political activity as a 'school' and Social Democratic leadership as, in essence, an enlightened pedagogy. Proletarian self-activity imbued the political struggle with consciousness of class and so enacted the resolution of the contradiction between means and end. The class-conscious political activity of the workers prefigured the socialist revolution; the aim of social democracy was thus immediately present in the democratic revolution in the form of the workers' consciousness of their independent class interests. This chain of argument effectively assimilated the struggle for proletarian hegemony in the bourgeois-democratic revolution to the development of working-class consciousness.

The themes evoked by Axelrod were taken up and embroidered in a number of Menshevik works, most elaborately by Leon Trotsky in his lengthy *Our Political Tasks*, issued in August 1904 under the imprimatur of the Menshevik *Iskra* and dedicated to Axelrod. Trotsky sought to analyse the growth and prospects of the RSDLP, he said, not in accordance with the consciousness that the Social Democrats had of themselves, but in terms of the real content of Social Democratic activity. Hitherto, he argued, Social Democratic energies in Russia had been absorbed in activities that were properly the historical vocation of bourgeois democracy. First, the practice of 'economic' agitation had awakened the 'elementary revolutionary instincts' of the workers but had displaced their

---

52 Axelrod 1903–4, pp. 49–50.
53 Axelrod 1903–4, p. 51.

political education; second, *Iskra*'s preoccupation with the affairs of the radical bourgeois opposition and its corresponding practice of 'political denunciation' had imbued the 'awakened instincts with the character of a conscious *civic protest*'.[54] Such activity did little more than give effect to the political programme of the *Credo*, a division of labour between the economic struggle of the workers and the liberal-democratic political protests of the intellectuals. It expressed the domination of the Social Democratic movement by a revolutionary intelligentsia which, cloaked in Marxist phrases, substituted itself politically for the proletariat. Rather than constituting themselves as the subject of the political struggle, the workers remained its object. Lenin's organisational plan sanctified and institutionalised this form of practice.[55]

Only the self-activity of the proletariat could resolve the antinomy of Economism and 'political substitutionism', practice and theory. The 'objective interests' of the workers, determined by their conditions of existence, must ultimately find conscious expression in their 'subjective interests', but the process, more complex than either Economist or 'politician' could grasp, was full of 'knocks and blows, errors and disappointments, vicissitudes and defeats. The tactical astuteness of the Party of the proletariat lies wholly between these two factors and consists in easing and abridging the road from one to the other'.[56] The politics of Social Democracy was thus, in essence, the education of the workers to their objective interests through the cultivation of proletarian self-activity. The Economists, though immersed in practice, had proven incapable of transcending the subjective aspirations of the workers; the Bolshevik politicians, though armed with a theoretical knowledge of objective proletarian interests, would not engage with the practice of real workers.[57] It was not the Social Democrats, *pace* Lenin, who 'must go among all classes of the population', but the workers themselves;[58] Social Democratic politics consisted in

---

54 Trotsky 1904a, p. 58.
55 See Trotsky 1904a, pp. 87–90.
56 Trotsky 1904a, p. 117.
57 See Trotsky 1904a, pp. 118–20.
58 In support of this position, Trotsky cites (1904a, p. 117) the following passage from Axelrod's 'Present Tasks and Tactics of the Russian Social-Democrats' (1897): 'In order to gain an influence over these strata ... it is not at all necessary that Social-Democrats go and work among them, in their midst. The task before the Russian Social-Democrats of gaining adherents and direct and indirect allies among the non-proletarian classes will be solved principally by the character of agitational and propaganda activity *among the proletariat itself*'. Lenin had cited the same passage in *What Is to Be Done?*, tellingly omitting the first sentence, in arguing the position Trotsky disputes (see Lenin 1902, p. 433).

'acting through the proletariat and not in its name'.[59] The constitution of a substantively proletarian political party must proceed by 'searching among the masses for forms of action that contain in themselves the possibility of their subsequent development and their transformation from methods of education into primers of [political] tactics'. The logic of such forms of action would 'lead the most conscious strata of the proletariat to oppose themselves politically to the institutions of the dominant classes in the very process of the general democratic struggle against Tsarism'.[60]

Not only would the educational activity of the Social Democrats thus assume an objective political significance, but the hegemony of the proletariat in the bourgeois-democratic revolution was thus also expressed in and through the self-activity of the workers. Trotsky went on to spell this notion out with striking clarity:

> Only the free Russia of the future, in which we will evidently be obliged ... to play the role of an opposition party rather than a party of government, will permit the class struggle of the proletariat to expand to its full measure. But so that the proletariat, led by Social-Democracy in its battle for this 'free Russia' is already prepared for the struggle for the dictatorship [of the proletariat], the proletariat must at once stand opposed to all the institutions, standing or provisional, of the class which will tomorrow assume the helm of state. Limiting our opposition to the plane of the theoretical principles of our programme or the purely literary plane of our press is not enough; our opposition must be a living fact in the reality of politics.[61]

Paltry though the *zemstvo*, the municipal duma, the liberal press and similar institutions might be in the struggle against Tsarism, they were all that existed in the manner of 'direct organisation of the will of the bourgeoisie' and as such, continued Trotsky, they were the 'only real point of departure for the self-determination of the proletariat in the existing regime'.[62] It was thus incumbent upon Social Democrats to work out the tactics whereby workers could themselves act upon these institutions and thereby bring revolutionary pressure to bear upon the bourgeois opposition. Of course, the practical effect of such action was limited by the very powerlessness of the bourgeois

---

59 Trotsky 1904a, pp. 116–17.
60 Trotsky 1904a, pp. 108, 109.
61 Trotsky 1904a, p. 110.
62 Trotsky 1904a, p. 112.

opposition – but this very limitation can serve to point up the distinctiveness of the Menshevik conception of hegemony, which consisted essentially in the prefiguration of the proletariat, in its very self-activity, as a class-for-itself – that is, conscious of itself as an independent political actor with its own historical vocation.

Although *Our Political Tasks* went unmentioned in Trotsky's autobiography, in which he remembers having 'spent the whole year of 1904 arguing with the leading group of Mensheviks on questions of policy and organisation',[63] it spells out with some rigour a theoretical foundation for the distinctive tactics the Mensheviks would evolve. The Tsar's ill-fated war with Japan exacerbated the contradictions of the autocratic state and, as winter approached amidst rising popular discontent, the liberal opposition was set to embark upon a campaign of meetings that would urge more or less far-reaching political reforms upon the government. To the Menshevik tacticians, chiefly Axelrod and Dan, this campaign provided a perfect occasion for demonstrations of workers to exert proletarian pressure on the liberal opposition.[64] It could thus become the focal point of Social Democratic political activity provided, first, that the demonstrators 'fully understand the radical difference between an everyday demonstration against the police or government, on the one hand, and on the other a demonstration designed to combat absolutism by the direct influence of the revolutionary proletariat on the political attitude of liberal elements', and second, that the leadership ensured the necessary self-discipline and informed the liberals of the action so as to avoid a fiasco in which panicky bourgeois would call in the police.[65] Only those 'affected with bourgeois revolutionism, for which the external effect is everything and the process of the systematic development of the class consciousness and the initiative of the proletariat is nothing', could object to the apparently cautious 'external' form of such revolutionary activity.[66] Making the bourgeois opposition the focus of working-class political action was thus fully consonant with a notion of the struggle for hegemony as the expansion of class consciousness through

---

63 Trotsky 1930, p. 170.
64 By this time, Trotsky had already parted company with the Mensheviks over this very question of the relation between bourgeois liberals and the working class, although he had not yet worked out his notion of permanent revolution. At the time, his views on tactics were closer to Lenin's than to the Mensheviks', calling for a 'political strike of the proletariat' as the fulcrum of the impending revolution, drawing the urban masses, the peasantry and the liberal opposition into 'a political demonstration of the population ... to stop the war and call a National Constituent Assembly' (see Trotsky 1904b, p. 49).
65 See Ascher 1976, p. 55.
66 Cited in Lenin 1904c, p. 514.

appropriately concrete forms of self-activity, but if the strategic significance of the form of self-activity was indeterminate, its contextualisation and concretisation would do nothing to undercut the assumptions of the unilinear historical logic of Marxist orthodoxy.

Rosa Luxemburg's Critique

Written in response to Potresov's solicitations and to the appearance of Lenin's own account of the factional struggle in *One Step Forward, Two Steps Back*, the most celebrated critique of the Bolshevik position on party organisation, Rosa Luxemburg's 'Organisational Questions of Russian Social-Democracy' (1904) was published in Kautsky's *Die Neue Zeit* as well as in the Menshevik *Iskra*. It was perhaps the strategically indeterminate character of the notion of hegemony as class consciousness through self-activity that enabled Luxemburg to articulate the main themes of the Menshevik critique in an article addressed, despite its title, to organisational questions of Social Democracy in general. Indeed, the problem of hegemony, though not entirely absent from the article, is indiscernible to those not already familiar with the background of the argument – apart from the fact that the working-class movement was in its early stages, virtually the only specific feature of Russia with which Luxemburg deals is the alleged proclivity of its intelligentsia to equate discipline with humiliation of the ego.[67]

She describes the difficulty facing the Russian Social Democrats, as Axelrod did, in terms of the 'abstract character' assumed by socialist theory and practice where 'the domination of the bourgeoisie is veiled by absolutist force'. Without the 'political raw material...supplied by bourgeois society itself', they must nonetheless 'make up by [their] own efforts an entire historical period...[and] lead the Russian proletarians from their present "atomized" condition...to a class organization...Like God Almighty they must have this organisation arise out of the void, so to speak'.[68] Rephrasing a line of argument advanced by Axelrod and Martov at the Second Congress, Luxemburg claims, 'Social-Democracy is not *joined* to the organization of the proletariat. It is itself the proletariat'. Since organisation is thus simply the form assumed by the substantive process of independent working-class activity, the only appropriate centralism is 'the self-centralism of the advanced sectors of the proletariat. It is the rule of the majority within its own party...It is a *tendency*, which becomes

---

67 Luxemburg 1904, p. 125.
68 Luxemburg 1904, pp. 114, 115.

real in proportion to the development and political training acquired by the working masses in the course of their struggle'.[69]

In an argument that recalls the transformation of Axelrod's party members into 'so many cog-wheels, nuts and bolts', Luxemburg, citing Lenin's claim that the factory accustoms workers to organisation and discipline, dissects the confusion allegedly implicit therein between the 'spontaneous coordination of the conscious, political acts of a body of men' and the 'absence of thought and will in a body with a thousand automatically moving hands and legs'. It is not in imitating the 'old habits of obedience and servility' inculcated by the division of labour, bureaucracy and army but in tearing them up root and branch that the workers will come to grasp 'the freely assumed self-discipline of the Social-Democracy'.[70] Reliance upon two procedures or 'principles', according to Luxemburg, enabled Lenin to replace social-democratic centralism with conspiratorial centralism and transpose the latter mechanically onto the working-class movement. First, an 'air-tight partition', suggesting the Menshevik caricature of Lenin's definition of party membership, is erected 'between the class-conscious nucleus of the proletariat already in the party and its immediate popular environment, the nonparty sections of the proletariat'; there follows the 'blind subordination, in the smallest detail, of all party organs, to the party center, which alone thinks, guides, and decides for all'. Subjected to organisational automatism, the self-activity and the consciousness of the working-class movement are eviscerated; organisation is severed from the mass struggle, form from substance.

'The unconscious comes before the conscious' and the 'directing organs of the socialist party [tend] to play a conservative role', merely preserving the conquests already made by the movement but reluctant to venture into uncharted territory.[71] Since socialist consciousness, the substance of social-democratic self-centralism, arises only through the independent activity of the workers, the appropriate measure of centralism increases only as the working-class movement grows and develops. The opportunist danger to the movement posed by bourgeois intellectuals thrives under just the opposite conditions: where, as in Russia, 'the workers still lack cohesion', it seeks to impose 'a rigorous, despotic centralism' upon them; but where the party of labour is already strong, decentralisation represents its best chance to secure a foothold. Lenin's fetishistic anxiety about the form of organisation, conceived in abstraction from the historical phase of the class struggle, is not only an inadequate

---

69   Luxemburg 1904, pp. 119, 120.
70   Luxemburg 1904, pp. 119–20.
71   Luxemburg 1904, p. 121.

defence against opportunism but itself constitutes the opportunist danger. Thus, while stricter centralisation and party discipline would be appropriate for the mature German movement, in Russia the same policy would merely stifle the as-yet-untried self-activity of the workers.[72]

It is striking that, thus abstracted from its specific Russian context, what is essentially the same argument as that put by Axelrod, Martov and Trotsky loses remarkably little of its rhetorical force. Indeed, its logic is perhaps more easily discerned. Something like the Menshevik notion of proletarian hegemony resounds in Luxemburg's exaltation of the creative powers of the workers ('in the beginning was "the act"'), something inattentive readers have even confused with advocacy of a premature socialist revolution. In other contexts, notably in her analysis of the mass strike, the theme of self-activity might serve her as a means of calling conventional assumptions about the limits of working-class struggles into question. But in the present argument, the contrast she draws between Russian aspiration – her reference to the god-like powers required of the Social Democrats to form an organisation *ex nihilo* – and German experience suggests that the creative powers of proletarian self-activity do not transcend the unilinear historical logic of orthodox Marxism and, hence, that the Social Democratic claim to hegemony in the impending Russian Revolution is implicitly waived. The definition of available alternatives is subordinated in Luxemburg's argument to a concern about the conception of agency required to grasp the relation between the end of socialist revolution and the appropriate means thereto: is revolutionary activity to be conceived, according to the view she attributes to Lenin, in mechanistic terms, such that the relation between means and the end is an external, technical and hence merely contingent one? Or is socialist activity essentially 'organic', self-conscious, such that the end must be implicit in, prefigured by, the means employed? To pose the issue in this way, however, as a choice between mutually exclusive alternatives, is to spirit away the relation between 'organic' self-activity and the 'mechanistic' circumstances in which it must unfold.

Lenin and the Logic of Factional Struggle

The very form of Lenin's rejoinder might seem to confirm the charge that Bolshevism was predicated on a pettily formalistic understanding of the role of organisation in the class struggle. His major statement, *One Step Forward, Two Steps Back*, took the form of a narrative history of the controversies and

---

72   Luxemburg 1904, pp. 126, 127.

decisions of the Second Congress, complete with painstaking analysis of voting patterns, designed to bolster the contention that the Mensheviks' refusal to work with the central party institutions violated party decisions and subverted the very principle of party, as distinct from mere circle, organisation. He would later complain that Luxemburg, following suit with the Mensheviks, 'puts in my mouth commonplaces, general principles and conceptions, absolute truths, and tries to pass over the relative truths, pertaining to perfectly definite facts, with which alone I operate'.[73] His preoccupation with form, precedent and the facts of the case – to the apparent detriment of the political content at issue – might seem to betoken a narrowly formalistic perspective. I will argue, on the contrary, that this optic, permitting him to locate his opponents' criticism in relation to a strategic logic of the political struggle as it developed during and after the Congress, enabled Lenin not simply to condemn their political conduct but to controvert the substance and the method of the Menshevik critique. The premises of this critique were not just dismissed as erroneous. Such notions as proletarian self-activity and the priority of political content over organisational form were, he concurred, the ABC of Marxism. Considered as a guide to the concrete political situation confronting the Russian Marxists, however, they were lamentably, even dangerously, abstract. In the context of Lenin's 'relative truths, pertaining to perfectly definite facts', the political and theoretical significance of the Mensheviks' 'general principles and conceptions' would be decisively transformed.

Each party to the controversy thus contrasted the abstraction of the opposing position unfavourably with its own attentiveness to the concrete. The connotations at work in each case were not unrelated, but they were quite distinct and even opposed. When the Mensheviks and Luxemburg argue that the Leninist project of distinguishing an organised vanguard party from the working class itself merely stifles the self-activity of the workers and thus perpetuates the abstract character of Russian Social Democracy, the 'abstract' designates the merely nominal, the formal, the insubstantial, the theoretical and the 'concrete', conversely, the real, the effective, the substantial, the practical. The abstract indicates an aim, an intention to be 'realised'; the concrete is the 'realisation' of the abstract aim through the medium of the increasingly self-conscious activity of the proletariat. Since the concrete end is thus implicit in the abstract aim, the accusation of abstraction bears the implication of hypocrisy, betrayal and manipulation.

In his controversies with the Economists and now with the Mensheviks, however, Lenin's criticism of their abstraction was typically directed at an

---

73   Lenin 1904b, p. 477.

alleged failure to modify theoretical analysis or political stance to take into account some new, or newly important, aspect of the conjuncture. To invoke the concrete, in this context, was to call for clarity and precision, for determinate analysis that would guide specific action. But the dialectical assertion that the truth is concrete was not simply an injunction to subordinate abstract rules to the concrete case, for the very efficacy and truth of an analysis that had served hitherto as a concrete guide to action might help to bring about circumstances that would now render it abstract. Lenin's dialectical orientation to the concrete also expressed, therefore, an imperative to criticise and to modify the concrete analyses of yesterday in conformity with the social and political struggles of today. It is not enough to qualify an analysis as abstract or concrete; one must also assess *how concrete* it is. The concreteness of an analysis is thus itself a relative magnitude and one that may be transformed, either unconsciously as it is outrun by developments or consciously through the cognitive appropriation of the new or the hitherto unknown.[74] The appropriate determinations may be specified in accordance with the politico-strategic logic that serves to situate political struggles in the context of the social and political order considered as a whole.

No aspect of the socio-political totality was immune to seizure in the strategic sights of an adversary; hence none, especially not internal disagreements in the Social Democratic camp, was beyond the reach of this logic of struggle. 'Without an analysis of the political groupings, without having a picture of the Congress as a struggle between definite shades, the divergence between us cannot be understood at all.'[75] Although not explicit in Lenin's analysis, the struggle for hegemony was implicit in the way he delineated the contending groups. The delegates were broken into a majority who adhered to the strategic and organisational perspective of *Iskra*, a minority consisting of those (the Bund and the Economists of *Rabochee delo*) who had consistently opposed *Iskra*, and the 'centre' or 'marsh', a variety of groups and individuals who, pursuing plans of their own, wavered between the opposing tendencies. The Congress may have altered the terms of struggle between tendencies but could not do away with the struggle itself: '[u]nder these circumstances, the Congress could not but become an *arena of struggle for the victory of the "Iskra" trend*',[76] that is, for the recognition of the strategic project of proletarian hegemony in the bourgeois-democratic revolution and its practical implementation through the agency of a Marxist vanguard party.

---

74   See Shandro 2001, pp. 216–20.
75   Lenin 1904a, p. 214.
76   Lenin 1904a, p. 211.

Lenin's survey of voting patterns was designed to show that *Iskra*'s opponents had, with considerable effect upon the unstable centre, urged derogation wherever possible from the centralism required for the authoritative implementation of Congress decisions. 'An issue had only to arise which did not quite come within the already established and customary pattern and which called for some independent application of Marx's theory ... and *Iskra*-ists who proved equal to the problems only made up three-fifths of the vote'.[77] Still, had the *Iskra* contingent held together, the consistent adoption of its perspective would have been assured. But Martov's definition of a party member, not coincidentally with the support of most of *Iskra*'s adversaries, yielded hostages to fortune; that is, it yielded scope for initiative to those, such as the Economists, whose demonstrated lack of initiative in working out an independent political position for the working-class movement would in effect have conceded the struggle for hegemony to the bourgeoisie. The Congress's adoption of this definition thus raised the spectre of a party unable to distinguish itself from, and therefore effectively subordinated to, the spontaneous movement. In itself the error was remediable, a mere chink in the party's armour that could be repaired, and Lenin sought to repair it by ensuring a working majority in the central institutions of the party for the most reliable activists. This move, 'a double knot to bind tight the pot broken by Martov',[78] put the strategic logic of the struggle for hegemony to work. The application of this logic to the incipient rift between 'hard' and 'soft' adherents of *Iskra* extended its practical reach into the councils of the Social Democratic Party itself.

The Mensheviks' refusal to cooperate with the central party institutions authorised by the Congress was tantamount to a refusal to recognise the authority of the Congress. Although justified as a democratic revolt against bureaucracy, it was in fact a revolt of 'aristocratic or intellectualist anarchism' against central authority and thus, on any reflective definition of the term, itself a perversion of democratic principle. It was a revival of the circle spirit and, once fitted out with an elaborate theoretical justification, it generalised the original mistake over party membership into 'a quasi-system of opportunist views on matters of organisation'.[79] In so doing, the Mensheviks breathed new life into the remnants of Economism: '[t]he philosophy of tail-ism', or, to recur to the terminology of Lenin's earlier polemic, of spontaneism, 'which

---

77 Lenin 1904a, p. 237.
78 Lenin 1904a, p. 299.
79 Lenin 1904a, p. 411.

flourished three years ago in questions of tactics, is being resurrected today in relation to questions of organisation'.[80]

Instead of addressing the specifics of the current controversy, the Mensheviks paraded an elaborate defence of such commonplace truths as the greater importance of the content of ideological struggle relative to its organisational form. The content of Social Democratic political practice had outgrown the Economism of the old circle days, argued Lenin, '[b]ut the form?... The lame and undeveloped character of the form makes any further development of the content impossible; it causes a shameful stagnation, leads to a waste of energy, to a serious discrepancy between word and deed'.[81] To counterpose content to form, practice to organisation, in the abstract was not simply to misconstrue the process of political struggle but to debate it as though from the outside, without situating oneself in relation to it: 'Does not this remind you very much of the character in the folk tale who, on seeing a funeral, cried, "Many happy returns of the day"?'[82] It was to mistake the very context of political debate. The point at issue, wrote Lenin, was 'whether our ideological struggle is to have forms *of a higher type* to clothe it, the forms of party organisation, binding on all, or the forms of the old disunity and the old circles'.[83] The higher organisational form, comprising a party organised by a central authority 'from the top down' and therefore clearly demarcated from the spontaneous movement of the working class, could only enhance the content of its political practice:

> precisely because there are differences in degree of consciousness and degree of activity, a distinction must be made in degree of proximity to the Party... [T]here can be no talk of throwing anyone overboard in the sense of preventing them from taking part in the movement. On the contrary, the stronger our Party organisations, consisting of *real* Social-Democrats, the less wavering and instability there is *within* the Party, the broader, more varied, richer, and more fruitful will be the Party's influence on the elements of the working-class *masses* surrounding it and guided by it.[84]

The idea of organising the party 'from the top down', that is, 'from the Party Congress to the individual Party organisations', did not proceed from an

---

80 Lenin 1904a, p. 388.
81 Lenin 1904a, p. 390.
82 Lenin 1904a, pp. 389–90.
83 Lenin 1904a, p. 388.
84 Lenin 1904a, p. 260.

assumption that rank-and-file party members were politically incompetent; it was meant, rather, to signal the need to hold the self-professed leadership of Russian Social Democracy accountable for the conduct of the Party. Despite its democratic resonance, Martov's alternative of building the Party 'from the bottom up' amounted in practice not to democracy, but to 'self-enrolment in the Party' and hence to an abdication of the responsibility of leadership. Lenin had already, in *What Is to Be Done?*, expressed confidence that the rank and file of the movement would understand and appreciate the need for specialised training of the leadership. Indeed, the division of labour correlative to centralised leadership was presented not as a politically neutral technique that could be efficiently substituted for the self-activity of the workers, but precisely as the most effective means, under the given circumstances of autocratic repression, to facilitate the conscious participation of the masses in the movement.[85] He now added that the workers could understand better than intellectuals the need for party discipline – the Mensheviks were guilty of a form of opportunism characteristic of intellectuals: 'Having gained some understanding of our programme and our tactics, the proletariat will not start justifying backwardness in organisation by arguing that the form is less important than the content'.[86] It was in this context, and not as a model of party organisation and discipline, that Lenin invoked the workers' experience of factory life, which taught them something intellectuals learned only with difficulty: to distinguish between 'the factory as a means of exploitation (discipline based on fear of starvation) and the factory as a means of organisation (discipline based on collective work united by the conditions of a technically highly developed form of production)', between discipline imposed mechanically from above and consciously assumed self-discipline.[87] Accordingly, he had already called for a thorough airing of the opposing points of view in the party press in order to enable the rank and file of the party to sort out the quarrels among the leaders. Only such open discussion could make it '*impossible* for the workers to cease to understand us; only then will our "general staff" really be backed by the *good* and *conscious* will of an army that follows and at the same time directs its general staff!'[88]

If the Menshevik approach to organisation abstracted from the play of opposing political tendencies in the working-class movement, the Menshevik tactical innovation of selecting the bourgeois opposition's protest campaign as

---

85 See Lenin 1904a, pp. 465–6, 469–70.
86 Lenin 1904a, p. 389.
87 Lenin 1904a, p. 391.
88 Lenin 1903c, p. 117.

the focal point of Social Democratic activity was an attempt to seize proletarian hegemony in abstraction from the strategic logic of the political struggle. The leading influence of working-class democrats first took the form of rousing the liberal democrats to political life; later, after liberalism took on a distinct public profile with the appearance of Struve's *Osvobozhdenie*, it had to assume the form of a persistent critique of the half-heartedness and inconsistency of liberal protests. Now, amidst a rising current of popular discontent, the government had conceded a measure of free speech to the *zemstvos*, though not to the workers. But without the forceful intervention of the working-class masses against the state, this measure would prove merely another ploy to divide and crush the opposition. The protests of the liberal opposition could be sustained through revolutionary struggle of the workers against absolutism, not vice versa:

> The bourgeois opposition is merely bourgeois and merely an opposition because it does not itself fight, because it has no programme of its own that it unconditionally upholds, because it stands between the actual combatants (the government and the revolutionary proletariat with its handful of intellectual supporters) and hopes to turn the outcome of this struggle to its own advantage.[89]

By concentrating the workers' political attention upon the institutions of the bourgeois opposition, the Mensheviks conceded the political initiative to the bourgeoisie – indeed, to the government itself – and effectively abdicated the struggle for hegemony. By the same token, rather than expanding the workers' consciousness to the full scope of the revolutionary struggle against the autocratic state, they restricted it to the constitutional charades of the liberal opposition. The independence of the proletariat is forged through its resistance to bourgeois attempts to divert and canalise its revolutionary struggle; the class consciousness of the proletariat cannot be conceived in abstraction from the strategic logic of the struggle for hegemony in the bourgeois-democratic revolution.

Two Orientations to Hegemony

In the course of the struggle between factions in the RSDLP, the ambiguities that ran through the notion of proletarian hegemony in the bourgeois-democratic

---

89 Lenin 1904c, p. 505.

revolution began to crystallise into distinct and opposing political and theoretical orientations. It was not simply, as Dan would write in his insightful history, that the problem occupying the Bolsheviks was the assertion of Social Democratic leadership of the armed uprising against Tsarism, while the problem for the Mensheviks was educating a workers' vanguard that could take over the leadership of the Social Democratic movement from the radical intelligentsia and thus secure the workers' class interests.[90] Sustaining this disagreement was the incommensurability of two ways of acting toward and thinking about the struggle for hegemony; what each side would construe as an exercise of proletarian hegemony appears, when evaluated according to the standards of the opposing side, as a forfeiture of hegemony.

The idea of proletarian self-activity was at the core of the Menshevik notion of hegemony and, as the selection of the opposition rather than the state as the focus of Social Democratic intervention attests, Menshevik politics consisted essentially in creating venues where the workers' self-activity might display itself. Through their self-activity – that is, in manifesting themselves directly as an autonomous presence in political life – the workers become conscious of their independent interests, of the essential connection between their class struggle and the goal of socialism, their historic mission. Consciousness figures here not as an attentiveness to and understanding of the circumstances in which one acts but as an awareness that, whatever the circumstances, one can act independently and effectively in one's interests; one has the capacity to determine and to effect one's own purposes; one is not a mere plaything of heteronomous circumstance. The workers' supreme expression of this capacity is socialism; hence their consciousness of this capacity is a prefiguration of socialism. There is thus an essential harmony between socialist consciousness and the working-class movement. On this assumption, Lenin's willingness not only to wage ideological warfare within the movement but also to press an advantage in this struggle by means of disciplinary measures and the authority of a Party Congress could not but appear as a bid by the revolutionary intelligentsia for ascendancy over the nascent workers' movement.

If the working-class movement could act with the unity of purpose of an individual, even a confused and fumbling individual, then organisational questions would properly be posed in instrumental or technical terms; the terms of the Menshevik critique of Lenin, substituting technique for politics, intellectuals for workers, means for the end, would clearly follow. If, however, the unity of the movement could not be assumed, then organisational questions would have to be understood, with Lenin, as inherently political.

---

90   Dan 1970, p. 260.

But the force of the Menshevik argument depends upon conflating two different senses of self-emancipation: individual and collective, individual self-activity and the autonomous movement of the workers as a class. It is not clear why a claim by bourgeois intellectuals to leadership in the workers' movement should pose a particular problem if self-emancipation is understood in individual terms; in those terms, an attempt by 'advanced workers' to assume the authority of the vanguard of the class should be no less repugnant. But if self-emancipation is to be understood as a collective process, the unity of the working class cannot simply be assumed – it must be forged and sustained through political struggle and embedded in determinate organisational forms and modes of decision-making that are always subject to political controversy. By conflating individual and collective self-emancipation, the unity of the working-class movement, achieved only through political struggle, can be made to appear as a unity of consciousness, an organic given. This conflation sustains and at the same time draws support from the Menshevik inclination to identify politics with facilitating the self-activity of the workers and thereby stimulating their class-consciousness – that is, with a kind of enlightened pedagogy.

Subordinating the struggle for hegemony to this pedagogical conception of self-activity, the Mensheviks were less and less able to operate as an independent, much less a leading, force in the arena of revolutionary politics. They never renounced their programmatic commitment to the idea of proletarian hegemony in the democratic revolution, invoking it in their literature and incorporating it in their political calculations.[91] But as the revolutionary upheaval of 1905 subsided, they felt increasingly constrained to align themselves behind the liberal bourgeoisie, the Kadets (Constitutional Democrats). In the political doldrums that followed, Menshevik activists, absorbed in the arduous daily struggle to organise trade unions, cooperative societies and other legal expressions of working-class self-activity, relegated the political struggle for hegemony, along with the illegal party organisation itself, to the background.[92] The equivocal character of their notion of proletarian self-activity rendered it protean, capable of assuming any form, from humble petitioning to the political general strike. Without deploying a strategic logic of the political struggle for hegemony, these forms of self-activity could not be situated in relation to the strategic projects of adversaries; the Mensheviks were consequently obliged to subordinate themselves to circumstances created by others. Though they could as easily adapt themselves to the more militant as to the more prosaic

---

91 Dan 1970, p. 262.
92 See Dan 1970, pp. 392–4.

forms of proletarian self-activity and would do so with some enthusiasm amidst the revolutionary mobilisation of 1905, the circumstances were powerfully shaped by the forces of economic and cultural backwardness and autocratic political repression – that is, by the historical imperatives of bourgeois revolution. In the absence of the tools to forge more concrete analyses of the political struggle in the bourgeois revolution, the substance of working-class self-activity could not serve to challenge the terms of the unilinear historical logic of Marxist orthodoxy. The Mensheviks had therefore in substance to concede the political struggle for proletarian hegemony.

This might not amount to such a damaging criticism had the Mensheviks been able in fact to organise a political forum in which to nurture proletarian self-activity. But this seems not to have been the case. According to David Lane's thorough empirical study of the RSDLP to 1907, Menshevik party organisations were no more democratic or proletarian in composition and actually less open than their Bolshevik counterparts.[93] The author of the most extensive biography of Rosa Luxemburg claims that, at the time she was taking Lenin to task for 'conspiratorial centralism', her Social Democracy of the Kingdom of Poland and Lithuania 'was in fact like a South American army – all generals and few soldiers'; her leadership of it differed from Bolshevik practice only because 'instead of controlling local organisations, she simply ignored them altogether'.[94] And in the pre-war years, as the working-class movement began to recover after a harsh period of counterrevolutionary repression, the workers and their organisations were drawn not to the professed champions of self-activity, but to the Bolsheviks.[95]

Lenin's approach to proletarian hegemony begins with the political struggle around state power whose strategic logic, although grounded upon the antagonism of class interests, further prescribes that contenders try to define the context for the actions and consciousness of other parties to the struggle. Hegemony involves seizing and maintaining the initiative in the political struggle, where the initiative consists in imposing in practice a definition of the object of struggle in terms of the independent interests of a class. Since all parties can be expected to innovate in pursuit of their own interests, the logic of their struggle is relatively open-ended and what is required in order to assert hegemony can be expected to change in the course of the struggle. The indispensable condition of proletarian hegemony is the political ability to act independently as a class and hence, if Lenin was right, an organised

---

93 Lane 1969, p. 215.
94 Nettl 1966, vol. I, pp. 275, 288.
95 Getzler 1967, pp. 134–5.

vanguard informed by Marxist theory and capable of diagnosing and acting upon significant movements in the logic of struggle. Since these movements would certainly reflect the intervention of adversarial class projects and could not fail to call into question the relation between Marxist theory, the Social Democratic Party and the spontaneous working-class movement, the Marxist vanguard party could no longer be conceived as representing the resolution of the essential contradictions of the historical process. It would have to be seen, instead, as a guide to action, organising the independent political intervention of the working class within a complex and shifting web of interrelated contradictions. What type and what locus of activity might properly be characterised as proletarian self-activity could only be determined in the context of a concrete analysis, informed by the politico-strategic logic of the struggle for hegemony, of a concrete situation. Considered in abstraction from such an analysis, even such an eminently orthodox concept as 'proletarian self-activity' was of indeterminate political bearing. Arguably, too, conceived thus abstractly, self-activity was necessarily misconceived because autonomy cannot be achieved, nor the awareness of it attained, except by grappling with the given circumstances. Self-activity cannot become an end in itself except in and through the pursuit of more concrete, proximate aims; it is, then, as Jon Elster has argued, essentially a by-product.[96] To press such an abstraction into service as a barometer of political action was unwarranted in theory and ingenuous in practice. To urge it against the organisation of the Marxist vanguard was to decry the very possibility of strategic initiative in the political struggle; it was to abdicate the struggle for hegemony. In political reality, proletarian self-emancipation could only be grasped concretely in terms of the logic of the struggle for hegemony, hence as an essentially collective process articulated in relation to determinate organisational forms.

From Orientation to Revolution

In subordinating the assumption of harmony between Marxist theory and the spontaneous development of the working-class movement to a dialectic of political struggle, the politico-strategic logic of the struggle for hegemony introduced a breach into the unilinear historical logic of Marxist orthodoxy. This breach forged an opening – the possibility of a more concrete mode of political analysis and, consequently, of a more dynamic relation between the logic of class struggle and the practice of political intervention in determinate

---

96   See Elster 1983, pp. 86–100.

conjunctures. Lenin had not replaced one integral historical conception with another, nor had he abandoned the historical materialist claims of orthodox Marxism. What he had done, rather, was to disarticulate some of the theoretical elements of orthodoxy and thereby forge a certain critical distance within it. This enabled him to fabricate new analytical tools and to adopt a more hands-on stance in practice. The result was not a new theoretical system but a new political and methodological relation to the extant system, bearing the possibility of its progressive reorganisation and transformation. The central claims of historical materialism would now function as raw materials in political analysis. The Social Democratic Party and Marxist theory would no longer serve to knit them into a closed system but would function, instead, as instruments to work the raw materials up and transform them in light of the requirements of concrete conjunctures. Theory no longer supplies its own principle of unity; the unity of theory would have to be established and re-established in practice. If the metaphor of reflection – social consciousness reflects social being – had served to affirm the harmony and synchrony of the objective and subjective aspects of the class struggle, it might now designate a process of critical re-evaluation and a practice of transformation.

This breach in the logic of Marxist orthodoxy emerged under the pressure of a conjuncture of crisis in the strategic project of proletarian hegemony in the bourgeois-democratic revolution. But the mere opening of a conceptual space represented by the politico-strategic logic of the struggle for hegemony could not, in itself, resolve the antinomies of this project. Lenin's approach to proletarian hegemony, although innovative and full of possibility, still did not elaborate a coherent account in historical materialist terms. The problem of hegemony was posed in terms of the logic of political struggle as it unfolds around the state power, but the range of this struggle was narrowly portrayed. Thus, asked how the class character of the movement would be expressed if the Social Democrats undertook to organise the systematic political exposure of the autocracy, Lenin replied,

> [W]e social-democrats will organise these nation-wide exposures; all questions raised by the agitation will be explained in a consistently social-democratic spirit, without any concessions to deliberate or unintended distortions of Marxism; the all-round political agitation will be conducted by a party which unites into one unbreakable whole the assault on the government in the name of the entire people; the revolutionary training of the proletariat, and the safeguarding of its political independence; the guidance of the economic struggle of the working class, and

the utilisation of all its spontaneous conflicts with its exploiters which rouse and bring into our camp increasing numbers of the proletariat.[97]

The drawing power exerted by the vanguard of the democratic revolution upon non-proletarian social strata – 'in order to become the vanguard, we must attract other classes'[98] – was to be combined in a single organisation with the political education of the workers. But the movement of the contradictory social forces comprising 'the entire people' is consistent with 'one unbreakable whole' only in rhetoric. The organisational cast of the response is inadequate to the terms of the problem: even if a Marxist vanguard organisation did seize the initiative in the democratic revolution, how could this initiative mould the work of the revolution durably, in conformity with the independent interests of the working class? Elaborating a coherent foundation in historical materialism for the political project of proletarian hegemony would have to take into account the full diversity of the social forces at work in the bourgeois-democratic revolution, to differentiate between the effect of peasant and liberal intellectual, oppressed national and disenchanted noble, upon the process of socio-political transformation and to explain how the independent class interests of the workers could so deeply shape the course of the bourgeois revolution that they might endure under the rule of a bourgeoisie already only too eager to compromise with the forces of Tsarism. The advent of a Marxist vanguard organisation capable of strategic initiative in the struggle for hegemony did not yet plumb the socioeconomic depths of the problem.

Lenin's mode of political analysis was inextricably bound up with the hegemonic political project of Russian Social Democracy; it could not be neatly separated from the concrete analyses in which it was set to work. If the range of his political analyses was restricted, this is comprehensible in terms of the fact that oppositional politics was still very largely the preserve of the underground, where an apparently personal matter such as the split between Peter Struve and the editors of *Iskra* could be understood – and under the circumstances, rightly understood – as an event of major political importance, representing relations between social classes. But the very terms that Lenin used to distance himself from the reassuring harmonies of the logic of orthodoxy were also marked by the latter. *What Is to Be Done?* conceived the spontaneous movement of the working class as a contradictory unity of proletarian

---

97 Lenin 1902, p. 432.
98 Lenin 1902, p. 431.

experience and the ideological influence of the bourgeoisie, but expressed the relation of proletarian experience to revolutionary socialism only as *receptiveness* to the established truths of Marxist theory,[99] not yet as the site of a capacity for creative innovation. In *One Step Forward, Two Steps Back*, Lenin insisted that Marxism develops in the course of struggle – but at the same time he portrayed the struggle as pertaining to the more-or-less-consistent application of a given theoretical and political position; he did not see himself as a locus of innovation. It was as though the history of Marxist theory were governed by an essentially internal logic. That Lenin should have cloaked the factional struggle in the Hegelian negation of the negation – 'not only do oats grow according to Hegel, but the Russian Social-Democrats war among themselves according to Hegel'[100] – is strangely appropriate; if everything happens in the realm of ideas, then nothing essentially new can take place. Expressing the logic of the class struggle in a complex and shifting politico-strategic field of contradictions, Lenin's thesis of consciousness from without performed a critical and materialist role in the development of Marxist political thought. But Marxist theory was located at the margins of this field rather than in its midst; it acted but was not acted upon. The thesis of consciousness from without was not, therefore, a sufficient condition for absorbing the creative energies of the spontaneous movement and using them to fuel the reorganisation of Marxist theory required to ground the project of proletarian hegemony, but it was, as previously argued, a necessary condition. Pious genuflection before the self-activity of the proletariat could never generate a coherent historical materialist foundation for the hegemony of the working class. Only through sober recognition of the real contradiction between Marxism and the spontaneous movement of the working class could the dialectic of their interpenetration be consciously enacted. This in turn would require that the incipient Leninist theory show itself able to learn from the masses.

---

99   Lenin 1902, p. 386n.
100 Lenin 1904a, p. 411.

CHAPTER 7

The Mechanics of Proletarian Hegemony: Solidarity in the Class Struggle

> Revolutions are festivals of the oppressed and exploited. At no other time are the masses of the people in a position to come forward so actively as creators of a new social order, as at a time of revolution... We shall be traitors... if we do not use this festive energy of the masses and their revolutionary ardour to wage a ruthless and self-sacrificing struggle for the direct and decisive path.
> – VLADIMIR LENIN[1]

∴

> Revolution teaches.
> – VLADIMIR LENIN[2]

∴

As one military defeat followed another in the Tsar's war with Japan, initial patriotic enthusiasm waned and gave way to a wave of disaffection from the regime. The liberal campaign for constitutional reform took on momentum; emboldened by the heady atmosphere of increasingly open political debate, the representatives of educated society were drawn to the democratic demand for universal, direct, free and equal suffrage.[3]

A more forceful movement for change was meanwhile quietly gestating in the working-class suburbs of the capital. Taking in contradictory advice from the 'police socialism' of Sergei Zubatov, from Social Democratic agitation and from the example of political 'spring' in liberal society, the workers began to articulate their grievances with political, even revolutionary, overtones. A minor dispute over unfair dismissal at the Putilov works in St. Petersburg erupted, as 1905 began, into strikes and protests across the city. The workers of

---

1 Lenin 1905m, p. 113.
2 Lenin 1905n, p. 146
3 See Galai 1973, pp. 232–6; Harcave 1965, pp. 52–60.

the capital, led by the enigmatic figure of Father Gapon, priest and labour organiser, Zubatovite police agent and sometime revolutionary,[4] resolved to petition the Tsar for measures to ease the hardships of life in the factory but also for freedom of speech, press and assembly, equality before the law, inviolability of the person, transfer of land to the people, separation of church and state, and responsibility of government ministers to the people.[5] Hundreds of thousands assembled peacefully under the banners of Tsar and Church to accompany Gapon to present the petition on 9 January. The demonstrators were charged by Cossack troops and those who reached the Winter Palace were fired upon; hundreds were killed or wounded.[6] At a stroke, 'Bloody Sunday' had shattered the workers' naïve faith in the Tsar; 'the revolutionary education of the proletariat', wrote Lenin, 'made more progress in one day than it could have made in months and years of drab, humdrum, wretched existence'.[7]

Throughout the empire, workers struck in solidarity with the victims of Bloody Sunday. Protest demonstrations and meetings were held everywhere, sometimes escalating into clashes with the authorities. Further repression was met with defiance, which in turn sustained the workers striking for wage increases and the right to organise; the strike wave spread. The autocracy was obliged to make concessions to popular representation, even if only for consultation. In the countryside rebellious peasants used the landlord's pasture and cut his timber illegally. Rent strikes broke out repeatedly. Here and there land-hungry peasants even set upon administrative offices and officials.[8] The authorities could no longer contain the situation; the revolution had begun.

The revolution would shift the ground upon which politics moved in Russia and Lenin's political thought would move with it, but the explosion of revolutionary energy onto the stage of open political activity would not render superfluous politico-strategic analysis of the struggle for hegemony in the bourgeois-democratic revolution. Indeed, the advent of revolution meant for Lenin that the logic of this struggle would be played out across a wider arena

---

4   For Gapon, see Sablinsky 1976, pp. 34–55, 292–322.
5   As Harcave writes, the petition was 'a strange mixture of monarchist, liberal, and socialist sentiments and goals' (1965, p. 80). Its authorship has been contested and has even been attributed (by Galai 1973, p. 239n) to Kuskova, but the thorough account in Sablinsky 1976 (especially pp. 132–8, 183–91) makes Gapon the author. The petition is reproduced in Sablinsky 1976, pp. 344–9.
6   See Sablinsky 1976, pp. 261–8.
7   Lenin 1905b, p. 97.
8   See Harcave 1963, pp. 99–109.

and with consequently greater intensity. Throughout the course of the revolution he would repeatedly claim confirmation for analyses laid out in *What Is to Be Done?* In the aftermath of Bloody Sunday, the 'revolutionary instinct' and 'spirit of solidarity' of the workers pushed them 'towards revolutionary Social-Democracy'. In fact, the 'spontaneous growth of the strike [movement] ... was far, far in advance of the planned participation ... of the organised Social-Democrats',[9] yet without the intervention of an organised social-democratic political leadership, the spontaneous revolutionary struggles of the working class would simply have lent 'a new lease of life' to the constitutional political project of the liberal bourgeoisie. Liberal public opinion, accustoming itself to the new balance of forces but desirous of limiting the working-class movement to the confines of this project, was busily extolling the fighting valour of the workers: '[T]he liberal bourgeoisie acknowledges the proletariat as hero *for the very reason* that this proletariat, though dealing a blow at Tsarism, is not yet strong enough, not yet Social-Democratic enough, to *win* for itself the kind of freedom *it* wants'.[10] The struggle for hegemony could no longer be regarded as a struggle for recognition of the proletariat as hero, as leader. It implied taking on the responsibilities of leadership and this would now require, first and foremost, the political and military organisation of armed uprising. To this end Lenin called for a dramatic expansion of party membership and inveighed against formalism and lack of initiative in its ranks:

> We must broaden the cadres of our army, we must advance them from peace strength to war strength, we must mobilise the reservists, recall the furloughed, and form new auxiliary corps, units, and services. We must not forget that in war we ... inevitably have to put up with less trained replacements, very often to replace officers with rank-and-file soldiers, and to speed up and simplify the promotion of soldiers to officers' rank.[11]

This preoccupation with the 'military-technical' details of armed insurrection drew predictable objections from Menshevik quarters, with Martov arguing that the essential thing was 'arming the people with the one irreplaceable weapon – [a sense of] the burning necessity of attacking the autocracy and of

---

9   Lenin 1905b, pp. 114, 117.
10 Lenin 1905d, p. 170. Lenin returned to this theme again and again, for example in 'The Proletariat and the Bourgeois Democrats', where he wrote that 'the bourgeois democrats are striving more than ever now to gain control of the working-class movement' (Lenin 1905g, p. 228).
11 Lenin 1905e, p. 217.

arming itself for that [purpose]'.¹² The theme of self-activity thus re-emerges in the guise of 'self-arming'. But, claims Lenin, 'the harder we strive to take full control of the conduct of the uprising, the greater will our share in the undertaking be, and ... the less will the influence of the anti-proletarian or non-proletarian democrats be';¹³ in abstracting the 'military-technical' side of things from the struggle for hegemony the Mensheviks 'evade a direct reply to the pressing questions of the day by repeating the word "class" over and over again' and thus provide a conduit for bourgeois hegemony in the working-class movement.¹⁴ The tone of the analysis may differ from that of *What Is to Be Done?*, but its logic is the same. The political struggle for hegemony in the democratic revolution was still to be fought out on the terrain of the spontaneous working-class movement and even in the councils of the vanguard party of the proletariat.

The logic of the struggle for hegemony, however, was not itself immutable. 'Undoubtedly', Lenin wrote, 'the revolution will teach us and will teach the masses of the people. But the question that now confronts a militant political party is: shall we be able to teach the revolution anything?'¹⁵ Lenin would learn something from the revolution and from the masses in the course of the revolution, but learning requires something more than exposure to new experience and opinion. Something new could be assimilated from the phenomena of revolution only because they were grasped in the context of a political project informed by a conceptual framework elaborate enough to respond to conjunctural variations in the revolutionary process and consequently capable of formulating the appropriate questions. To express the same point somewhat paradoxically, it was only because he was ready to teach the revolution something that he was able to learn from it what he did. The hegemony of a proletarian political project is *established only in struggle with the hegemonic project of an adversary*; insofar as the agency of the proletariat figures in the strategy of the adversary and the working-class movement is thus targeted, the spontaneous movement and even factional divergences among an aspiring vanguard

---

12 Cited in Dan 1970, p. 304.
13 Lenin 1905d, p. 173.
14 Lenin 1905c, p. 155. He contextualised this charge in the following terms: 'There are two kinds of independent activity. There is the independent activity of a proletariat possessed of revolutionary initiative, and there is the independent activity of a proletariat that is undeveloped and is held in leading strings: there is a consciously Social-Democratic independent activity, and there is a Zubatovist independent activity. And there are Social-Democrats who to this day contemplate with reverence the second kind of independent activity'. See also Lenin 1905f, p. 222.
15 Lenin 1905m, p. 18.

can enter into the logic of the struggle for hegemony. Now, extending his analyses of that logic so as to incorporate the experience of the revolutionary mass movements of workers and peasants, Lenin was able to work out a coherent historical materialist conception of proletarian hegemony. The movement of the peasantry enabled him to conceive hegemony as *embodied in a determinate alignment of heterogeneous social forces*, with the implication that the exercise of hegemony involves *acknowledging the distinct character and encouraging the initiative of subaltern forces*. To accommodate theoretically the unexpected sweep of the peasant movement, he was led to reformulate his account of capitalist development in rural Russia to reflect the *imprint of the struggle for hegemony in the socio-economic structure itself*. The initiative of the workers' movement in establishing organs of revolutionary power – soviets – enabled him to grasp how hegemony is exercised not only through the coercion of arms and the persuasiveness of agitation and propaganda but also *through the very forms of social and political organisation that structure the material possibilities for cooperation and conflict, alliance and fragmentation*, encouraging some and inhibiting others, and thereby also structuring the way these possibilities are perceived.

In thus drawing upon the experience of the spontaneous movements of the workers and peasants to hammer out a coherent Marxist conception of proletarian hegemony in the bourgeois-democratic revolution, the movement of consciousness, in the event, the movement of Lenin's thought in relation to his political practice must itself be understood as an aspect of the struggle for hegemony. Accordingly, in tracing the evolution of Lenin's orientation toward a proletarian-peasant alliance and the corresponding movement of his analyses of the agrarian question, I will criticise the widespread view that this alliance – and consequently Leninist strategy in 1905–7 – follows directly from the analysis of the development of capitalism in Russia he worked out during the previous decade.[16] The author of the most thorough exposition of this view, Neil Harding, asserts that, for Lenin, the revolutionary events of 1905–6 were 'but history's realization of the prognostications of prior theory... only to be understood as manifestations of underlying trends whose basic direction theory had long previously discerned'. Both before and during the revolution, his writings exhibited 'an almost unbelievably dogmatic prediction and appraisal of the way things *must* turn out'.[17] Indeed, in a later book Harding would attribute 'a philosophy of certainty' to Lenin – and, indeed, to Marxism – in virtue of the overweening project of reshaping the

---

16 See, for example, Lefebvre 1957, p. 248; Hill 1971, pp. 69–73; Bettleheim 1974, p. 100.
17 Harding 1977, p. 248.

world according to the dictates of theory.[18] Harding accurately renders Lenin's analysis of capitalist development in terms of 'an almost Aristotelian teleology' (in my terms, the unilinear historical logic of Marxist orthodoxy) but he doesn't see that the proletarian-peasant alliance simply isn't given with that analysis; the alliance and the strategy of hegemony would have to be constructed, politically and theoretically. In an essential movement that escapes Harding's reading, the 'almost Aristotelian teleology' would have to be subordinated to the politico-strategic logic of the struggle for hegemony and thereby reworked so as to accommodate the lessons of revolutionary practice.

For the same reason, in tracing the movement of Lenin's orientation toward the spontaneous working-class movement and its invention of the soviets, I criticise the common interpretive procedure of more or less systematically contrasting the Lenin of the mass democratic revolution of 1905 to the prerevolutionary party politician of *What Is to Be Done?*[19] Perhaps the foremost practitioner of this method, Marcel Liebman, has portrayed 1905 as 'Lenin's first revolt ... against Leninism'.[20] Captivated by the spontaneity of the proletariat, Lenin, Liebman claims, would now discard his previous distrust for the spontaneous working-class movement. His calls for a thoroughgoing democratisation of the RSDLP are supposed to belie his earlier 'elitist conception of the party'.[21] Reliance upon professional revolutionaries from the intelligentsia is said to give way to enthusiasm for the influx of revolutionary workers into the party as a tonic to relieve the bureaucratic lethargy of the committee. Whereas intervention on behalf of centralised control from above had seemed so essential in the underground, in the light of revolutionary reality Lenin would make himself the spokesman for creative initiative from below. The previous supposition that revolution 'must necessarily be the work of a vanguard group rather than a mass party' would now be replaced by recognition of the soviets, broad organisations of the power of the working masses, as vital centres of revolutionary activity.[22] Thus was 1905 'a revolution that shook a doctrine'.[23]

This procedure, abstracting spontaneity and consciousness, workers and intellectuals, democracy and centralism, party and class, and so on from the context of Lenin's orientation to the strategic problems of the revolution, is not well designed to grasp the movement of his thought. Thus abstracted, these

---

18 See Harding 1996, pp. 219–42.
19 See, for example, Carlo 1973; Menashe 1975.
20 Liebman 1970, p. 73.
21 Liebman 1975, p. 29.
22 See Liebman 1975, pp. 29–31.
23 Liebman 1970.

concepts no longer occupy a determinate place in Lenin's Marxist project of grasping theoretically, so as to transform politically, the complex and shifting constellation of class forces; they figure, instead, as a set of essentially moral distinctions, each of whose terms represents a contrasting value, repeated shifting of emphasis between them serving merely to enact the drama of a soul torn between the demands of conflicting political moralities. To the extent that this procedure draws upon the conventional caricature of *What Is to Be Done?*, its bases have already been undermined. Here, by situating the movement of Lenin's thought in the context of the politico-strategic logic of the struggle for hegemony, it becomes possible to show just what it was that he learned from the spontaneous movement of the working class and so render the Liebman approach dispensable. By incorporating the experience of the spontaneous revolutionary movements of the workers and peasants into his analyses of the logic of the struggle for hegemony, Lenin would work out a Marxist conception of proletarian hegemony in the bourgeois-democratic revolution. In so doing he would come to grasp his own Marxism reflexively, as itself situated in the midst of the struggle for hegemony, and thus rectify his account of the relation of spontaneity and consciousness. He would do so not because he had abdicated the thesis of consciousness from without, but precisely because he was able to pursue its logic to further conclusions and thereby develop it.

An Alliance of Workers and Peasants

In 'The Workers' Party and the Peasantry', written in 1901 and described by a populist writer as 'a landmark in the evolution of Marxist views on the rural masses',[24] Lenin distinguished between 'two kinds of class antagonism exist[ing] side by side' in the Russian village, 'the antagonism between the agricultural workers and the proprietors' and that 'between the peasantry as a whole and the landlord class as a whole'. The former, although 'becoming more acute', lay in the future, while the latter, 'gradually diminishing', already belonged largely to the past.[25] Yet the antagonism between landlords and peasantry was of greater practical significance for the present: the agricultural labourers 'are still too closely connected with the peasantry... still too heavily burdened with the misfortunes of the peasantry as a whole to enable [their] movement... to assume national significance, either now or in the immediate

---

24   See Treadgold 1976, p. 79.
25   Lenin 1901a, p. 423.

future'.²⁶ Implicit in this analysis was the possibility of a revolutionary movement of the peasantry as a whole. But as yet it was only implicit and only a possibility, not yet a reality and perhaps not even a probability. And a possible alliance with the peasantry was not yet counterposed to other potential alliances, notably with the bourgeois opposition; indeed, during the *Iskra* period, Lenin devoted much more attention to the latter than to the former. Even after a wave of peasant unrest swept across the south of Russia from the Ukraine to the Urals in 1902, he reserved his judgment: '[W]e cannot ... say in advance whether, when the revolution awakens them to political life, our land-holding peasants will come out as a democratic revolutionary party or as a party of Order'.²⁷ This reserve was expressed in the agrarian programme of the RSDLP, drawn up by Lenin and adopted at the Second Congress, in which figured prominently a demand for the return of the 'cut-off lands' [*otrezki*], lands expropriated from the peasants in 1861 as part of the payment exacted for their legal emancipation. Criticised at the Congress as both meagre and impractical, this demand did not reflect concerns about the propriety of peasant land seizures, but doubts about the revolutionary capacity of the peasants.²⁸

The same reserve characterised Lenin's initial reaction to the peasant movement in 1905. From its inception, the peasant movement left the mere *otrezki* in its dust. 'All land to the people!' So spoke a Ukrainian peasant sailor, Matinishenko, expressing his impatience with the *otrezki* proposal while visiting Lenin with Father Gapon.²⁹ Lenin reiterated the claim that the solidarity of the peasantry as a whole would surely exhaust itself in the demand for the return of the cut-off lands, beyond which antagonism would flare up between the rural proletariat and the incipient peasant bourgeoisie. But wishing to avoid anything that might appear to constrain the revolutionary initiative of the peasant movement, he urged the replacement of the *otrezki* demand in the party programme with a more adaptable, open-ended call for the formation of revolutionary peasant committees that could set about dismantling the remnants of serfdom and reorganising rural society along democratic lines.³⁰ For the same reason, he rejected agitation for nationalisation of the land, although this was the most far-reaching measure of agrarian reform consistent with capitalism. A call to nationalise the land could not serve to focus the revolutionary struggle for democracy, 'for it does not place the stress on the peasants'

---

26   Lenin 1901a, p. 424.
27   Lenin 1903a, pp. 444–5.
28   See RSDLP 1904, pp. 249–95.
29   Krupskaya 1930, p. 110.
30   Lenin 1905i, pp. 247, 248.

relations to the landlords (the peasants take the land of the landlords) but on the landlords' relations to the state'.[31] Lenin was evidently still labouring under the impression that the peasants did not yet grasp their 'relations to the landlords'. Only after the breadth and resilience of their movement had demonstrated the contrary would he revisit the issue of nationalisation in light of the peasants' relation to the state.

Only after he had examined, through the optic of the struggle for hegemony, how the 'two kinds of class antagonism' intersected to shape the terrain of the bourgeois-democratic revolution could Lenin assign the peasantry a determinate position in the strategic matrix of the political struggle. The results of this examination were spelled out, characteristically, through a critique of the hegemonic posture of the Mensheviks, most fully in *Two Tactics of Social-Democracy in the Democratic Revolution*. The Mensheviks expressed the same reservations about participation in a provisional revolutionary government as they had about organising armed insurrection. So as not to '[tie] its hands in the struggle with the inconsistent, self-seeking policies of bourgeois parties and not allow ... itself to become merged in bourgeois democracy', the RSDLP should eschew the responsibilities of governmental office and 'remain a party of extreme revolutionary opposition'.[32] In thus asserting the political independence of the proletariat, the party would be in a position to bring pressure to bear upon the parties of the bourgeoisie for a 'decisive victory of the revolution'; in this sense the Mensheviks, although increasingly reticent about it, continued to advocate a hegemonic role for the working class.[33]

The danger to the political autonomy of the working class did not lie, according to Lenin, 'in the formal stand which Social-Democracy will take in the struggle, but in the material outcome of the entire present revolutionary struggle'; if Social Democracy was unable, despite its distinct organisation, 'to place the imprint of its proletarian independence on the course of events ... in the last analysis, its "dissolution" in bourgeois democracy will nevertheless be a historical fact'.[34] Even the most thorough revolutionary transformation would not 'depart from the framework of the bourgeois, i.e., capitalist socio-economic system' or touch 'the foundations of capitalism ... without a series of intermediary stages of revolutionary development'.[35] It was nonetheless possible, within these limits, to distinguish between a form of 'democratic revolution ...

---

31 Lenin 1905q, p. 312; see Lenin 1905i, pp. 249–50.
32 See Ascher (ed.) 1976, pp. 57–8.
33 See Larsson 1970, pp. 339–45.
34 Lenin 1905m, p. 54.
35 Lenin 1905m, pp. 49, 56.

advantageous mainly to the big capitalist, the financial magnate, and the "enlightened landlord"' and 'a form advantageous to the peasant and the worker'.[36] In accordance with the predominance of one or the other form, as determined by 'the objective combination of the operation of the various social forces', Lenin counterposed 'two possible courses and two possible outcomes of the revolution in Russia'.[37]

For the big bourgeoisie and the landlords, factory owners and the fashionable 'society' that followed Struve's *Osvobozhdenie*, fettered by their private property and thus dependent upon the apparatuses of the state to repress those who were not thus fettered, it was advantageous that

> the necessary changes in the direction of bourgeois democracy...take place more slowly, more gradually, more cautiously, less resolutely, by means of reforms and not by means of revolution; [that] these changes spare the 'venerable' institutions of the serf-owning system (such as the monarchy) as much as possible; [that] these changes...develop as little as possible the independent revolutionary activity, initiative, and energy of the common people.[38]

It would be to the advantage of the working class and of the peasantry, by contrast, that these changes be accomplished in a revolutionary fashion without the 'delay, procrastination, the painfully slow decomposition of the putrid parts of the national organism' attendant upon the farrago of reform. The workers and peasants, who would 'suffer first of all and most of all from that putrefaction', would be better served by a revolutionary 'amputation'.[39] The workers were obliged by their very class position to wage a consistent struggle for democracy, while the peasantry's struggle against the old order in the countryside rendered it revolutionary and potentially a force for republican democracy.[40] The decisive victory of the revolution would necessitate an insurrection of 'the [armed] people, i.e., the proletariat and the peasantry', culminating in a provisional government with the will to employ the dictatorial measures required to break the counterrevolutionary resistance of the landlords and the big bourgeoisie, to ensure 'a radical redistribution of land in favour of the peasantry', to establish 'consistent and full democracy, including a republic', and to extirpate 'all the oppressive features of Asiatic bondage'

---

36   Lenin 1905m, p. 48.
37   Lenin 1905m, p. 55.
38   Lenin 1905m, pp. 50–1.
39   Lenin 1905m, p. 51.
40   Lenin 1905m, pp. 51–2.

in the factory as well as the countryside, so as to 'lay the foundation for a thorough improvement in the conditions of the workers' and to spread the spark of revolution into Europe.[41] Such a provisional government could only be a revolutionary-democratic dictatorship of the proletariat and the peasantry. Should the strength, the determination and the cohesion of the populardemocratic forces prove inadequate to the task, however, their revolutionary ferment would have served the liberal-monarchist bourgeoisie as a bargaining counter in its negotiations with Tsarism. The deal already assiduously sought by the Bulygins[42] and the Struves would be concluded with 'some form of representative assembly convened by the Tsar, one that could be called a constituent assembly only in derision ... a docked constitution, or, if the worse comes to the worst, even [with] a travesty of a constitution'.[43]

Social Democracy was inextricably implicated in a strategic matrix of political struggle organised around state power and structured by the struggle around these two possible forms of the bourgeois-democratic revolution. The struggle for hegemony was waged through the constitution and disaggregation of class alliances with the potential to determine the predominance of one form or the other in the course of the revolutionary transformation. This struggle was reflected within the working-class movement in the divergence between Bolsheviks and Mensheviks, and Lenin never failed to note the complementary positions adopted by the liberal *Osvobozhdenie* and the Menshevik new-*Iskra*,[44] not infrequently linking this alignment to the persistence of spontaneist (now styled 'tailist') themes in Menshevism.[45] The politics of Social

---

41   Lenin 1905m, pp. 56–7.
42   Alexander Bulygin, appointed Interior Minister in the aftermath of Bloody Sunday, was the author of a project for a state duma, a representative body to be elected on a narrow franchise and with a merely consultative mandate, as a sop to rising middle-class aspirations to political inclusion. The so-called Bulygin Duma never met; the project never came to fruition, a victim of the rising revolutionary tide.
43   Lenin 1905m, pp. 47, 58.
44   See Lenin 1905m, pp. 65–74, 115–22.
45   Lenin's critique of Menshevism is best grasped as a prolongation of his analysis of Economism under the new circumstances of the struggle for hegemony. He returned again and again to parallels – and filiations, making great play of the influence in Menshevik councils of the former Economist Martynov – between Economism and Menshevism, drawing analogy, for example, between the Economist notion of 'tactics as process' and the Menshevik approach to the process of revolution. Where the original 'theory of stages' envisaged passage from a struggle for rights to political agitation to political struggle (or, Lenin added heavy-handedly, from the ten-hour day to the nine-hour day to the eight-hour day), it had now been updated along the following lines: '1) the Tsar convenes a representative institution; 2) this institution "decides" under pressure of the "people" to set up a constituent assembly; 3) ... the Mensheviks have ... forgotten that the

Democracy are unthinkable, Lenin wrote, 'without marching, in certain cases, *side by side* with bourgeois democracy'. But where the tactics of the Bolsheviks enabled them to 'march side by side with the republican and revolutionary bourgeoisie, without merging with it', Menshevik tactics condemned them to 'march side by side with the *liberal and monarchist bourgeoisie*, without merging with it either'.[46] The Mensheviks' failure to distinguish between the two forms of the bourgeois-democratic revolution undermined their efforts to escape the political orbit of the liberal-monarchist bourgeoisie and allowed them to serve as a conduit for bourgeois influence in the working-class movement. The independence of the proletariat could be expressed only in and through a decisive victory over Tsarism and, consequently, only in fostering the spontaneous revolutionary movement of the peasantry and educating it to the political struggle for democracy:

> [T]o avoid finding itself with its hands tied in the struggle against the inconsistent bourgeois democracy the proletariat must be class-conscious enough and strong enough to rouse the peasantry to revolutionary consciousness, guide its assault, and *thereby* independently pursue the line of consistent proletarian democratism... If it is not strong enough for this the bourgeoisie will be at the head of the democratic revolution and will impart an inconsistent and self-seeking nature to it. Nothing but a revolutionary-democratic dictatorship of the proletariat and the peasantry can prevent this.[47]

---

revolutionary pressure of the people will meet with the counter-revolutionary pressure of Tsarism and that therefore the "decision" will remain unfulfilled or the issue will be decided after all by the victory or the defeat of a popular insurrection' (1905m, pp. 34–5). In neither case is the object of Lenin's criticism properly characterised in terms of specific forms of struggle; what he sought to deconstruct, rather, was an underlying political tendency in the working-class movement, crystallised in differing forms in accordance with the circumstances and identified though the politico-strategic logic of the struggle for hegemony. Thus he discerned in Menshevism a tendency to spontaneism, to a corporatist circumscription of proletarian horizons and, therefore, to the forfeiture of the strategic political initiative: 'Good marchers but poor leaders, they disparage the materialist conception of history by ignoring the active, leading and guiding part which can and must be played in history by parties that have realized the material prerequisites of a revolution and have placed themselves at the head of the progressive classes' (1905m, p. 44).

46 Lenin 1905m, p. 46.
47 Lenin 1905m, p. 60; emphasis added.

The hegemony of the proletariat was thus redefined in terms of the course and outcome of the revolution, made dependent upon an alliance with the peasantry and articulated with the factional struggle inside the RSDLP. This analysis brings together two ideas already separately present in Lenin's conceptual armoury. The politico-strategic logic of the struggle for hegemony is deployed to theorise the conjunction of the two distinct kinds of class antagonism underpinning the revolutionary process. This brings about a certain integration of the political and socioeconomic aspects of his analysis of the class struggle. Lenin was thereby able to specify the class content of the strategic matrix of political struggle and endow the idea of hegemony with more determinate political significance.

Class Alliance in Theory and Practice

It has often been assumed by commentators concerned to situate Lenin's political thought in the context of class analysis that the alliance of proletariat and peasantry was the political conclusion that followed from the analysis of the development of capitalism in Russia he had already worked out by the turn of the century. This claim has been argued at some length by Neil Harding, according to whose accurate account the 'dialectical teleology' that structured Lenin's early analysis of emergent capitalism enabled him to identify the worker in large-scale capitalist industry as the natural representative of all Russia's exploited: '"natural" in that his life situation was already that which the life situation of the other strata must become, "natural" in terms of an almost Aristotelian teleology where the developed and already realised characteristics of the proletarian life situation were but immanent in the life situation of the other exploited strata'.[48] I have already shown in relation to Kautsky and to the young Lenin that the implicit equation of the merely positional quality of being ahead of others with the activity of leading them simply papers over a theoretical gap. Here, however, what is noteworthy is the implication, properly drawn by Harding, that the exploited masses who were to follow the industrial proletarian must be accounted 'rural semi-proletarians who were part petty-bourgeois and part proletarian'. This imparts a very specific sense to the claim that Lenin's analysis of the development of capitalism in Russia 'led him directly to the unique potentialities of a proletarian-peasant alliance which he was to canvass so aggressively in 1905 and 1917'.[49] The alliance

---

48 Harding 1977, pp. 80, 104.
49 Harding 1977, p. 106.

in question is understood as a bloc of workers and *poor* peasants: '[O]nly the proletariat and the poor peasantry were wholeheartedly committed to the destruction of landlordism. The bourgeoisie would prevaricate, make concessions, but would ultimately side with the landlords'.[50]

Only the logic of Harding's argument as a whole, which requires a Lenin for whom the revolutionary events of 1905–6 'were but history's realisation of the prognostications of prior theory',[51] could suggest an alliance of the proletariat with the poor peasantry. He cites no evidence to back it up; what evidence there is – and there is a great deal of evidence – contradicts this interpretation comprehensively. Lenin's revolutionary strategy rested upon an alliance with the whole peasantry, not only with the poor peasants, and the logic of his political theory and practice is rendered opaque if this is not fully grasped.[52]

---

50 Harding 1977, p. 216.
51 Harding 1977, p. 248.
52 In his major statement, *Two Tactics of Social-Democracy in the Democratic Revolution*, Lenin saw fit to emphasise the following formulation of Social Democratic strategy in the revolution: 'The proletariat must carry the democratic revolution to completion, allying to itself the mass of the peasantry in order to crush the autocracy's resistance by force and paralyze the bourgeoisie's instability. The proletariat must accomplish the socialist revolution, allying to itself the mass of the semi-proletarian elements of the population, so as to crush the bourgeoisie's resistance by force and paralyze the instability of the peasantry and the petty-bourgeoisie' (1905m, p. 100). The revolutionary process is here construed with reference to the specific alignments and alliances of class forces in such a way that, had Lenin defined these forces as Harding says he did, he would in logic have had to reckon Russia's revolution socialist. The Menshevik writer Martynov in fact placed such a construction upon Lenin's strategic orientation at the outset of the revolution. Lenin's rejoinder accused Martynov of conflating the two distinct revolutionary periods by obscuring 'the diversity of wills of the various strata of the bourgeoisie which is just emancipating itself from absolutism' and, more specifically, overlooking 'the existence of that immense peasant and petty-bourgeois population which is capable of supporting the democratic revolution, but is at present incapable of supporting the socialist revolution' (Lenin 1905j, pp. 282–4). In the same article may be found a formulation that is as close as Lenin comes to something that might be reconciled with Harding's interpretation: '[I]t is not the proletariat alone, as distinct from the "bourgeoisie" ... but the "lower classes", which are the active motive force of every democratic revolution. These classes are the proletariat *plus* the scores of millions of urban and rural poor whose conditions of existence are petty-bourgeois' (1905j, p. 286). But confusing a descriptive reference to the poor with the analytical class concept of the poor peasantry is to be avoided and, as if to ward off just such confusion, Lenin immediately adds, 'Without a doubt, very many representatives of these masses belong to the bourgeoisie'. Harding's mistake is the exact converse of the one committed by those who understand the proletarian-peasant alliance more or less correctly but ascribe it erroneously to Lenin's works of the 1890s. For my

The peasantry, as Lenin defined the term, was a social estate encompassing the rural semi-proletariat, the peasant petty bourgeoisie (or middle peasants) and a nascent peasant bourgeoisie, and unified in the struggle against the institutions and practices of serfdom since the 'oppression of one social-estate by another can be destroyed only by the whole of the lower, oppressed estate'.[53] From his earliest response in March 1905 to the revolutionary actions of the peasantry, Lenin consistently advocated an alliance that included the peasant bourgeoisie. He eschewed any notion that *this* bourgeoisie would side with the landlords: though the independent organisation of the rural proletariat was always on the agenda of the Social Democrats, in the democratic revolution it was also incumbent upon them to act together 'with the peasant bourgeoisie against all manner of serfdom and against the serf-owning landlords'.[54] As land seizures and attacks upon landlords and officials spread and the peasant revolt intensified, this position was asserted with increasing confidence: 'The struggle against the bureaucrat and the landlord can and must be waged together with all peasants, even the well-to-do and middle peasants';[55] 'class-conscious socialists must unconditionally support the revolutionary struggle of all, even the prosperous, peasants against the officials and landowners'.[56]

That Lenin understood the peasant movement in this way indicates that the alignment of class forces in the democratic revolution was not to be read immediately from the current phase in the development of the capitalist mode of production, a procedure that would subsume diverse social strata in the simple polarisation between the proletariat and the bourgeoisie. The peasantry with which Lenin sought to cement a revolutionary alliance was no mere semi-proletarian tail of the industrial workers but a distinct social force, albeit one comprised of divergent elements and formed through a struggle specific to it.

> [I]t is not two contending forces that form the content of the revolution, but two distinct and different social wars: one waged within the present autocratic-feudal system, the other within the future bourgeois-democratic system, whose birth we are already witnessing ... An arduous and formidable task thus devolves on the socialists – to wage two wars

present purpose, a focus on Harding is more useful, since he proceeds from a more precise account of the point of origin of Lenin's theoretical development.

53   Lenin 1905i, p. 250.
54   Lenin 1905h, p. 233.
55   Lenin 1905t, p. 443.
56   Lenin 1905u, p. 177.

simultaneously, wars that are totally different in their nature, their aims, and the composition of the social forces capable of playing a decisive part in either of them.[57]

The alliance of workers and peasants was not founded upon an identity, even an immanent identity, of class interest but upon the combination of diverse and conflicting interests. The strategy of proletarian hegemony had to be deployed politically, and the alliance with the revolutionary-democratic peasantry constructed politically, around the conjunction of the 'two distinct and different social wars'. This alliance did not exemplify and therefore could not have followed from Lenin's early analysis of the development of capitalism in Russia. It could have been conceived only in response to the experience of the revolutionary peasant movement.

Indeed, Lenin would subsequently invoke that experience to justify the need to rectify both the analysis of capitalist development and the agrarian programme based on it. The distinction between the two forms of bourgeois-democratic revolution, in terms of which the worker-peasant alliance was articulated, was ungrounded in that analysis; in consequence, the political form of the distinction was more clearly delineated than its social and economic content. It would seem relatively straightforward to determine whether 'the necessary changes in the direction of bourgeois democracy' were carried out by worker and peasant or by bourgeois and landlord. The difference between a democratic republic and a liberal monarchy is definite; that between the organisation of an armed insurrection and the exertion of revolutionary pressure upon bourgeois negotiations with the Tsar, while perhaps difficult to judge in practice, is still clearly drawn. But what in Lenin's analysis of the development of capitalism in Russia could underpin the distinction between these political forms, and so lend it historical weight and resonance, is less apparent. In virtue of the unilinear historical logic running through this analysis, the 'necessary changes' in social relations were identified with the elimination of the 'remnants' of pre-capitalist relations, mere remnants playing no constitutive part in the dynamic of historical development; what thus differentiated the two forms of revolution was not the socioeconomic substance of the transformation but its political form and tempo. The strategic distinction between the two forms of revolution was not, therefore, situated in terms of historical materialism.

---

57   Lenin 1905q, pp. 307, 308.

Proletarian Hegemony and Historical Materialism

The comprehensive sweep and sheer resilience of the peasant movement led Lenin to reassess the depth of its roots, to revise his analysis of the social relations of the Russian countryside and to reformulate his agrarian programme accordingly. In so doing, he refined the idea of two paths of bourgeois-democratic revolution, relating it to the theory of capitalist development and thereby equipping the Marxist political project of proletarian hegemony, for the first time, with a solid historical materialist armature. The new analysis was first adumbrated in *Revision of the Agrarian Programme of the Workers' Party*, written for the Fourth (Unity) Congress of the RSDLP, held in April 1906. The peasant movement was given there as grounds for retracting the call for the return of the cut-off lands in favour of a more radical approach and for an implicit but unmistakable critique of his earlier analysis of the development of capitalism in Russia: 'Taken as a whole, the landed estate in Russia today rests on a system of feudal bondage rather than on the capitalist system. Those who deny this cannot explain the present breadth and depth of the revolutionary peasant movement in Russia'.[58]

The critique was made explicit the following year in *The Agrarian Programme of Social-Democracy in the First Russian Revolution, 1905–1907*, where Lenin attributed 'the mistake' of the earlier programme to the fact that,

> while we correctly defined the *trend* of development, we did not correctly define the *moment* of that development. We assumed that the elements of capitalist agriculture had already taken full shape in Russia, both in landlord farming (minus the cut-off lands and their conditions of bondage...) and in peasant farming, which seemed to have given rise to a strong peasant bourgeoisie and therefore to be incapable of bringing about a 'peasant agrarian revolution'... But the survivals of serfdom in the countryside have proved to be much stronger than we had thought: they have given rise to a nation-wide peasant movement and they have made *that* movement the touchstone of the bourgeois revolution as a whole. Hegemony in the bourgeois liberation movement, which revolutionary Social-Democracy always assigned to the proletariat, had to be defined more precisely as leadership that rallied the *peasantry* behind it. But leading to what? To the bourgeois revolution in its most consistent and decisive form. We rectified the mistake by substituting for the partial aim of combating the *survivals of the old* agrarian system, the aim of

---

58 Lenin 1906b, p. 177.

combating *the old agrarian system as a whole*. Instead of purging landlord economy, we set the aim of abolishing it.[59]

It had now become necessary, Lenin argued, to think the new estimate of the progress of agrarian capitalism through 'to its logical conclusion'. If the elements of capitalist agriculture were still only in formation and bourgeois landlord economy had not yet been consolidated, he reasoned, two types of agrarian capitalist evolution remained open: the 'American path', consisting in the free development of small peasant farming along capitalist lines, or the 'Prussian path', consisting in the gradual evolution of landlord estates into large-scale capitalist farms.[60] The two pertinent transitional forms – the formation of the bourgeois farmer through the differentiation of the peasantry and the passage of the landlord from feudal to capitalist economy – had already been distinguished in *The Development of Capitalism in Russia*.[61] They figured there, however, as mutually reinforcing elements of an integral process.[62] Only the experience of the peasant movement would lead Lenin to consider them as defining the lines of battle in a social war between landlord and peasant, as conflicting objectives in the strategic logic of political struggle, and therefore as opposing paths of socioeconomic development.[63] 'If the demand for the confiscation of all the landlord estates proved to be historically correct' – and this was just what the peasant movement demonstrated – then 'the beginnings of capitalism in landlord economy can and must be sacrificed to the wide and free development of capitalism on the basis of renovated small farming'.[64] Where the American path implied the radical demolition of all fetters upon capital, both the infrastructure of feudal bondage and oppression and the Tsarist state superstructure, the Prussian path signified the indefinite survival of the socioeconomic taproot of political reaction. The American path was

---

59   Lenin 1907d, pp. 291–2.
60   Lenin 1907d, p. 239.
61   Lenin 1899a, pp. 172–87, 191–251.
62   See Lenin 1899a, pp. 185–6, 207–8, 210.
63   In the course of the debate on the agrarian question at the Second Congress of the RSDLP, one of the delegates, Gorin, did draw a contrast between two 'methods' of transition from feudalism to capitalism, either direct or through petty proprietorship. He did not, however, draw any political implications from the contrast and if he exhibited any preference for one of the methods, it was for the former, roughly corresponding to Lenin's 'Prussian' path. He did not, in any case, envisage the distinction as a focus of social and political struggles (see RSDLP 1904, pp. 277–8). For Marx's discussion of the forms of transition to capitalist agriculture, see Marx 1894, pp. 782–813.
64   Lenin 1907d, p. 292.

the historical materialisation of *'narodnoye tvorchestvo* (the creative activity of the people)',[65] of the revolutionary-democratic dictatorship of the proletariat and the peasantry and of the hegemonic political project of Russian Marxism.

Citing a resolution of the Inaugural Congress of the All-Russian Peasant Union, Lenin asserted that the peasants, in the course of 'their struggle against the private ownership of the large estates ... necessarily arrive, and through their foremost representatives have already arrived, at the demand for the abolition of all private ownership of land in general'.[66] Judged in terms of his initial estimate of the development of agrarian capitalism, nationalisation of the land had seemed a mere paper project, a distraction from the class antagonism between peasant and landlord.[67] Thus, although insistent upon its progressive economic significance, Lenin had hitherto resisted its inclusion in the Social Democratic agrarian programme. But since the idea had now arisen spontaneously among the peasants themselves, from the very circumstances of small peasant ownership weighed down by medieval exactions, it had to be reckoned with not as an agrarian socialist utopia, but as an expression of the most radical aspirations of the bourgeois agrarian revolution. Indeed, without nationalisation of the land the bourgeois revolution could not triumph in Russia: in the struggle between the two paths of bourgeois revolution, it represented a radical 'clearing of the estates' by the peasantry so that relations corresponding to 'the conditions of free commercial agriculture' could be established.[68] Nationalisation of the land, Lenin claimed, was the measure that would give fullest effect to the American path; he could back the claim with the Marxist theory of capitalist ground rent.

Marx distinguished two forms of rent, differential and absolute.[69] Differential rent is based upon differences between better and worse soils in production and consists of the difference between the individual price of production on the better soils and the highest price of production on the worst soil. It arises inevitably in capitalist agriculture through the action of competition, whether the land is privately owned or not. Absolute rent, by contrast, arises through the monopolistic relation of private property in land. Capitalist

---

65 Lenin 1907d, p. 346.
66 Lenin 1906b, p. 180.
67 Lenin 1905i, pp. 249–50.
68 Lenin 1907d, p. 277.
69 See Marx 1894, pp. 614–781, especially 640–7 and 748–72. The theory of ground rent is also the subject of the greater part of Marx 1968. Lenin's discussion of Marx's theory, while polemical, is quite accurate; it also draws upon the account in Kautsky 1898, pp. 101–20.

agriculture is historically characterised by a lower organic composition of capital, lower productivity of labour, and hence a higher rate of surplus value than industry. The institution of private property in the land, however, constitutes a significant barrier to the free penetration of capital into agricultural production and effectively prevents agricultural capital from entering into the formation of the average rate of profit. The sale of agricultural products at a price above even the highest price of production is thereby possible, with the difference accruing to the landowner in the form of absolute rent. Tantamount to the abolition of absolute rent, nationalising the land would promote the application of capital to agriculture more consistently than any other measure: money capital that would otherwise be tied up in the purchase of land could be invested directly in production and the subjection of the peasant to usury capital would thus be eroded.[70]

Although nationalisation of the land corresponded to a definite phase of the peasant struggle against feudal landlordism, it was bound to come into contradiction with the desire in the emergent class of petty capitalist farmers for their own privileges of ownership. This contradiction, expressed in the farmers' demands for the restoration of private property and division of the land, would sap the worker-peasant alliance. Absent a socialist revolution in Europe, the requirements of capitalist development would at some point overcome all the influences counteracting the demand for restoration. Nationalisation would nonetheless have demonstrated enduring historical significance; in shattering the carapace of medieval social relations that weighed upon the Russian countryside, it would have established the most advantageous point of departure for the American path of agrarian capitalist development, and in helping to dislodge one form of private property the working class would have made its aspirations felt everywhere.[71] Lenin's analysis of the peasant struggle for nationalisation of the land thus vindicated in historical materialist terms not only the moral but also the material significance of the struggle for proletarian hegemony in the bourgeois-democratic revolution.

Proletarian Hegemony and Peasant Ideology

When Lenin incorporated nationalisation of the land into the agrarian programme he proposed to the Unity Congress, Plekhanov taunted him with the spectre of *Narodnaia volia*.[72] Along with the majority of delegates, Plekhanov

---

70 Lenin 1907d, pp. 295–316.
71 Lenin 1907d, pp. 323–5.
72 See Baron 1963, pp. 265–7; Lenin 1906d, pp. 283–4; Lenin 1906e, p. 331.

backed a Menshevik agrarian programme whose centrepiece was the notion of 'municipalisation', the transfer of the landed estates to 'organs of local self-government'. Isolated even among the Bolsheviks in espousing nationalisation, Lenin lent his vote to the 'divisionists' who advocated the formation of peasant committees and the seizure and division of the land by the peasants themselves: 'municipalisation is wrong and harmful; division is wrong but not harmful'.[73] Since the proposal for municipalisation did not designate the mode of agrarian transformation – it referred neither to peasant committees nor to the direct seizure of the land, and the transfer of land was not conditioned upon a democratic republic[74] – Lenin estimated that it amounted in practice to a call for transfer of the landed estates to the *zemstvos*, something the peasants would never accept. The prospect, stressed by Plekhanov, that municipalisation would constitute an institutional guarantee against counterrevolution was illusory, Lenin argued, for the only real guarantee would be a socialist revolution in the West, while the only guarantee within the power of the Russians themselves was the thoroughness of the revolutionary transformation 'effected by the revolutionary class directly'.[75] He would later buttress this argument with the trenchant observation that municipalisation, applied only to the

---

73 Lenin 1906d, p. 286.
74 See Ascher 1976, pp. 64–5.
75 Lenin 1906d, p. 281. Lenin repeatedly savaged as 'bureaucratic' any approach to the agrarian question that did not proceed from the formation of revolutionary peasant committees and the immediate seizure and disposition of all the landed estates by the peasants themselves, pending the convocation of a constituent assembly, and as 'utopian' any that did not arrive at the revolutionary-democratic dictatorship (see, for example, 1906b, pp. 190–2; 1906e, pp. 343–4; 1907d, pp. 355–8, 374–80): 'The standpoint of the police official and of the Russian liberal is: how to provide the *muzhik* with an allotment? The standpoint of the class-conscious worker is: how to free the *muzhik* from feudal landlordism? How to break up the feudal latifundia?' (1907d, p. 230). Harding is therefore mistaken in regarding nationalisation as 'the centre-piece of Lenin's strategy' during the period 1905 to 1907 (Harding 1977, p. 217), an error he could hardly have avoided given his more basic mistake as to the nature of the peasant movement. The centrepiece of Lenin's strategy was proletarian leadership of the revolutionary-democratic peasantry; the call for nationalisation would become a significant element in this strategy, but in isolation from the organisation of peasant committees – which goes unmentioned by Harding – it would have amounted to another bureaucratic utopia. Despite his estimate of the economically progressive character of nationalisation, Lenin rejected its use as a revolutionary slogan throughout 1905. Considered in abstraction from his re-evaluation of Russian peasant ideology, itself intimately bound up with his reassessment of rural social relations – which Harding does not mention and cannot accommodate – in light of the experience of the peasant movement, Lenin's reversal on this question is incomprehensible, as is the politico-strategic significance he would come to assign to nationalisation.

landed estates, would leave intact the existing demarcation between landlord and peasant lands, itself an integral element of the system of medieval land-ownership: '[I]t is necessary to "unfence" *all* the land, landlord as well as allotment land... The whole land must be "cleared" of all medieval lumber'.[76]

Agreed in their support for the formation of peasant committees and for the peasants' direct seizures of the landed estates, Lenin and the proponents of 'division' of the land diverged in their assessment of the potential latent in peasant ideology. For the 'divisionists', noteworthy among whom was the young Stalin, the decisive issue was working-class support for the legitimate and progressive demands of an ally in the revolutionary struggle: 'If the emancipation of the proletariat must be the act of the proletariat itself, then the emancipation of the peasants must be the act of the peasants themselves'.[77] Despite this appreciation of peasant self-activity, the 'divisionists' did not take the peasants at their word. But without taking them at their word, the divisionists were ill-equipped to recognise, and consequently to respond to, the political challenge of establishing a connection between the peasant agrarian revolution and the struggle for a democratic republic, the challenge of political leadership in the worker-peasant alliance.

'The peasant says: "The land is God's, the land is the people's, the land is nobody's"'.[78] This idea sustained the populist belief in the socialist propensities of the Russian peasants. According to Lenin, the 'divisionists' correctly diagnosed the material interest underlying it: peasant socialism was a matter of mere words. Talk about 'God's land' was the ideological expression of the peasants' desire to enlarge their small farms at the expense of the landed estates; behind the words, what they really wanted was the right to buy and sell land. '[T]he advocates of division *rightly* understand what the peasants say about nationalisation... [but] they do not know how to convert this correct

---

76   Lenin 1907d, p. 424. Harding is mistaken in characterising Lenin's proposal as the 'nationalisation of all the landlords' lands' (Harding 1977, p. 217). Along with the most politically articulate representatives of the peasant movement, who aimed to nationalise *all* the land, not only the landed estates, Lenin would doubtless have regarded such a proposal as another bureaucratic project: 'Not only is landlordism in Russia medieval, but so is the peasant allotment system... The *whole* system of medieval landownership must be broken up... The greatest possible facilities must be created for the exchange of holdings, for the free choice of settlements, for rounding off holdings, for the creation of new free associations instead of the rusty, tax-levying village communes' (Lenin 1907d, p. 424; see also pp. 317, 328–9, 423).
77   Stalin 1906, p. 240.
78   Lenin 1906d, p. 287.

interpretation into *an instrument for changing the world*.⁷⁹ Including division in the programme would leave Social Democratic activists in the anomalous position of trying to persuade crowds of peasants who insist that the land belongs to God, the people or nobody of the advantages of division, whereas including nationalisation would provide activists with the means to connect the agrarian demands of the peasantry with political education in favour of a republic.

> You say that everybody ought to have the right to use the land? You want to transfer the land to the people? Excellent! But what does transferring land to the people mean? Who controls the people's wealth and the people's property? The government officials, the Trepovs. Do you want to transfer the land to Trepov and the government officials? No. Every peasant will say that it is not to them that he wants to transfer the land ... Hence – we will explain to the peasants – if the land is to be transferred to the whole people in a way that will benefit the peasants, it is necessary to ensure that all government officials without exception are elected by the people.⁸⁰

The 'divisionist' approach to the peasantry relied upon the same sort of procedure that Lenin had employed in dissecting populist ideology into progressive (bourgeois-democratic) and reactionary (utopian-socialist) elements and advising its proponents to retain the former while eschewing the latter. Thus had Lenin encouraged the 'legal populists' of the *Narodnoe pravo* party to cast off the utopian-socialist verbiage in which they cloaked an essentially constitutional-democratic political project and to merge with the political representatives of the liberal bourgeoisie;⁸¹ this is just what the leading *Narodopravtsi* did, rallying to Struve's *Osvobozhdenie*.⁸²

Simply disregarding the utopian-socialist idiom of the peasant movement in favour of a diagnosis, even though ultimately correct, of its material interest in private property, the 'divisionists' were proceeding, albeit implicitly, in the same fashion. It was still necessary, in order to foster the independence of the agricultural proletariat and to appreciate the dynamic of the agrarian revolution, to distinguish the revolutionary-democratic force of the peasant conviction that 'the land should belong to the whole people' from its freight of

---

79 Lenin 1906e, p. 345.
80 Lenin 1906d, p. 287.
81 See Lenin 1894a, pp. 329–32.
82 See Galai 1973, pp. 192, 219.

utopian-socialist illusion. But since the idea, however illusory, had gripped the masses, the illusion was inextricably intertwined with the force; it was not possible, in practice, simply to dispense with it. Lenin would later cite Engels in this connection: 'What formally may be economically incorrect, may all the same be correct from the point of view of world history'.[83] The distinction between the two aspects of populist ideology could be transformed into 'an instrument for changing the world', but only on the condition that it not be reduced to a distinction between the emancipatory power of the truth and the chains of mere illusion. 'We must say [to the peasants]: there is a great deal of truth in what you say about the land being God's, nobody's or the state's; but we must look at the truth very closely'.[84] The politics of alliance with the peasants was no simple matter of acting upon their interests, correctly conceived, and leaving their illusions to the logic of spontaneity; it necessitated reckoning with illusion, though not as a mere token of respect, working with it as a condition of collective action and a function of political leadership.

Through the experience of the revolutionary movement of the peasantry, Lenin incorporated into the politico-strategic logic of the struggle for hegemony not only the war over the agrarian social structure, but even the ideology that actuated the peasant masses in that war. The peasantry would enter ubiquitously and in some respects quite intricately into his political calculations. This was exemplified when in the summer of 1905, in an effort to forestall demands for a constitution and pacify the revolutionary movement, the Tsarist government conceded a merely consultative assembly to be elected on a severely restricted property franchise, the projected Bulygin Duma. The liberal bourgeoisie responded in conciliatory fashion, but the liberal professions and the employees, grouped in 'the most comprehensive organisation of the bourgeois intelligentsia', the Union of Unions, decided upon a boycott of the Duma. In an effort to deepen the split between the liberal bourgeoisie and the bourgeois intelligentsia and thereby buttress the elements from which a political leadership of the revolutionary peasant movement might be drawn, Lenin urged support for the boycott idea and Social Democratic efforts to radicalise

---

[83] Cited at Lenin 1909b, p. 401. Lenin comments that 'the conditions of life of the Russian peasantry being what they are, its bourgeois-democratic revolutionary spirit could not be ideologically expressed otherwise than in the form of 'belief' in the sovereign virtue of land equalization... Our Mensheviks have never been able to understand these words of Engels. While exposing the *falsity* of the Narodnik *doctrine*, they closed their eyes like pedants to the *truth* of the contemporary struggle in the contemporary bourgeois revolution, which is expressed by these quasi-socialist doctrines'. See also Lenin 1912b, p. 357.

[84] Lenin 1906e, p. 345.

the boycott campaign. The bourgeois intelligentsia 'could become an important force in the struggle ... against the autocracy ... *provided it draws closer to the people* ... Powerless by itself, it could nonetheless give quite considerable sections of the petty bourgeoisie and the peasantry just what they lack – knowledge, programme, guidance, and organisation'.[85]

This analysis provided an early indication of a course of action Lenin would pursue consistently across the shifting conjunctures of the struggle for hegemony, at least until the world war: encouraging the formation of an independent political party of the peasantry and fostering, with advice and criticism, the emergence and radicalisation of a non-proletarian political leadership for the peasants.[86] It anticipated, and perhaps it suggested, the celebrated analysis of intellectuals and the peasantry in Gramsci's 'Some Aspects of the Southern Question'.[87] Recognising the autonomy of the peasant movement enabled Lenin to pursue apparently opposing modes of intervention in tandem: by subjecting peasant populism to historical materialist critique, he demonstrated its formal economic or utopian illusions and asserted a distinction between proletariat and peasantry; by encouraging the emergence of the peasantry as an independent, non-proletarian political force, he fuelled its world-historical truth – that is, its historically progressive illusions. '[E]xtract[ing] the sound and valuable kernel of the sincere, resolute, militant democracy of the peasant masses from the husk of [populist] utopias'[88] proved no simple operation, either in theory or in political practice.

'Permanent Revolution'

Lenin was not the only Marxist seeking to learn something from the revolution. The spontaneous surge of working-class struggles, mass strike activity punctuated by the formation of soviets, vortices of oppositional innovation whose very existence constituted a challenge to the authority of the state, prodded Russian Marxists, especially outside Bolshevik ranks – as well as SPD members like Parvus, Kautsky and Luxemburg, who took an interest in Russian affairs – to question and try to rethink a number of the assumptions and

---

85   Lenin 1905o, pp. 214, 215.
86   That the struggle for proletarian hegemony should have embraced the constitution of an independent political party of the peasantry is not mentioned by Harding and is, indeed, incomprehensible in terms of his interpretation.
87   See Gramsci 1926.
88   Lenin 1912b, p. 359.

distinctions that had been built into Social Democratic strategy and encrusted socialist practice. Locutions multiplied blurring distinctions between economic and political struggle, between the aims of democratic and socialist revolutions. Parvus exemplified both the probing and the equivocation:

> Workers' democracy includes all of the most extreme demands of bourgeois democracy, but imparts to some of them a special character and also includes new demands that are strictly proletarian ... [T]he revolution in Russia creates a special connection between the minimum programme of Social-Democracy and its final goal ... We are not yet ready in Russia to assume the task of converting the bourgeois revolution into a socialist revolution, but we are even less ready to subordinate ourselves to a bourgeois revolution.[89]

Thus Luxemburg: 'Being formally bourgeois-democratic, but essentially proletarian-socialist, [the Russian revolution] is, in both content and method, *a transitional form* from the bourgeois revolutions of the past to the proletarian revolutions of the future'.[90] And Kautsky: '[W]e do not yet have complete power, the dictatorship of the proletariat; we do not yet have the socialist revolution, but only its beginnings'.[91]

This current could draw strength from the confluence of several streams of thought and sensibility. As the wave of revolutionary activity crested, Economist infatuation with the elemental spontaneity of the working-class movement mutated into what Reidar Larsson has termed 'revolutionary Economism':[92] the injunction to unmask the class context of platforms on behalf of 'the entire people' and to destroy 'all illusions of some community of political goals' among all classes, particularly workers and bourgeois, could be followed up with an imperative to destroy the state duma.[93] The Menshevik theme of proletarian self-activity expressing a consciousness of specifically 'class', specifically socialist aims was radicalised as Menshevik workers and

---

89 Parvus 1905, p. 493.
90 Luxemburg 1905, p. 526.
91 Kautsky 1905b, p. 531.
92 Larsson 1970. It should be remembered that Lenin's argument in *What Is to Be Done?* assumed that forms of Economism were consistent with participation in revolutionary politics, although not with proletarian hegemony in the revolutionary process; there is nothing in the emergence of 'revolutionary Economism' that would embarrass that analysis or even require its revision.
93 Riazanov 1905, p. 475.

even leaders like Dan and Martynov flirted with the notion of a 'workers' regime'.[94] David Riazanov infused the discourse of 'the revolution *in Permanenz*' into typically Menshevik themes of working-class independence: 'In concentrating all its efforts on completing *its own* tasks, [Social Democracy] simultaneously approaches the moment when the issue will not be *participation* in a provisional government, but rather the seizure of power by the working class and conversion of the "bourgeois" revolution into a direct prologue for the social revolution'.[95] The notion that the workers first of all – most often, the workers alone – were driving the revolution, perhaps beyond its anticipated limits, was sometimes intertwined with hard-edged dismissal of the thought of subordinating the daring, determination and inventiveness of the newly awakened masses to the narrow perspectives or bureaucratic schemes of party politicians, as when Luxemburg invoked the dynamism of the Russian mass strikes, at once economic and political, to try to shake the German trade unions from their routine.[96]

Although this current was broad and its resonance diffuse, it was most enduringly instantiated by Trotsky and conceived with the greatest clarity from his perspective of permanent revolution. Drawing upon Kautsky's reflections on the unevenness of working-class movements in America and Russia,[97] Trotsky reasoned from the international context of capitalism in less-developed Russia that the victory of the bourgeois-democratic revolution would be conditional upon its being 'telescoped' into a proletarian-socialist revolution, a circumstance that could be expected to trigger workers' revolutions in Europe, initiating a process of socialist revolution on a world scale.[98] Capitalism had progressed to a point where the proletariat, escaping the political ineptitude of the other social forces, displaced the bourgeoisie as the driving force of the democratic revolution. Once power is assumed by 'a revolutionary government with a socialist majority, the division of our programme into maximum [socialist] and minimum [democratic measures] loses all significance, both in principle and in immediate practice';[99] the working class is driven 'by the very logic of its position... toward the introduction of state management of industry' and the construction of a socialist order,[100]

---

94   Dan 1970, p. 343.
95   Riazanov 1905, p. 473.
96   See Luxemburg 1906.
97   See Kautsky 1906a.
98   See Trotsky 1906, pp. 65–6.
99   Trotsky 1906, p. 78.
100 Trotsky 1906, p. 67.

transcending the differences between Bolsheviks and Mensheviks and rendering the factional division obsolete. Consistent with this logic, Trotsky sought persistently in the aftermath of 1905 to broker a reconciliation between the opposing political tendencies, earning him Lenin's epithet 'centrist' – the same label Lenin would later affix to Kautsky's quixotic quest to maintain an illusory unity of the working-class movement after the outbreak of the world war. In later years, Trotsky would attribute his misguided efforts to conciliate the factional opponents to 'a sort of *social-revolutionary* fatalism ... [in] questions of the inner development of the party'.[101] The logic of his position might be more accurately expressed, in the terms of the present argument, as the assumed resolution of the contradictions of the working-class movement implicit in the logic of Marxist orthodoxy.

Although the elemental struggles of the peasantry for land might wear away at the props of absolutist rule, this was a process profoundly lacking in consciousness and political will; the peasants were 'absolutely incapable of taking up an *independent* political role'.[102] Since the countryside had never engendered a class capable of undertaking the revolutionary abolition of the relations of feudal society, upon its ascension to power the working class would 'stand before the peasants as the class which had emancipated them'.[103] The peasants would be left with no political choice other than to rally to the rule of the workers and it would not matter greatly if this was done with 'a degree of consciousness not larger than that with which [they] usually rally to the bourgeois regime'.[104] The struggle of the workers for political influence over the

---

[101]   Trotsky 1930, p. 231; see also Trotsky 1929, p. 173.
[102]   Trotsky 1906, p. 72.
[103]   Trotsky 1906, p. 71.
[104]   Trotsky 1906, p. 73. In criticising the Bolshevik strategy of revolutionary democratic dictatorship of the proletariat and the peasantry, Trotsky asserted, first, that the nature of the revolutionary government was a matter of 'who will determine the content of the government's policy, who will form within it a solid majority', to which the only viable answer was the proletariat, and second, that a worker-peasant coalition 'presupposes either that one of the existing bourgeois parties commands influence over the peasantry or that the peasants will have created a powerful independent party of its own', neither of which was a possibility (1906, pp. 69, 74). While he would maintain that a peasant party had already taken shape in the course of the revolution, if only in embryo, and could be expected to grow and strengthen – along with the political knowledge and activity of the peasants – as the revolution developed, the really decisive point of Lenin's response was that '[a] "coalition" of classes *does not at all* presuppose *either* the existence of any particular powerful party, *or* parties in general' (Lenin 1909a, p. 371). Coalitions between workers and peasants could and did assume the most diverse forms of joint action between, say,

peasantry was acknowledged, of course, but it did not deflect the logic of Trotsky's conception. The instinctive proprietorial urges of the petty-bourgeois peasant mass would not bend to the organic collectivism of the industrial proletariat; this contradiction could not be resolved within the limits of one country, especially such an economically backward one as Russia, and would sap the foundations of proletarian rule unless it was reinforced by the victory of the international working class. While the proletarian socialist revolution and the peasant revolts against landlordism might be temporally 'telescoped', they were not thereby conceptually interwoven.

The logic of the struggle for hegemony constrains political actors to adapt hegemonic political projects to shifting conjunctures of struggle and renders disagreement over the definition/redefinition of a political project potentially deeply trenchant. Understood in these terms, the project of proletarian hegemony in the democratic revolution was open to the influence of the people, and the proletariat's relation to them, especially to the peasantry, may be partially constitutive of its revolutionary political project and hence of its political identity. Political relations between classes, in particular the relation between proletariat and peasantry, are cast in Trotsky's theory of permanent revolution in more rigid terms. The theory seems addressed to political actors who were able, because adversaries and allies had no margin of manoeuvre, to calculate their own actions leaving no margin for uncertainty. Such an inflexible grasp of political agency may help to account for the lack of political suppleness that Lenin later criticised as an 'excessive preoccupation with the purely administrative side of the work';[105] it yields an inability to engage effectively with other political actors and hence a politics conducted as though its 'author' were looking at the process of history from the outside.[106]

---

    primarily non-party organisations such as Soviets of Workers' Deputies or strike committees and soldiers' or peasants' soviets. The governmental form appropriate to the revolutionary democratic dictatorship could not be understood in abstraction from the struggle to transform the social relations in agriculture; a governmental majority in the cities could not enforce its decisions in the countryside without the agency of the peasants' struggle (Lenin 1909a, pp. 370–4). Accordingly, Lenin had specified the organisation of the democratic dictatorship: 'Workers' governments in towns, peasant committees in the villages (which at a certain moment will be transformed into bodies elected by universal, etc., suffrage) – such is the only possible form of organization of the victorious revolution, i.e., the dictatorship of the proletariat and peasantry' (Lenin 1907d, p. 392n).

105 Lenin 1922–3, p. 595.
106 Carr 1970, p. 162. The present account is, I think, congruent with the following, admittedly rather enigmatic, passage on 'permanent revolution' from Gramsci's *Prison Notebooks*: 'With respect to the "Jacobin" slogan formulated in 1848–9, its complex fortunes are worth

The various tendencies among Russian Marxists were all eager to have their positions receive the imprimatur of Karl Kautsky. When Plekhanov circulated a questionnaire seeking the views of prominent West European Social Democrats on the nature of the Russian revolution and the appropriate Social Democratic orientation to it, he must have been disappointed with Kautsky's response, printed in several Russian editions as 'The Driving Forces of the Russian Revolution and Its Prospects'.[107] But Trotsky and Lenin were each comfortable writing a preface for different editions of the essay; each could with some justice associate quite a distinct position with Kautsky's views. Trotsky characterised Kautsky's essay as 'the best theoretical statement of my own views'.[108] As capital progressed, 'the proletariat had become independent and had been powerfully strengthened while ... an enormous gulf had opened up between the petty bourgeoisie and capital',[109] a process accentuated by the concentration of foreign capitalist investment in Russia[110] and leaving no class with the capacity to unite bourgeoisie and proletariat in 'the common struggle for political liberty'. The working class emerged from the beginning as Social Democratic, the bourgeoisie 'intimidated by the slightest stirring on the part of the proletariat'.[111] Leadership of the revolutionary movement fell to the workers and, in the sense that the bourgeoisie was not a driving force, the revolution could not be termed bourgeois. The working class of Russia was, however, too weak and backward to accomplish a socialist revolution on its own, although 'you cannot struggle successfully if you renounce victory in advance'. The victory of Social Democracy would depend on the support of another class; it could implement only as much of its programme as the interests of

---

studying. Taken up again, systematized, developed, intellectualized by the Parvus-Bronstein group, it proved inert and ineffective in 1905, and subsequently. It had become an abstract thing, belonging in the scientist's cabinet. The tendency which opposed it in this literary form, and indeed did not use it "on purpose", applied it in fact in a form which adhered to actual, concrete, living history, adapted to the time and the place; as something that sprang from all the pores of the particular society which had to be transformed; as the alliance of two social groups with hegemony of the urban group. In one case, you had the Jacobin temperament without an adequate political content; in the second, a Jacobin temperament and content derived from the new historical relations, and not from a literary and intellectualistic label' (Gramsci 1929–35, pp. 84–5n).

107 Kautsky 1906c.
108 Cited in Donald 1993, p. 91.
109 Kautsky 1906c, p. 601.
110 Kautsky 1906c, p. 594.
111 Kautsky 1906c, p. 602.

that class would permit.[112] That class was, of course, the peasantry; its interests, far from ripe for socialism, lay in private ownership of the land, although Kautsky left the door open to possible surprises to be delivered by the length of the revolutionary process or its repercussions upon the workers of Western Europe and their reaction in return upon Russia. The Russian revolution was most appropriately understood, he concluded, 'as neither a bourgeois revolution in the traditional sense nor a socialist one but as a quite unique process which is taking place on the borderline between bourgeois and socialist society, which requires the dissolution of the one while preparing the creation of the other'.[113]

The Kautskyan propositions that the bourgeoisie was not a driving force of the revolution; that the victory of the proletariat required an alliance with the peasantry; and that, consequently, the revolution was not a socialist revolution constituted, according to Lenin, 'a brilliant confirmation of the tactics of the revolutionary wing of the Russian Social Democratic Party', their vindication against the Mensheviks' political orientation toward the liberal bourgeoisie, which the Bolsheviks had fought since the very beginning of the revolution.[114] Kautsky did not himself draw any implications from his analysis for the political division between Bolsheviks and Mensheviks, and his presentation of it could lend itself to either a Bolshevik or a Trotskyist reading. In any case, whether simply through the caution appropriate to an outsider – he termed himself 'a novice...when it comes to Russian affairs'[115] – or, as my reading of the logic of his Marxism indicates, also for deeper political and theoretical reasons, he steered clear of anything that might challenge the unity of the RSDLP. While with Lenin he recognised the struggle of the peasantry as the single most important factor shaping the context of the hegemonic project of the Russian working class, unlike Lenin he did not engage with the political aspects of the construction of an alliance of workers and peasants. What prepared a change in the peasant's outlook from 'sleepy and unthinking creature of habit' to 'restless...warrior for the new' was the transformation of economic relations through the late nineteenth century; the isolation of the village came to an end as it was linked to world trade. The influence of the workers appeared in sociological rather than political terms: 'large numbers of peasants or peasant children who had lost their land turned to the factory and the mine and thus joined the proletarian class struggle and they conveyed their

---

112   Kautsky 1906c, p. 605.
113   Kautsky 1906c, p. 607.
114   Lenin 1906g, pp. 410–11.
115   Kautsky 1906c, p. 604.

impressions of it to their comrades left behind in the villages back home'.[116] Kautsky's sketch of the post-revolutionary progress of Russian agriculture was drawn along similar lines to the American path of capitalist development Lenin envisaged, but he shared the concern of the Bolshevik 'divisionists' to avoid standing in the way of the peasants' struggle for private property in land, like them foregoing the kind of political engagement with the contradictions of peasant ideology with which Lenin embroidered his proposal for nationalisation of the land.[117]

But as with all those whose political trajectory reflected the gravitational pull of 'permanent revolution', issues of revolutionary agency were framed in Kautsky's discourse as a matter of identifying which class, bourgeoisie or proletariat, could drive the revolution forward and how far it could push the process. Once it was determined that the proletariat had succeeded the bourgeoisie or the petty bourgeoisie as the principal driving force of the revolutionary process, debate over political tactics was framed in terms of the distance the proletariat could travel, under given or foreseeable circumstances, along the revolutionary path. The bourgeoisie, lacking the strength to lead the revolutionary forces, went over to the side of reaction; it was no longer capable of mounting a hegemonic project. The struggle was framed as one between revolution and reaction rather than as between adversarial hegemonic projects. The real distinction between Lenin and those, including Kautsky, who looked at the revolution through this optic was his *articulation* of the worker-peasant alliance with a political logic of struggle between two paths of revolutionary development, two adversarial projects of hegemony. Like his colleagues, Lenin did frame the alternative as between less and more thoroughgoing processes of revolutionary transformation, but this kind of formulation was supplemented, in his case, by the struggle between bourgeois hegemony and proletarian hegemony, between a landlord-bourgeois path and a proletarian-peasant path of the revolution, between the Prussian path and the American path of capitalist development.[118] There was more than one way forward; the struggle was not only a matter of forward or back but also of direction. Alternatively put, the distinctiveness of Lenin's position consisted not in the recognition of proletarian revolutionary agency alone but of the enduring potential of a class-antagonistic bourgeois political project as well, with the

---

116   Kautsky 1906c, p. 603.
117   See Donald 1993, pp. 93–106, 150–7.
118   The earliest reference I have noticed to the struggle between two paths of capitalist development contrasts, interestingly, Italian and American rather than Prussian and American paths (Lenin, 1905k, p. 319).

implication that the self-understanding of the proletariat must take this circumstance into account. That is, the working-class movement must understand itself not only as a protagonist with its own revolutionary project to enact but also as targeted by its class antagonist, acted upon through its agency, and consequently under an obligation to rethink its project and reshape its own agency reflexively in virtue of the logic of this struggle.

It is not that Lenin supposed the bourgeoisie capable of throwing up a latter-day equivalent of the Jacobin Clubs, an alternative focal point for popular mobilisation, any more than did any of the proponents of permanent revolution; bourgeois hegemony operated, instead, by utilising the popular insurgency as a kind of bargaining chip to negotiate a constitutional rearrangement of state power along liberal lines and facilitate the transition to an agriculture organised around capitalist latifundia, relying upon the narrowness or diffidence nurtured in the nascent working-class movement by corporatist – Economist, spontaneist, Menshevik – influences to seize the political initiative and turn it to bourgeois advantage at key junctures in the revolutionary process. On such an understanding of the logic of the struggle for hegemony, ideological and political divisions within the working-class movement are not simply assignable to an undeveloped phase of the movement to be transcended in the further course of its evolution; since they also figure as potential objects of strategic contention, the lines of demarcation of the political unity of the working-class movement are always subject to redefinition in terms of the struggle for hegemony. While such divisions do not translate automatically into a split, and a rising tide of revolutionary struggle could do much to accommodate them, neither is there a historical logic that could underwrite their transcendence. To reckon without the possibility of splits in the working-class movement (the orthodox – centrist – metaphysics of class unity to the contrary notwithstanding) is to misconstrue the politico-strategic logic of the struggle for hegemony and hence also the struggle between the two paths of the democratic revolution.

The Advent of the Soviets

At the Inaugural Congress of the All-Russian Peasant Union in August 1905, it was proposed to send greetings to 'our brothers the workers, who have for so long been spilling their blood in the struggle for the people's freedom'. But when a Social Democratic delegate intervened in the discussion with the claim that '"without the factory workers the peasants will achieve nothing", he was met with shouts from the floor that "on the contrary, without the peasants the workers can achieve nothing".[119] Apparently, proletarian hegemony was not exercised just in being asserted, even where there was a measure of good will and recognition of common interests. The sophistication of Lenin's socio-economic analysis and political calculations would seem a thin thread, in historical materialist terms, upon which to hang a claim to proletarian leadership in the bourgeois-democratic revolution; even if the organisation of the RSDLP had responded reliably to these calculations, it would still have been in no position to bring their insight to bear in the villages. The hegemony of the proletariat would have to be spread through a more extensive and deeply rooted network than the party. It would require, therefore, a reappraisal of the spontaneous working-class movement and such a reappraisal would be occasioned by the emergence of the soviets.

The most prominent exemplar of this institution, the St. Petersburg Soviet of Workers' Deputies, emerged at the height of the October general strike. The rumoured arrest of several delegates to a conference of railroad employees triggered a strike of Moscow rail workers which quickly assumed a general and political dimension. Industrial workers came out in solidarity across the country and the dwindling St. Petersburg strike movement gained a new lease of life. As postal workers, telephone and telegraph workers, service and commercial employees, professionals and students, and even groups of peasants joined in, the protest movement attained an unprecedented breadth. The workers of the capital were acquainted with the idea of electing representatives in the factory. Under a 1903 law, factory elders [*starosti*] could be chosen by management from candidates nominated by the workers to negotiate their grievances. Committees of deputies had been organised in a number of factories since the January strike, and in the aftermath of Bloody Sunday, the workers took part in two-stage elections for representatives to the abortive Shidlovskii Commission, established by the government to investigate the causes of unrest among the factory workers of St. Petersburg.[120] In addition to this practical experience, the workers had been exposed during the summer to Menshevik efforts to popularise slogans in favour of a 'workers' congress' and 'revolutionary self-government'.[121]

As the strike wave reached St. Petersburg, a number of factories spontaneously elected deputies. When the Mensheviks initiated a workers' committee to lead the general strike and, seeking to broaden its representation, agitated for the election of one deputy per 500 workers, they did so under the rubric of

---

119   See Perrie 1976, pp. 110–11.
120   See Harcave 1965, pp. 181–6; Anweiler 1974, pp. 24–7, 32–7.
121   See Anweiler 1974, pp. 45–6.

'revolutionary self-government'. The Soviet of Workers' Deputies thus came into being as a strike committee, but one already animated by a broader political vision.[122] In response to the practical imperatives of the general strike, the Soviet began to act like a 'second government', ruling on matters of everyday life and issuing instructions to the post office, railroads, even policemen.[123] The momentum of the strike movement was such that the Tsar was obliged, in order to bring the moderate opposition into the camp of order and pacify the situation, to issue the Manifesto of 17 October, conceding civil liberties, universal suffrage, a representative assembly with legislative powers, and ministerial responsibility. The revolutionary impetus of the working class was not broken. The soviets continued to spread through urban Russia. In taking up the everyday concerns of the masses, they won the allegiance of broad strata of workers and attracted sympathy and support among the non-proletarian population of the cities. They renewed strike activity against state repression and martial law, for the eight-hour day and 'a people's government', and encroached more and more upon the prerogatives of the state. In accordance with the logic of an illegal confrontation with the Tsarist state, they began to assume a new dimension as an agency of insurrection and an organ of revolutionary state power. Before the autocracy could restore its order and deploy its forces against the peasant risings in the countryside, it would have to put down workers' insurrections in Moscow and other cities.[124]

By the time Lenin returned from exile in early November, the terms in which Bolsheviks and Mensheviks debated the significance of the Soviet had already been defined. Partially constitutive of the new institution were the Menshevik watchwords calling for 'revolutionary self-government' and a 'workers' congress'. They entered, through the early influence of the Mensheviks in organising the Soviet, into its self-conception. A plan for revolutionary self-government called upon workers' organisations to take the initiative in organising, parallel to the official duma elections, an electoral process open to the masses. Not only would this bring the pressure of public opinion to bear upon the official electors but, at an auspicious moment, the people's representatives could declare themselves a constituent assembly. Whether or not it reached this 'ideal objective', such a campaign would 'organise revolutionary self-government, which will smash the shackles of Tsarist legality, and lay the foundation for the future triumph of the revolution'.[125] Axelrod presented the idea of a workers' congress

---

122 See Schwarz 1967, pp. 168–78.
123 See Anweiler 1974, pp. 55–8.
124 See Harcave 1965, pp. 233–42; Trotsky 1908, pp. 249–64.
125 Cited in Lenin 1905p, p. 224; see Schwarz 1967, pp. 168–71.

as an alternative to the Bolsheviks' 'active boycott' of the elections to the Bulygin Duma. An embodiment of proletarian self-activity, the congress was to be comprised of delegates elected by assemblies of workers to 'adopt specific decisions concerning the immediate demands and plan of action of the working class'. It would debate the stance to be adopted toward 'the government's caricature of a representative assembly', the appropriate terms for agreements with liberal-democratic bodies, the summoning of a Constituent Assembly and the kinds of economic and political reforms to be advocated in elections to that body, and other such current public issues. Agitation around this idea, Axelrod wrote, could 'captivate tens of thousands of workers', a mass large enough in a period of revolution to 'endow the congress, its decisions and the organisation set up by it with tremendous authority, both among the less conscious masses of the proletariat and in the eyes of the liberal democrats'. Even if the congress did not come to fruition, by contributing to 'the political enlightenment of the working masses, strengthening their combative spirit and developing their ability and readiness to meet force with force in defence of their rightful demands', such agitation might occasion an uprising.[126]

The Mensheviks hoped that such proposals, by providing a forum for working-class self-activity, might culminate in the formation of a mass party of labour. Seen in this perspective, the institution of the soviet had essentially to do with the relation between the working class and its political party. Unable to grasp the new institutional form in different terms than those proposed by the Mensheviks, the Petersburg Bolsheviks were obliged to react defensively. Fearful that the influence of an amorphous, non-socialist political organisation among the workers could undermine their political evolution toward Social Democracy, they greeted the formation of the Soviet with suspicion. Their leader, Alexander Bogdanov, favoured setting the Soviet an ultimatum: accept the programme and leadership of the RSDLP or the Bolsheviks would withdraw.[127] In the end they stayed in the Soviet with a view to correcting

---

126   Axelrod 1905, pp. 65–7.
127   Bogdanov would figure prominently in subsequent Bolshevik history as the intellectual driving force behind a leftist current that expressed itself philosophically in an inclination to ground socialism in the specifically proletarian experience of collective labour in large-scale industry and to subordinate historical materialist analysis to proletarian will and experience, and politically in resistance to participation in bourgeois elections and parliaments. Read out of the Bolshevik faction, in the aftermath of October Bogdanov would play a seminal role in the Proletcult, a movement that sought to work out a new culture, grounded in specifically proletarian experience, for the new socialist society (see Bogdanov 1906–24). He is instructively discussed in Craig Brandist's forthcoming

spontaneous anti–Social Democratic tendencies and expounding the party's ideas. Perhaps mindful of Lenin's earlier warnings about the danger of non-partisan political organisations serving as conduits for bourgeois influence over the proletariat, they sought to distinguish the need for the Soviet as 'the executive organ for a specific proletarian action' from presumptuous 'attempts on its part to become the political leader of the working class'.[128] But by the time Lenin arrived, the Soviet had concluded the 'specific proletarian action' for which it had been formed and showed no sign of withdrawing from the field of political action.

Lenin's Intervention

Read in terms of the debate between Mensheviks and Petersburg Bolsheviks over the Soviet, Lenin's intervention is bound to seem unstable, ambivalent and ultimately incoherent. It is this circumstance, I think, that has given rise to the invention of his alleged 'revolt against Leninism'. I will argue on the contrary that, by setting the Soviet in the context of the strategic logic of the struggle for hegemony, Lenin envisaged it as an apparatus for the exercise of proletarian hegemony and thereby shifted the terms of the debate. The case for his 'revolt against Leninism' depends upon neglecting this shift. Once it is taken into account and the relation between the spontaneous working-class movement and the Marxist party is re-examined in its light, the real movement of Lenin's thought can be established.

Lenin cautiously advanced his reading of the situation in a long letter, 'Our Tasks and the Soviet of Workers' Deputies', submitted to the editorial board of the Bolshevik *Novaia zhizn'* [New Life] but not published. After beginning as a strike committee, the Soviet had spontaneously assumed the features of a hub

---

Dimensions of Hegemony as the proponent of a project of cultural hegemony that developed separately from but in parallel with Lenin's political project of hegemony, until the proletarian assumption of power occasioned a limited and rather uneasy conjunction of the two projects. But it should be noted that, however things may have stood with other Bolsheviks, Lenin himself would never have ceded the cultural dimension to Bogdanov and his co-thinkers. His own approach in this area proceeded from an insistence, consistent with the politico-strategic logic of the struggle for hegemony, that 'genuine proletarian culture' could not be grown in hot-house isolation but developed only by engaging, assimilating and reworking 'everything of value in the more than two thousand years of... human thought and culture' (Lenin 1920d, p. 317).

128   Gvozdev cited in Schwarz 1967, pp. 186, 187; see Lenin 1905l, pp. 507–8.

of revolutionary politics capable of unifying 'all the genuinely revolutionary forces' and serving as the medium for an uprising against the state. It should be regarded, consequently, as 'the embryo of a *provisional revolutionary government*'. But considered in this light, the broad, non-partisan composition of the Soviet was no disadvantage. On the contrary, '[w]e have been speaking all the time of the need of a militant alliance of Social-Democrats and revolutionary bourgeois democrats. We have been speaking of it and the workers [in bringing forth the Soviet] have done it'. The question as to whether the Soviet or the party should lead the political struggle was ill conceived: both the party and a reorganised Soviet were equally necessary. Indeed, the Soviet, considered 'as a revolutionary centre providing political leadership, is not too broad an organisation but, on the contrary, a much too narrow one'. It must constitute a provisional revolutionary government and must 'enlist to this end the participation of new deputies not only from the workers, but ... from the sailors and soldiers ... from the revolutionary peasantry ... and from the revolutionary bourgeois intelligentsia'.[129]

This estimate of the Soviet was accompanied by a call to reorganise the party in line with the new, albeit precarious, conditions of political liberty. While its secret apparatus would have to be preserved, the party must be opened up to Social Democratic workers and their initiative and inventiveness engaged in the task of devising new, legal and semi-legal forms of organisation, broader and less rigid than the old circles and more accessible to 'typical representatives of the masses'. Accordingly, it must adopt democratic practices, including electing rank-and-file delegates to the forthcoming Congress.[130] The limits of underground politics had made the party torpid: 'Let [the worker] delegates put new life into the ranks of our central bodies, let the fresh spirit of young revolutionary Russia pour in through them'. The working class having demonstrated in action its readiness to struggle 'consistently and in a body for clearly-understood aims, to fight in a purely Social-Democratic spirit', the workers who joined the party would be dependable socialists or amenable to socialist influence. 'The working class is instinctively, spontaneously Social-Democratic, and more than ten years of work put in by Social-Democracy has done a great deal to transform this spontaneity into consciousness'.[131] The workers, who – unlike intellectuals – would not rest content with a mere solution in principle, must take the issue of party unity in hand. 'We have "theorised" for so long (sometimes – why not admit it? – to no use) in the unhealthy

---

129 Lenin 1905v, pp. 21–3.
130 Lenin 1905w, p. 34.
131 Lenin 1905w, p. 32.

atmosphere of political exile, that it will really not be amiss if we now "bend the bow" slightly... "the other way" and put practice a little more in the forefront'.[132]

The Soviet figured in Lenin's analysis not only as an organiser of the general strike but also as a non-partisan political organisation. Within days of this assessment, however, he would support the Bolshevik critique of '"non-partisan" class organisations' by declaring 'Down with non-partisanship! Non-partisanship has always and everywhere been a weapon and slogan of the bourgeoisie'.[133] Shortly thereafter he would pronounce the Soviet 'not a labour parliament and not an organ of proletarian self-government, nor an organ of self-government at all, but a fighting organisation for the achievement of definite aims'.[134] He had pronounced the Soviet just as necessary, in order to provide the movement with political leadership, as the party and had indicated that the party was itself in need of revitalisation through the influx of 'typical representatives of the masses'. Yet he could, at the same time, issue a warning that the 'need for organisation which the workers are feeling so acutely will', without the intervention of the Social Democrats, 'find its expression in distorted, dangerous forms'. He could acknowledge that, were the party inclined to demagogy or lacking a solid programme, tactical precepts and organisational experience, a sudden influx of untried and untested new members could threaten the dissolution of the conscious vanguard of the class into the politically amorphous masses.[135] Though the workers were 'instinctively, spontaneously Social-Democratic', it was still necessary to reckon with 'hostility to Social-Democracy within the ranks of the proletariat', hostility that often assumed the form of non-partisanship. The transformation of the proletariat into a class was dependent upon 'the growth not only of its unity, but also of its political *consciousness*' and the transformation of 'this [social-democratic] spontaneity into consciousness' was still envisaged in conjunction with the intervention of the Marxist vanguard in the spontaneous class struggle.[136]

That some of Lenin's readers, in order to make sense of the apparent contortions of his political stance, should have had recourse to the interpretive device of a doctrinal rebellion that shook but did not displace an entrenched dogma is not too surprising. Considered in abstraction from the logic of the struggle for hegemony, his response to the Soviet and to the spontaneous working-class

---

132 Lenin 1905w, p. 38.
133 Lenin 1905x, p. 61.
134 Lenin 1905y, p. 72.
135 Lenin 1905w, pp. 29, 32.
136 Lenin 1905x, pp. 60–1.

movement that had called it into being would seem not to incorporate a dialectic of contradictory tendencies, but to collapse into a welter of conflicting formulations. Instead of reconciling apparent contradictions, Lenin's theoretical discourse is partitioned into elements reflective of the reality of the spontaneous class struggle and those marked by the resistance of the Bolshevik apparatus. This procedure, reducing Lenin's discourse to a battleground for contending political forces, is most systematically deployed by the Menshevik historian Solomon Schwarz, but it is implicit in the interpretive apparatus of a Leninist doctrinal rebellion. It becomes dispensable, however, once Lenin's stance toward the soviet is re-examined in the context of the struggle for hegemony.

The Spontaneous Movement and Hegemony

The 'instinctively, spontaneously Social-Democratic' disposition that Lenin ascribed to the working class in the immediate triumphant aftermath of the general strike would not seem to consist in its pursuit of specifically socialist objectives. In an essay written to explain the prevalence of non-partisan ideology and institutions in the revolutionary movement, he was prepared to acknowledge 'the striving of the workers towards socialism and their alliance with the Socialist Party ... [even] at the very earliest stages of the movement' as being a consequence of 'the special position which the proletariat occupies in capitalist society'. He claims at the same time, however, that an examination of the petitions, demands and instructions emanating from factories, offices, regiments, parishes and so on throughout Russia would show a preponderance of 'demands for elementary rights' rather than 'specifically class demands':[137]

> [E]ven the proletarian demands are limited, in most cases, to reforms of the sort that are fully realisable within the framework of capitalism. What the Russian proletariat is demanding now and immediately is not something that will undermine capitalism, but something that will accelerate and intensify its development ... [P]urely socialist demands are still a matter of the future ... Even the proletariat is making the revolution, as it were, within the limits of the minimum programme and not of the maximum programme.[138]

---

137   Lenin 1905z, p. 76.
138   Lenin 1905z, p. 77.

If the working-class movement was spontaneously Social Democratic, it was so not in virtue of its consciousness but of its practice, not in virtue of what it thought but of what it did and how it acted. In order to grasp how this could be so, the practice of the spontaneous working-class movement must be situated in relation to the politico-strategic logic of the struggle for hegemony, specifically in relation to the struggle between the two paths of the bourgeois-democratic revolution. In the first place, the general strike rendered unworkable the Bulygin Duma and thereby disrupted the compromise it represented between Tsar and bourgeoisie. The workers' revolutionary struggle thus escaped the strategic hegemony of the liberal bourgeoisie spontaneously – by its fighting spirit, its tenacity and its 'plebeian' methods – although not yet consciously and not, therefore, durably. In the aftermath of 'the first great victory of the urban revolution', it was incumbent upon the proletariat to

> broaden and deepen the foundations of the revolution by extending it to the countryside... Revolutionary war differs from other wars in that it draws its main reserves from the camp of its enemy's erstwhile allies, erstwhile supporters of tsarism, or people who blindly obeyed tsarism. The success of the all-Russian political strike will have a greater influence over the minds and hearts of the peasants than the confusing words of any possible manifestoes or laws.[139]

Not only did the spontaneous movement of the general strike open up the possibility of a decisive revolutionary transformation, but in so doing it exemplified the exercise of hegemony materially through the production/imposition of *faits accomplis*, not simply ideologically through the generation and transmission of consciousness, belief and conviction. It foreshadowed the hegemony of the proletariat as a reorganisation of the system of alliances of social and political forces, both destabilising the adversary's forces and mobilising an incipient revolutionary coalition. The working class was 'spontaneously Social-Democratic' to the extent that its spontaneous struggle was congruent with the strategic orientation of Russian Social Democracy toward the hegemony of the proletariat in the bourgeois-democratic revolution.

In the second place, the Soviet thrown up in the course of the general strike provided an institutional form through which the alliance of revolutionary democrats could be concluded on a mass scale, the revolutionary-democratic dictatorship of the proletariat and the peasantry exercised and, consequently, the 'imprint of proletarian independence' placed upon the path of the

---

139 Lenin 1905s, p. 433.

revolution. Though it emerged from the working-class movement, Lenin did not treat the soviet as a specifically proletarian class institution, a form of organisation exclusive to the workers. Indeed, what was decisive in his analysis was that, as a mode of organisation, the soviet constituted an opening to the masses of workers and peasants, intellectuals and petty bourgeois, sailors and soldiers, a political terrain upon which a coalition of revolutionary democrats could take shape. As such and only as such did it represent an embryo of revolutionary-democratic state power.

This estimate of the Soviets of Workers' Deputies was pointedly formulated in a Bolshevik resolution prepared for the April 1906 Unity Congress of the RSDLP and elaborated more fully in a lengthy pamphlet distributed to Congress delegates, *The Victory of the Kadets and the Tasks of the Workers' Party*.[140] According to the resolution, the soviets, which arise 'spontaneously in the course of mass political strikes as non-party organisations of the broad masses of workers', are necessarily transformed, 'by absorbing the more revolutionary elements of the petty bourgeoisie... into organs of the general revolutionary struggle'; the significance of such rudimentary forms of revolutionary authority is completely dependent upon the efficacy of the movement toward insurrection.[141] In the context of this movement, however, the 'Soviets of Workers', Soldiers', Railwaymen's and Peasants' Deputies' really were new forms of revolutionary authority:

> These bodies were set up exclusively by the *revolutionary* sections of the people; they were formed irrespective of all laws and regulations, entirely in a revolutionary way, as a product of the native genius of the people, as a manifestation of the independent activity of the people which... was ridding itself of its old police fetters. Lastly, they were indeed organs of *authority*, for all their rudimentary, spontaneous, amorphous and diffuse character, in composition and in activity... In their social and political character, they were the rudiments of the dictatorship of the revolutionary elements of the people.[142]

Established without the authorisation of, indeed in struggle against, the *ancien regime*, the authority of the soviets and kindred institutions derived neither from the force of arms nor the power of money nor the habit of obedience to entrenched institutions, but from nothing other than 'the confidence of the

---

140 Lenin 1906a.
141 Lenin 1906a, p. 156.
142 Lenin 1906c, p. 243.

vast masses' and the enlistment of 'all the masses' in the practice of government. Unlike the old, the new authority did not shroud its operations in ritual, secrecy or professions of expertise: 'It concealed nothing, it had no secrets, no regulations, no formalities... It was an authority open to all, it carried out all its functions before the eyes of the masses, was accessible to the masses, sprang directly from the masses, and was a direct and immediate instrument of the popular masses, of their will'. Since 'the masses' also included those who had been cowed by repression, degraded by ideology, habit or prejudice, or who simply inclined to philistine indifference, the revolutionary authority of the soviets was not exercised by the whole people but by 'the revolutionary people'. The latter, however, explained patiently and in detail the reasons for their actions and 'willingly enlist[ed] the *whole* people not only in "administering" the state, but in governing it too, and indeed in organising the state'.[143] This account of the soviets implies that the new authority constituted not only and not so much an embryonic state as an embryonic anti-state. The implication was not yet drawn – as it would be in *The State and Revolution* – but a sense of the dissolution of the opposition between society and the apparatus of politics, between the people and the organisation of state power, is conveyed. The soviet provided an institutional form in which the social, economic and cultural struggles of the masses – workers and peasants – could combine with the revolutionary struggle for political power, amplifying and reinforcing each other.

If Lenin's analysis of the soviet in 1905–6 is supposed to contradict his criticism of 'revolutionary self-government', the 'workers' congress' and the principle of non-partisanship, neither its analytical force and elegance nor the extent of its affinity with the theory of the state elaborated in *The State and Revolution* can be appreciated. Properly understood – that is, understood in terms of the politico-strategic logic of the struggle for hegemony – the criticism does not contradict but follows logically from the analysis. To invoke the theme of 'revolutionary self-government' in order to characterise the soviets was to invoke the political orientation of those, the Mensheviks, who gave it currency. As Lenin saw it, in their hands, the exercise of 'revolutionary self-government' was simply juxtaposed with cooperation in the rites of the Tsarist government with no strategic forethought as to the inevitability of counter-revolutionary repression. Thus conceived in abstraction from the logic of the struggle for hegemony, however, it represented a denial of the need to organise the revolutionary insurrection or, at best, a refusal to take the initiative in organising it. In this context, revolutionary self-government is not an approximation to the

---

143 Lenin 1906c, pp. 244–5, 247.

dictatorship of the revolutionary people, but its subordination to an experiment in political pedagogy, and precisely this was the target of Lenin's criticism.

The same holds *a fortiori* for such formulations as 'labour parliament' and 'workers' congress', which bear the additional disadvantage of identifying the soviets as non-partisan organisations of the working class. Framed in this way, the soviets would exclude the non-proletarian masses and detract from the leadership of the RSDLP. The non-partisan structure of the soviet was essential, in Lenin's analysis, precisely because it provided a political arena in which a coalition of the proletarian, petty bourgeois and peasant masses could take shape. Non-partisanship was indeed a bourgeois principle, but inasmuch as the revolutionary process called for an alliance of the workers with bourgeois democrats, this was not a drawback but an asset; in order to preserve the political independence of the working class, the leadership of the Social Democratic Party remained essential. However paradoxical it may seem, this leadership was exercised precisely in orchestrating a class alliance around the organisation of a revolutionary insurrection and, consequently, in unravelling the strategic confusion represented by the notion of a 'workers' congress' and so on.

As demonstrated in the emergence of the soviets, the spontaneously Social Democratic bent of the working-class struggle could not be reduced to mere receptiveness to the political lessons of Marxist class analysis: 'We have been speaking all the time of the need of a militant alliance of Social-Democrats and revolutionary bourgeois democrats. We have been speaking of it and the workers have actually done it'.[144] What the workers had done was not simply to put into practice advice supplied by Marxist theory; they had shown themselves capable of political innovation and, in so doing, they had generated a solution in practice to a key problem on the agenda of Marxist theory. But what they had done in Social Democratic fashion was done spontaneously, not consciously. It was Lenin who, by situating their innovation in the context of the politico-strategic logic of the struggle for hegemony, would provide the theory of their practice. Just what was it that the working class had done? Not only had it momentarily disrupted the hegemony of the liberal bourgeoisie and gained for itself some experience of political life, it had erected a new institutional form through which the diverse revolutionary-democratic forces could mesh together in a coalition of the masses, the worker-peasant alliance, and assume state power. It had thereby evinced its own aptitude for hegemony in the bourgeois-democratic revolution.

---

144 Lenin 1905v, p. 22.

This hegemonic potential of the soviet form of organisation could be durably realised only through action in conformity with the politico-strategic logic of the struggle for hegemony. It would require, therefore, the deployment of armed force to meet and defeat the violence of the counterrevolution and the deployment of Marxist analysis to seize the shifting conjunctures of the political struggle and hold the springs of ideological confusion in check. The soviet could not render the intervention of the Marxist vanguard party superfluous, but the soviet and similar forms of organisation had come to embody an aspect of the struggle for proletarian hegemony that was hardly less requisite. What they did, in displacing the conventions that gave politics its shape and texture, was in a sense to reorganise the space of political life: opening the process of political decision-making to the scrutiny of the popular masses, they encouraged the masses to enter politics; merging the social, economic and cultural demands and grievances of the people in the assault upon the autocratic regime, they palpably expanded the range of the political struggle; dispensing with formalities that barred the path to participation in the struggle, they permitted the confluence of popular forces in all their contradictory diversity. In all these ways, they restructured the terrain of political struggle along lines that enabled the Marxist vanguard party to pursue the political project of proletarian hegemony more effectively. In thus transforming the terrain of struggle, the institution of the soviet represented a connection between the idea of proletarian hegemony as the project of a party and the material inscription of proletarian hegemony in the path of the bourgeois-democratic revolution. Theorising the soviet in this context enabled Lenin to pull together at last a coherent historical materialist conception of the hegemony of the proletariat.

Some years later he would have recourse, albeit without specific reference to the soviets, to a spatial metaphor in order to define the idea of proletarian hegemony:

> He who confines the class to an arena, the bounds, forms and shape of which are determined or permitted by the liberals, does not understand the tasks of the class. Only he understands the tasks of the class who directs its attention (and consciousness, and practical activity, etc.) to the need for so reconstructing this very arena, its entire form, its entire shape, as to extend it beyond the limits allowed by the liberals... [T]he difference between the two formulations... [consists in] the very fact, *among other things*, that the first *excludes* the idea of 'hegemony' of the working class, whereas the second deliberately defines this very idea.[145]

---

145 Lenin 1911–12, pp. 422, 423.

The politico-strategic logic of the struggle for hegemony was grounded upon the struggle of social classes; it was only played out through the struggle between adversarial hegemonic projects. It dictated preparedness for armed conflict, readiness to deploy the arts of insurrection. It engaged a battle of ideas, waged with the science of Marxist analysis and the arts of persuasion. But it could not be disengaged from a struggle over the very shape, the contours and dimensions, of the battlefield. This struggle might be waged consciously according to the arts of organisation, but it would most often unfold spontaneously, the product of impromptu variations upon or challenges to established convention whose bearing would be reinforced or transformed in unforeseen ways by the sheer weight of popular involvement. The conventions governing political actors' expectations of one another, deployed upon the material environment of politics, shape an arena for political action which, although subject to change at the hands of those implicated in it, both offers various possibilities for action and exerts a kind of structural constraint upon the plans of actors. This arena is encountered by individual actors, like baseball players having to adjust to an idiosyncratic stadium, not exactly as persuasion and not exactly as coercion but as something like the force of circumstance. Thus, the exercise of hegemony could make itself felt not only in consent to persuasion or fear of coercion but also in adaptation to the force of circumstance. The spontaneous working-class movement, in throwing up the soviets, had transformed the circumstances of political action in ways that made some constraints more pressing and others less so, some possibilities more real and others less so, some threats more plausible and others less so, some arguments more persuasive and others less so; in thus reconstructing the political arena, it enabled/required actors – not only workers themselves but also peasants, soldiers, sailors, employees, intellectuals (and, of course, landlords and bourgeois) – to reorient themselves in relation to the political struggle for hegemony in the bourgeois-democratic revolution.

Theory and Practice in the Struggle for Hegemony

Applying this politico-strategic logic to the analysis of the spontaneous revolutionary movements of the peasants and the workers, Lenin was able to endow the project of proletarian hegemony with a more concrete orientation. Prior to the revolution, he had characterised the exercise of hegemony by analogy with a tribune of the people, whose function it was to articulate any and all popular grievances against the regime; this universal role is preserved but the menace of a rival project of bourgeois hegemony, on the one hand, and the emergence of a revolutionary peasant movement, on the other, required that hegemony take the specific form of an alliance between the working class and the peasantry. The object of proletarian hegemony need no longer be designated only in abstract and teleological terms as the more or less thorough bourgeois-democratic transformation of Russian society but could be understood, through the intermediary of the peasant revolution, in determinate relation to variant forms of extraction of capitalist ground rent and the social relations generated thereby. Hegemony figured earlier as a kind of generalised proletarian influence, liable to be confused in practice with the mere dissemination of party propaganda, but with the emergence of an institutional form, the soviet, capable of enacting the proletarian-peasant alliance and exercising revolutionary state power, hegemony could be conceived concretely as embracing the mass action of the working class.

The politico-strategic logic at work in Lenin's political analyses dictated receptiveness to conjunctural variations in the class struggle. This endowed his theoretical stance with a degree of reflexivity, enabling him to bring the practical experience of the spontaneous mass movements to bear upon the lacunae of Marxist theory. The idea of proletarian self-activity that formed the substance of the Menshevik notion of hegemony was adaptable in quite another sense. Conformable to the limits of any situation, it manifested itself differently in accordance with variations in the circumstances of the class struggle. Whatever form it assumed, however, since the self-activity of the working class was always asserted in opposition to the hegemonic orientation of Bolshevism and thus never conceived in relation to the strategic logic of the struggle for hegemony, what defined it was that it prefigured the socialist aim, contained it in intention. In this sense there was no distance between theory and reality, no theoretical lacunae, but also no possibility of theoretical growth. The form of self-activity appropriate to the given situation would have to develop spontaneously, in an ad hoc fashion. The call for proletarian self-activity would be adjusted to an arena of struggle imposed by the defeat of the revolution; instead of contesting the boundaries of that arena, the Mensheviks would allow the illegal party apparatus to fall into disuse and disrepair. Menshevism had long figured, on Lenin's strategic map, as a conduit for the hegemony of the liberal bourgeoisie – but this, he claimed, amounted to an abandonment of the very project of proletarian hegemony in the bourgeois-democratic revolution. The Mensheviks would increasingly abandon the language of hegemony. But they had never held, and so could not have abandoned, the concept of hegemony as Lenin had come to employ it.

The Menshevik stance in relation to the institution of the soviets invites comparison with the eighteenth-century chemists Joseph Priestley and Carl

Wilhelm Scheele. Although they were the first to produce oxygen experimentally, they were unable to comprehend their accomplishment in scientific terms. Captive to the categories of the prevailing theory, according to which combustion consisted not in the consumption of oxygen but in the release of an absolute combustible, phlogiston, Scheele termed the product 'fire-air', Priestley 'dephlogisticated air'. It fell to Antoine Lavoisier, by using the experimental evidence his colleagues produced, to criticise the terms of the old theory and elaborate a new conceptual apparatus, to identify 'fire-air' as a new chemical element and accomplish the scientific discovery of oxygen. Similarly, although the Mensheviks took a hand in the constitution of the soviets, they were able to locate them theoretically only as a forum for the political education of the working class through self-activity. By siting the soviets in the context of the politico-strategic logic of the struggle for hegemony, Lenin was able to specify in what their self-activity consisted, perhaps thereby playing Lavoisier to the Mensheviks' Priestley; he could criticise their characterisation as forms of revolutionary local self-government and discern in them the capacity to embody an alliance of revolutionary democrats and hence to assume state power.[146]

Through analyses of the peasant movement and especially of the constitution of the soviets by the spontaneous working-class movement, the logic of spontaneity and consciousness worked out in *What Is to Be Done?* was extended and thereby rectified. The recognition that spontaneous movements innovate in ways that not only anticipate but also challenge 'consciousness' placed Marxist theory itself within the logic of political struggle. Identified through its contradictory relation to consciousness, spontaneous innovation need not call for the reassertion of consciousness but for its rectification and development. It was not despite, but just because of, the need to import consciousness into the spontaneous working-class movement that its converse, the need to import the innovative capacity of the spontaneous movement into consciousness, could be recognised. This contradictory relation forms the context for Lenin's insistence upon the concrete analysis of the concrete situation:

> Absolutely hostile to all abstract formulas and to all doctrinaire recipes, Marxism demands an attentive attitude to the *mass* struggle in progress, which, as the movement develops, as the class consciousness of the masses grows, as economic and political crises become acute, continually

---

146 The oxygen/phlogiston analogy is prompted by the example of Engels ('Preface' to Marx 1885, pp. 5–16) and Althusser (1970c, pp. 149–57), who invoked it to illuminate the relation between Marx's concept of value and its Ricardian antecedent.

gives rise to new and more varied methods of defence and attack.... Under no circumstances does Marxism confine itself to the forms of struggle possible and in existence at a given moment only, recognising as it does that new forms of struggle, unknown to the participants of the given period, *inevitably* arise as the given social situation changes. In this respect Marxism *learns*, if we may so express it, from mass practice... To attempt to answer yes or no to the question whether any particular means of struggle should be used, without making a detailed examination of the concrete situation of the given movement at the given stage of its development, means completely to abandon Marxism.[147]

The circumstances of struggle shift independently of the dictates of any, even a hegemonic, political actor. A position established today can always be transformed tomorrow in accordance with the strategic calculation of an adversary, the unforeseen consequences of one's own actions, or the logic of spontaneous innovation. So a hegemonic project presumes the ability to adapt to the changing conjunctures of political struggle. To engage with the concrete conjuncture, a politics of hegemony must combine awareness of the underlying structures that drive and resist change with openness to diverse sites and sources and forms of social and political innovation. Such a politics describes a dialectical relation of vanguard and masses, and the logic of this relation must shape the relation of theory and practice. To the extent that Lenin was able to redeploy theory in this way in the midst of class struggles, he acknowledged in practice its necessarily situated and hence limited character; that theory was situated in this way represented a critical distance from the abstract harmonies of orthodox Marxism and so facilitated the work of probing, and thereby pushing further, its limits. And if theory must indeed be situated in relation to the class struggle, this work is properly understood as another aspect of the struggle for hegemony.

---

147 Lenin 1906f, pp. 213–14.

CHAPTER 8

Imperialism and the Logic of Hegemony: The 'People' in the Class Struggle

> 'A shift in the structure of experience...'
> As I pass down Broadway this misty late-winter morning,
> the city is ever alluring, but thousands of miles to the south
> the subsistence farms of chickens, yams and guava
> are bought by transnationals, burst into miles
> of export tobacco and coffee; and now it seems the farmer
> has left behind his plowed-under village for an illegal
> partitioned attic in the outer boroughs. Perhaps
> he's the hand that emerged with your change
> from behind the glossies at the corner kiosk;
> the displaced of capital have come to the capital.
>
> A shift in the structure of experience
> told the farmer on his Andean plateau
> 'Your way of life is obsolescent.' – But hasn't it always been so?
> I inquire as my column spills from page one
> to MONEY&BUSINESS. But *no*, it says here the displaced
> stream now to tarpaper *favelas*, planetary barracks
> with steep rents for paperless migrants, so that they
> remit less to those obsolescent, starving
> relatives on the *altiplano*, pushed up to ever thinner air and soil;
> unnoticed the narrative has altered.
>
> — ANNE WINTERS[1]

∴

The War and the Split in Socialism

The assassination of Archduke Franz Ferdinand of Austria by Serbian nationalists occurred against the backdrop of a system of military alliances that

---

[1] Winters 2004, pp. 11–12.

enmeshed the great powers of Europe. It served to trigger a war whose ultimate stakes, Lenin would claim, were the terms of the division and re-division of the world among the powers; this made it a struggle whose roots could be traced to a new, imperialist stage of capitalism. The conflict had been brewing for years and had been expected, not least by the Marxist thinkers and the social-democratic parties of the Second International. The phenomenal growth of militarism had been traced in Rudolf Hilferding's *Finance Capital*[2] and Rosa Luxemburg's *Accumulation of Capital*[3] to a capitalist mainspring that set in motion the imperialist pursuit of colonies and of domination more generally. In *The Road to Power* Kautsky had already established a link between imperialism, militarism and the intensification of class antagonisms: the growth of proletarian power and the trepidation it inspired among the bourgeois had held back a European war for three decades, but 'the great powers are heading toward a situation in which the rifles will finally fire of themselves'.[4] It was the duty of the international proletariat to fight imperialism and militarism: 'war means revolution', and the proletariat could 'no longer speak of a *premature* revolution when it has drawn from the existing governmental framework as much strength as could be drawn from it, when a transformation of this framework has become a condition of its further advancement'.[5] The 1907 Stuttgart Congress of the International adopted a resolution on 'Militarism and International Conflicts' that enjoined Social Democrats to treat the crisis provoked by war as a means to hasten the downfall of capitalism.[6] The 1912 Basel Congress produced a 'Manifesto' predicting that war would engender economic and political crisis, enjoining the workers to regard as criminal any violence against each other for the sake of capitalist profit, dynastic honour or secret diplomatic treaties, committing socialists to take advantage of the wartime difficulties of the government and the indignation of the masses to further socialist revolution, and threatening bourgeois governments with the examples of the Paris Commune and the 1905 revolution in Russia as indicating what might be reaped from the seeds of war.[7]

If the World War was a tangible expression of the crisis of capitalism, it brought to maturity, with a rapidity that stunned Lenin, among others, what had been for some time a *crise larvée* in international socialism.

---

2   Hilferding 1910.
3   Luxemburg 1913.
4   Kautsky 1909, p. 80.
5   Kautsky 1909, p. 84.
6   See, for example, the account in Joll 1955; see also Lenin 1907a, p. 80; 1907b, p. 92.
7   See Lenin 1915b, p. 213; 1915d, pp. 307–8; see also Luxemburg 1914–15, pp. 293–301.

The incantation to international proletarian solidarity was broken up in the storm of patriotic fervour that raged through the belligerent countries. The call to arms offered the workers a taste of adventure, respect as the defenders of the fatherland, and the dream of heroic glory.[8] For many a Social Democrat the war effort signalled the end of an increasingly uncomfortable exile from the national community, from society and citizenship.[9] Some Social Democrats simply acquiesced to what they saw as the inevitable. Others, like Plekhanov, evinced more enthusiasm: '[I]f I were not old and sick I would join the army. To bayonet our German comrades would give me great pleasure'.[10] Thus did the parties of the Second International surrender, whether reluctantly or with enthusiasm, at the first shots of war; only in Russia and Serbia did the Social Democratic parliamentary delegations refuse to vote war credits to their respective governments. This socialist patriotism was everywhere decked out in colours of freedom, progress and democracy. The Germans could even adorn it with quotations from Marx and Engels urging war against Tsarism. The French and English had to settle for more general references to the defence of democratic liberties which, they had no doubt, were threatened by Prussian militarism. This kind of argument presented certain problems for the Russians, but there were those who thought they could overcome them by seconding the cause of their entente colleagues. With whatever degree of enthusiasm or reluctance, however shady or acute the reasoning, the alignment of a majority with the war aims of the ruling classes was a betrayal that split the working-class movement irrevocably. Rosa Luxemburg was among the first to pronounce the post-mortem judgment: 'On August 4th, 1914, German Social-Democracy abdicated politically, and at the same time the Socialist International collapsed. All attempts at denying or concealing this fact ... tend objectively to perpetuate, and to justify, the disastrous self-deception of the socialist parties, the inner malady of the movement, that led to the collapse'.[11]

A Hegelian Epiphany?

The wartime crisis of socialist internationalism signalled, not only the collapse of the Socialist International, but also, according to an influential current of interpretation, the collapse of the theoretical coordinates that had defined Lenin's pre-war Marxism. A political exile in a neutral country, Lenin retreated

---

8   This point is well discussed in Mitchell and Stearns 1971.
9   See Mitchell and Stearns 1971; see also Roth 1963, Chapters XI and XII.
10 Cited in Baron 1963, p. 324.
11 Luxemburg 1915, p. 197.

to the silence of the public library in Berne, where he set out to struggle through the dialectic of Hegel's most abstract work, *The Science of Logic*. From this encounter would spring a newfound understanding of dialectics and a corresponding rethinking of Marxism. For Raya Dunayevskaya, Lenin's notebooks on *The Science of Logic* constituted 'the philosophical foundation for the great divide in Marxism', a complete reconceptualisation of the relation between material, economic forces and 'human, subjective forces, the relationship between science and human activity', that turned on 'a restoration of truth to philosophic idealism against [the] vulgar materialism' of his pre-war philosophy.[12] The Leninist dialectic did not negate only those who had betrayed socialist internationalism: 'The collapse of the Second International meant the breakdown of all previous thought and method of thought which called itself Marxist, i.e., *all* established Marxism' – not only Kautsky, but also Bukharin and even Lenin's own pre-war Marxism.[13] From the ashes of Lenin's critique would emerge a series of innovative analyses, evincing the creativity of revolutionary subjectivity: the contradictions of imperialism, the anti-imperialist agency of oppressed nationalities, the revolutionary activity of the soviets against bureaucracy and the working masses against the state.[14] Kevin Anderson fleshes out this line of thought, linking it with the conventional wisdom about the Lenin of *What Is to Be Done?*, in a book-length treatment of Lenin's encounter with Hegel. The inability of Second International Marxism to comprehend the dialectic and, consequently, revolutionary subjectivity is held responsible for the alleged authoritarianism of Lenin's vanguardist politics; only the engagement with Hegel enabled Lenin 'to point the way toward the only type of Marxism that is viable today: one with a multiple concept of subjectivity rather than an exclusive reliance on the traditional industrial working class'.[15] More recently, Slavoj Žižek has enveloped the theme of Lenin's Hegelian epiphany in a Lacanian pathos: 'the Lenin we want to retrieve is the Lenin-in-becoming, the Lenin whose fundamental experience was that of being thrown into a catastrophic new constellation in which old reference points proved useless, and who was thus compelled to *reinvent* Marxism'.[16] This 'dialectical return to Lenin aims at repeating, in the present global conditions, the 'Leninian' gesture of reinventing the revolutionary project in the

---

12 Dunayevskaya 1971, pp. 168, 171.
13 Dunayevskaya 1971, p. 172.
14 Dunayevskaya 1971.
15 K. Anderson 1995, p. xiv.
16 Budgen, Kouvelakis and Žižek (eds.) 2007, p. 3; see also Löwy 1976; Michael-Matsas 2007; K. Anderson 2007; Kouvelakis 2007; and Balibar 2007.

conditions of imperialism, colonialism, and world war'.[17] The 'gesture' to be repeated is, however, neither a re-enactment nor a readjustment of political strategy but the sheer experience of revolutionary subjectivity, openness to the future: 'What Lenin did for 1914, we should do for our times... "Lenin" stands here for the compelling *freedom* to suspend the stale existing ideological coordinates, the debilitating *Denkverbot* in which we live. It simply means being allowed to start thinking and acting again'.[18]

Inasmuch as readings organised around a Hegelian epiphany rely upon a caricature of the Marxist orthodoxy of the Second International as lacking a subjective dimension, and insofar as it draws sustenance from the conventional wisdom about *What Is to Be Done?*, it runs into significant obstacles in consequence of the argument developed – and the evidence deployed – in the preceding chapters. It also sits uneasily with the form of Lenin's wartime critique of Kautsky, at once a critique of failure to rethink Marxist positions in the light of the dramatically changed context and conjuncture of the war and a critique of the abandonment in the face of hostilities of revolutionary positions already well established by Marxist orthodoxy. Not *all* the old coordinates were to be cast aside as useless. Lenin did not frame his intervention as iconoclastic but as defence of a tradition, a revolutionary tradition that not only allowed but even insisted upon innovation in the face of the new, but a tradition nonetheless. This circumstance allows Lars Lih to make the argument that the theory of imperialism, widely understood as a Leninist innovation, is already to be found 'lock, stock and barrel' in Kautsky's *Road to Power* of 1909.[19] Now, whatever else may be said about this contention, it is simply deaf to the Leninist claim that 'the standpoint of the division of the international proletariat into two camps' was 'the key position in the epoch of imperialism'.[20] From this standpoint, whence Lenin's critique of imperialism is enunciated, the split in the international proletariat – to which the SPD's political collapse and Kautsky's theoretical retreat, deferring the revolutionary culmination of the contradictions of capitalism, were integral – figures as an essential aspect of the imperialist epoch. The split in the international proletariat was thus part of the *explanandum* of the Leninist theory of imperialism and it will be seen that Lenin's *explanans* was conceived (as Kautsky's was not and, if I am

---

17 Budgen, Kouvelakis and Žižek (eds.) 2007, p. 3.
18 Budgen, Kouvelakis and Žižek (eds.) 2007, p. 4. A similar conflation of the issue of the requisites of agency in general with the issue of the concrete analyses requisite to effective action under definite circumstances is criticised in Shandro 1998.
19 See Lih 2011.
20 Lenin 1916c, p. 343.

right, could not have been) with this aspect in view. *Something* shifts, between Kautsky and Lenin, in the understanding of revolutionary political agency; Lenin's approach to imperialism was reflexive in a way that Kautsky's was not. So the idea of Lenin's Hegelian epiphany, while overdrawn, represents a response, albeit exaggerated and unfocussed, to a real movement in Leninist practice and theory.

If any theoretical coordinate was swept aside in the Leninist critique of imperialism, it was the orthodox Marxist assumption of the political unity of the working-class movement and of the Marxist party of the proletariat. But this movement was anticipated in Lenin's practice within Russian Marxism of drawing lines of political demarcation, by his thesis of consciousness from without, and by the politico-strategic logic of the struggle for hegemony. Now, the claim of Perry Anderson's formative article on the 'antinomies' of Gramsci's political thought, that the term 'hegemony', '[f]orged to theorise the role of the working class in a bourgeois revolution, was rendered inoperative by the advent of a socialist revolution'[21] resonates with the theme of Lenin's wartime epiphany. That Lenin should have worked out a form of vanguard organisation appropriate to a socialist revolution while labouring under a misconception as to the very aim of the revolution is something Anderson treats as merely ironic. If he is correct, the practical and theoretical contradictions through which the notion of hegemony emerged had little bearing upon the most evident movements of Lenin's practice and theory, the wartime split in the International, his break with Kautsky and the Bolsheviks' reorientation in 1917 from bourgeois-democratic to socialist revolution. This judgement, however, depends upon treating the notion of hegemony narrowly as a particular strategic orientation, not as a mode of analysis or a meta-strategic logic of struggle, and certainly not as a 'philosophical fact'.

But the role of Marxist theory as Lenin understood it was not simply to indicate the aim of struggle but to situate that aim in the context of action – the class struggle – and to revise it reflexively in accordance with the concrete circumstances and the logic of the struggle. The relation between political actor and political aim was always mediated by the strategic logic of the struggle. Marxism was not simply an injunction to action – go, workers, go! – but a guide to action, with map and compass, as it were. A careful examination of the emergence of Lenin's theory of imperialism and of the theory of the state he articulated in the midst of the 1917 revolution will turn up the imprint of the politico-strategic logic that he had worked out in the struggle for hegemony in the bourgeois-democratic revolution. This logic required that the political

---

21 P. Anderson 1976, p. 17.

activity of the Marxist vanguard party of the proletariat take into account the reflexivity of political action and the complex, uneven and contradictory intersection of a diverse and changing cast of political actors, adversaries, allies and neutrals. The theory of imperialism enabled Lenin to reconceive socialist revolution – and socialism – in terms of this logic. If Lenin de-emphasised the terminology of hegemony for political reasons after some of his Bolshevik critics deployed it to urge completion of the bourgeois-democratic revolution in contrast to the struggle for socialist revolution, this is not true of the distinctive meta-strategic logic of political analysis and engagement that informed it. If the language of hegemony is appropriate not only to the strategy but also to the logic, then the theory of imperialism and the practice of socialist revolution do not mark Lenin's abandonment of the politico-strategic logic of the struggle for hegemony, but his extension and even generalisation of it.

The logic of hegemony facilitates an account of Lenin's wartime reorientation as a moment of decision inscribed in a process of struggle, as well, indeed, as an appreciation that a moment of innovation (a revolution in the revolution, as it were) presumes its inscription in a process of struggle that carries with it a tradition of self-understanding. It may also facilitate a clearer understanding of what Lenin was looking for in Hegel and what he thought he found there. The first sentence of an unpublished manuscript in which Lenin summed up his encounter with Hegel reads: 'The splitting of a single whole and the cognition of its contradictory parts... is the *essence*... of dialectics'.[22] Although this claim indicates that the questioning and reconceptualisation – the transformation – of lines of demarcation is essential to the process of knowledge in general, it is impossible to read it in awareness of the context in which it was written without seeing its reference to the split in the socialist movement, in the international proletariat. But this split had its local precedent in Lenin's practice of drawing and redrawing lines of demarcation in the pre-war Russian movement. In this light, Lenin's *Philosophical Notebooks* might be understood as a kind of coming-to-(self-)consciousness of some of the broader dialectical implications of his pre-war political practice. Thus, after characterising the struggle of opposites as absolute, their unity as relative, he rested the distinction between 'subjectivism' and dialectics upon the dialectical recognition that 'the difference between the relative and the absolute is itself relative. For objective dialectics there *is* an absolute *within* the relative'.[23]

---

22 Lenin 1915e, p. 359.
23 Lenin 1915e, p. 360.

'Kautskyism' and the Highest Stage of Capitalism

With his analysis of imperialism, Lenin aimed to provide the means for revolutionary Social Democrats to reorient themselves in the critical new conjuncture. To that end, he sought to explain the connection between the logic of capitalist development, the war and the crisis of international socialism. In concluding his major work on the subject, Lenin pulls together a definition of 'the economic essence of imperialism' as 'capitalism in transition, or more precisely, as moribund capitalism'.[24] Imperialism is 'the monopoly stage of capitalism', a transitional stage to socialism.[25] And in a preface added after the fall of Tsarism, Lenin writes more forthrightly of 'the fact that imperialism is the eve of the socialist revolution'.[26] The characterisation of imperialism as 'the highest stage of capitalism' is neither an afterthought nor mere rhetorical flourish. It is not only congruent with the political function of Lenin's theory – if imperialism is the eve of the socialist revolution, identifying with the social-democratic allies of empire is unthinkable – but built into its conceptual structure.

The primary target of Lenin's theory of imperialism was not the 'social chauvinism' of those like Plekhanov who sided with their respective imperialist governments – 'One does not analyse arguments in favour of a pogrom; one only points them out so as to put their authors to shame in the sight of all class-conscious workers'[27] – but 'Kautskyism', the Social Democratic current whose opposition to the war was conceived apart from the struggle for socialist revolution and undertaken instead with a view to preserving the conditions for an eventual fraternal reunification of the Socialist International once hostilities had concluded. The workers of each country, Kautsky wrote, had a pressing interest, like their compatriots, in fending off enemy invasion; 'the independence and unity of its national area ... [constituted] an essential part of democracy' and hence of the struggle for socialism. So as not to give grounds for future wars, the Social Democrats in each nation were duty-bound to regard the war 'only as a war of defence' and to seek its causes 'not in the personal depravity or inferiority of the opponent, but in objective conditions ... that is, [in] imperialist conflicts and the armaments race'.[28]

---

[24] Lenin 1916b, p. 302.
[25] Lenin 1916b, p. 266.
[26] Lenin 1916b, p. 187.
[27] Lenin 1914, p. 97.
[28] Kautsky 1915, pp. 94, 95.

Kautsky's conception of 'ultra-imperialism' endowed this stance with a theoretical rationale: a drive to export capital from industrial states to agrarian regions was inherent in the logic of capitalist development and sustained an imperialist aspiration to subordinate those regions politically, but the export of capital need not generate an armaments race between contending powers or imperialist war. Indeed, such militaristic competition was increasingly inimical to the development of capitalism. Though it was the preferred policy of finance capital, the very contradictions it engendered could provoke the strongest imperialist powers to abandon the arms race and conjugate their efforts in the joint, and therefore peaceable, exploitation of the world – a sort of cartelisation of foreign policy, ultra-imperialism. Like imperialism, ultra-imperialism was grounded in the exploitation of labour by capital and, though it posed distinctive dangers, the Social Democrats would fight against it 'just as energetically as we fought imperialism'.[29] In keeping with the logic of orthodox Marxism, the import of this line of thought was to consign the socialist revolution to a future in which political forces align themselves clearly and unambiguously along the lines of social class and thereby, in the present, merely to palliate the contradictions of the international socialist movement; it thus conceived the socialist class struggle in abstraction from the complex, uneven, contradictory conjunctures in which it was, inevitably, concretised and hence, just as inevitably, modified, displaced and diffracted.

Lenin's characterisation of imperialism as the highest stage of capitalism asserts, against Kautsky, the impossibility of any subsequent ultra-imperialist phase of capitalism.[30] This assertion derives, I will argue, from a more fundamental critique of certain Kautskyan or orthodox Marxist modes of thinking about the limits of capital, about the end of capitalism or, to put the same point another way, a critique of a certain way of thinking about – or failing to think about – socialist revolution. Lenin's claim that imperialism is the highest stage of capitalism, read in terms of the unilinear historical logic of Marxist orthodoxy, translates to a claim about the inability of capitalism to further the development of the productive forces. In the years after Lenin's death something like this line of thought would come to inform the politics of the Communist International.[31] More recently Bill Warren has claimed to derive 'the underlying logic of Lenin's theory', presented in abstraction from the struggle over the division of the world between monopoly capitalist combines,

---

29   Kautsky 1914, p. 86.
30   Competent summaries of Lenin's theory may be found in Nabudere 1977, pp. 101–28; and Kemp 1967, pp. 63–85; also of note is the treatment in Palloix 1970.
31   See Kemp 1967, pp. 106–33.

from the characterisation of capitalism as 'overripe' in a few countries: competition engendered monopolies whose control of domestic markets was so tight that the competitive incentive to innovate had dried up, the living standards of the masses were bound to stagnate and the monopolists could find no profitable spheres of domestic investment.[32] Neil Harding concurs, attributing to Lenin the claim that monopoly capitalism extinguished free competition and with it the engine whereby capital augments the forces of production.[33] He further reads the highest stage of capitalism as implying the dissolution of all intermediate social strata and the complete differentiation of society into bourgeoisie and proletariat.[34] But this is to mistake one tendency, always subject to modification through the workings of the politico-strategic logic of the struggle for hegemony, for the analysis as a whole and thus to miss the essential complexity of Lenin's strategic orientation: imperialism was the highest stage of capitalism and thus the stage of transition to socialism not by virtue of a supposed inability to stimulate technological progress or enhance economic growth, but because it restructured the arena of class struggles, extended the contradictions of capitalist production to the furthest corners of the world and thus reorganised irreversibly the pattern of contradictions that would shape the transition to socialism. What is crucial to his analysis is not some dogma concerning the level of production allegedly already attained, but the manner in which the logic and the structure of imperialist contradictions grow out of the social form of monopoly capitalism within which production is organised and moves.

The immanent tendencies of the capitalist mode of production, as analysed by Marx, provide the groundwork for the claim that imperialism is the highest stage of capitalism. The anarchy of capitalist production necessarily results in the concentration of production. Concentration of production is evident in a number of phenomena, both in the increasing scale of production and the dominance of the market by a relative handful of enterprises capable of reaching monopolistic agreements and in the combination of different branches of production in the same enterprise, facilitating corporate planning and technical improvements and strengthening competitive positions in the search for raw materials.[35] By means of agreement, cartels can dictate terms of sale and payment, fix prices and production schedules and divide profits. The associated monopolists have the resources, the connections and the research

---

32 See Warren 1980, pp. 50–2.
33 Harding 1981, p. 46.
34 Harding 1981, p. 316.
35 See Lenin 1916b, pp. 197–8.

capacity to estimate and control access to sources of raw materials, to estimate the capacity of markets and share them out, and to monopolise means of transportation and pools of skilled labour.[36] As monopolists strive to subordinate all aspects of the process of production, productive activity is increasingly organised and rationalised: the process of technical innovation is socialised and, with the introduction of 'scientific management' practices – Taylorism, time-and-motion study, and so on – the labour process itself is tightly enmeshed in capitalist rationalisation.[37] Through the process of concentration in banking, the money revenues of the entire society – capital, small business, employees and the upper stratum of workers – are placed at the disposal of monopoly capital. Thus is established 'the form of universal book-keeping and distribution of means of production on a social scale, but solely the form'.[38] The banks and industry coalesce into a financial oligarchy, finance capital; '[s]cattered capitalists are transformed into a single collective capitalist' and the banks themselves are transformed from modest executors of auxiliary operations into guardians of the money capital of the whole capitalist class, enjoying access to and, by facilitating or obstructing credit, wielding control over the financial position of the various capitalists.[39] 'Capitalism in its imperialist stage leads directly to the most comprehensive socialisation of production'. Inasmuch as its apparatus of production, accounting and planning limns the skeletal form of the socialist organisation of production, it 'drags the capitalists, against their will and consciousness, into some sort of a new social order, a transitional one from complete free competition to complete socialisation'.[40]

Since 'appropriation remains private', the growth of monopoly capitalism does not do away with the competitive struggle between capitalists, but since 'production becomes social', it does fundamentally transform the scope and the stakes and the means of the struggle and, consequently, how it is waged.[41] The field of battle upon which the contest over raw materials, labour and markets is joined has now grown to global dimensions. The stakes of victory or

---

36 See Lenin 1916b, pp. 202, 205.
37 Lenin did not deal directly with the phenomenon of 'scientific management' in his *Imperialism*; but it figured prominently in his original plans for the book and in his preparatory notebooks on imperialism (see Lenin 1915–16, pp. 152–60, 230–43). A perceptive discussion of Lenin's engagement with Taylorism may be found in Linhart 1976, especially pp. 84–94).
38 Marx 1894, 606, cited at Lenin 1916b, p. 216.
39 Lenin 1916b, pp. 216, 214.
40 Lenin 1916b, p. 205.
41 See, for example, Lenin 1916b, pp. 276, 300.

defeat, both financial and other, have grown in tandem and the intensity of the struggle is correspondingly heightened. More significant, however, is the fact that the competitive struggle need no longer be conducted 'blindly': it no longer pits scattered producers against each other, producing for an unknown market and perhaps unknown even to one another. The size, resources, and connections of the monopolies do not shield them from competition, but do provide them with some room for manoeuvre. The socialisation of production makes it possible, and hence necessary, to wage the struggle more strategically and thus more 'consciously'. Agreements are concluded between the various monopolists, but these agreements do not conclude the competitive struggle between them; they are to be understood, rather, as one form of that struggle. As the circumstances of competition – the availability of raw materials and cheap labour, the accessibility of markets and the most advanced techniques of production – shift, so too do the relative bargaining positions of the competitors. Monopolists strive not just to find new sources of raw materials or cheap labour or to open new markets or to discover new techniques but to monopolise these, to deny them to their competitors: agreement is always conditional, competition a given. Lenin's analysis of monopoly capitalism as the highest stage of capitalism follows on Marx's characterisation of the phenomenon of joint stock companies as 'the abolition of the capitalist mode of production within the capitalist mode of production itself, and hence a self-abolishing contradiction, which presents itself *prima facie* as a mere point of transition to a new form of production'.[42] Those features of monopoly capital, bound up with the socialisation of production, that create the possibility of socially planned production and hence prefigure socialism are precisely what serves, in the context of private appropriation, to render competition more conscious, more strategic, more intense and, in this sense, more political – and consequently more dangerous.

Capitalism is an inherently expansive mode of production. It is Lenin's contention that the growth of monopoly capitalism transforms the form of capitalist expansion: whereas the period of free competition was characterised by the export of goods, the dominance of monopolies brings with it the export of capital. The export of capital depends upon the uneven development of capitalist production. This unevenness is evident in an enormous accumulation of 'surplus capital' in a few wealthy countries: surplus in the sense that it will not be applied to meet the needs of the working masses when higher profits are to be sought in investment abroad, as they always are where capital is scarce and land, labour power and raw materials are plentiful. Although the export of

---

42   Marx 1894, p. 438.

capital is most usually read in quantitative terms as the export of quantities of money capital,[43] and it does sometimes take the form of loan capital, it assumes the entry of the recipient countries into 'world capitalist intercourse', the construction of railways, the establishment of the preliminary conditions for industrial development.[44] Its primary significance in Lenin's argument is as the export of a social relation of production, the relation between wage labourer and capitalist. The colonial countries are henceforth drawn not only into commodity exchange but into capitalist production: 'Imperialism is...the export of capital. Capitalist production is being transplanted to the colonies at an ever increasing rate'.[45] The export of capital thus signifies the extension of the contradictions of the capitalist mode of production throughout the world. Quantitative analysis of capital exports is thus appropriately situated in the context of – and hence subordinate to – analysis of the logic of strategic competition between contending monopoly capitalist groupings and imperialist powers.

Monopoly capitalist struggle over the economic division of the world and imperialist contention over its division into spheres of control and influence are fuelled, on Lenin's account, by the imperatives of capital investment – but no more and perhaps less than by the need to secure access to markets, to labour power and especially, in view of the rapidity of technological development, even to sources of merely potential raw materials.[46] This need for access, nurtured by the sheer scale, the connections, and the capacity of the capitalist monopolies for strategic planning, must give rise to the ambition to deny access to competitors, to adversaries. Once this ambition had arisen somewhere, it was transformed by the logic of competitive struggle from a mere possibility into a necessity everywhere. Lenin often cited the dictum of the Austrian Marxist Rudolf Hilferding: 'Finance capital does not want liberty, it wants domination'.[47] That the territorial division of the world should have reached completion with the onset of the epoch of monopoly capitalism is, in the logic of Lenin's argument, anything but a coincidence. That capital can only develop unevenly renders unavoidable shifts in the relative strength of

---

43 See, for example, Michalet 1985, pp. 261–72, 313–16.
44 Lenin 1916b, pp. 241–2.
45 Lenin 1916c, p. 337.
46 This part of Lenin's analysis has been widely criticised for its alleged one-sided emphasis upon economic processes and in particular upon the export of capital (see, for example, Fieldhouse 1972). However, Stokes 1969 has shown that Lenin's formulations are sufficiently supple to invalidate this criticism.
47 Cited at Lenin 1916b, p. 262.

the contending powers, and consequently, once the world has been divided, struggles to shift the division in accordance with the new relation of forces. Under capitalism, Lenin argues, such a struggle can be decided only by force. The implantation of the machinery of colonialism and the export of capitalist social relations of production give rise to movements of resistance, where class struggles mesh with opposition to national and colonial oppression and draw the peoples of the colonies into a global arena of struggle. Imperialism is thus the highest stage of capitalism in the additional sense that it extends the contradictions of capitalism to the furthest reaches of the world and pushes them, in the form of imperialist war, to their highest intensity.

Parasitism and Social Decay

That imperialism breeds a parasitic tendency to the decay of the social body constitutes a further sense in which it is the highest stage of capitalism. Although Lenin does not invoke the passage, his use of the terminology of parasitism suggests the *Communist Manifesto*'s condemnation of the bourgeoisie as 'unfit to rule because it is incompetent to assure an existence to its slave within his slavery, because it cannot help letting him sink into such a state that it has to feed him, instead of being fed by him'.[48] This tendency is easily misconstrued as a simple collapse into economic stagnation unless it is situated within the dynamic interaction of contradictory tendencies that intensify the uneven development of capitalism. Parasitism and decadence do not figure in Lenin's argument as synonyms for economic stagnation, but serve to suggest a social organism whose dominant elements depend essentially upon, but nonetheless cannot exist without sapping, the productive activity of others. The real significance of imperialist parasitism is as a set of permutations in the field of class forces and something like a politico-strategic logic of the struggle for hegemony is indispensable to their analysis. The advent of monopoly curbs the forces of 'technical and, consequently, of all other progress' and gives rise to 'the *economic* possibility...of deliberately retarding technical progress'. Always counteracted, this tendency to stagnation does not, on the whole, predominate, but it nonetheless 'continues to operate and in some branches of industry, in some countries, for certain periods of time, it gains the upper hand'.[49] The unevenness of this process meshes with the tendency of finance capital to accentuate the separation of ownership from production and to

---

48   Marx and Engels 1848, pp. 495–6.
49   Lenin 1916b, p. 276.

engender a stratum of people who live on their holdings, without taking any part in productive enterprise: 'The export of capital ... still more completely isolates the rentiers from production and sets the seal of parasitism on the whole country that lives by exploiting the labour of several overseas countries and colonies'.[50] The conjunction of these tendencies in imperialism gives rise to a 'rentier' or 'usurer' state, a militarist machine that safeguards the lucre of empire and envelops it in an ideology of chauvinism.

To bring out the parasitical character of the process Lenin borrows from the English critic of imperialism J.A. Hobson the image of 'a group of advanced industrial nations, whose upper classes drew vast tribute from Asia and Africa, with which they supported great tame masses of retainers, no longer engaged in the staple industries of agriculture and manufacture, but kept in the performance of personal or minor industrial services under the control of a new financial aristocracy'.[51] Parasitism does not, in Lenin's estimation, preclude the rapid growth of capitalism – '[o]n the whole, capitalism is growing far more rapidly than before; but this growth is ... becoming more and more uneven ... [and even] manifests itself ... in the decay of the countries which are richest in capital'.[52] It does, however, express a mutation in the pattern of class struggle and class alliance. In particular, the super-profits accrued to monopoly capital through the super-exploitation of cheap labour in the colonies provide a material basis for a counter-tendency to the tendency of capital to equalise wages and working conditions and hence for the formation of a stratum of relatively well-to-do workers distinct from the mass of wage labourers, a 'labour aristocracy'. Bribed by 'the capitalists of the "advanced" countries' with crumbs from their imperialist super-profits, 'the labour leaders and the upper stratum of the labour aristocracy ... are the real agents of the bourgeoisie in the working-class movement, the labour-lieutenants of the capitalist class, real vehicles of reformism and chauvinism'. Lenin characterises '[t]his stratum of workers-turned-bourgeois', the labour aristocracy, as the principal locus of opportunism in the working-class movement and 'the principal social ... prop of the bourgeoisie'.[53]

---

50 Lenin 1916b, p. 277.
51 Hobson 1902, cited at Lenin 1916b, p. 280. That Lenin's treatment of imperialist parasitism and the labour aristocracy draws upon Hobson's work is well known; less known but worthy of note is the use he makes in this context of the important work *Immigration and Labor* (1912) by Isaac Hourwich, a Russian-American statistician and Bolshevik sympathiser.
52 Lenin 1916b, p. 300.
53 Lenin 1916b, p. 194.

Lenin does not elaborate a systematic analysis of the process whereby workers turn bourgeois; taken individually, some of his formulations suggest a simple, straightforward transaction, a crude bribe, and hence an equally simple, transparent realignment of forces in the class struggle. Thus construed, the notion of an aristocracy of labour bears the implication that the temptations of opportunism and the reach of bourgeois influence are localised in specific strata of the working class.[54] But Lenin indicates that the bribery takes place 'in a thousand different ways, direct and indirect, overt and covert' and the characterisation of labour aristocrats as 'vehicles' implies that the influence of 'reformism and chauvinism' is more broadly diffused.[55] The role of a labour aristocracy is assumed by specific strata of the working class but just how these strata are characterised – indeed, just which strata these are – is subject to significant variation across Lenin's analyses. The labour aristocracy could take the form, as in imperial England, of skilled workers defending a monopoly of craft privilege, but even where the position of skilled labour was eroded by the application of science to production and the imposition of 'scientific management' techniques, the tradesman's wages, paid by monopoly capital to secure access to 'unskilled' labour, could express the process of bourgeoisification.[56]

What emerges across these variations is a tendency toward hierarchy within the class of wage labourers and consequently a process of division, of the hierarchical fragmentation of the working-class movement. The lines around which hierarchies form (skilled versus unskilled, national versus immigrant, white versus black, and so on), as well as the advantages accruing to the better positioned (higher wages, better conditions, greater security, social respectability, political rights, and so on), are subject to endless variation because they are not the simple product of a series of deals but the outcome of social struggles. Imperialist super-profits furnish capital – and the state – with the wherewithal to concede some of the workers' most pressing demands, though in forms that typically reflect and reproduce division and hierarchy. They constitute a material basis for the belief, most congenial to the better-off workers but

---

54 The concept of the labour aristocracy and its use by Lenin have been widely criticised, but the criticism typically relies upon reducing its referent to a particular social stratum considered in abstraction from the logic of class struggle and the struggle for hegemony – which form the essential context of Lenin's analysis – even where it is not also misleadingly conflated with the personnel of the trade-union and Social Democratic party apparatus, the so-called 'labour bureaucracy'; for a recent example, see Post 2010. Generally reliable accounts of Lenin's concept of the labour aristocracy may be found in Nicolaus 1970 and Elbaum and Seltzer 2004, pp. 3–48.
55 Lenin 1916b, p. 194.
56 See Lenin 1915–16, p. 157.

available also to others who may hope to emulate their gains, that economic improvement and social reform are more generally attainable under capitalism and, consequently, for the opportunist belief that socialism can be attained through the peaceful accumulation of reforms.[57] The struggle for socialist revolution, for the general interest of the working class, is thus effectively subordinated to the struggle for social reform, for particular improvements benefitting particular groups of workers. The resulting inability of Social Democrats to meet the imperialist war with a declaration of class war effectively disorganised the proletariat as an independent social force, allowing its fragments to be consolidated into a system of social control in which the leaderless masses were confronted one by one, as isolated individuals, with the organised power of the state.[58] Putting forth a critique of the war and imperialism while refusing to call into question the practice of unity with proponents of chauvinism under the banner of Social Democracy, indeed holding forth the prospect of reconciliation in conditions of peace, Kautskyism serves to hold this alignment in place, absorbing the grievances of the masses while refusing to challenge their subordination to an opportunist leadership.[59]

Thus opportunism is engendered in the working-class movement not merely through the influence of petty-bourgeois milieus and newly proletarianised or backward strata, but decisively through the influence of the 'stratum of workers-turned-bourgeois', a stratum generated by the most developed forms and tendencies of capital with influence crystallised in the leading economic, cultural and political organisations of the working-class movement. The function of imperialist parasitism in Lenin's argument is to underwrite the claim that the influence of opportunism in the working-class movement and hence the need to struggle against this influence are inescapable under capitalism: the logic of the uneven development of imperialism renders inconceivable a future stage in which the logic of capital, levelling the conditions of the workers and hence unifying them as a class, might erode the roots of opportunism and render the struggle against it unnecessary. The workers are constituted as a class not by excluding the stratum of labour aristocrats but by establishing a political context within which the struggles of that stratum can

---

57 See Lenin 1915b; and 1916b, pp. 276–85.
58 See Lenin 1915b, pp. 240–50. This aspect of Lenin's analysis has received sparse attention but it finds an echo in the thoughtful treatment of the working-class movement in nineteenth-century England in Foster 1975; see also the critique of Foster in Jones 1975. The historical literature on the labour aristocracy in Britain is reviewed in McLennan 1981, pp. 206–32.
59 See, for example, Lenin 1915b, p. 249.

be integrated with and thus subordinated to a project of proletarian socialist revolution. Such a context can be established, Lenin insists, only in the course of a political struggle against opportunism and hence also against Kautskyism.

'Imperialist Economism'

In the context of imperialism, as in the context of bourgeois-democratic revolution, the political struggle to constitute the proletariat as a class is shot through the working-class movement, but also extends far beyond it. The advent of imperialism helps to generate new configurations of alliance and contention among the propertied classes, reorganising their reservoirs of strength and redistributing the sites of their vulnerability. The logic of struggle between monopolies is entwined in a field of contradictions between cartelised and non-cartelised industry, between monopoly and the free market, between the operations of finance capital and the manoeuvres of independent traders and so on, and drives finance capital and the monopolies to seek not simply freedom but domination. This tendency results everywhere, '[w]hatever the political system ... [in] reaction and an extreme intensification of [political] antagonisms ... Particularly intensified become the yoke of national oppression and the striving for annexations, i.e., the violation of national independence'.[60] Reaction in turn generates democratic resistance. In the colonies, intensified national oppression elicits a political awakening of the popular masses – peasant, proletarian and bourgeois – in the form of movements of national liberation. In developed countries the intensification of capitalist contradictions is expressed in 'the high cost of living and the tyranny of the cartels',[61] in the erosion of political democracy and liberties and pervasive reaction, as well as in the heightened oppression of nationalities. These manifestations of parasitism and decay give rise to 'a petty-bourgeois-democratic opposition to imperialism'.[62] '[R]eactionary in its economic basis', this current exhibits a utopian yearning to restore the imagined peace and harmony of the era of free competition. Its struggles for peace and democracy, conducted independently of the proletarian political project of socialist revolution, are animated by a forlorn hope of palliating the contradictions of imperialism. Since his speculative construction of a post-war ultra-imperialist future excludes the perspective of socialist revolution from the present, Kautsky

---

60 Lenin 1916b, p. 297.
61 Lenin 1916b, p. 300.
62 Lenin 1916b, p. 287.

effectively assumes a petty-bourgeois democratic stance.[63] In articulating what amounts to petty-bourgeois ideology in a Marxist idiom, Kautskyism provides a sort of ideological cement to bind the workers to organisations dominated by an alliance of labour aristocrats and petty-bourgeois democrats and hence a prophylactic against the emergence of an independent working-class political project. Whence the decisive strategic significance, in Lenin's eyes, of targeting Kautsky in the critique of imperialism.

Reactionary as the petty-bourgeois economic basis of this democratic resistance to imperialism may be, the resistance itself need be no more reactionary than struggles waged by sections of the aristocracy of labour against capital. Indeed, when situated in the context of the class struggle between proletariat and imperialist bourgeoisie, each can be made to serve as a source of fuel for the fires of revolution. To grasp them in this way presumes the political posture of a proletarian vanguard capable of animating an independent political project of socialist revolution even while embracing the process of revolutionary struggle, warts and all – that is, as an inevitably uneven and contradictory conjunction of heterogeneous forces. In a defence of the right of nations to self-determination penned just after his *Imperialism*, in a passage occasioned by the failed Easter 1916 Irish uprising against British colonial rule, Lenin argued that social revolution is inconceivable 'without revolts by small nations in the colonies and in Europe, without revolutionary outbursts by a section of the petty bourgeoisie *with all its prejudices*, without a movement of politically non-conscious proletarian and semi-proletarian masses' against various forms of oppression. The point is set in relief by a Leninist lampoon of leftist expectations for a 'pure' social revolution: 'So one army lines up in one place and says, "We are for socialism", and another, somewhere else and says, "We are for imperialism", and that will be a social revolution!'[64] The 'army' of revolution is assembled only on the field of battle, in the course of hostilities, from whatever elements are available, drawn often from the ranks of the opposing forces. The job of revolutionary political leadership is thus in part a work of bricolage, requiring both a clear awareness of one's situation enveloped in a complex, uneven, shifting ecology of battle and the independence of judgement to act decisively in its midst.

The point is argued by reference to the experience of the bourgeois-democratic revolution of 1905 in Russia and then extended to the 'socialist revolution in Europe'. The logic of social polarisation does not render marginal the political significance of intermediary forces between bourgeoisie and

---

63   Ibid.
64   Lenin 1916c, pp. 355–6.

proletariat; contradictions among revolutionary forces, both between the working class and the petty bourgeoisie and within the working class itself, persist throughout the process of socialist revolution, shaping the course and tempo of its development; the unevenness and fragmentation of the movements leave them open to the logic of strategic rivalry between imperialist camps (as in German efforts to assist the Irish insurrection).[65] 'Capitalism is not so harmoniously built that the various sources of rebellion can immediately merge of their own accord'.[66] But only the diversity of popular struggles, of their participants and their forms and of the sites and rhythms of their development, can assure the breadth and depth of the revolutionary process; only individual, sporadic, untimely and therefore unsuccessful actions will enable the masses to ready themselves, gain political experience and size up 'their real leaders, the socialist proletarians'. Articulating the disposition of these 'variegated and discordant, motley and outwardly fragmented' movements of the masses in the logic of the struggle against capital, the 'class-conscious vanguard' strives to unite them, provide them with direction, and engage them in the struggle to 'capture power, seize the banks, expropriate the trusts ... and introduce other dictatorial measures which in their totality will amount to the overthrow of the bourgeoisie and the victory of socialism, which, however, will by no means immediately "purge" itself of petty-bourgeois slag'.[67]

There is, then, no moment at which the would-be leadership of the socialist revolution would not have to reckon with the fact of heterogeneity, both within and without the working-class movement, and hence to understand itself as situated on a field of battle subject to a complex, uneven and contradictory logic of the political struggle for hegemony. This is the burden of Lenin's critique of 'imperialist Economism', a trend of thought in some Bolshevik quarters expressed in a rejection of the 'bourgeois-democratic' right of nations to self-determination. Nikolai Bukharin and Iurii Piatakov defended this position on the grounds that exercising a right to self-determination was impossible in an era dominated by imperialism and that calling for it was unnecessarily divisive when an impending socialist revolution could command the wherewithal to put an end to national oppression and bring nations together. Although it was advanced specifically in relation to national self-determination, Lenin discerned in this defence the outlines of a familiar logic of political analysis, one that would not preclude political, even revolutionary action, but would

---

65 See Lenin 1916c, p. 357.
66 Lenin 1916c, p. 358.
67 Lenin 1916c, p. 356.

constrict it within narrow, corporate boundaries: 'just as the Economism of blessed memory could not link the advent of capitalism with the struggle for democracy', the newly emergent imperialist Economism 'cannot solve the problem of *how to link the advent of imperialism with the struggle for reforms and democracy*'.[68]

This inability, Lenin argues, grows out of an abstract and undifferentiated understanding of imperialism and a corresponding failure to grasp the uneven development of the national question in the advanced countries of Western Europe and the United States where bourgeois national movements had long accomplished their progressive tasks, in Eastern Europe where 'the awakening of the masses to the full use of their mother tongue and literature...is *still* going on' and in the colonial and semi-colonial countries where national self-determination is 'largely a thing of the *future*'.[69] Not only is solidarity with struggles for bourgeois-democratic rights – Lenin instances a republic, political democracy and freedom of divorce in addition to national self-determination – necessary so that the workers ready themselves for socialist revolution, it is imposed by the strategic necessity of constructing the unity of the revolutionary forces, and hence of denying to adversaries the leverage needed to pry it apart. The context of uneven development implies that social revolution unfolds as a combination of 'civil war by the proletariat against the bourgeoisie in the advanced countries and a *whole series* of democratic and revolutionary movements, including the national liberation movement, in the underdeveloped, backward and oppressed nations'.[70] Recognition of a right of nations to self-determination is neither unrealistic – since imperialist domination can assume a variety of political forms – nor divisive, since '[i]n *real life* the International is composed of workers *divided* into oppressor and oppressed nations', where joint action in defence of the nation, including joint action with a bourgeoisie, may carry very different political implications.[71] Unity of the working class can be forged across national divisions only if workers of the oppressed nation make support for the exercise of self-determination conditional upon freedom to resist the dangers of bourgeois nationalism, while workers of the oppressor nation make criticism of the movement of the oppressed nation conditional upon recognition of its right to self-determination, just as unity of action 'against the tsarist army near

---

68 Lenin 1916d, p. 15.
69 Lenin 1916e, pp. 38, 39.
70 Lenin 1916e, p. 60.
71 Lenin 1916e, p. 56.

Moscow, say, requires that the revolutionary forces march west from Nizhni-Novgorod and east from Smolensk'.[72]

Thus must would-be revolutionary leaders understand not only that political action is subject to a complex, uneven and contradictory logic of struggle, but also that it is affected by where they themselves are situated in the field of battle. Political action must be adjusted not only to the temporal succession of concrete conjunctures but to the dispersion of forces within the political space of the conjuncture; this must lead differently situated actors to adopt different, even 'contradictory' courses of action in order to attain a common aim. Awareness of this circumstance also lies behind Lenin's insistence that consistent revolutionary opposition to the war supposed not only a willingness to 'turn the imperialist war into a civil war' but a preference for the defeat of one's own government: to the criticism that this stance, when generalised to all the belligerent states, collapsed into incoherence,[73] Lenin could reply that only revolutionary defeatism allowed political actors consciously to assume the initiative – to begin the revolution – somewhere in particular rather than defer it – that is, forfeit it – to a hypothetical agreement between hypothetical revolutionaries everywhere in general. Only revolutionary defeatism clearly acknowledged the potential consequences of assuming the initiative anywhere and thereby galvanised the distinction between real and merely hypothetical – Kautskyan – revolutionaries.[74]

The continuity of terminology evident in Lenin's critique of 'imperialist Economism' gives pointed expression to the reading proposed here. In *What Is to Be Done?* Lenin did not criticise Economism as the renunciation of political struggle but as the subordination of political struggle to narrowly trade-unionist concerns, hence to the hegemony of the bourgeoisie in the democratic revolution, and thus as a form of proletarian subalternity. In so doing, he reconceived the politics of the class struggle through an optic I have termed the politico-strategic logic of the struggle for hegemony. His analysis of imperialism implies a similar rethinking of the relation between democratic struggles and socialist revolution: while the logic of imperialist domination fuels a reaction against democracy everywhere, parasitic dependence upon imperialist super-profits nourishes a split in the working-class movement. The socialist revolution does not announce itself through a simplification of class alignments; it must take the form, rather, of the conjunction of the proletarian struggle for socialism with a variety of revolutionary-democratic movements.

---

72   Lenin 1916e, pp. 57–8.
73   See Draper 1996.
74   See Lenin 1915c; Lenin 1915–16, pp. 734–5; Shandro 1998–9.

The mantle of leadership in the struggle for bourgeois-democratic rights does not fall by default to the forces of proletarian socialism. Since imperialism gives rise to bourgeois movements of national liberation and to a petty-bourgeois democratic opposition, the revolutionary vanguard of the proletariat must seek to assume the political leadership of the democratic struggles of heterogeneous or even of non-proletarian strata of the people while waging a political and ideological struggle against the hegemony of petty-bourgeois democracy – more precisely, of an alliance of petty bourgeois and labour aristocrat – in the struggle against imperialism. The dynamic of political struggle inherent in imperialism, understood as the eve of the socialist revolution, reproduces on an extended scale the politico-strategic logic of the struggle for hegemony in the bourgeois-democratic revolution. A consequence of Lenin's analysis of imperialism – and of the critique of 'imperialist Economism' that flows from it – is thus the generalisation of the politico-strategic logic of the struggle for hegemony. Imperialism is therefore the highest stage of capitalism in the further sense that there can be no socialist revolution whose political leadership does not emerge through its engagement in the complex, uneven, contradictory logic of the struggle for hegemony.

The State and the Logic of Revolution

When Lenin's most abstract work of political theory is read in light of the context of its genesis and composition, or when it is simply read with care, it is possible to discern the politico-strategic logic of the struggle for hegemony at work even, or perhaps especially, in its pages. *The State and Revolution*, however, is rarely read in context or with the kind of care political thinkers other than Lenin are accorded as a matter of course. Read in abstraction from the strategic issues that confronted Lenin in the class struggle, it has sometimes been portrayed as an anarchic, even 'idyllic' utopia, incongruous with Lenin's usual absorption in the hard-nosed politics of organisation, tactics and power in the here-and-now: to discuss the dissolution of the state as a practical proposition is surely to signal the dissolution of the rationale for strategic political calculation and, with it, the theoretical basis of the vanguard party.[75] Proponents of this sort of reading have been able to point to the relative paucity of references to the party in the text of *The State and Revolution*. A.J. Polan, however, who asserts that the meaning of the text can only be sought in a history 'temporally situated *after* the appearance of the text, not prior to and

---

75 See, for example, Ulam 1969, pp. 462–3; and Conquest 1972, pp. 85–7.

simultaneous with its production', varies this approach by arguing that Lenin's theoretical dissolution of the state is tantamount to dismantling the rule of law, the elementary condition of political liberty, and hence to a dystopian prefiguration of 'the subsequent history of the Soviet Union' congruent with the elitist Lenin of conventional wisdom.[76]

Whether reading it as utopian or dystopian, this interpretive optic relies upon the assumption that the object of the text is to advocate an ideal type of social organisation; the logic of Lenin's argument is thereby supposed to turn upon a comparison between pre- and post-revolutionary institutional models, between the state and the stateless communist society of the future. It is as though Lenin thought it possible to understand revolution by standing back from the historical process of its unfolding – to occupy a position of 'absolute knowledge' – so as to compare before and after; revolutionary consciousness would thereby be reduced to consciousness of a post-revolutionary aim, abstracted from the reflexive action of grasping the logic of the revolutionary process and one's implication in it. It is in this very text, however, that Lenin takes Kautsky to task for using just this kind of analytical procedure in order to deal with or, as Lenin would have it, to evade the question of the state and revolution. He recounts how Kautsky responded in 1912 to the leftist contention that the workers' struggle is also a struggle against state power by distinguishing two issues, the Social Democratic stance of opposition to the present state and 'the form the "future state" will be given by the victorious Social-Democrats'.[77] Lenin glosses this response as follows: '[A]t present we are an opposition; what we shall be after we have captured power, that we shall see', and comments, *'Revolution has vanished!'*[78] The criticism is not that Kautsky fails to specify the form of the future state, or even of a future non-state – after all, Lenin himself defers this very question[79] – but that by formulating the issue as an antithesis between present and future states of society, he evades the question at issue, the transition from one to the other, the relation of the state and revolution. But this is just how the issue is constructed in the utopian/dystopian reading of *The State and Revolution*. It would thus seem possible, for those endowed with the requisite understanding of its future, to determine the meaning of the text not only without regard to 'its origins, its motivations or its intentions',[80] but also apparently without regard to much of

---

76 Polan 1984, p. 52.
77 Cited at Lenin 1917i, p. 490.
78 Lenin 1917i, p. 491.
79 See Lenin 1917i, pp. 474–5.
80 Polan 1984, p. 52.

what it says – as if this future and how it is to be understood could be anything other than products of struggle and objects of contention.

The State and Revolution was written in August and September 1917 while Lenin was in hiding. After Bolshevik workers and soldiers paraded their armed might through the streets of St. Petersburg over two days in July, the Socialist Revolutionary and Menshevik leadership of the Soviets acquiesced as the General Staff dispatched cadets and Cossacks to close down Bolshevik newspapers and moved to disarm the workers and revolutionary soldiers, as the bourgeois and monarchist press slandered Lenin and other Bolshevik leaders as German spies, and as the provisional government ordered them arrested. As Lenin was writing in the underground, rail workers and soldiers, attentive to Bolshevik warnings of impending counterrevolution and despite the dithering leadership of the soviets, managed to derail General Kornilov's attempted *coup d'état* before it really got on track.[81] With the counterrevolution beaten back and any other claim to revolutionary leadership discredited, the masses looked to the Bolsheviks for leadership in the soviets, setting in motion the 'political crisis – the eve of the October revolution' – that would interrupt the writing of *The State and Revolution* before Lenin could complete more than the title of a projected final chapter on 'The Experience of the Russian Revolutions of 1905 and 1917'.[82] The currency of the utopian reading might be attributed in part to the fact that this chapter remains unwritten, but this fact ought to bring home more forcefully the necessity of reading the text together with Lenin's preparatory notebook, plans for the unwritten chapter and contemporaneous writings – that is to say, reading it in context.[83]

The circumstances of its composition suggest the inadequacy of the notion that *The State and Revolution* owes its inception to revolutionary intoxication amidst the 'festival of the masses'. This notion has been effectively refuted by Marion Sawer, who traces the impetus for Lenin's return to the classical Marxist writings on the state to a controversy with Bukharin in 1916.[84] In 'The Imperialist Robber State', a brief article published against Lenin's advice, Bukharin argued that Marxist socialism distinguished itself from anarchism not by its support for the state, which must be 'abolished' [*gesprengt*], but only by its support for

---

81 See Rabinowitch 1968.
82 See Lenin 1917i, pp. 496–7. The dynamic of the revolutionary process in the capital is well discussed in Rabinowitch 1976.
83 This material is not included in the English edition of Lenin's *Collected Works*, a translation of the fourth Russian edition, but is available in English translation as *Marxism on the State: Preparatory Material for the Book 'State and Revolution'* (Lenin 1917a).
84 See Sawer 1977.

'a centralised, that is, technically more progressive' organisation of production after the revolution. He portrayed the contemporary state as a 'modern leviathan' capable of absorbing all the other organisations of the ruling class, material and spiritual as well as coercive, into itself and 'penetrating into every pore of finance-capitalist society'. Remarking 'how deeply the roots of state organisation have sunk into the minds of the workers', he insisted upon Social Democratic 'hostility in principle to the state'.[85] Lenin took the young Bolshevik theorist to task on two grounds: first, the anarchist prescription simply to *abolish* the state is not shared by socialists since the dictatorship of the proletariat, indispensable in the transition from capitalism to socialism, is also a form of state, albeit one that would *wither away*; second, the Social Democratic stance was stated abstractly – 'hostility in principle to the state' versus the grip of 'the state idea' upon the minds of the workers – instead of being placed in the context of the split between opportunist and revolutionary trends in the working-class movement. The thrust of the criticism was to situate the state in relation, first, to the *process* of revolution and, second, to the process of *class struggle*.[86]

Lenin concluded by indicating a desire to return to the subject at greater length. In the weeks leading up to the February 1917 revolution he compiled an extensive notebook, gathering the materials and rehearsing the arguments that would figure in *The State and Revolution*. The notebook shows that Bukharin prompted Lenin to rethink his position on the state but it does not show – Sawer, Stephen Cohen and Neil Harding notwithstanding[87] – that Lenin adopted the position of his younger colleague. Lenin did acknowledge that '[i]n essence...Bukharin is closer to the truth than Kautsky' and repeatedly underlined the importance of smashing the military-bureaucratic state machine; otherwise he attributed the same mistakes to Bukharin as he had earlier, with the result that 'instead of exposing the Kautskyites, he *helped* them'.[88] What concerned him, both in the notebook and in *The State and Revolution*, was to think through the destruction of the state machine together with the withering away of the state as elements cohering in an integral process of revolution.[89] He tried to do this by distinguishing, as

---

85 Bukharin 1916, pp. 103–4, 106–7.
86 Lenin 1916f, pp. 165–6.
87 See Sawer 1977, pp. 216–18; Cohen 1975, pp. 41–3; and Harding 1981, pp. 114–17.
88 Lenin 1917a, p. 26.
89 See Lenin 1917a, pp. 24–5, 48–52; Lenin 1917i, pp. 404–5.

Bukharin had not done, between state power and the apparatus of the state[90] and then thinking through the movement of these terms in relation to the process of the class struggle. That he examined the process of class struggle, as Bukharin did not, under the optic of the politico-strategic logic of the struggle for hegemony enabled him to bring the rich experience of 1905 to bear upon the question of socialist revolution and the state; indeed, even before beginning his preparatory notebook, he was looking to consult the 1906 Bolshevik resolution on the soviets.[91]

War accelerated the amalgamation of the state with capitalist associations and transformed the hinterland of the advanced countries into 'military convict prisons for the workers', while the opportunist leaders of the official socialist parties adapted themselves to the imperialist interests of their respective national states. Although the forces of proletarian revolution were ripening, working people would not escape the influence of the imperialist bourgeoisie without a struggle against 'opportunist prejudices concerning the "state"'.[92] A return to classical Marxist analysis of the state was called for. Lenin begins by locating the state expressly *not* as a technically indispensable instrument of coercion in the context of 'the growing complexity of social life [and] the differentiation of functions', but rather politically in the context of the class struggle, as a product of 'the irreconcilability of class antagonisms'.[93] Thus situated, the state can be understood as 'a power which arose from society but places itself above it and alienates itself more and more from it' and be seen to consist of 'special bodies of armed men' equipped with such institutional means of repression as prisons. This state apparatus operates directly or, in a parliamentary democracy, through the myriad conduits of wealth and an ensemble of petty constraints and exclusions that squeeze the poor out of politics, indirectly in the service of the ruling class.[94] It cannot establish order by

---

[90] Balibar 1974a uses the distinction between state power (a relation of power, the domination of one social class over another), and the state apparatus (the institutional 'machinery' in which the relation of state power is crystallised, subject to historical change but, as a *state* apparatus, essentially separate from the body of society) to explicate Marx's thesis, derived from the experience of the Paris Commune and introduced into later editions of the *Communist Manifesto*, that 'the working class cannot simply lay hold of the ready-made state machinery and wield it for its own purposes'; the distinction is developed with reference to Lenin's attempts to grapple with the soviet experience of the transition to socialism in Balibar 1976. See also Miliband 1970 and Colletti 1972b.

[91] Lenin 1916g, p. 589.

[92] Lenin 1917i, pp. 387–8.

[93] Lenin 1917i, pp. 393–4.

[94] Lenin 1917i, 397–8, p. 466.

reconciling the antagonistic classes, only hold their irreconcilable antagonism in check by oppressing the exploited classes. In this sense, the state apparatus is an institutional precipitate of the social dominance of property owners over those who must live by working for them, a transformed form of social power, alienated from class society and so beyond its control.

Class antagonism eventuates in socialist revolution when the working class seizes state power and appropriates the means of production on behalf of society, doing away with class distinctions and thereby setting in motion the process of the withering away of the state. But since its hierarchical and exclusive mode of organisation fits the military-bureaucratic apparatus of the state to the purposes of a dominant minority, 'the working class cannot simply lay hold of the ready-made state machinery and wield it for its own purposes'.[95] Since class antagonism is irreconcilable, these purposes cannot be accomplished without suppressing the resistance of the exploiting class – and since this resistance is conducted in the first instance through the agency of the ready-made state apparatus, the latter cannot simply be replaced but must be destroyed, 'smashed', its organisation shattered, its operation rendered impossible. To accomplish these purposes, the workers must therefore organise themselves as the ruling class, that is, as a state – but this is a state apparatus 'so constituted that it begins to wither away immediately and cannot but wither away'.[96] The working class initiates a decisive shift in social power: it seizes state power, precisely in smashing the ready-made state apparatus, and it organises its own domination in such a way that it gradually sheds the antagonistic, state-like form of social power alienated from society.

To understand how the destruction of the bourgeois state apparatus and the withering away of the state are conceived as aspects of an integral process of revolution, it is necessary to grasp what 'the working class organised as the ruling class' means. While Lenin expected the transition from capitalism to communism 'to yield a tremendous abundance and variety of political forms', he followed Marx's recognition of the Paris Commune as 'essentially a working-class government, the result of the struggle of the producing against the appropriating class, the political form at last discovered under which to work out the economic emancipation of labour'.[97] Its first decree suppressed the standing army and replaced it with the armed people; whereas the suppression of the majority by the minority required a special apparatus, separated from the people and centralised bureaucratically from above, no special apparatus was

---

95   Cited at Lenin 1917i, p. 419.
96   Lenin 1917i, p. 407.
97   Cited at Lenin 1917i, p. 436.

needed in order for the majority of the people to suppress the exploiting minority: nothing other than the action of the armed people themselves, consciously and voluntarily centralised through democratic forms of popular organisation.[98]

The parliamentary rituals of bourgeois democracy served merely to lend legitimacy to the rule of capital and to dignify the privileges of deputies who could not be held to account, since the 'real business of government' was conducted 'behind the scenes' in the military-bureaucratic machine.[99] The Commune, having dismantled the repressive instrumentation of the state, sought to restore the 'legitimate functions' of government power to 'the responsible agents of society': it was composed of municipal councillors chosen locally by universal suffrage, responsible and subject to recall at short intervals; for the most part workers or their acknowledged representatives, its members enjoyed no special privileges and were paid workers' wages like all other public functionaries, who were also to be elected, responsible and revocable. 'The Commune was to be a working, not a parliamentary, body, executive and legislative at the same time':[100] since its members would help put the laws they approved into practice and would be directly accountable to their constituents, freedom of opinion, discussion and debate would not breed fraud. By permitting, indeed requiring, that its agents and representatives be held accountable, the Commune did away with 'parliamentarism'.

The Commune was thus 'a thoroughly expansive political form', open to society, subject in principle to its direction and therefore well suited to wither away. But this political form takes on its 'full meaning and significance only in connection with the "expropriation of the expropriators"'.[101] The socialisation of production implicit in monopoly capital and the financial system and explicit, albeit in alienated form, in such state-capitalist monopolies as the postal service, generates a 'mechanism of social management' that, once prised from the grip of private property and the tentacles of bureaucracy, 'can very well be set going by the united workers themselves, who will hire technicians, foremen and accountants' at workers' wages.[102] All citizens having become employees of the association of armed workers, the basic requisite is 'accounting and control' to ensure that all 'do their proper share of work and get equal pay'. These functions – which Lenin takes care to distinguish from scientific

---

98 See Lenin 1917i, pp. 423–4, 434–5.
99 Lenin 1917i, p. 428.
100 Marx 1871, p. 331, cited at Lenin 1917i, pp. 423–4, 427.
101 Lenin 1917i, p. 426.
102 Lenin 1917i, pp. 431–2.

and technical work – having been simplified by capitalism, reduced to the 'simple operations... of supervising and recording... arithmetic and issuing appropriate receipts', could be undertaken by any literate person. As the workers themselves further simplify 'the more important functions of the state' and as 'the *majority* of the people begin independently and everywhere' to keep accounts and exercise control, the former capitalists and 'the intellectual gentry who preserve their capitalist habits' will be left with 'nowhere to go'. As independent participation not only in voting and elections, but also in state administration, becomes 'universal, general and popular', the state as a power separate from society as a whole withers away. '[A]ll will govern in turn and will soon become accustomed to no one governing'.[103]

The Logic of Revolution and Hegemony

If *The State and Revolution* is reduced to Lenin's commentary on the experience of the Commune, however, its account of the revolutionary process may be construed too narrowly and the need for political struggle and political leadership in the process rendered opaque. Such a reading is misleading, not only because the text was left incomplete, but also because the text itself, read attentively, points beyond it, as it does when Lenin underlines the indispensability of political leadership:

> The proletariat needs state power... both to crush the resistance of the exploiters and to *lead* the enormous mass of the population – the peasants, the petty bourgeoisie, and semi-proletarians – in the work of organizing a socialist economy.
> By educating the workers' party, Marxism educates the vanguard of the proletariat, capable of assuming power and *leading the whole people* to socialism, of directing and organizing the new system, of being the teacher, the guide, the leader of all the working and exploited people in organizing their life without the bourgeoisie and against the bourgeoisie.[104]

Such leadership cannot be taken as given, Lenin continues, but must be established in the course of political struggle against the prevalent opportunist temptation for parties of the working class to represent the interests of 'the

---

103 Lenin 1917i, pp. 478–9, 492–3.
104 Lenin 1917i, p. 409.

better-paid workers', narrowly construed, in isolation from the struggles of the masses of the people. Lenin's insistence upon leadership not only of the masses of the working class but of the whole people is quite categorical.

Lenin's point makes eminent sense when read in the context of his analysis of imperialism and his defence, against imperialist Economism, of the inherently complex, uneven, contradictory process of the revolutionary struggle against imperialism. There is no mass struggle without the participation of strata of the petty bourgeoisie and backward workers, with 'their prejudices, their reactionary fantasies, their weaknesses and errors' and with their energy and enthusiasm, their sheer mass.[105] It may be low wages, poor working conditions or unemployment that actuates the backward workers or it may be, as with their petty-bourgeois confrères, the high cost of living, the petty tyranny of the bureaucracy or police brutality, or as with their student or intellectual or even bourgeois compatriots, national oppression or racial or religious prejudice, or as with their peasant and soldier comrades, the simple desire for peace and bread and to live a normal life, etc., etc. The consciousness of workers taking part in the spontaneous movements of the masses cannot but reflect the diversity and the contradictions of the movements themselves – but, if solidarity born of struggle should reflect itself in their consciousness of being part of 'the people', this would not be an illusion or a 'reactionary fantasy' but the simple recognition of an essential truth about the mass struggle. And if, as Lenin argued, the process of socialist revolution were inconceivable without 'variegated and discordant, motley and outwardly fragmented mass struggle', this would also be an essential truth about the process of socialist revolution. Not the whole truth, certainly, but a part of it and hence also a part of the political identity of the proletariat as a class. The proletariat constitutes itself as a class only in aggregating the people around itself as a kind of political penumbra. To characterise the process of class formation in this way is to look at it from within; examined from without, on the contrary, individuals and groups might simply be subsumed under the appropriate Marxist class categories. But where lived experience reflects a contradictory combination of class practices and positions, workers may well see themselves as workers but, perhaps at the same time, as would-be petty bourgeois or lumpen proletarians 'on the make', and certainly without knowing how they will be seen, and where they will be ranked, by those who would lead them. If assuming the political leadership of the backward workers is a duty incumbent upon the vanguard of the proletariat, it cannot be fulfilled by segregating the workers from the mass

---

105   Lenin 1916c, p. 356.

struggles of the people but only by seeking the political leadership of the revolutionary movement of the people as a whole.

When Lenin invokes the soviets, along with the Commune, as a form of organisation of the proletariat as the ruling class,[106] the proletarian character of these institutions is to be sought not in the class exclusiveness of their membership, but precisely in their openness to the heterogeneous ensemble of the people. In *The State and Revolution*, even while excoriating the petty-bourgeois penchant for place-hunting as one of the springs of bureaucracy, he follows Marx in criticising the Commune for its inability to conclude an alliance with the peasantry and appeal to the peasant and petty-bourgeois desire for cheap government which, he argues, could be satisfied only by the proletarian state-in-the-process-of-withering-away.[107] As the medium for the revolutionary political participation of the popular masses, this institutional openness is a necessary condition both of the dictatorship of the proletariat and of the withering away of the state. Openness – 'expansiveness' is Marx's term, 'flexibility' Lenin's – is simply an enabling condition: the emergence of a forum in which the practical concerns of the masses can be given political expression and their political aims can be debated in practical terms does not by itself accomplish the revolutionary seizure of state power, nor does it destroy the 'ready-made state machine'. What it does do, however, is permit a dramatic expansion of the limits of political participation and political debate, including debate about these very issues. And the engagement of the masses in political struggle and political debate cannot take place without the influence of petty-bourgeois democracy, an influence expressed both in the erosion of the institutions of popular power by bureaucratic place-hunting cloaked in parliamentary bombast and in trepidation before the revolutionary seizure of state power. The participation of the masses is thus at once an agency indispensable to the process of the socialist revolution and the object of a political struggle that runs through the logic of this process from revolutionary crisis to the seizure of power to the withering away of the state. The revolutionary process, including the withering away of the state, is thus governed by the politico-strategic logic of struggle for hegemony. Suggested by the incomplete text of *The State and Revolution*, this point is abundantly demonstrated in Lenin's preparatory notebook and plans and in his contemporary writings.

Working through the logic of Marx's account of the Commune in his preparatory notebook, Lenin notes as '[t]he condition' for the conquest of political power by the proletariat the political 'awakening... of the *majority* of the

---

106 See Lenin 1917i, pp. 491, 495.
107 See Lenin 1917i, pp. 413, 422, 426.

population, *their* active participation *instead* of the officials in state affairs', though this will require 'proletarian guidance, they must be guided by organised and centralised proletarians'. This would require a reduction of the working day and participation by everyone in both productive labour and state administration. 'The Russian Revolution', he adds, 'has *approached* this very device, on the one hand, in weaker fashion (more timidly) than the Paris Commune; on the other hand, it has shown *in broader fashion* the "Soviets of Workers' Deputies", of "Railwaymen's' Deputies", of "Soldiers' and Sailors' Deputies", of "Peasants' Deputies". This *Nota bene*'.[108] Written prior to the revolution of 1917, these notes refer to the soviets of 1905: 'timid' in not having seized power, 'broad' nonetheless in their adaptability to the heterogeneity of the people. Lenin recurs to the same point in his plans for the unwritten chapter of *The State and Revolution*: 'Experience of 1917. Mass enthusiasm, Soviets. (Their wide scope and their weakness: petty-bourgeois dependence)'.[109] This contradiction is essential to the political logic of the revolutionary process: the weaknesses of the soviets derive from the very aspect that sustains their strengths, their constitutive openness to the popular masses. Lenin ascribed to petty-bourgeois influence the acquiescence of the Menshevik and Socialist Revolutionary leadership in the counterrevolutionary repression of the Bolsheviks and the resulting utilisation of the soviets as vehicles of bourgeois domination, and counselled the temporary withdrawal of the Bolshevik slogan 'All power to the soviets!' Under the heading 'Prostitution of the Soviets by the S.R.s and Mensheviks', his outline of the unwritten chapter adverts to their acquiescence in the disarming of the people, to the bureaucratisation of the soviets themselves and to soviet non-partisanship, the 'authorities' "independence" of parties'.[110]

The outline would be fleshed out in 'Can the Bolsheviks Retain State Power?', a pamphlet penned just after Lenin set aside the manuscript of *The State and Revolution*. Among the virtues that qualify the soviets as a new state apparatus, he lists the close connection they afford between the armed workers and peasants and the people, their democratic mode of operation and lack of bureaucratic formalities, the participation of 'the most varied professions' encouraging implementation of 'the most varied and most radical reforms' and the function of the soviets as 'an organisational form for the vanguard ... of the *oppressed* classes, the workers and peasants ... [to] elevate, train, educate, and lead the entire vast mass of the classes, which has up to now stood completely outside

---

108   Lenin 1917a, p. 50.
109   Lenin 1917a, p. 94.
110   Lenin 1917a, pp. 94–5.

of political life and history'. The very features that render such leadership possible, however, render it also necessary: left unchecked, the illusions of petty-bourgeois democracy would exhaust the promise of the soviets in a purgatory of concessions, vacillation, double-dealing and pretence. The vanguard of the proletariat would have to exercise leadership in order to forestall the exhaustion of the revolution and unfetter the soviets, which could 'display their potentialities and capabilities to the full only by taking over *full* state power;... otherwise they have nothing to do... they are... simply embryos (and to remain an embryo too long is fatal)'.[111]

Evoking an image of the new soviet apparatus undertaking the work of state administration by enlisting the popular masses in the tasks of accounting and control of production and distribution, Lenin contrasts the eviction of a working-class family by the capitalist state with the forcible installation of a destitute family in a rich man's apartment. The former presents the spectacle of military forces imported from outlying areas (so as to preclude sympathy with the tenants) to protect the bailiff from the anger of the people. The latter is pictured in more prosaic fashion: Lenin would have us imagine a squad of workers' militia fifteen strong, two soldiers, two sailors, two class-conscious workers, one a party sympathiser, a student, and the rest poor working people, at least five women, domestic servants, unskilled labourers. They inspect the apartment, arrive at a reasonable allocation of space, socialise access to the telephone, and assign light duties to the unemployed members of the wealthy family; this 'state order' is drawn up in duplicate by the student and a written declaration of compliance with the order demanded.[112] Here participation in state administration is not made conditional upon literacy, or arithmetical competence, or employment by the state, or employment at all. 'The chief thing', Lenin tells us, is not knowledge or education or technique but 'to imbue the oppressed and the working people with confidence in their own strength', with a conviction of their responsibility and a sense of their ability, despite the inevitable mistakes and setbacks, to administer the state, oversee production and ensure distribution.[113] This self-confidence of the people, their courage for politics, might be supposed simply to grow in a romance of revolutionary self-discovery only if it is conceived in abstraction from the logic of the political struggle for hegemony. In Lenin's analysis, it can only grow in the soil of the class struggle, through the destruction of the 'ready-made state apparatus' but also through the everyday work of crushing the active and passive resistance of

---

111 Lenin 1917k, pp. 103, 104.
112 Lenin 1917k, pp. 112–13.
113 Lenin 1917k, pp. 114–15.

the propertied classes, leaving them with nothing to do but resign themselves to 'observing the simple, fundamental rules of the community', a practice that will of necessity 'soon become a *habit*'.[114]

Spelled out in this way, the withering away of the state is not a narrowly technical process of administration that would succeed the politics of smashing the state machine and exercising proletarian dictatorship. These are two aspects of the same process and, although reduction of the working day and technical education of the people are necessary means, their bearing on the process is governed by a political logic of struggle. Lenin's understanding of the state in the process of socialist revolution replicates the logic of his analyses of 1905–6. Indeed, this connection is made explicit in Lenin's notebook, where he compares the experience of the soviets in 1905 to the Commune, and in his plans for *The State and Revolution*, where he refers specifically to the Bolshevik resolution of 1906 on the soviets – and to theses of 1915 reiterating the substance of this resolution – and adds, '*Nil* in West-European literature on the state'.[115] The soviets arose, in 1917 as they did in 1905, from the spontaneous movement of the working class and spontaneously drew in or spread to soldiers, sailors, peasants, the people, an exemplification of proletarian leadership in the revolution. The promise of the soviets could be redeemed and proletarian leadership of the people consolidated, in 1917 as in 1905, only through the seizure of state power. The class struggle of the workers could be directed effectively against the power of the state, in 1917 as in 1905, only through the intermediation of a Marxist vanguard in struggle against the influence of petty-bourgeois democratic ideology over the masses. The full development of the soviets, drawing the masses of the people into the work of government and state administration would, in 1917 as in 1905, erode the barrier between the people and the state apparatus and thereby also the distinction between society and the state.

Only in 1917, however, after he had worked out the conception of imperialism as the highest stage of capitalism, was Lenin able to situate the soviets in the context of the transition to socialism and hence to conceptualise this process as the withering away of the state. But although the language of hegemony was muted (when associated with the argument of some Bolsheviks that victories won in the bourgeois-democratic revolution must be consolidated

---

114   See Lenin 1917k, p. 109; Lenin 1917i, p. 479.
115   Lenin 1917a, p. 86. The influential claim of the Menshevik chronicler of 1917, N.N. Sukhanov, that, prior to Lenin's arrival at the Finland station, 'no one had ever dreamt of [the soviets] as organs of state power' (Sukhanov 1955, p. 283) is misleading; not only had the notion been dreamt, it had been incorporated in the Bolshevik resolution of 1906.

before entering upon socialist revolution), the politico-strategic logic of the struggle for hegemony was still at work in Lenin's political analyses. If the soviets now figured as forms of the dictatorship of the proletariat rather than as forms of the revolutionary-democratic dictatorship of the proletariat and the peasantry, this was in part because he had come to think of the socialist revolution as a movement of the people; it was proletarian, to be sure, but the proletariat was now conceived, in the socialist revolution of 1917 as it had been in the bourgeois revolution of 1905, as constituting itself as a class only in and through the political project of leading a people's revolution. Deployed on the uneven terrain described in his analysis of imperialism, the politico-strategic logic of the struggle for hegemony enabled Lenin to imbue his understanding of socialist revolution with the experience of the Russian people's revolution of 1905.

A People's Revolution

The popular character of the revolution does not serve, in Lenin's political practice, to designate a particular alignment of class forces but rather a process of popular-revolutionary struggle governed by the politico-strategic logic of hegemony. The class content of the concept of 'the people' could vary significantly in accordance with the dynamic of the class struggle and the struggle for hegemony, as it had done in the course of the bourgeois-democratic revolution: 'the people' represented an opening to those engaged in democratic struggle. Prior to 1905 Lenin was uncertain as to whether the peasantry would act as part of the people but held open the possibility that the bourgeoisie, or significant parts of it, might do so; in the course of the revolution, the bourgeoisie aligned itself with the landlords against the people, while the struggle of the peasants – including the peasant bourgeoisie – for land would constitute one of the essential fronts in the popular revolution.

The revolution of February 1917 deposed the Tsar and gave rise to the peculiar situation in which a provisional government dominated by the bourgeoisie could rule only with the agreement of the soviets thrown up by the workers, joined by the peasants in uniform and led by Mensheviks and Socialist Revolutionaries. Lenin's call for the workers to assume state power in a transition to the second phase of revolution aroused dissent even among the Bolshevik leadership, with Kamenev raising the question of hegemony, insisting that the incomplete tasks of the bourgeois-democratic revolution, in particular the revolution in agrarian social relations, be addressed. The effect of Lenin's response was to sharpen the focus of debate. 'The Bolshevik slogans and ideas *on the whole* have been confirmed by history; but *concretely* things have worked out *differently*; they are more original, more peculiar, more variegated than anyone could have expected':[116] the old Bolshevik proposal for a 'revolutionary democratic dictatorship of the proletariat and the peasantry' formulated a '*relation of classes* and not a *concrete political institution implementing* this relation, this cooperation'. In the form of the soviets, however, the rule of the proletariat and peasantry, instead of succeeding the rule of the bourgeoisie, was interlaced with it.[117] With no armed forces apart from the people, the provisional government could not use violence against the workers and soldiers in the capital; the soviet, meanwhile, swept up in the intoxication of revolution, eager to safeguard its fragile achievement and its promise, and under the petty-bourgeois leadership of Mensheviks and SRs, voluntarily ceded power to the bourgeois government, allowing it in the name of 'revolutionary defencism' to prosecute the imperialist war.

To gear the aims of revolutionary strategy to the completion of the democratic revolution was to abstract from the international aspect of the conjuncture, from the imperialist war, and to make the political struggle of the working class conditional upon the ability of the peasantry to act independently of the bourgeoisie, a political possibility but far from a certainty. It was thus to cede the political independence of the proletariat, to adopt in effect the political stance of the petty bourgeoisie. The political independence of the proletariat required that the spontaneously 'defencist' alignment of the proletariat with the petty-bourgeois peasantry behind the bourgeoisie be broken. Whether the peasantry would prove itself capable of breaking with the bourgeoisie or continue indefinitely wavering between capital and labour, the Marxist vanguard was obliged, in order to carve out the space for an independent working-class political stance, to set about '*disentangling* the proletarian line from the defencist and petty-bourgeois "mass" intoxication'.[118] The Bolsheviks could do this, in the condition of political freedom prevailing under 'dual power', simply by waging '*a struggle for influence within* the Soviets of Workers', Agricultural Labourers', Peasants', and Soldiers' Deputies', simply by patiently explaining, in terms 'adapted to the *practical* needs of the *masses*', that a democratic peace was impossible without the defeat of capital and the passage of power to the soviets.[119]

---

116 Lenin 1917e, p. 44.
117 Lenin 1917e, pp. 44–6.
118 Lenin 1917e, pp. 51, 54.
119 Lenin 1917e, pp. 48–9.

Disentangling the proletarian line and winning over the people were thus two aspects of the same political stance. From this stance Lenin would approach the popular masses and in particular the agrarian masses under a number of different, indeed contradictory, descriptions – soldiers and peasants, poor peasants and agricultural labourers, the petty-bourgeois peasantry, semi-proletarians, working people, the petty bourgeoisie, poor people and so on and on.[120] The contradictory formulations do not indicate an atheoretical pragmatism, but rather a theoretically informed practice of probing the movements of the masses amidst the uncertainties of war and revolution, feeling them out so as to ascertain their composition and direction and so be in a position to act effectively upon them. 'What is the peasantry?' Lenin asked a Bolshevik audience upon his return from exile, acknowledging the as-yet-indeterminate disposition of the agrarian struggle with the striking admission, 'We don't know, there are no statistics, but we do know it is a force'.[121] Had the capitalist agrarian policy of Stolypin succeeded in splitting the peasant commune into a nascent bourgeoisie and an agricultural proletariat? Was the peasantry still capable of acting ensemble against the landlords or would its component parts align themselves with the class struggle in the cities? Would petty-bourgeois aspirations and revolutionary patriotism prove strong enough to bind the peasants to the imperialist bourgeoisie? On the whole Lenin was inclined to regard the peasant movement as semi-proletarian, a movement of the poorer peasants, perhaps interpolating an international alignment of forces – on the erroneous supposition that a common interest in imperialist war aims would suffice to align the peasant bourgeoisie with the landlords – into the Russian countryside, or perhaps simply reflecting his belief in the primordial importance of the political independence of the proletariat. But as it became clear that the peasantry would rise as a whole against the landlord regime, nothing in his prior analyses would preclude, or even embarrass, the inclusion of this movement in the Bolshevik project of a people's revolution.[122]

Indeed, the openness of Lenin's political stance to the movements of the people, his repeated admonitions to the Bolsheviks to learn from the masses and his own attentiveness to the specifics of popular struggles fostered the

---

120   See, for example, Lenin 1917b, pp. 307, 314, 329, 341; Lenin 1917d, p. 22; Lenin 1917e, pp. 47, 53; Lenin 1917f, pp. 71–2; Lenin 1917g, 150; Lenin 1917h, p. 246. There is an interesting discussion in Frankel 1969a; see also Kingston-Mann 1979.
121   Lenin 1917c, p. 441.
122   See Lenin 1917j, pp. 77–81.

breadth and diversity of the revolutionary process. The very feature that qualified the soviets as a proletarian state-in-the-process-of-withering-away, their institutional flexibility or expansiveness, is what enabled them to accommodate themselves to the scope and variety of popular struggles and thus to incorporate the concrete concerns expressed by those struggles into the revolutionary process. Something like this would seem to be the import of the following passage of *The State and Revolution*, in which Lenin took to task critics of the democratic right of nations to self-determination and of other democratic institutions and practices:

> Taken separately, no kind of democracy will bring socialism. But in actual life democracy will never be 'taken separately'; it will be 'taken together' with other things, it will exert its influence on economic life as well, will stimulate its transformation; and in its turn it will be influenced by economic development, and so on. This is the dialectics of living history.[123]

Lenin's ability to situate a conscious vanguard within concrete conjunctures of struggle and, consequently, to foster its responsiveness to diverse and contradictory currents of popular struggle and to open the prospect of its dynamic merger with the movement of the masses sets to work more than just a personal knack for discerning the feel of political situations. It has roots in the practical-theoretical space he opened up for analyses of the politico-strategic logic of the complex, uneven and contradictory struggle for hegemony. The very features of this logic that obliged the Marxist vanguard to adapt its hegemonic political project in response to the shifting conjunctures of struggle and rendered disputes over the definition of that project more significant also made the political project more adaptable, more open to the influence of the people. Thus understood, the relation of the vanguard of the proletariat to the people is in part constitutive of its revolutionary political project and hence its political identity. There is no incongruity, then, in the fact that Lenin should have worked out the idea of the vanguard party of the proletariat in the course of a bourgeois-democratic revolution, but a fundamental truth about the logic of socialist revolution – and perhaps even about socialism.

---

123 Lenin 1917i, pp. 457–8.

CHAPTER 9

The Arm of Criticism and the Criticism of Arms: Courage in the Class Struggle

> Friends, I'd like you to know the truth and speak it.
> Not like tired, evasive Caesars: 'Tomorrow grain will come'.
> But like Lenin: By tomorrow
> We'll be done for, unless...
> — BERTOLT BRECHT[1]

...

> The dictatorship
> of the proletariat
>   you need to say that
>   need to hear that
>   not be scared of that
>   cause that's gonna save your life
>
> you need to talk about that
> you gonna have to fight for that
> — AMIRI BARAKA[2]

∴

In the aftermath of the Bolshevik seizure of power, the focus of international debates around the split in the working class movement shifted from imperialist war to the dictatorship of the proletariat. Lenin's intervention in this debate reproduced the logic of his turn-of-the-century critique of the appeal for 'freedom of criticism' in *What Is to Be Done?* The transition to a classless society figures in Lenin's argument as the construction of a proletarian-popular community capable of assuming and transforming the social functions hitherto performed by the former ruling classes. The difficulty of pulling

---

1 Brecht 1987b, p. 441.
2 Baraka 1991, pp. 256, 258.

this community together under circumstances of revolution and counterrevolution, of incipient civil war, as well as the operation of the politico-strategic logic of the struggle for hegemony in Lenin's attempts to come to grips with the process of transition, may be clarified by following through the tension between the two assumptions of his earlier argument, the desirability of constitutional liberties and the irreconcilability of the class struggle. Understood in terms of the logic of hegemony, the process of transition is responsive to the struggles and the innovations of the actors engaged in it and, in that sense, it is open-ended. That is, of course, also to say that the process comes with no guarantees of success and, in the event, while the Bolsheviks were able to fashion useful analytical tools and plough up a wealth of experience and insight upon which future attempts can draw, they proved unable to master its contradictions.

Karl Kautsky's *The Dictatorship of the Proletariat*, published in 1918, did as much as any other work to set the terms of the social-democratic critique of the Bolshevik Revolution and the experience of soviet power. Though painted on a broader canvas, his advocacy of democracy (as opposed to Bolshevik dictatorship) follows in essential respects the lines of the Bernsteinian call for 'freedom of criticism' from the weight of Marxist dogmatism, the refutation of which set the scene for Lenin's polemic against the Economists in *What Is to Be Done?* Lenin's response to Kautsky follows the logic of his earlier anti-critique. As Chapter 5 showed, the initial argument of *What Is to Be Done?* was shaped by two assumptions. It assumed a moral consensus, at least among the 'advanced parties', on the value of such constitutional principles as freedom of criticism or freedom of association as constraints upon the conduct of the political struggle and it assumed that the significance of appeals to such principles, like political watchwords and practices in general, depended upon the balance of political forces and must therefore be assessed with reference to the logic of the class struggle and the struggle for hegemony. The consensus of the former assumption implies no unity of purpose among political actors; indeed, it implies openness, if not impartiality, to the pursuit of diverse and conflicting purposes and interests. It therefore implies drawing some distinction between the pursuit of individual or partisan interests that may come into conflict and a consensual framework of freedom beyond which these interests may not be legitimately pursued. Since, however, the antagonism of class interests is irreconcilable, the latter assumption implies that there is nothing in the social whole that could not, in principle, be required as a weapon in the class struggle; compliance with a moral consensus on constraints on the political struggle is not exempt from such strategic assessment. There is thus some tension between the two assumptions, but where, as in the argument of *What Is to*

Be Done?, the moral consensus appealed to has to do with relations between non-state actors, this tension need not affect the argument.

Where state power is the immediate stake in the struggle, however, the tension is inescapable: could a moral consensus be supposed to hold once class struggle intensifies to the point of struggle between revolution and counter-revolution? Framed in these terms, Bernstein's challenge to Marxism appears as an attempt to resolve the tension by subordinating the Social Democratic conduct of the class struggle to a moral consensus around liberal democratic or constitutional norms. Such a consensus, by conciliating the class interests of workers and liberal bourgeoisie would avoid the ravages of revolution. A theoretical guarantee of liberal-democratic freedoms could thus be established – but at the cost of supposing, against all evidence, that a bourgeoisie would respect a moral consensus even as it was dispossessed of its monopoly of the means of production. This position was tantamount, in Lenin's view, to abandoning the political independence of the working-class movement; his own political stance implied, by contrast, subordinating constitutional norms to the logic of the class struggle. In the 1918 debate, however, Lenin's interlocutor was Kautsky.

Class Struggle and the Rule of Law

The socialist parties, according to Kautsky, shared the goal of 'emancipating the proletariat, and with it humanity, through socialism'. The division between Social Democrats and Communists turned upon the opposition of 'two fundamentally distinct methods, that of democracy and that of dictatorship' – the one pluralistic and inclusive, open to discussion, the other autocratic and exclusive, relying upon forcible suppression; the one promising a peaceful transition, the other only civil war.[3] Democracy will naturally be the appropriate form of its rule once the proletariat has attained 'the strength and intelligence to take in hand the regulation of society, that is...the power and capacity to transfer democracy from politics to economics'.[4] Until that point is reached, it is through their struggles 'to win, maintain and extend democracy' and to make use of every democratic reform achieved 'for organization, for propaganda, and for wresting social reforms' that the workers develop the political strength and intelligence to rule.[5] In addition to governance and

3 Kautsky 1918, pp. 1–3.
4 Kautsky 1918, p. 23.
5 Kautsky 1918, p. 21; see also p. 96.

political pedagogy, democracy serves a crucial epistemological function in Kautsky's argument: while democracy can neither reconcile class antagonisms nor forestall their ultimate transcendence in socialism, it provides 'a clear indication of the relative strength of the classes and parties' and thereby 'serves to prevent the rising classes from attempting tasks to which they are not [yet] equal and ... restrains the ruling classes from refusing concessions when they no longer have the strength to maintain such refusal'. This does not deflect the direction of historical development, but it does smooth its pace.[6]

The method of dictatorship, by contrast, is better suited than democracy to waging war.[7] The socialist revolution is not, however, to be identified with civil war; transforming the mode of production is necessarily a protracted process most effectively accomplished in circumstances of peace. Dictatorship is not only a method to cope with civil war but also, through its exclusiveness and restriction of freedoms, itself generates civil war where it does not generate apathy: '[c]ivil war becomes the method of adjusting political and social antagonisms'.[8] That bourgeois revolutions, fought against despotic governments, should have taken the form of civil war is simply the nature of the case; that the Russian Revolution should have done so is an expression of the immaturity of social conditions in Russia.[9] 'The less the material and intellectual conditions existed for all that they aspired to, the more [the Bolsheviks] felt obliged to replace what was lacking by naked power, by dictatorship'.[10] Kautsky evokes the rule of the Jesuits in Paraguay, whose authoritarian socialism was possible only 'where the rulers are vastly superior to the ruled in knowledge and where the latter are absolutely unable to raise themselves to an equal standard'.[11] If the Bolsheviks' dictatorial method is not an expression of historical immaturity and political impatience, it is an expression of patriarchal authoritarianism.

Kautsky distinguishes dictatorship as a form of government from dictatorship as a state of sovereignty.[12] Since 'a class is a formless mass' and government requires the organisational capacity of a party, 'a class can rule' – that is, hold sovereignty – 'but not govern'.[13] Dismissing as inapplicable to an entire class the historical sense of dictatorship – derived from the Roman republic –

---

6   Kautsky 1918, p. 36.
7   See Kautsky 1918, p. 57.
8   Kautsky 1918, p. 52.
9   See Kautsky 1918, pp. 54–5.
10 Kautsky 1918, p. 65.
11 Kautsky 1918, p. 6; see also p. 48.
12 See Kautsky 1918, p. 45.
13 Kautsky 1918, p. 31.

as a temporary suspension of democracy in favour of the rule of an individual unfettered by any laws, Kautsky presents the Marxist use of the term 'dictatorship of the proletariat' as a figurative designation of the democratic election of a government supported by a proletarian majority among the electorate.[14] Once this clarification has been made, the contrasting methods, democratic and dictatorial, translate straightforwardly into two opposite forms of government. Democracy signifies the rule of the majority, but the nature of this rule mandates protecting the political rights of minorities, freedom of speech and association, and universal and equal suffrage in elections to a parliament capable of controlling the activities of the executive power. As a form of government, dictatorship can only be the rule of an individual or an organisation, a party; opposition is disarmed by denying opponents the requisite political freedoms, the franchise, freedom of speech and association.[15] When the proletariat is divided between parties, the dictatorship of one proletarian party is tantamount to 'a dictatorship of one part of the proletariat over the other'.[16] As the criteria for political rights become elastic, arbitrary rule is encouraged and the advent of an individual dictator, a socialist Tsar, is foreshadowed.[17]

Lenin's response, delivered most fully in his *Proletarian Revolution and the Renegade Kautsky*, shifts the issue of dictatorship from the institutional sphere of governmental forms to the more encompassing sphere of state forms: that is, to the relation of forces in the class struggle as it is expressed in the institutional arrangements and practices of government and in the intersection of those arrangements and practices with the institutions, practices and ideologies through which class domination and subordination are woven into the fabric of society.[18] The wider focus is consonant with a political project that envisages a transition not only from one form of state to another but to a form of state that is already in process of withering away, where the alienation of government from society is in the process of dissolution.[19] By treating democracy, identified with the institutions of parliamentary democracy,

---

14 Kautsky 1918, p. 43.
15 See Kautsky 1918, p. 45.
16 Kautsky 1918, p. 46.
17 See Kautsky 1918, pp. 81, 132.
18 See Lenin 1918e, p. 237. By contrast with the extensive literature targeting Lenin's argument in *State and Revolution*, students of political thought seem to have found little to interest them in *The Proletarian Revolution and the Renegade Kautsky*. Donald is representative in asserting that '[t]he work actually amounted to very little in terms of any theoretical development of Lenin's views on the nature of Soviet power' (Donald 1993, p. 218). By way of exception, Claudin 1977 offers a thoughtful engagement with some of the theoretical issues at stake in the polemic between Lenin and Kautsky.
19 See Lenin 1918e, p. 323.

as an independent standard of measurement of the balance of class forces, Kautsky effectively abstracts the *form* of government – at least, *that* form of government – from the relations of class society with which it is essentially bound up and, consequently, from the class struggle. But the instantiation of the abstract principles of democracy in some set of constitutional forms, conventions and rules of conduct not only expresses but also enforces a determinate balance of the class forces in struggle. It moralises the differential access of the opposing forces to the means of political action, thereby organising a hierarchical distribution of political space and sanctifying the domination of one class or another; in form as well as in substance, democracy is always either bourgeois democracy or proletarian democracy. Where the relations between social classes are irreconcilably antagonistic, there is, in principle, no aspect of the social order that may not enter into the strategic calculations of one or another adversary and so become an object of struggle: no institution, no convention, no rule of conduct, no constitutional guarantee, however democratic its form, is immune from investment by the power of the dominant class and deployment against subordinate classes. While constitutional norms may permit the various class forces some room for political manoeuvre, in a class-divided society there can be no consensual criterion according to which the distribution of constitutional rights might be deemed impartial.

Lenin does claim that the soviet form of proletarian dictatorship, inasmuch as it alone is open to working people, the plebeian majority, taking responsibility for ruling and for administering public affairs into their own hands, is more democratic than the most democratic bourgeois state. But the dictatorship of the proletariat is 'merely a more historically concrete and scientifically exact formulation of the proletariat's task of "smashing" the bourgeois state machine'.[20] Thus Lenin's argument does not rest, most basically, upon a comparison between state forms; it turns fundamentally upon the irreconcilable antagonism of interests between the class forces invested in and expressed through the opposing forms of state. The Kautskyan procedure of assessing the more or less democratic character of political forms independently of the struggle between them assumes that the unfolding of the revolutionary process is to be understood from the perspective of an impartial, and therefore an external, observer without reference to the stance of political practitioners having to orient themselves and to act upon it from within. That is, it abstracts from the politico-strategic logic of the revolutionary struggle. Where the antagonism of class interests is irreconcilable, no durable relation of trust can be established; where the right to dictate a settlement upon the terms of one

---

20   Lenin 1918e, p. 233.

or another antagonist is itself contested, there can be no guarantee that the adversary will not try to impose a settlement by force. The possibility of irreconcilable disagreement over the constitutional forms through which consensus might be achieved and the will of the people recognised as legitimate is implied in the very notion of revolution; from it follows Lenin's definition of dictatorship as 'rule based directly on force and unrestricted by any laws'.[21]

That dictatorship is unrestricted by law does not make it synonymous with arbitrary rule: in revolution the political community is reconstituted around the dominance of one or another social class, and the power of a social class does not exist separate and apart from its embodiment in *some* set of norms and institutional forms. That the rule of the proletariat is to be unrestricted by any laws does not imply the absence of legal forms as normal conduits of proletarian rule. The dictatorship of the proletariat implies neither unconcern with the problem of working out constitutional forms to foster the emergence of a proletarian-popular community-in-struggle nor lack of recourse in trying to address it. Indeed, Lenin's encouragement of the working people to take the administration of the law into their own hands was designed to discover and test out forms of rule appropriate to their newfound power, although these forms, too, would always have to be revisited in light of changing circumstances, needs, capacities and dangers: 'Thousands of practical forms and methods of accounting and controlling the rich, the rogues and the idlers must be devised and put to a practical test by the communes themselves, by small units in town and country'.[22] Inasmuch as the objects of proletarian rule are necessarily bound up with the repression of bourgeois resistance, proletarian refusal to be restricted by legal forms might well be read as a kind of materialist historicisation of Aristotle's notion of equity, in which 'the standard applied to what is indefinite is itself indefinite, as the lead standard is in Lesbian building, where it is not fixed, but adapts itself to the shape of the stone; likewise, a decree is adapted to fit its objects'.[23] Establishing some historical perspective on Kautsky's accusations of 'arbitrariness' in the Russian workers' and peasants' constitution after only a few months in power, Lenin notes that the British bourgeoisie had taken several hundred years to work out the forms of its constitution and over the course of those centuries had entrenched in legal form and thus normalised myriad instances of arbitrary treatment, domination and control of the 'common labouring people'.[24]

---

21   Lenin 1918e, p. 236.
22   Lenin 1917m, p. 414.
23   Aristotle 1985, 1137b 29–32.
24   Lenin 1918e, p. 274.

The British experience, and in particular the example of the great theorist of the British bourgeois revolution, John Locke, may help to provide some perspective on Lenin's defence of proletarian dictatorship.

Although less forthright than Lenin, Locke, perhaps the pre-eminent bourgeois theorist of limited government, was unable to spell out the practical operation of the rule of law without having to fall back upon the expedient of prerogative, a 'power to act according to discretion, for the public good, without the prescription of the law, and sometimes even against it'.[25] It should be noted that Locke introduces prerogative not to accommodate such relatively circumscribed issues as executive clemency or the discretionary authority of public officials to act in emergency situations, but, under the portentous standard *salus populi suprema lex* ('let the good of the people be the supreme law'), to underwrite the power of the prince – and ultimately of the people – to regulate the 'measures of representation' in the legislature even against the opposition of the legislature itself.[26] His concern was to provide a remedy for the erosion of equal representation through the flux of time and unequal change, for example, against the danger of a parliament dominated by representatives of 'rotten [depopulated] boroughs' insulating itself from the will of the people.[27] Prerogative is needed, then, to ensure that government is established upon 'its true foundations'.[28] It is needed, that is, to address the foundational question of how the will of the people is to be expressed through institutional forms and hence made capable of being recognised. The use of prerogative was to be assessed in light of the law of nature by which all 'men' (in the language of Locke's time) are – and are to be treated as – free and equal as owners, each of his life, liberty and estate. By thus conceiving life and liberty as species of proprietary right, Locke was able to assert property right as the form in which recognition of human equality and freedom could be universalised and thereby to theorise the hegemony of bourgeois property. Writing in the context of nascent capitalism, Locke could suppose that this natural-law criterion would command the assent of all reasonable men but he acknowledged that intractable disagreement could be resolved only by 'appeal to heaven', that is, by trial of arms,[29] and stipulated that unjust recourse to arms

---

25   Locke 1690, ¶160. Locke's conception of prerogative is usefully discussed in Pasquino 1998 and illuminatingly applied to the so-called 'wars' on drugs and on terror in Arnold 2007.
26   Locke 1690, ¶158.
27   See Locke 1690, ¶157.
28   Locke 1690, ¶158.
29   Locke 1690, ¶168.

might be dealt with by execution or enslavement.[30] For Locke, as for Lenin, the rule of laws depends upon and is therefore limited by the possibility of resort to force. If Locke's prerogative power gives expression to the dictatorship of property, the dictatorship of the proletariat, as understood by Lenin and by Marx, might well be characterised as the prerogative of labour.

Class Power and Political Form

The thrust of Lenin's reply to Kautsky may be further clarified by reference to an event from recent political history: when the people of the barrios of Caracas rose in April 2002 against the pro-imperialist coup that briefly removed the democratically elected Venezuelan president, Hugo Chavez, from office, they seized the television stations that, after having legitimated the coup, had proceeded in its aftermath with programming as usual, and obliged them to report news of resistance to the coup.[31] They did so, in Lenin's sense of the term, 'dictatorially' – that is, they imposed their will upon the owners of the television stations by force, without seeking to gain their consent by persuasion and without regard to the authority of the law. Yet such 'dictatorial' measures, suppressing freedom of speech, were arguably indispensable to the restoration of 'democratic' rule. One need not be insensitive to the rhetorical force of the language of democracy in order to suggest that violence is done to the texture and the logic of the political struggle of the popular masses by attempting to squeeze them, analytically, into an exclusive alternative of democracy or dictatorship. Such a perspective occludes, rather than clarifies, a whole series of questions that arise in historical materialism about the relation between class power (the question of dictatorship) and the apparatuses through which it is exercised (the question of democratic – and non-democratic – political forms). The point is not to suggest that the interaction and variation of political forms are unaffected by the democratic or undemocratic political leadership and culture of popular movements, but precisely that this effect is exerted, in historical materialist terms, within the class struggle – not upon a choice between democracy and dictatorship in the abstract, but upon varying conjunctions of democratic (or non-democratic) political institutions with the power, the rule (the dictatorship) of one or another social class.

---

30   Locke 1690, ¶172.
31   See Bartley and Ó Briain 2003.

Kautsky's account of the dispersal of the Constituent Assembly by the Bolshevik soviets is the centrepiece of his critique, dramatically exemplifying his pivotal contrast between democratic and dictatorial methods. After being postponed (despite protests, most vociferously from the ranks of the Bolsheviks) throughout the year of revolution, elections to the Constituent Assembly took place in the immediate aftermath of the seizure of power by the Bolshevik-led soviets. Conducted on the basis of universal suffrage and organised through a system of proportional representation on lists of candidates proposed by each political party, the elections, as portrayed by Kautsky, were a straightforwardly, indeed self-evidently, accurate expression of the popular will. With the issue constructed in these terms, the Bolsheviks' dispersal of the Constituent Assembly could appear only as an arbitrary derogation from democratic norms and Lenin's justification of it as not only wrong-headed but disingenuous.[32] Consistent with the logic of his rebuttal, Lenin responded by situating the Constituent Assembly, the elections and the terms of Kautsky's critique in the context of the politico-strategic logic of the class struggle.

The Bolsheviks had been arguing the superiority of the soviet form to parliamentary-type institutions such as the Constituent Assembly since the spring, calling at most points for a soviet assumption of power. At the same time, seeing the Constituent Assembly as more open than the provisional government to the force of the insurgent masses and hence preferable either as a context in which to advance the struggle for soviet power or, failing that, a form in which the bourgeois-democratic revolution could be driven as far as possible, Lenin called for its convocation. Correlatively, the bourgeois forces around the provisional government sought repeatedly to defer the Constituent Assembly elections, which took place only days after the soviets seized power in the capitals. While Lenin had earlier argued that the power of the soviets was a necessary condition for the success of the Constituent Assembly, the fact of the soviet seizure of power and the initial measures adopted triggered a series of shifts in the balance of class forces. The October Revolution was driven by, and in turn greatly multiplied, the impetus behind a 'mighty movement of the exploited people for the reconstruction of the leading bodies of their organisations', a movement reflected in the rise of the Bolsheviks in the soviets and still in the ascendant as knowledge of the new revolution spread to the outreaches of the empire.[33] This movement produced a split in the party of the peasant majority, the Socialist Revolutionaries, with the Left supporting the soviet assumption of power and the Right opposed. Coming after the closing date

---

32   See Kautsky 1918, Chapter VI.
33   Lenin 1917l, p. 381.

for the submission of party lists of candidates for the Constituent Assembly elections, however, the split could not be reflected in the party list. Meanwhile, in reaction, elements of the officer corps had commenced operations against the revolution and a campaign of white terror had begun even before the elections, perhaps drawing confidence from the initial generous leniency of the new soviet power. As the bourgeoisie and landowners coalesced around the Kadet Party, 'All power to the Constituent Assembly' had become the rallying cry of the counterrevolution. When the elections returned a majority of deputies dominated by the Right SRs, whose inability to chart a political course independent of the bourgeoisie had been amply demonstrated in the unfolding of the revolution from February to October, a political crisis ensued. The divergence between the election results and 'the will of the people and the interests of the working and exploited classes' could be resolved peacefully, Lenin claimed, only by new elections organised under the authority of the Soviet power.[34] The refusal of these terms by the Right SRs, Kadets and Mensheviks presented the Bolshevik-led soviets with the alternative of recognising the authority of the Constituent Assembly or asserting their own authority in dispersing it.

According to Lenin's analysis of the dynamics of the revolutionary process, the dispersal of the Constituent Assembly followed upon an irreconcilable antagonism of class interests, here revealed in disagreement about the institutional forms and practices through which the will of the people is most legitimately expressed, accurately recognised and effectively implemented. Kautsky's protestations notwithstanding, this kind of disagreement, once engaged, cannot be resolved by appeal to the notion of equality. Abstracted from the context of class antagonism, the principle of equality cannot adjudicate between the procedural guarantees and formal universality of suffrage of the Constituent Assembly elections and the responsiveness (through such provisions as the recall of deputies, bearing the possibility of reflecting shifts in dynamics of popular politics as the split between Right and Left SRs) and the openness to plebeian initiatives of the soviets. Overlooked in Kautsky's insistence upon the principle of equality as the hallmark of democratic legitimacy is the prior issue in the Leninist political calculus: through the institutions and practices bound up with the interests of which of the opposing classes – bourgeoisie or proletariat – is the political community to be reconstituted? Subordinating the class struggle to an abstraction of political equality, in which Kautsky indulges here, gives expression to a quixotic yearning for an imaginary reconciliation of class interests characteristic of the petty bourgeois – part

---

34 Lenin 1917l, p. 383.

owner, part worker, incapable of sustaining an independent conception of modern society and thus condemned to waver politically between its two fundamental classes.

Lenin does invoke the real equality of a classless society but its function in his argument was not as an alternative standard for the distribution of political rights but rather as an index of the incongruity of assessing the institutions of class society by standards appropriate to a classless society.[35] Spelling out a 'truth' that 'forms the essence of socialism', he declared, 'The exploited and the exploiter cannot be equal... [T]here can be no real, actual equality until all possibility of the exploitation of one class by another has been totally destroyed'.[36] Lenin gauges variant distributions of political rights not as approximations to or departures from some ideal distribution, but according to their openness to the exercise and the extension of working-class power. This does not imply that considerations of equality or freedom can play no role in Lenin's analysis, but the role they play is subordinate to the politico-strategic logic of the class struggle. Since that logic requires that the part be subordinated to the politico-strategic whole, it follows that any particular right may have to be sacrificed to maintain the power of the working class and to sustain the dynamic of the revolutionary process. The universalist promise of freedom of criticism and other democratic constitutional norms can thus be reconciled with the politico-strategic logic of the struggle for hegemony only in virtue of the expansiveness of the socialist project of the working-class movement.

---

35 The practice of interpolating utopian ideals into the class struggles of the popular masses and then bemoaning the tragic dilemmas that will of necessity confront attempts to realise these ideals by revolutionary means has long since become a standard trope of counterrevolutionary rhetoric; this may have been what particularly provoked Lenin's ire against Kautsky's critique. The very next year Max Weber, in a striking and influential example of the genre, would frame the revolutionary political project of the Spartacists and the Bolsheviks in terms of the pacifist ethic of the Sermon on the Mount, the better to show his audience, students who might staff a leadership cohort for the liberal democratic regime rising out of the ashes of Imperial Germany, that he who would enter the political world had best act on an 'ethic of responsibility' (Weber 1919). The currency of this trope would seem to reflect an ingrained assumption that the process of revolution and the genesis of revolutionary violence can be grasped without reference to counterrevolution and the roots of violence in the structure of class society. Arno Mayer's work stands virtually alone – at least among non-Leninist students of revolution – in framing the process as driven by an open-ended dynamic of struggle between revolution and counterrevolution; although marred by a rather Nietzschean preoccupation with 'vengeance', his comparative study of violence in the French and Russian revolutions is instructive (A. Mayer 2000). More generally, on the paradoxes of counterrevolutionary rhetoric, see Hirschman 1991.

36 Lenin 1918e, p. 252.

The Russian proletarians would have to engage the vast masses of the petty bourgeoisie and other semi-proletarian strata in constructing a classless society while preventing the forces of bourgeois restoration from instrumentalising the illusions, whether 'realist' or utopian, and the vacillations generated by petty-bourgeois social circumstances. The reconciliation of proletarian power and democratic and constitutional rights is thus a contested and therefore a contingent outcome of the logic of the political struggle for hegemony.

Class Struggle and Political Community

The coercive exercise of political power is certainly repressive, but inasmuch as it is partially constitutive of a community organised around the domination of a social class, it can also, on Lenin's account, be productive. Dictatorship need not imply 'the abolition of democracy for the class that exercises the dictatorship', but it does, Lenin stipulates, imply 'the abolition (or very material restriction, which is a form of abolition) of democracy for the class over which, or against which, the dictatorship is exercised'.[37] The 'very material restriction' of democracy under bourgeois rule is manifested, even where workers have managed to win some political rights in capitalist society, in a panoply of organisational forms, rules, conventions, habits and practices well calculated to subordinate the operation of the state to the logic of capital and to seal it off from the possibility of working-class participation and influence, in the systematic repression of working-class parties and organisations, whenever necessary, in recourse to exceptional measures, states of siege, martial law, and in the underlying weight of property and money in channelling the exercise of political rights.

The dictatorship of the proletariat entails, conversely, 'the *forcible* suppression of the exploiters as a *class*, and, consequently, the *infringement* of "pure democracy", i.e. of equality and freedom, *in regard to* that *class*'.[38] The 'material restriction' upon democracy for the class of capitalists takes the form, most basically, of expropriating its property and hence forcibly eliminating the prerogative of property in matters political. This implies, for example, the elimination of a bourgeois press, that is, the refusal to recognise any right of the ownership of capital, as such, to a voice in politics. But it need not take the form of restricting the franchise. This, Lenin wrote, was 'a nationally specific and not a general question of the dictatorship'.[39] The disenfranchisement of

---

37 Lenin 1918e, p. 235.
38 Lenin 1918e, p. 256.
39 Lenin 1918e, p. 256.

the bourgeoisie was an outcome of the specific path of development of the Russian Revolution, of the antagonism of the bourgeoisie to the soviets even when led by the Mensheviks and, in particular, of bourgeois participation in Kornilov's attempted counterrevolutionary coup.[40] The franchise and, by extension, such other political rights as freedom of speech or freedom of association were conditional upon whether their exercise was consistent with the political power of the proletariat. This turns, however, not simply upon the class character of state power but also upon the politico-strategic situation and the logic of the revolutionary process. The distribution of political rights would have to be worked out in the course of the revolution.

While disenfranchising the bourgeoisie was 'not an *indispensable* characteristic of the logical concept "dictatorship"', after the experience of the war and the revolution in Russia, it was, Lenin acknowledged, likely.[41] Its likelihood follows from the terms in which Lenin conceived the revolutionary process: since the production and extraction of surplus labour in the form of value is the axis around which turns the whole of the social and political order dominated by the bourgeoisie, the process of socialist revolution consists essentially in exercising proletarian power in working out the forms of a classless society in which production is socially organised and regulated and in which it will no longer be possible to draw an income – and to dominate others – by virtue of owning property: that is, a state of affairs 'in which it will be impossible for the bourgeoisie to exist or for a new bourgeoisie to arise'.[42] Bourgeois property might be expropriated at a stroke, but the springs from which bourgeois ownership could draw would not be exhausted unless and until the workers took over the social functions hitherto performed by the bourgeoisie and reorganised them so as to accommodate proletarian-popular interests. Dominance of these (managerial, organisational, technical, educational and military) functions by the former ruling classes constitutes solid grounds for their political self-confidence and resistance to proletarian rule, and nurtures hopes for and attempts at restoration. The bourgeoisie remained, even after the proletarian seizure of state power, stronger in important respects than the working class. The constructive activity of working out the forms of the new social order cannot but be intimately intertwined, therefore, with the destructive activity of breaking the political power and uprooting the social power of the capitalist class.

---

40   See Lenin 1918e, p. 272.
41   Lenin 1918e, p. 256.
42   Lenin 1918c, p. 245; see also Lenin 1918e, pp. 252–3.

The rule of the working class would thus need to be open-ended, that is, unrestricted by any laws – dictatorial – not only in order to deter attempts at counterrevolution, to break the resistance of the bourgeois and their entourage, but also in order 'to *lead* the enormous mass of the population ... in the work of organising a socialist economy',[43] to inspire the labouring population with confidence in the authority of the armed workers, stiffen the resolve of the workers themselves and steady the wavering middle strata. Such repressive measures of the proletarian dictatorship as the imposition of compulsory labour duty upon the former bourgeois or the appropriation of bourgeois housing stock to lodge the homeless put the bourgeois on notice that their property and their persons were no longer sacrosanct. This provided tangible confirmation for working people that things had indeed changed; it might thereby help inspire them to shuck off the ingrained plebeian habits of diffidence, deference, cynicism and 'sour grapes', a political culture of subordination inherited from the social relations and institutions of class society that wore upon the solidarity and determination of the working people. Such confirmation was all the more important as the newfound and still-fragile political confidence of the popular masses had had to endure accumulated frustration at the apparent irresolution of nominally 'socialist' and even 'Marxist' leaderships faced with the responsibility of power. Repression of the exploiting classes was thus necessary not only in order to stymie resistance but also in order to unleash popular self-confidence, the people's courage for politics. Thus understood, force may not only be repressive but also enabling, encouraging. It need not be counterposed to but may serve as an integral element in the struggle for hegemony, whereby the working class 'constitutes itself as the nation' by constituting the people as a community around itself.

It is not just that the use of coercion, in repressing some people, enables others. The dictatorship of the proletariat, as it functions in Lenin's discourse, cannot be grasped in such narrowly instrumental terms. He could be – and often has been – construed in such terms, but only when his instrumental language is read in abstraction from the political analyses informed by a politico-strategic logic of the struggle for hegemony in which it is typically embedded. When striking workers enforce a policy of retribution against strike-breakers, it may be a warning to other workers to stay away, but each worker knows that, should she or he cross the picket line, she or he would become an 'other'. They direct the threat at themselves as much or more than at others – but the constraint can serve, if not as the foundation of their confidence in each other, then as a more or less effective means of consolidating it against the

---

43   Lenin 1917i, p. 409.

employer's attempts to play upon the disintegrating effects of debt, desperation and personal tragedy. It can serve to knit together the threads of the strike community. Force functions then as a conduit of solidarity and as a resource for collective action and collective heroism. But here, too, where the exercise of force has a 'consensual' aspect, force is directly exercised by some individuals against others, by an 'apparatus', however embryonic, and the excessive or poorly judged use of force can snap the ties that bind the strike community together – when its repressive aspect eclipses its enabling aspect, force, no longer encouraging, becomes demoralising.

The following claim from Lenin's 'Immediate Tasks of the Soviet Government' of April 1918 was showcased by Kautsky: the 'form of coercion' required in the transition from capitalism to socialism is 'determined by the degree of development of the given revolutionary class' and by such 'special circumstances' as the 'legacy of a long and reactionary war and the forms of resistance put up by the bourgeoisie and petty bourgeoisie. There is, therefore, absolutely *no* contradiction in principle between Soviet (*that is*, socialist) democracy and the exercise of dictatorial powers by individuals'.[44] As it figures in a passage cited by Kautsky, in a version mangled by clumsy translation, spirited out of its context by hidden ellipses of sometimes several pages and reframed in terms of the old Marxist trope of a politically passive peasantry as the mainstay of imperial rule,[45] the claim serves to insinuate the spectre of a socialist Tsar. An overly confident Lenin allowed the outbreak of the German Revolution to stand in place of a written response to this part of Kautsky's argument; the insinuation was left unanswered. But to re-establish the context an answer might have invoked, recourse may be had to the original pamphlet from which Kautsky extracted the claim. It may thus be seen that the same logic at work in the strike community, though played out on a much broader stage, is engaged in the exercise of proletarian dictatorship.

Lenin produced a first draft of 'The Immediate Tasks of the Soviet Government' just after a peace treaty was signed with Germany at Brest-Litovsk. However onerous its terms, the treaty offered the Soviets a respite in which to turn to the positive task of constructing a socialist order of production and society. This task was presented, in the first draft, as a matter of combining the knowledge and experience of (formerly) bourgeois technical experts, consultants, and advisors with 'the initiative, energy and work of the broad masses of the working people'.[46] '[T]he force of example' was brought

---

44 Lenin 1918c, p. 268.
45 Compare Kautsky 1918, pp. 131–2, with Lenin 1918c, pp. 265–8.
46 Lenin 1918a, pp. 77–8.

to the fore as 'a morally essential...pattern for organising labour';[47] the transition to socialism thus appeared as a process of experimentation in re-contextualising and re-forming the institutions and practices of bourgeois society, notoriously including an attempt to mobilise the techniques of Taylor's 'scientific management' – extracting the most efficient labouring motions from current practices by means of time and motion studies and then redesigning the working environment so as to impose the resulting efficiencies upon the workers as a kind of best-practice straitjacket – for the ends of a classless society.[48] If the permissibility of 'one-man managerial authority (which could be called dictatorial)' and of coercion was invoked in connection with establishing labour discipline and self-discipline, the necessity of recourse to coercion was argued primarily, in the first draft, in relation to the resistance of former members of the exploiting classes.[49] As grain destined for Russia's hungry cities had to negotiate its way across a rail system fragmented into a patchwork of fiefdoms under 'workers' control' and Menshevik influence, the threat of famine reached critical proportions. The famine crisis over-determined the context and the argument of Lenin's second draft:[50] resistance to socialist construction was cast not only and not so much in the form of bourgeois defence of class privilege but also, and with greater emphasis, in the form of 'petty-bourgeois anarchy', of the forces of social disintegration unleashed by the war and crisis of revolution and expressed in 'an increase of crime, hooliganism, corruption, profiteering and outrages of every kind'.[51] The Soviet government sought to address the crisis by delegating 'dictatorial powers in matters relating to railway transport' to the People's Commissar of Ways and Communications[52] and by generalising the practice of one-man management and reliance upon the expertise of bourgeois professionals.

At stake in the individual exercise of dictatorial power, then, was the coercive exercise of managerial discretion. The proposal unleashed a storm of protest from Left Socialist Revolutionaries and anarchists, Mensheviks and the

---

47 Lenin 1918b, p. 204.
48 A sense of this openness to experimentation and of the narrowness of the (material and ideological) constraints within which experimentation was undertaken at the emergence of the Soviet system of production are remarkably evoked in Robert Linhart's discussion of the complexity of Lenin's 'Taylorist' position in 1918 (Linhart 1976, especially pp. 105–16); see also Bettleheim 1974.
49 See Lenin 1918b, pp. 211–18.
50 The shift from the first draft to the second draft is helpfully contextualised and discussed in Linhart 1976, pp. 117–37.
51 Lenin 1918c, pp. 264, 265–6.
52 See Bunyan and Fisher 1961, p. 655.

Left Communist grouping led by Bukharin: while the assumption of dictatorial powers by individuals might be squared with bourgeois democracy, it could only signal the abandonment of the higher principles of socialist democracy. Lenin's concern was to redirect the discussion from issues of principle to the pressing tasks of the moment, but to this end he had to reframe the issue of principle so that the principle invoked could be brought to bear upon the current moment. This was the context of Lenin's denial, cited by Kautsky, of a contradiction in principle between socialist democracy and the exercise of dictatorial powers by individuals. The denial is directly accompanied by a distinction, not cited by Kautsky, between proletarian and bourgeois dictatorship. The dictatorship of the proletariat 'strikes at the exploiting minority in the interests of the exploited majority' *and* 'it is exercised – *also through individuals* – not only by the working and exploited people, but also by organisations which [like the soviets] are built in such a way as to rouse the people to history-making activity'.[53] The distinction is drawn with a view not only to the *class interests* advanced through the exercise of coercion but also to the *political location* of the individual 'dictators' in relation to the organised struggle of one or another social class. It thus refers both to consciousness of class interest and to the constitution of a class as a political community of struggle.[54] To draw the distinction according to the individual or collective face of coercion is to misconceive the nature of political rule – social forces always rule through individuals and the actions of these individuals are always mediated by organisations that both convey and structure the influence of the broader social relations at work – and to constrain unnecessarily the political choices available to the workers. The example of the striking workers illustrated that the exercise of coercion need not be simply instrumental but may also be constitutive of a political community in struggle; coercion is repressive but it can also, depending upon the context, be enabling. If the analogy fits, the individual exercise of dictatorial powers is not inconsistent with and may even, depending upon context, facilitate the rule of the proletariat as a class.

---

53   Lenin 1918c, p. 268.
54   The absence of this essential context is what allows Bolsinger (2001) to reduce Lenin's strategic orientation to a simple calculus of means and ends, facilitating a comparison of his political thought to that of the right-winger Carl Schmitt; with the context restored, the comparison collapses.

Community and Class Consciousness

The relevant context is determined by the transitional character of the current moment and by the logic of the transition from capitalism to a classless communist society. Any ready-made socialist blueprint for industrial organisation would not be worth the paper it was printed on; a transition to new modes of conceiving and organising working life could be accomplished only in assimilating and testing out the existing (bourgeois) forms of organisation and adapting them to the possibilities and necessities of working-class power, learning by means of 'reversions to the old' to distinguish and to nurture 'the rudiments (not always immediately discernible) of the new'.[55] The technology of large-scale industry and of the railways in particular prescribes a 'strict *unity of will*' that could be ensured only '[b]y thousands subordinating their will to the will of one'.[56] This subordination could take different forms: '[g]iven ideal class consciousness and discipline on the part of those participating in the common work ... [it] would be something like the mild leadership of a conductor of an orchestra [but it] may assume the sharp forms of a dictatorship if ideal discipline and class consciousness are missing'.[57] Sharp forms of subordination were suited, Lenin suggests, to the psychology of the ordinary worker in the aftermath of the initial victory over the exploiters, eager to relax and take 'the blessings of life that were [at last] there for the taking', persuaded intellectually, perhaps, but not yet fully seized by the realisation that the reflex of simply 'taking' would only result in economic dislocation and thereby facilitate the return of the exploiters.[58] If relations of subordination in production bear the seeds of bureaucratic rule, soviet power is the force that enables the workers to winnow them out: the more imperative the need for 'the dictatorship of individuals *in definite processes of work*, in definite aspects of *purely executive* functions, the more varied must be the forms and methods of control from below'.[59] The role of the Marxist vanguard, 'the class-conscious spokesman for the strivings of the exploited for emancipation', is pivotal in this process; it is to combine 'the "public meeting" democracy of the working people – turbulent, surging, overflowing its banks like a spring flood – with

---

55   Lenin 1918c, pp. 269, 273.
56   Lenin 1918c, pp. 268, 269.
57   Lenin 1918c, p. 269.
58   Lenin 1918c, pp. 269–70.
59   Lenin 1918c, p. 275.

iron discipline while at work, with *unquestioning obedience* to the will of a single person, the Soviet leader, while at work'.[60]

The exercise of discretionary authority – of dictatorial powers – by individuals is consistent with the rule of the proletariat and socialist democracy only on the assumption that the 'individual dictators' can be understood as organs of the political power of the working class, as exercising functions on its behalf. Lenin's argument thereby assumes some account of the political unity of the working class, of the working class as a political community, conceived in relation not only to the current conjuncture, with its constraints and possibilities, but also to the logic of the class struggle as it unfolds through successive conjunctures, constraining and enabling the construction and the emergence of a society beyond class. But the political community of the working class is never simply a given; it is always constituted as a pattern of unity and disunity through the politico-strategic logic of the struggle for hegemony. If an account of the cohesion of the working-class community is thus presumed by Lenin's argument, it is present only obliquely, allusively, through a series of references to 'class consciousness', a term whose significance here is itself much in need of clarification. 'Class consciousness' figures at two different stages in the argument and takes on distinct content and plays a distinct role at each stage. At an initial stage, 'ideal class consciousness' denotes an awareness of the demands imposed by the current conjuncture of the class struggle and a willingness to assume the responsibilities incumbent upon the working class in the transition to a classless society; in this sense, 'ideal class consciousness' does not make 'unquestioning subordination' superfluous but is, rather, at least in part consciousness of the need for 'unquestioning subordination' to a single will in the production process as the form of working-class unity appropriate to the task of the moment.

'Class consciousness' is predicated of the Communist Party, at a second stage, in virtue of its role as 'spokesman for the strivings of the exploited for emancipation'. The 'ideal class consciousness' of the previous stage of the argument is here sublated in the reflexive consciousness of the vanguard's relation to the 'strivings of the exploited'. Played out through the politico-strategic logic of the struggle for hegemony, the spontaneous striving for emancipation is refracted by the grip of petty-bourgeois habit upon plebeian experience; class consciousness is always less than ideal. In grasping the circumstances that distinguish the consciousness of the 'average, ordinary representative of the toiling and exploited masses' from 'ideal class consciousness', the Marxist vanguard becomes conscious, reflexively, of its own situation and task; to facilitate a

---

60   Lenin 1918c, pp. 270, 271.

transition from the 'discipline forced upon them by the exploiters to conscious, voluntary discipline', the vanguard must guide the process of 'co-ordinating the task of arguing at mass meetings *about* the conditions of work' with the task of unquestioning obedience '*during* the work'. The political consciousness of the 'spokesman', of the vanguard, is thus understood with reference both to an aim (understood in varying degrees of concreteness) to be realised in practice and to the process whereby it is enacted, including, reflexively, the political practice of 'arguing' with fellow workers. Though the process is shadowed by the threat of coercion, the threat is tempered by the practice of 'arguing', of criticism and debate, and the spontaneous movement of the masses in its contradictory diversity may be pulled together into a political community upon the terrain of 'the "public meeting" democracy of the working people'.

What ensured the expansiveness of the proletarian-popular community and made the soviets an appropriate form for the political power of the working class, Lenin argued prior to the seizure of power, was the openness of this kind of democracy to the diverse currents of the plebeian struggle and aspiration, 'turbulent, surging, overflowing its banks like a spring flood'; he still scorns the inability of bourgeois and Mensheviks to see in the popular 'mania for meetings' only the 'chaos, the confusion and the outbursts of small-proprietor egoism'.[61] The unruliness that marked the soviet form as an arena for popular political experiment and innovation, and hence as an appropriate vehicle of proletarian political power, was thus inseparable from its openness to the diverse currents of plebeian politics, even those that embodied the spectre of indiscipline and anarchy and thus menaced the foundations of working-class power. Charged with orchestrating the play of criticism and coercion, discipline and debate, the Marxist vanguard is placed by the logic of Lenin's argument in the contradictory position of having to sustain the authority to exercise coercion over the very people whose critical challenge it must invite and even encourage. This contradiction fires an inherent ambiguity as to whether the authority of the vanguard derives from the persuasiveness of its example and its arguments to the workers or from the threat of coercion standing behind them: the proletarian character of state power is thus constitutively, and not merely contingently, contestable.

Where the proletarian-popular community-in-struggle endures, this contradictory position can be sustained and even drive the process of revolutionary transformation. The endurance of such a community may be consistent even with very severe measures of repression as long as a belief in their necessity can bind the community together. But the more severe such measures, the

---

61   Lenin 1918c, p. 270.

more they test the bonds of community: as the space necessary for spontaneous innovation (and for the criticism implicit in the fact of innovation) is constrained by the demands of discipline, the spontaneity of the masses comes to be expressed in resistance to 'individual dictators' or else its innovative capacity simply withers. Conversely, as social and economic dislocation, aggravated by resistance, renders even more imperious the need for discipline, the ability of the vanguard to discern in the spontaneous activity of the masses something beyond 'not-yet-consciousness' is eroded. 'Consciousness' thus comes to be invested in an apparatus of rule increasingly closeted from the unfettered criticism and effective participation of the masses; as the parameters of free criticism progressively narrow, the springs of self-critical capacity dry up. Thus insulated from the forces underlying the politico-strategic logic of the struggle for hegemony, the capacity of the conscious vanguard to grasp the distinctiveness of new conjunctures of struggle and hence to establish hegemony effectively within and across them is subordinated to and increasingly imprisoned by the antiquated assumptions of its former analyses. The logic of the struggle for hegemony can thus work so as to transform difference into antagonism, dissent into resistance, driving potential allies into the adversary's camp or reducing friends to indecision or the active support of loyalists to sullen automatism, stoking the ambitions of the adversary.[62] When political actors are unable to correct their mistakes in good time, they can find these errors confirmed, through the operation of this logic, as the truth of their position and a corresponding realignment of forces entrenched against them.

The Bolsheviks would never master this contradiction. The difficulty of their task was certainly multiplied by the deadweight of Tsarist culture and technical backwardness, by long years of civil war fought amidst the ruins of imperialist war, by famine and disease, by a desperate reliance upon the personnel of the old regime, by the militarisation of institutions and attitudes, by the defeat of the revolution in Europe and by the ever-present threat and the reality of imperialist intervention. But no revolution unfolds apart from circumstances of profound crisis.

---

62 'Antagonism and contradiction are not at all the same thing', Lenin would note in the margin of Bukharin's *Economics of the Transformation Period*. 'The former disappears, the latter remains under socialism' (Bukharin 1920, pp. 51, 214). For analyses of antagonistic and non-antagonistic contradictions, see Mao 1937; for the transformation of non-antagonistic into antagonistic contradictions – and vice versa – in the transition to socialism, see Mao 1957.

Class Consciousness and Courage

That Lenin's account of working-class unity, of proletarian-popular community, is conveyed – and the context of his reference to 'individual dictatorship' is consequently established – through a series of references to 'class consciousness' carries with it a significant ambiguity. Depending upon whether the pivot of his account is identified with 'class consciousness' as it functions at one or another stage of the argument, his account of consciousness – and consequently of the proletarian-popular community essential to his account of the dictatorship of the proletariat – may be construed in two very different ways. If the 'ideal class consciousness' of the first stage – a perspicuous grasp of the direction, stakes and current circumstances of the class struggle and of the duties incumbent upon the working class in these circumstances – is taken as the standard by which consciousness is to be measured, then the conscious vanguard is called upon, at a second stage, to grapple with the impediments that hold fellow workers back from action in accordance with that ideal. The storminess of the public-meeting democracy through which the workers are to be unified around the ideal is to be accounted for by the force of these impediments. If, however, what is pivotal in 'class consciousness' is its reflexive implication in a practical process of struggle, investigation, debate and (re)assessment – here the process of 'arguing about the conditions of work' – then the workers' distance from the initial 'ideal' consciousness does not necessarily constitute a drawback or limitation but may bear the seeds of a concretised or even a rectified consciousness and the stormy meetings bear witness to the intensity of commitment amidst the diversity of situations and circumstances that constitutes the proletarian-popular community.

Something like this distinction was seen at work in Chapter 6 in Lenin's critique of the 'divisionists' in the debate over the RSDLP agrarian programme during the revolution of 1905–7: where the young Stalin and other divisionists diagnosed, correctly in Lenin's view, a desire to divide the land into individual parcels beneath the socialist idiom of the peasants' ideology, Lenin discerned the possibility, by taking the peasants at their word, however illusory, of intervening to help the peasants consciously draw the implications of the struggle over the land for the political struggle over the state, for a revolutionary-democratic dictatorship of the proletariat and the peasantry. The logic of the divisionist position yields an account of revolutionary transition in which the goal of the process, conceived independently of the self-consciousness of the agents, remains the standard by which the process is assessed; the self-understanding of the agents makes no significant difference to the unfolding and the general result of the process. While the peasants may well emancipate themselves according to this standard, they are not capable of redefining the criteria of their emancipation. By this logic, the revolutionary process is a kind of materialisation of the 'ideal class consciousness' prescribed by initial Marxist analysis. On Lenin's analysis, however, the self-understanding of the peasants, despite or perhaps even because of its illusory character, could sustain or maybe even suggest a redefinition of the aims and possibilities of the revolutionary process. The process of revolution is open to redefinition in accordance with the reflexive implication of 'class consciousness' in the process of struggle. Similarly, the very lack of partisanship of the spontaneous working-class movement, its mass rather than its class consciousness, is what gave rise, on Lenin's account, to the soviets in the first Russian Revolution and gave expression to their openness and their hegemonic possibilities, leading him to broaden and rethink his own analysis of hegemony.

Extending the logic of an 'ideal class consciousness', the transition to socialism might be conceived as the historical realisation of a 'vision', a plan or blueprint consciously formulated by a vanguard. Understood as a vision in which the diverse and possibly conflicting concerns of different sections of the working people – whether productivity or transcending alienated labour, investment or leisure, individuality or de-commodification, community or preservation of the natural environment, health, education, social justice, peace and so on – are finally reconciled without contradiction or residue in a harmonious social order, socialism figures as a utopian goal distant from the immediate reality of the class struggle. In this context, characterising the vanguard as representing the working masses means that it plans and sets priorities, it makes the hard decisions for them, it acts politically on their behalf. If, however, Lenin's stormy meetings and the soviets figure among the 'political form[s]' Marx thought necessary 'to work out the economical emancipation of labour'[63] – and it is in the spirit of Marx's insight to add that the 'working out' would always have to be resumed and revised in light of altered needs, capacities and circumstances – then 'class consciousness' can only be identified through its reflexive implication in the practice of 'working out'. The function of a vanguard, understood in this context, might be characterised as generating 'concrete analyses of concrete situations' and, armed analytically and with the political arts of audacity, humility, organisation, persuasion, negotiation and compromise, orchestrating the diverse currents of the working class and the various strata of the people in the political process of 'working out'. A claim to bear socialist consciousness, unless it is identified with the visionary consciousness of a utopian goal, need not imply a claim to clairvoyance. The consciousness of a vanguard does not signify an impossible freedom from error

---

63   Marx 1871, p. 334.

but the commitment, by learning the lessons of practice and by developing the political skill of listening to the needs, suggestions, criticisms and resistance of the masses, to correct errors and to adjust analyses to changing realities. In this context, the notion of a vanguard does not designate a particular institution or set of individuals but, fundamentally, certain political functions in the movement of the class. In this sense, any member of the masses could join the vanguard simply by performing vanguard functions, without thereby eroding the distinction between vanguard and class. Socialist consciousness is to be understood correspondingly not as a set of propositions that could be claimed as the property or the brand of a certain group, but more basically as a capacity to reconfigure the socialist project to the changing circumstances of the class struggle; it develops through the interaction of vanguard and masses. Here, if the vanguard may be said to represent the working people, it is not only by standing for them but also by working with them; it is as a deputy rather than a sovereign.

This understanding of 'class consciousness' suggests, if it does not quite imply, that socialism is to be conceived not as an ideal form against which attempts to transcend capitalist society are to be measured but as marked by the inevitable unevenness of the transition and as engaging a diversity of partial perspectives and necessarily assuming a variety of forms. Lenin makes this conception explicit in ' "Left-Wing" Childishness' of May 1918. Chiding Bukharin and the 'Left Communists' for their theoretical failure to move beyond the abstract contrast of capitalism and socialism to an analysis of 'the concrete forms and stages of the transition that is taking place in our country', he asserts that 'the new society' emergent 'after prolonged birth-pangs' from the womb of capitalism is 'an abstraction which can come into being only by passing through a series of varied, imperfect concrete attempts to create this or that socialist state'.[64] Again, 'in the development of nature as well as in the development of society' there would always be some 'discrepancy' such as that between the political strength of the Bolsheviks and the economic weakness of Soviet Russia; the logic of change implies that 'only by a series of attempts – each of which, taken by itself, will be one-sided and will suffer from certain inconsistencies – will complete socialism be created by the revolutionary co-operation of the proletarians of *all* countries'.[65]

By attending to the internal complexity of the concept of 'class consciousness' and its complex and contradictory function in Lenin's approach to the transition to socialism, it becomes possible to construe his political theory and practice in terms either of the urgent certainties of a dogmatic and incipiently

---

64 Lenin 1918d, p. 341.
65 Lenin 1918d, p. 346.

authoritarian 'consciousness' or of the 'conscious' play of its more open-ended, dialectical and potentially democratic threads. While the latter provides the more accurate and encompassing reading, it would be too simple to equate it with an 'authentic' Leninism and counterpose it to the former, portrayed as a product of later Stalinist reification. The fact that both aspects of Lenin's approach – the theoretically-informed concrete analysis of the concrete conditions and the political dialectic of struggle and debate, whereby analysis is adjusted from one conjuncture to the next – are subsumed under the umbrella term 'consciousness' can serve to mask and thus to facilitate a kind of conceptual slippage from one to the other. This usage would come to function as a kind of epistemological obstacle to a clear recognition of the process whereby the ties knitting together the proletarian-popular community come undone and, by closeting the 'consciousness' of the would-be vanguard from the logic and circumstances of the struggle in which it is necessarily engaged, play into that process.

The lack of a guarantee of political rights more absolute than the political intelligence and maturity of the working people and their leaders might seem, in light of the unfortunate history of democratic rights in the Soviet Union, a profound lacuna in Lenin's political thought. It is far from obvious, however, that a rhetorical guarantee lacking theoretical coherence and practical purchase would be preferable: this sort of criticism begins with a retreat from the politico-strategic logic of the struggle for hegemony, that is, from the openness and the uncertainty inherent in the practice of politics, certainly in the practice of revolutionary politics. The truths that pertain to this domain, Lenin always insisted, are not absolute but relative. His occasional recourse in later years to the Napoleonic dictum *'On s'engage et puis... on voit'* – 'First engage in a serious battle and then see what happens'[66] – may suggest that the understanding of absolute truth that emerged from his wartime reading of Hegel's *Science of Logic* confirms this implication of the politico-strategic logic of the struggle for hegemony: what we can know absolutely is the finitude of our insertion in an infinite process; no one – neither Bonapartist nor revolutionary – can know everything that is (or is not) germane to action, in particular how others will react to one's own act. In the light of this truth we can appreciate the essential role Lenin accorded the revolutionary courage of the proletariat: not only the physical courage to risk life and limb in the uncertainties of a revolutionary leap, but also the moral courage to act – and to assume the responsibility of ruling – on merely relative truths.

---

66   Cited in Lenin 1923, p. 480.

CHAPTER 10

A Modern Prince to Discourses of Resistance... and Back?

> Unnoticed, the narrative has altered,
> but though the city's thus indecipherably orchestrated
> by the evil empire, down to the very molecules in my brain
> as I think I'm thinking, can I escape morning happiness,
> or not savor our fabled 'texture' of foreign
> and native poverties? (A boy tied into greengrocer's apron,
> unplaceable accent, brings out my coffee.) But, *no*, it says here
> the old country's 'de-developing' due to its mountainous
> debt to the First World – that's Broadway, my cafe
> and my table, so how can I today
> warm myself at the sad heartening narrative of immigration?
> Unnoticed, the narrative has altered,
> the displaced of capital have come to the capital.
>   – ANNE WINTERS[1]

∴

> Seen from the outside, establishment appears obvious: you get yourself hired and you organize. But here, this insertion 'into the working class' dissolves into a multitude of little individual situations where I don't manage to find a firm handle. These very words, 'the working class', no longer have the same immediate meaning in my eyes as they did in the past. It is not that I have come to doubt they cover a profound reality, but the variegation and the mobility of this population of the 'unskilled' in the midst of which I find myself thrown has shaken me, submerged me. Here, each one is a case. Each one has a story. Each one ponders his tactic and gropes around in his own fashion looking for a way out.
>   – ROBERT LINHART[2]

∴

---

1 Winters 2004, p. 12.
2 Linhart 1978, pp. 60–1.

The post-Marxist project of detaching the Gramscian concept of hegemony from its Leninist moorings is parasitical upon uncritical acceptance of the conventional caricature of Lenin; once Lenin's politico-strategic logic of the struggle for hegemony is explicated and the caricature thereby unveiled as such, it becomes possible to diagnose post-Marxist 'hegemony' as a disavowal in theoretical form of the burdens and responsibilities of leadership in the class struggle and, consequently, as a form of subaltern celebration of mere resistance consistent with the continuing domination of capital. Amplified by the fall of the Soviet Union and the Chinese turn to capitalism, similar efforts to purge 'Lenin' from the self-definition of the 'left' have had the effect of purging the kinds of questions raised by Lenin and in Leninist experience from the 'leftist' imagination. Absent some appreciation of the logic of the struggle for hegemony, issues of radical or revolutionary agency are typically posed unproductively in terms of an abstract opposition between direct action and vanguard representation; Lenin's vanguard and his politics generally are construed as seeking to represent – in the sense of 'acting on behalf of' as opposed to 'acting together with', and of thereby disempowering and distorting – proletarian and popular agency. The traditional terms of bourgeois political debate are left undisturbed, mere resistance is conflated with popular hegemony, and the status of the exploited as subaltern is reproduced. The same logic plays itself out even in quarters where an orientation to the struggles of working people and to the horizon of a society beyond class divisions has a much firmer grounding than in post-Marxism, for example in one of the most comprehensive and reflective engagements with recent transformations of capitalism and the class struggle, the *Empire* trilogy of Michael Hardt and Antonio Negri. I will argue that a preoccupation with getting beyond Leninism renders Hardt and Negri, in this respect at least representative of the mainstream of left-wing opinion, unable to draw upon or engage productively with the history of proletarian and popular struggles of the past century and that this fixation functions as a kind of distorting lens on their effort to portray the current shape of class and popular struggles. I go on to suggest, with reference to Gramsci's resurrection of Machiavelli's prince in the light of Lenin's vanguard, that these kinds of difficulty may be addressed – and perhaps partially redressed – by raising Leninist questions: the politico-strategic logic of the struggle for hegemony forged in Lenin's experience of the class struggle, by enabling political actors to grasp the spontaneous and the conscious aspects of revolutionary agency in relative terms and thereby making it possible to grasp their interpenetration, may assist leaders in contemporary movements of resistance in concretely analysing their concrete circumstances and in grounding and orienting themselves even amidst conjunctures of disorientation, prostration and merely fragmented resistance, analogous to the Italy that Machiavelli hoped to unify.

From Empire to Commonwealth?

Seeking to chart a third way between capitalism and statist communism, Hardt and Negri delineate the transmutation of social productive power under the auspices of Empire and, immanent within it, the emergence of a 'process of the multitude learning the art of self-rule and inventing lasting democratic forms of social organization'.[3] The inaugural volume, *Empire*, released in the aftermath of the triumphant debut of the anti-globalisation movement at the Seattle WTO meetings in 1999, seemed to want to announce 'autonomist Marxism', if not as the new spirit of the age, at least as the new spirit of anti-capitalist resistance. Together with its successor volumes, it has become a key point of reference in discussions of globalisation, postmodernity, political agency and the state; the debate it has triggered reflects a profound yearning for theoretical synthesis. If it is to yield more than mere yearning, however, a work of synthetic ambition must, like Marx's *Capital* or Lenin's oeuvre, impose, through the rigour of its logic and its theoretical command of the most outstanding issues of the time, a transformation in the terms in which the constituent issues are debated. The Hardt-Negri trilogy, while well designed to amplify the echoes of contemporary debates, is vitiated by pervasive ambiguity in a set of categories forged with a view as much to marking a distance from Leninist vanguardism as to rendering comprehensible the movement and logic of contemporary social relations.

Hardt and Negri begin their exposition with the transformation in the shape and organisation of social and political power attendant upon the process of globalisation of capitalism. While this process signifies a decline of the sovereign nation-state, it does not, they claim, signify a decline in sovereignty as such but rather that 'sovereignty has taken a new form, composed of a series of national and supranational organisms united under a single logic of rule'.[4] The claim is to be construed broadly as designating 'a new inscription of authority and a new design of the production of norms and legal instruments of coercion that guarantee contracts and resolve conflicts'.[5] Thus understood, the transformation in the form of sovereignty draws its impetus from the activity of the ruled every bit as much as from the rulers. The new form of sovereignty, in this encompassing sense, is what the authors mean by 'Empire'. Capitalist imperialism, which presupposed the form of the sovereign nation-state, is transformed through the logic of capitalist globalisation into Empire. Empire

---

3 Hardt and Negri 2009, pp. vii–viii.
4 Hardt and Negri 2000, p. xii.
5 Hardt and Negri 2000, p. 9.

erodes not only the boundaries between nation-states but also those between production and reproduction, culture and industry, and so on.

The logic of rule under Empire is distinguished from imperialism in being deterritorialised, decentred, immanent and all-encompassing. Rule is no longer exercised primarily through the establishment of control over clearly demarcated territories; it is not that borders have disappeared, but those that remain are both less rigid – they shift constantly in response to the varied functional requirements of capital – and more permeable to capital and labour, ideas and images. Deterritorialisation blurs the distinction between the deployment of force in home and foreign policy as the latter increasingly takes the form of 'police actions', while in the former the rule of law is shaped by multiplying exceptions – 'wars' on crime, drugs, etc. – and renders defunct the logic whereby contention between imperialist powers leads to war. It is not that the number of imperialist powers has been reduced to one; since capital and the state are no longer anchored to a particular territory, what distinguishes Empire is rather the absence of a sovereign centre from which decisions can be imposed upon peripheral territories. Capitalism still develops unevenly, but its unevenness has itself become more uneven, distributing inequalities and obstacles along a multiplicity of fractured lines.

If the United States is nonetheless indispensable to the logic of Empire, this is so not in virtue of its imperialist might but inasmuch as it establishes a kind of constitutional template for the expansive tendency of republican liberty. The point may be understood through a distinction the authors repeatedly invoke between a modernist and European (Hobbesian or Rousseauian) conception of power in which sovereignty is portrayed, appropriately in the case of the nation-state, as an entity that transcends the immanent movements of labour and capital and the 'new political science' of the *Federalist Papers*, which proposed that 'the order of the multitude must be born not from a transfer of the title of power and right, but from an arrangement internal to the multitude, from a democratic interaction of powers linked together in networks'.[6] In a move that might have surprised Madison, Hamilton and Jay, the republican separation of powers is thus made to anticipate the openness and hence expansiveness of postmodern networking arrangements, a protean but axiomatic system of social control immanent in the productive life of society, at once liberating and pervasively dominating.[7] The opposition between the immanent and the transcendent that organises this argument runs together a political-science distinction between constituent power and constituted

---

6 Hardt and Negri 2000, p. 161; see Hamilton, Madison and Jay 1787–8.
7 Hardt and Negri 2000, pp. 326–7.

power (that is, the 'multitude' and the state apparatus alienated from it), a cultural distinction between the postmodern and the modern and an ontological distinction between doing and being, creative subjectivity and ossified objectivity. It is never quite clear whether (or to what extent) the mutation in the form of social power has to do with a reorganisation of state power or with its dissolution into the flux of social activity.

The agential form of resistance appropriate to the age of Empire is drawn out in the second volume, *Multitude*. Appearing at a conjuncture reshaped by 9/11 and by the beginnings of the imperial response, in order to reconcile the appearance of *Pax Imperii* with the realities of perpetual war, it reemphasises persisting unevenness and fractures in the Empire. Hardt and Negri multiply metaphors – 'swarm', 'network', 'guerilla warfare' – to convey the mobility, the multi-dimensional diversity and the decentredness of the emergent agency of resistance, the 'multitude'. These characteristics, they claim, distinguish the logic of contemporary resistance to Empire from the centralising and homogenising logic of the 'working class', the 'people', even the 'masses', correlates all of one or another form of hierarchical rule. However, their professed need to extract the guerrilla aspect of resistance from its historical and strategic insertion into the context of one or another 'people's army' calls into question their characterisation of the latter form of organisation as inherently reductive and homogenising.[8] Indeed, if, as they insist, resistance is to be understood as the force that most fundamentally drives capital forward, this extraction inevitably poses a question as to whether or not this kind of 'liberation' of the forces of resistance simply reduces resistance to the mere obverse side of the perpetual wars of Empire. If Hardt and Negri have a response to this kind of question, it is to be sought in the final volume, *Commonwealth*, which, by spelling out the notion of the commons, the social space that is the medium through which the multitude constitutes itself as agency beyond Empire, proposes 'an ethics of democratic political action', a kind of 'Becoming-Prince of the multitude'.[9]

The 'common' is a term of protean significance in the authors' rhetorical and argumentative strategy. It is said, first, to cut across the opposition between 'private' and 'public' that shaped the debates of the twentieth century. The 'common' thus represents a gesture toward a third way beyond the sterile opposition between capitalism and statist communism. Second, it extends the traditional sense of the commons as land accessible to all not only to the air, the water, indeed the common bounty of the natural world, but to the socially

---

8 See Hardt and Negri 2004, pp. 69–91.
9 Hardt and Negri 2009, pp. vii–viii.

constituted storehouse of common linguistic, cognitive, affective, and gestural resources. It thus serves, third, through a largely implicit invocation of Marx's notion of the social individual or species-being (the notion that the terms in which humans individuate themselves are only constituted in and through their social relations), as the context for the emergence of a multitude of 'singularities', equal, hence horizontal, open, self-determining, in constant movement, mixture and metamorphosis. To characterise the type of activity implicit in this context as the immanent form of emergence of a real communism, the authors have recourse to the notion of biopolitical production, here understood with reference to 'the hegemony... of immaterial production in the processes of capitalist valorization', to the 'feminization of work' in the sense not only of women's increased participation in the wage-labour market but also of increased flexibility of the working day and breakdown of the distinction between productive and reproductive, cognitive and affective labour, and to the emergence of 'new patterns of migration and processes of social and racial mixture'.[10] The Foucauldian concept of biopower is mobilised to express the immanent and capillary (rather than transcendent and sovereign) workings of contemporary power and to suggest a semblance of material unity and hence political efficacy in the notion of immaterial labour. Conceived thus in terms of biopolitical production, finally, the common provides a rhetorical conduit between the immaterial labour of 'postmodern' network society and the 'pre-modern' (transfigured, in this postmodern context, and by contrast with fundamentalist anti-modernism, into 'altermodern') labour associated with the traditional common.

By conceiving the common as emergent in and through biopolitical production, the authors are able to pose the transition to a classless society not only in the quantitative terms of the level of development of the productive forces but qualitatively, in terms of the social forms and forces immanent in the most advanced phase of capitalist production. In so doing, they revive an important – though little discussed of late – theme in Marx's account of modern industry in *Capital*.[11] Alas, in contrast to the analytical clarity of Marx's presentation, Hardt and Negri's argument relies upon allusion and equivocation. The transition is conceived as a kind of exodus from the domination of capital, conditioned by the autonomy of the biopolitical labour of the common; where industrial capitalism was characterised by the absorption and subordination of knowledge to a centralised system of command, biopolitical production is

---

10   Hardt and Negri 2009, pp. 132–7.
11   See Marx 1867, Chapter XV.

constituted in part by the productive force of a mass intellectuality whose productivity exceeds its utilisation by capital and escapes, at least tendentially, its system of control: 'Biopolitical production is an orchestra keeping the beat without a conductor, and it would fall silent if anyone were to step onto the podium'.[12] This account presents an unexpected homology with the Kautskyan trope of capital as increasingly vestigial to production and thus shucked off as naturally and as easily as a snake sheds its old skin. While it may resonate with the atmosphere of the in-house think tanks at an Apple or a Google, this account is a tragic mockery of the organisation of production experienced by call-centre workers. This point, the difficulty of conceiving a political convergence based upon the 'common' situation of biopolitical or immaterial labour, suggests a more basic problem: that the concept of biopolitical production itself, so far from constituting the anatomy of contemporary capitalism, is simply a muddled expedient.

At all essential points in the argument, Hardt and Negri explicate biopolitical production and its cognates by way of contrast with modern industrial production. The merely instrumental character of industrial labour serves to point up the inherently social and affective character of immaterial labour. Where the asocial character of industrial labour saps the roots of cooperative self-activity, underwriting the assumption of hegemony – the usurpation of political agency – by a would-be representative institution, the biopolitical production of the common renders possible, indeed instantiates, forms of action at once economic and political, in which the horizontal diversity of the singularities constituting the multitude renders hierarchy (and with it representation) superfluous. The openness and hence the claim to universality of the common demands that it be constituted not through any specific forms of activity but through any activity that is social in the egalitarian sense of not purporting to act for another, standing in opposition to industrial labour only insofar as the latter is utilised to sustain the pretensions of a would-be vanguard.

Shifting promiscuously between several different senses in which labour might be said to be social (or not), this line of thought is little more than an attempt to endow with the weight of sociological analysis what is really a moral argument on behalf of direct action against political representation. In some respects, it recalls Jürgen Habermas's distinction between instrumental and communicative action.[13] It has some affinities with the Bakuninist

---

12   Hardt and Negri 2009, p. 172.
13   See Habermas 1984, pp. 75–101.

dismissal of the industrial proletariat as bourgeoisified and the resulting anarchist chase after non-industrial agents of revolutionary change. But the real issue is not the industrial working class; Hardt and Negri are careful to note that, in the broader context of biopolitical production, industrial workers, too, are capable of cooperative self-activity. The real issue is the political instrumentalisation of the industrial working class by a self-appointed (canonically Leninist) vanguard.

The meaning and hence the coherence of categories as central to the argument as biopolitical production and immaterial labour would seem to rest less upon their capacity to clarify the movement of contemporary social forces than upon their utility in establishing a reassuring distance from (what is really a Cold War caricature of) the historical experience of Leninist vanguards. Judged by the standard of the authors' professed aim of establishing an ethic of democratic political action immanently in the analysis of the present moment, political agency is construed narrowly in terms of an opposition between direct action and representation. One might still have expected, in a work devoted to the political ethics of democratic agency, some account of leadership in terms of 'acting together with' rather than as 'acting on behalf of'. Yet despite a preface entitled 'Becoming-Prince of the Multitude', the authors have literally nothing to say about leadership, leaving us perhaps with nothing more than an apotheosis, concluding the initial volume, of St. Francis of Assisi, exemplifying 'in love, simplicity and also innocence...the joy of being communist'.[14] It would seem that Hardt and Negri are unable to get beyond an obsession with getting beyond Leninism. In this they arguably represent a trend of thought that is widely influential, if not hegemonic, in contemporary movements of resistance.

The Modern Prince and the 'Discourses'

The lessons of *realpolitik* that may be found in the pages of Machiavelli's *Prince* were already available, through experience, breeding and social connections, to 'those already in the know', to the ruling classes. And so, Gramsci reasons, the very act of writing down what is to be done without being said reveals Machiavelli's partisanship for the people, for 'those who are not in the know'.[15] *The Prince* is no dry scientific treatise whose results are offered indifferently to reactionary and democrat alike. Through the dramatic movement of the work,

---

14   Hardt and Negri 2000, p. 413.
15   Gramsci 1929–35, p. 135.

Machiavelli merges dialectically with the people, 'whose consciousness and whose expression he becomes and feels himself to be', with those persuaded by the force and logic of his call for a prince who would found a unified Italian state. The figure of the prince is the symbol that crystallises a 'concrete phantasy', which acts on a dispersed and shattered people to arouse and organize its collective will'. In his culminating 'invocation of a prince who "really exists"', the 'rigorous logic' and 'scientific detachment' of his power-political analyses assume the status of 'auto-reflection on the part of the people – an inner reasoning worked out in the popular consciousness, whose conclusion is a cry of passionate urgency. The passion, from discussion of itself, becomes once again "emotion", fever, fanatical desire for action'.[16] With this kind of dialectical movement in view Gramsci would try to extend Lenin's notion of the vanguard party of the proletariat into the vision of a modern prince. In the modern world, Gramsci argues, an individual could not incarnate the function of the Machiavellian prince. The kind of improvisation a mere individual is capable of executing is consistent only with the defensive, conservative work of restoring or reorganising an already existing, albeit decayed, political consensus. A modern prince must, by contrast, be capable of undertaking a political project with 'a long-term and organic character', such as the establishment of 'new states or new national and social structures', a project for which 'a new collective will must be created from scratch, to be directed towards goals which are concrete and rational'. This kind of project could only be undertaken by 'an organism, a complex element of society in which a collective will, which has already been recognized and has to some extent asserted itself in action, begins to take concrete form'. This organism is the political party, 'the first cell, in which there come together germs of a collective will tending to become universal and total'.[17]

The Prince was concerned not with the princely administration of an established regime, but with the construction of new political foundations, the creation of a new regime, and for this – Machiavelli was categorical – the concentrated will of a single political actor was a necessity. Machiavelli's insistence on this point suggests a difficulty with the Gramscian analogy, for the modern prince is, of course, a collective actor. The issue may be illuminated by recourse to Machiavelli's other great work of political analysis, *Discourses on the First Decade of Titus Livius*. The issue around which the *Discourses* are organised concerns the durability and expansiveness of a political power once established, best ensured, Machiavelli argued, by republican forms where

---

16 Gramsci 1929–35, pp. 126–7.
17 Gramsci 1929–35, pp. 129–30.

responsibility for ruling is decided in a public space of political struggle open to a plurality of actors. Not only could the popular tumults that surround political strife secure the people a share in administration and sustain political liberties, they enhance the civic virtue of the citizenry and hence the force and expansiveness of the republic.[18] What is more, the diversity of its citizenry enables a republic to adapt to changes in political circumstance better than a prince could do.[19] If, however, a new regime can only be founded by a single will, by a prince, the problem necessarily arises of how the transition from prince to a republic is to be understood. The problem may be addressed by treating the distinction between the prince and the citizen of a republic as a distinction most basically between two aspects of political agency, action upon political foundations and action in pursuit of political aims within foundational parameters, upon which the distinction between different types of political actor depends.

The possibility of acting outside the established conventions and prevailing assumptions of the political process – and hence, *a fortiori*, the possibility of calling them into question – may be available to any political actor, but it is constitutive of the political project of the Machiavellian prince. In order to enact its political project coherently, however, the prince must be able to communicate with some measure of confidence and to assign clear significance to the response to its attempts at enactment. It must, therefore, be conscious of acting in a practical inter-subjectivity, a community, and act so as to be(come) recognised as ruler: '[J]ust as those who paint landscapes place themselves in a low position on the plain in order to consider the nature of the mountains and the high places and place themselves high atop mountains in order to study the plains, in like manner, to know well the nature of the people one must be a prince, and to know well the nature of princes one must be of the people'.[20] To the extent that the project of the Machiavellian prince is launched in the context either of an absence of political community or of a political community organised around recognition of another actor as ruler, it consists in the (re)constitution of a community – but the newly reconstituted community could no longer be governed in accordance with traditional, unreflective authority. The new prince does not act alone, but may be the one actor in the emergent community who has assumed responsibility for having overturned – and, therefore, for having questioned – the traditional, or at least the given, arrangement of authority. In so doing, however, it reveals the horizon of a

---

18   See Machiavelli 1517, Book I, Chapter 4.
19   See Machiavelli 1517, Book III, Chapter 9.
20   Machiavelli 1513, p. 78.

political world in which questioning authority is conceivable and a politics incorporating such questioning is, in this sense, a possibility for others, a world with a potential plurality of Machiavellian political actors; an enduring arena for such a plurality could only be a republic.[21] The distinction between prince and citizen, principality and republic, is, at least in this sense, fluid.

As a modern prince lays out the scaffolding for the construction of a new classless social order, it begins to give shape to a public arena of political struggle, that is, it establishes the 'political form[s] ... under which to work out the economical emancipation of labour',[22] within which parameters the policies, practices and institutions of the new order may effectively be contested, reorganised, extended or even reversed. This process of 'working out' would always have to be resumed and revised in light of changing circumstances, needs and capacities; and in the process the parameters of the arena of political struggle are themselves subject to change. Such a process is the more necessary inasmuch as the project of a modern prince is not simply the materialisation of new values but also the practice of weaving together the threads of a new community informed by a plurality of interests, needs and aspirations and thus open to a variety of patterns, priorities and combinations. The point holds *a fortiori* in that the scope of the project embraces a transformation not just in the political but also in the social order and in the relation between politics and society. On the Machiavellian hypothesis that the expansiveness and durability of proletarian rule requires republican – that is, constitutional – forms of rule, the ability of the proletarian power to clothe itself in effective constitutional forms will depend in turn upon the strength and vitality – in Machiavellian terms, the civic virtue – of the proletarian-popular community. Civic virtue, political community, is not a given but waxes or wanes with the course of the struggle between revolution and counterrevolution; working out the forms of a socialist republic is thus subject to the complex, uneven and contradictory logic of the struggle for hegemony. What really confirms the hegemony of the modern prince is not the emergence of a consensus beyond dispute but the transmutation of the role of adversary of the new order into that of an opposition unable to challenge the parameters of public policy and public debate without spontaneously respecting the foundations of the new order. The prince will then have become one citizen among many in a socialist republic.

---

21 See Garver 1987, pp. 117–40.
22 Marx 1871, p. 334.

Prince and People

The fragmentation, disorientation and prostration of renaissance Italy before Machiavelli's invocation of the 'concrete phantasy' of a liberator-prince might recall, in some quarters, the circumstances of progressive forces under the current reign of finance capital. It is worth remembering, however, that Machiavelli did not find a prince to answer his call, and nothing is less likely than that our prince will come. In any case, the posture of expressing one's political agency through the symbolisation of a 'concrete phantasy' fits more comfortably with the Menshevik sense of agency as self-activity and with the unilinear logic of Marxist orthodoxy – or, for that matter, with the Whig view of history – than with the politico-strategic logic of the struggle for hegemony. Nor could an alternative course of action consist, on the Leninist logic of hegemony, simply of arrogating the title of prince to oneself, for a prince can only be prince when recognised by the people. The work of political leadership consists, in a sense, in building and defending a community of the people capable of bestowing such recognition; the construction of such a community is not undertaken from one perspective alone. Paradoxical as it may seem in light of the conventional caricature, Lenin's politico-strategic logic of the struggle for hegemony yields insights useful for thinking about the constitution of a proletarian-popular community through the struggles of an irreducible plurality of political actors.

Consider once again Lenin's discussion of the appropriate stances of revolutionary Marxists in relation to the right of nations to self-determination. He insisted, in his critique of 'imperialist Economism', that proletarian internationalism called for quite different courses of action from revolutionaries in oppressed nations and from those in oppressor nations: with the aid of a strategic-geographical analogy – concerted action against the Tsar's army at Moscow requires revolutionary forces to move east from Smolensk but west from Nizhni-Novgorod – he argued that the former must place a critique of nationalist illusions in the forefront of their struggle, while the latter accord priority to the right of the oppressed nation to self-determination. His point, of course, was that different, even 'contradictory', orientations and movements from differently situated actors need not subvert but may be necessary to reach a common goal. Taken literally, the geographical analogy might suggest that the aim of the international revolutionaries is, like Moscow, a fixed point, a given. One might then assume that the forces in Smolensk and Nizhni-Novgorod were simply different contingents of the same army acting under a unified command in accord with a preconceived plan. But then the analogy breaks down. When Lenin made this argument he was at the head of no revolutionary army. Indeed, there was no headquarters from which to issue directions; the Socialist International had collapsed with the collusion of most of its constituent parties in the war efforts of their respective governments. His aim was to knit together the threads of solidarity of the international proletariat that had been shredded in this betrayal. The (re)construction of international solidarity supposed certain objective bases to exist and would have to be worked out under more or less severe objective constraints, but it called upon the agency of workers of different nations to establish trust in one another, demonstrating to one another their feeling for the fears and aspirations, their understanding of the limitations and opportunities implicit in the circumstances of the other: in short, their mutual trustworthiness. If the substance of Lenin's argument is kept in mind, the aim that the variously situated actors seek to accomplish, although it can be located in a general way, is not fixed, not a given but constituted, at least in part, in and through the relations the actors establish with one another and among others they hope to influence; their aim, that is to say, is in part to establish their community.[23]

Differently situated amidst the spontaneous unfolding of the class struggle, Marxist political actors, conscious of the irreconcilable antagonism of classes, may thus have to orient themselves, to act, and to organise independently – indeed, along contradictory lines – concerting their varied approaches only in the course of practice rather than according to a prearranged design, in order to knit together the threads of proletarian-popular community. As Lenin observed in a related context, 'Capitalism is not so harmoniously built that the various sources of rebellion can immediately merge of their own accord'. He went on to suggest that such contradictory complexity, the 'variegated and discordant, motley and outwardly fragmented' character of mass struggles, is not a 'bug' but an essential feature of the process of socialist revolution and the constitution of revolutionary communities-in-struggle: '[T]he very fact that revolts do break out at different times, in different places, and are of different kinds, guarantees wide scope and depth to the general movement'.[24] There is every reason to suppose that amidst the unevenness, complexities and contradictions of the logic of the struggle for hegemony, orientations analogous to those set to work by Lenin to forge the international solidarity of the workers can be taken on by contemporary Marxists in order to situate themselves in the class struggle and to fortify other dimensions of proletarian and popular community.[25]

---

23 See Lenin 1916e, especially pp. 55–63.
24 Lenin 1916c, pp. 356, 358.
25 See Shandro 1998 and Shandro 2000.

The material circumstances in which working people find themselves are inevitably diverse and their experience and interests multi-faceted; these features are bound to express themselves in a proletarian-popular community. Any community presumes a capacity for solidarity, but such a community is not founded on some mutually-agreed vision in which diverse priorities are harmoniously reconciled. It assumes the existence of determinate material forces of production and it grows (or fails to grow) through the transformation (or reproduction) of the existing social relations of production, a process of class struggle refracted through the politico-strategic logic of the struggle for hegemony. Actions to accomplish particular aims will also have implications for the transformation and reproduction of the relations of production subtending potentially emergent proletarian-popular communities as well as upon the strength and breadth of solidarity that constitutes such communities. Action in pursuit of particular aims which does not take into account its implications for the transformation of the material bases of the proletarian-popular community, or concerting one's actions with the efforts of others with a view toward a particular aim but not toward organising and managing the cognate effects of those efforts upon the relations of production, might be characterised as being undertaken spontaneously or 'unconsciously'. But the transformation of relations of production is not something separate and apart from actions undertaken in pursuit of particular aims. Conversely, then, action undertaken with a view to introducing determinate transformations in the relations of production without taking into account the effect of the actions on others' pursuit of particular aims or without concerting one's actions with the efforts of others, with a view only to their effects upon the relations of production but not upon particular aims pursued, might be characterised no less appropriately – if nonetheless differently – as 'unconscious' or spontaneous. Lenin levelled the charge of 'spontaneism' in *What Is to Be Done?* not only against the Economists' orientation to the spontaneous working-class movement but also, it is worth noting in the present connection, against intellectuals who advocated individual acts of terror with a view to exciting the masses to revolutionary action.[26]

Since the spontaneous process is uneven, contradictory and multi-faceted, if, as Lenin asserted, 'the spontaneous element' represents in essence 'consciousness in an *embryonic form*',[27] then consciousness may be expected to emerge from its embryonic forms at various points in the process and in a

---

26 See Lenin 1902, pp. 417–21.
27 Lenin 1902, p. 374.

number of different shapes, perhaps not quite 'variegated and discordant, motley and outwardly fragmented' but without its unity being a given. Action in concert will always be marked by the unevenness of the process and will always be expressed in varying forms and combinations of cooperation and autonomy, organisation and innovation, unity and division. Whether and when action in concert is appropriately characterised as the advent of a 'modern prince' does not depend on a standard erected independently of the logic of the struggle for hegemony. Lenin made a related point at the Second Congress of the Communist International in addressing reservations about the leading role of the communist party expressed by representatives of the Industrial Workers of the World and the British Shop Stewards movement:

> [I]f Comrade Tanner says that he is opposed to parties, but at the same time is in favour of a minority that represents the best organised and most revolutionary workers showing the way to the entire proletariat, then I say that there is really no difference between us. What is this organised minority? If this minority is really class-conscious, if it is able to lead the masses, if it is able to reply to every question that appears on the order of the day, then it is a party in reality.[28]

The most important thing is not the name or the forms in which hegemonic agency is exercised but whether those forms, whatever they are, enable the class-conscious workers to undertake the functions of leadership 'in constant and real contact with the masses', whether they are in consequence really recognised by the masses as their leaders, whether they are really 'able to lead those masses'[29] through the class struggle in constituting a community beyond class.

---

28   Lenin 1920c, p. 235.
29   Lenin 1920c, p. 236.

APPENDIX 1

Karl Kautsky, 'The Revision of the Austrian Social Democratic Programme'[1]

At the Brünn Party Conference in 1899 our Austrian comrades passed a resolution to undertake a revision of the programme they adopted at Hainfield in 1888. A commission, consisting of comrades Adler, Daszynski, Ellenboggen, Schuhmeier and Steiner, was entrusted with this task. The result of their work was published at the end of August and put forward for criticism by party members.

As Victor Adler informs us in the Vienna *Worker Times* of 22 September, the wish of the Austrian comrades to revise the Party programme arose 'far less from a principled or practical than from a formal, one could almost say an aesthetic, need'. The old Hainfield programme consists of a statement of principles and two resolutions, one of which deals with political rights and the other with labour protection legislation, in a fashion that, in some respects, no longer corresponds to contemporary views. The principles have not changed but the fighting proletariat no doubt has a heightened sense of its power and its confidence as to what it can wring from the present-day state has grown. On the other hand, other resolutions are to be added to these two. In Brünn in 1899 our fraternal party decided upon a nationalities programme; in Graz a kind of agrarian programme was adopted by the Congress of the German party organisation; a municipal programme is being worked out: in view of all these changes the wish to refashion the demands of the programme on some other points and to standardise them is understandable.

We do not wish to talk about this side of the amended programme here. But the committee also deemed it necessary to alter the statement of principles, although our principles have in no way changed, merely in order to prevent misinterpretations in one or another point or to remove a few blemishes for aesthetic reasons.

One wonders whether this constitutes sufficient grounds to subject the statement of principles, which stands at the head of every socialist programme, to a change. What distinguishes our programme from all bourgeois programmes is not the individual demands but this statement of principles. It contains the 'ultimate aim' and the reasons that inspire our efforts. It has very important practical, and not merely decorative, functions to fulfil. It does not, as some latter-day socialists believe, have the same

---

[1] Karl Kautsky, 'Die Revision des Programms der sozialdemokratie in Oesterreich', in *Die Neue Zeit*, XX Jahrgang, I Band, Nr. 3, 1901–2, 68–82. Thanks to John-Paul Himka for assistance with the translation.

significance for us as does a holy icon for the peasant, who keeps it in his home and ritually makes the sign of the cross and lights his candle in front of it without ever giving it a thought in his practical activity. It has rather the great practical task of maintaining the unity of the proletarian movement.

And this in two ways. The more the proletarian movement grows, the more does the division of labour develop in it. Various functions fall to persons who occupy themselves exclusively with them and for whom these means to an end turn only too easily into ends in themselves. The more the various aspects of the proletarian movement become independent, the more easily friction and contradiction arise between them and this can very often sap the strength of the whole movement. This danger can be more easily overcome, the more alive are the ideas of all the participants about the ultimate aim – and everything in practical everyday work and detail work should contribute to this – and the more unified the conception of the ultimate aim.

But this has to bring unity, not only between the different functions, but also between the successive phases, of the proletarian movement. Every fluctuation in social and political life redounds upon this movement and the less solidly grounded in theory is its ultimate aim, the more dependent it becomes upon the conjuncture, public opinion and the fashion of the day. Those who most proudly parade their independence from all 'dogma' and 'received opinion' are the very ones who can be shoved around most recklessly by the currents of the time, ecstatic one day, suicidal the next, mocking the Marxists today from the anarchist standpoint as petty-bourgeois, armchair revolutionaries and denouncing the same Marxists tomorrow as Blanquists since they aren't all wrapped up in a cooperative store.

A solidly structured programme with a clear final aim puts a strong rein on this kind of zigzag course. The politicians of fashion and opinion occasionally experience it as a fetter, moan about dogmatic fanaticism, and equate the theorems of the programme with the articles of faith of the Catholic Church, but afterwards, when the fashion is past and the party, unwavering, has moved further along the road to its destination, they acquiesce in it.

But if the preservation of the unity of the movement is viewed as one of the functions of the ultimate aim and of our programme's statement of principles, then it already follows that patching up a statement of principles just for the sake of a few blemishes contradicts its purpose for no compelling reason.

In my opinion there are only two reasons that might lead a Social Democratic party to change the part of its programme that deals with principles if it is well thought out and precisely drafted. One is a fundamental change in its structure that must also be given public expression. That is especially the case where two quarrelling factions join forces. They won't set off without a new programme, even though it may not differ fundamentally from the previous programmes. Only a new programme can show that this is a new organisation, that one organisation has not been swallowed up in the other, that there is neither a winner nor a loser. The Gotha and the Hainfeld Programmes owe their origin to such an occasion.

But a programme must also be changed when a fundamental change has taken place in the party's theoretical orientation. This is what brought about the Erfurt Programme. Marxist theory, to which it gave expression, may already have been fully developed in the 1870s but it had not yet been assimilated into the thinking of the German Social Democrats. Long and arduous work was required before the unified Marxist conception superseded the old vulgar socialism. As soon as that occurred, the old programme also became intolerable.

Nobody would claim that either of these reasons for changing the programme applies now. Even those who are most taken with Bernstein's revisionist movement do not claim that he has given our party a new theoretical basis but only that he has supplied the necessary groundwork for it. Thus, even from the Bernsteinian standpoint, a reformulation of the programme would be premature.

But Adler himself explains that the new version of the programme is no concession to the Bernsteinian standpoint. Rather, insofar as that is taken into account, this merely betokens an effort to preclude misunderstandings to which some clauses of the old programme would have been exposed as a result of Bernstein's critical philosophy.

Once one had definitely decided to change the statement of principles, this concern would certainly carry a lot of weight and should no doubt be taken into consideration in the formulation of individual clauses. It does not by itself, however, constitute sufficient grounds for such a change.

Our programme will always be exposed to misunderstandings simply because of its inevitable brevity. Even a theory elaborated in a massive book can never exhaust life; it will always emphasise only the essential points and must disregard the inessential and accidental. Life is always more diverse than theory, let alone the quintessence of theory as set down in a statement of principles. People who have not fully grasped our theory or who cannot distinguish the essential from the inessential will always be in a position to misunderstand our statement of principles, however we may express it. If we wanted to respond to every misunderstanding that turns up by changing the programme, we could subject it to a revision every year.

But each year new blemishes will be discovered. It isn't possible to draft a clause that appears entirely faultless to everyone; very often the author himself soon finds a happier and more precise version. If this constitutes sufficient grounds for a revision, then we will never finish revising the programme. The more we want to improve it, the more we threaten its principal beauty, its unity and harmony.

As well thought out and unified a work of art as the Hainfeld Programme will most likely suffer damage in this respect through a revision. I may, incidentally, praise this programme so highly without being guilty of self-importance because it is not true, contrary to what Hertz says in the *Socialist Monthly*, that the Hainfeld Programme was written by Adler and me. Adler drafted it by himself and just obtained my opinion for the final edition. I had nothing to do with it, except for some small remarks where I was pleased with it.

Sufficient grounds for changing the statement of principles have not therefore been produced. This change was, in any case, a difficult and thankless business. Let us see what has come of it.

First, so that a comparison is possible, let us print the old programme and the new one side by side.

The Hainfield Programme

The Social Democratic Workers' Party in Austria strives for the liberation of the whole people, without distinction of nationality, race or sex, from the fetters of economic dependence, to do away with its political disenfranchisement, and to raise it out of spiritual atrophy. The reason for this shameful state of affairs is not to be sought in particular political arrangements but in the fact, dominating and conditioning the nature of the whole social order, that the means of labour are monopolised in the hands of the owners of private property. The owners of labour power, the working class, thereby become the slaves of the owners of the means of labour, the capitalist class, whose political and economic domination is expressed in the present-day state. Just as in politics private ownership of the means of production signifies the class state, in economics it signifies the increasing poverty of the masses and growing immiseration for ever broader strata of society.

Through technical development, the colossal growth of productive powers not only proves this form of property superfluous, but also effectively elimi-

The New Draft

Austrian Social Democracy strives for the liberation of the whole people, without distinction of nationality, race or sex, from the fetters of economic dependence, political disenfranchisement, and spiritual atrophy. The reason for the present state of affairs does not lie in particular political arrangements, but in the fact, dominating and conditioning the nature of the whole social order, that the means of labour are monopolised in the hands of the owners of private property. The owners of labour power, the working class, thereby become increasingly dependent upon the owners of the means of labour, including the land, the class of large landowners and the capitalist class, whose political and economic domination is expressed in the present-day state.

Technical progress, the increasing concentration of production and ownership and the unification of all economic power in the hands of capitalists and capitalist groups have the effect of dispossessing ever wider circles of previously independent small entrepreneurs and turning them into wage workers or employees directly or indirectly

(Continued)

nates it for the overwhelming majority of people while simultaneously securing the material and spiritual conditions necessary for the form of common property. The transfer of the means of labour into the social property of the whole people therefore signifies not only the liberation of the working class but also the culmination of a historically necessary development. The bearer of this development can only be the class-conscious proletariat organised as a political party. That is why the real programme of the Social Democratic Workers' Party in Austria is to organise the proletariat politically, to imbue it with the consciousness of its position and its mission and to render it and keep it spiritually and materially fit for action. All appropriate means that accord with the people's natural sense of justice will be employed to this end. The Party will, incidentally, have to adjust its normal tactics to the circumstances, especially to the behaviour of the enemy.

dependent upon capitalists and of transforming the small peasants into debt slaves. The living conditions of ever broader strata of working people are in increasingly striking contrast to the rapidly rising productive power of their own labour and to the burgeoning wealth they have themselves created. Crises springing from the planlessness of the capitalist mode of production and bringing unemployment and misery in their wake, accelerate and intensify this development.

But the more the development of capitalism swells [the ranks] of the proletariat, the more is the proletariat [both] able and obliged to take up the struggle against it. It becomes conscious that the supersession of private production makes private ownership increasingly superfluous and harmful, that both the spiritual and the material conditions necessary for new forms of cooperative production and common ownership have to be created, and that the transformation of the means of labour into the social property of the whole people must be the goal of the struggle for the liberation of the working class. The bearer of this necessary development can only be the proletariat itself, awakened to class consciousness and organised for class struggle. That is why the real programme of Austrian Social Democracy is to organise the proletariat politically, to imbue it with the consciousness of its position and its mission and to render it and keep it spiritually and materially fit for action. All appropriate means that accord with the people's natural sense of justice will be employed to this end.

(*Continued*)

> Austrian Social Democracy will always represent the class interest of the proletariat in all political and economic questions and will energetically counteract every attempt to obscure and disguise class conflict or to exploit the workers for the benefit of the ruling parties.
>
> Austrian Social Democracy is an international party: it condemns the privileges of nations just as it does those of birth, sex, property, and [ethnic] origin and declares that the struggle against exploitation must, like exploitation itself, be international. It condemns and struggles against all restrictions upon the free expression of opinion as well as every form of spiritual paternalism by state or church. It strives for legal protection of the living conditions of the working class and it struggles to gain due influence for the proletariat in all areas of public life.

That the name of the party should have changed stands out immediately in the comparison. 'Social Democracy' is supposed to take the place of 'Social Democratic Workers' Party'. Apparently, this has only been done for the sake of brevity. No one can claim that the proletarian character of Social Democracy in Austria has become less pronounced today than it was formerly.

Apparently, it is also only in order to remove an awkward expression that one now speaks of an Austrian Social Democracy and no longer of a Social Democracy in Austria. But even this latter term is very distinctive. It attests to the fact that the Social Democracy of Austria regards this country as a geographical concept, the framework within which it is condemned to work, but does not feel, as perhaps the Germans, French and English do, like the Social Democracy of a particular people. There is an Austrian state – even this does not express it exactly, since there is only an Austro-Hungarian monarchy – but no Austrian people, only peoples in Austria. Hence there is no Austrian Social Democracy in Austria, only German, Czech, Polish, etc. Social Democracies, which together form the Social Democracy of Austria. This peculiar situation is much better characterised if the statement of principles speaks of Social Democracy in Austria than if it speaks of Austrian Social Democracy.

The next change is the following: after enumerating the fetters from which the people are to be liberated, the old programme said, 'The reason for this shameful state of affairs is not to be sought in particular political institutions' but in the private ownership of the means of production. The new draft, by comparison, speaks of the 'reason for the present state of affairs'. This is a distinct weakening. Present state of affairs, how colourless! We struggle against this state of affairs because it is shameful, not because it is present.

However, the expression, 'present state of affairs', is not merely weak, it is also incorrect. Only some present circumstances, those that are characterised as shameful in the old programme, the oppression, exploitation and atrophy of the worker, have their ultimate cause in the private ownership of the means of production, but not all present circumstances. That Wagnerian operas are better received today than Meyerbeerian, that more mountain climbers fall each year, that there are people who believe that there is no god and that men may be descended from apes, are present circumstances that one would not want to trace back to the private ownership of the means of production.

The replacement of 'this shameful state of affairs' by the 'present state of affairs' is so completely inappropriate and thus so pointless that we could ascribe it to carelessness rather than to a particular intent.

Let us go on to the next innovation.

In the old programme we find the phrase, 'The owners of labour-power, the working class, thereby become the slaves of the owners of the means of labour, the capitalist class'. In the new draft it says, 'The owners of labour-power, the working class, thereby become increasingly dependent upon the owners of the means of labour, including the land, the class of large landowners and the capitalist class'.

Why this change? Unfortunately, since the new draft includes no indication of motive, one is obliged to guess the reasons for particular changes. Does the expression 'slaves' appear too strong to the Programme Committee? Since the wage labourer is obviously not legally a slave, whether one designates him as such depends entirely upon subjective opinion. The more passionately one feels, the greater the degree of freedom one demands, the more readily will one use the term 'wage slave' to describe the worker. That word is decidedly more powerful and expresses the relationship of domination and exploitation more vividly than does the colourless word, 'dependent'.

While, in one respect, the new version weakens the statement, in another it strengthens it. The old programme explains the fact of wage slavery by private property in the means of production, without discussing its tendency. The draft speaks of the increasing dependence of the worker. As the Programme Committee set itself the task, above all, of precluding the misunderstandings spread by revisionist discussions of the so-called theory of immiseration, this innovation is all the more unfortunate. As we will see later, an attempt was made to rule out these misunderstandings by adding a whole new paragraph and deleting an old one. [Yet] here a back door is opened up for them.

The clause concerning increasing dependence is correct or incorrect depending upon how it is interpreted. It is correct as a necessary tendency of the capitalist system that must strive incessantly to subjugate the worker more and more. The concentration of units of production and the centralisation of ownership and, especially, of control over them in a few hands already work in this direction. So does the replacement of skilled by unskilled labour, of men by women, of human labour power by machines, of culturally highly advanced labour power by the labour power of culturally backward nations and regions. But anyone who has read and understood Marx also knows that this is only one side, albeit a necessary one, of the dialectical process that social development engenders. Pressure mounts but along with it mounts the indignation of the burgeoning ranks of the proletarian masses who are schooled and organised by the very mechanism of the capitalist mode of production. Capital sets submissive woman in the man's place – but then woman, too, begins to enter into the struggle of the proletariat for emancipation. It puts Slavs and Italians in place of Germans – but now these, too, begin to go out on strike and organise themselves, etc.

The outcome of the struggle is uncertain; if the sentence about the increasing dependence of the worker is thus understood, not as the characterisation of a tendency, but as an acknowledgement of a conclusion to the social struggle, then it is incorrect. Here the dependence of the worker increases, there it diminishes; here a step is taken towards the 'constitutional factory' and there, a new factory feudalism develops. But what in any case grows is the opposition between capital and labour, the contradiction between the capitalist tendency to reproduce dependency and the growing proletarian need for independence, a contradiction necessitated, as long as capitalist society exists, by the class struggle and the repressive tendency of the capitalist class, a contradiction that can come to an end only in transcending that society.

The same thing holds for increasing dependence as for increasing misery; each is correct in the same sense and incorrect in the same sense. A characterisation of each of these tendencies is called for in a socialist programme because each of them constitutes a necessary factor in the social development of the capitalist mode of production. So if one is afraid that comment upon the increasing misery arising from capitalism could give rise to misunderstanding, then neither must one talk about increasing dependence.

This clause introduces an inconsistency into the new version of the programme. Its inclusion stands in contradiction to the next change we must discuss. To wit, the sentence stating that private ownership of the means of production signifies 'rising mass poverty and growing immiseration for ever broader strata of society' has been deleted and a whole new paragraph added that portrays capitalist tendencies in far greater detail.

The first part of this paragraph describes the expropriation of small entrepreneurs through the concentration of capital, [a prospect] with which the small peasants, whom capitalist development 'transforms into debt slaves', are confronted. The recent finding that, in the last decade, the supersession of small agricultural concerns by the big concerns has not proceeded in the same way as it formerly did, should surely be taken into account in this clause. It is now believed that debt slavery is found in place of the expropriation of small plots, so that the rape of the peasants by capital stands out as clear as day. But one has thereby exposed oneself to new misunderstandings. The impression is created that, among farmers, it is only the small peasants who get into debt. That is by no means the case. Mortgage indebtedness must occur in the capitalist mode of production, despite private landownership, wherever the leasehold system does not prevail. Capitalist development strives to make ground rent independent, to counterpose the pure landowner to the farmer as a distinct individual. This appears most clearly in the form of the relation between landlord and tenant; it appears furtively in the form of the relation between mortgage holder and debtor. But, just like the tenant, so, too, can the debtor be a big capitalist entrepreneur. Debt can be a product of need and engender further need, but this is not inevitable.

If agricultural indebtedness is not a phenomenon peculiar to small concerns, neither is it the only form in which their crisis manifests itself. One denies the expropriation of the small peasantry and yet it is proceeding in the most tangible form before our very eyes, only in other ways than in industry. It is seldom any longer [only] the competition of big business, but the whole economic and political life of capitalism that expropriates the small peasantry. Taxes and army service, as well as interest on debt, contribute to this process. The expropriation of the small peasants does not manifest itself immediately in the expansion of the big operations, but in the flight of the former from the land and in the industrialisation of the latter. For those who remain on the land, agriculture more and more often ceases being the mainstay of their income. It becomes a supplement to the household budget, which enters in alongside income from employment, either from wages (labour in the forests, railways, quarries, factories, etc.) or from domestic industry. On the other side, agriculture becomes more and more the appendage of an industrial concern, a sugar factory, a distillery, etc.

If one did not want to describe this highly complicated process or if one found that it was not clear enough as it stood, then perhaps one would do best to say nothing at all about the peasantry. The reduction of the distress of the peasants to mere indebtedness is misleading and that should happen least of all in a programme that was supposed to replace the existing one because of the misunderstandings it permitted.

But the clause that constitutes the point of the whole revision of the programme, that ought to make any misunderstanding of the 'theory of immiseration' impossible, permits even more serious misunderstandings. It reads: 'The living conditions of ever broader strata of working people are in increasingly striking contrast to the rapidly rising productive power of their own labour and to the burgeoning wealth they have themselves created'.

This proposition is irreproachable as a scientific hypothesis. But it stands here, not as the conclusion of a learned treatise on the living conditions of the proletariat, but in a Social Democratic programme in place of a clause that accused capitalism of producing growing mass poverty and increasing misery for broad strata of society. The latter clause made the struggle against mass poverty and the misery of the people the substance of the Social Democratic movement. In the new version this substance appears to be the struggle for a quicker tempo in the improvement of the living conditions of the workforce. One can interpret the draft clause as meaning that the affluence of the workforce rises but it does not rise quite as quickly as the 'rapidly rising productive power of labour'; the affluence of the capitalists rises faster than that of the proletarians who are peeved about that and so want to replace the capitalist mode of production with the socialist mode of production.

There is no indication here that the slightest improvement in the living conditions of the proletariat must be wrested with difficulty from capital and is always threatened anew; not a word about capital engendering among broad social strata, through its greed for profit, not only a tendency to immiseration, but an actual increase in poverty. If, here and there, capital raises wages or reduces labour time, then everywhere it strives to break up the worker's family, to push his wife into wage labour, to aggravate slum housing conditions. And the Austrian comrades themselves know best how great is the poverty of the foundering petty peasantry, in Galicia for instance, or of the petty artisans, in Vienna itself, or of domestic industries such as those of northern Bohemia. Improvement is restricted primarily to union-organised and younger workers. Younger labour power is sought after and is best able to establish a reasonable position for itself. But capital wears its slaves out quickly: a forty-five-year-old worker already counts as an elderly man who has nothing to expect but increasing poverty. His earnings fall off since the old are the first to be shown the pavement whenever there is a shortage of work and the last to be taken on when business revives. Intervals of unemployment occur more and more often and become longer and longer until, finally, the old worker, broken in body and soul, sinks into the poorhouse or breaks down completely.

In England, that much praised Eldorado of the labour force, half the old workers die in the poorhouse.

And do the younger, union-organised workers, whose position had decidedly improved, not always face the danger of a new machine, a new method of work, a new transportation route that brings new workers of lower status into the country, a new combination of employers or a new legal constraint, depriving them of the fruits of their struggle and thrusting them down into poverty? At this very moment the English workers provide a cautionary example. They grandly assumed that their unions were permanently established and beyond all dispute but were taught by the Lords, overnight, upon what shaky ground every proletarian organisation and every proletarian achievement stands in capitalist society.

The Programme Committee naturally knows all this just as well as we do. One can't say everything in a programme, which after all isn't a treatise. But everything about increasing mass poverty and the growth of hardship among broad social strata is laid out in the deleted clause and it is missing in the clause that is supposed to replace it.

Both clauses can be misunderstood: one can be interpreted as saying that every struggle against poverty in contemporary society is hopeless and that we expect radical social change to stem directly from the immiseration of broad strata of society. Conversely, the new clause can be interpreted as saying that we are of the liberal, optimistic opinion that poverty is nothing more than the growing pains of a capitalism that will, in the course of its development, rid itself of them through growing abundance but that this development is just not going quickly enough for us.

It almost makes me think that every clause of a programme is exposed to misunderstandings. Only the basic theoretical education of our agitators, of those who have to explain the programme, can cure that. It may be that, in a brief paragraph, there is no version of our conception of poverty that safeguards it against every misunderstanding and allows the apparent contradiction it contains to appear as arising from the subject matter itself and not as a mere subjective contradiction. That being the case, the old deleted clause still seems to me more acceptable than the new one. A full Social Democratic programme which does not show that capitalism engenders mass poverty and misery by natural necessity, that does not characterise the struggle against this poverty and this misery as the substance of Social Democracy's endeavours, says nothing about the decisive aspect of our movement and thus contains a serious gap.

The only sentence in which the new draft programme speaks of misery does not begin to narrow this gap. It follows the one just discussed and it says, 'Crises springing from the planlessness of the capitalist mode of production and bringing unemployment and misery in their wake, accelerate and intensify this development'. Thus is misery spoken of, in the draft, solely and exclusively as a concomitant of crises. One does not learn from the draft programme that there is constant and permanent mass misery in contemporary society, misery that threatens to grow if the proletariat does not strain all its powers against it.

The old programme is subject to misunderstanding in accordance with a pessimistic view of contemporary society, while the danger threatening the new one accords with an optimistic view. Which kind of misunderstanding is more alarming for a party struggling against this society needs no demonstration.

Apart from the misunderstanding of the 'theory of immiseration', there is another major misunderstanding that should be eliminated by the new draft. As Adler says in the above-mentioned article, it should 'express, where possible, more clearly than formerly, the fact that the social-democratic movement is not only a necessary product of capitalism, but also a consciously formed expression of the proletariat. It should also take up here the most fatuous of all the critical misunderstandings, according to which the recognised necessity of historical development and the effect of this recognition upon the consciousness and the will of the working class constitute an antithesis.'

The following sentence in particular ought to serve that purpose:

> It (the proletariat) becomes conscious that the supersession of private production makes private ownership increasingly superfluous and harmful, that both the spiritual and the material conditions necessary for new forms of cooperative production and common ownership have to be created, and that the transformation of the means of labour into the social property of the whole people must be the goal of the struggle for the liberation of the working class.

The old programme states, by comparison, that technical development makes the form of private property in the means of production increasingly superfluous and eliminates it for the mass of people, 'while simultaneously securing the material and spiritual conditions necessary for the form of common property. The transformation of the means of labour into the social property of the whole people therefore signifies not only the liberation of the working class but also the culmination of a historically necessary development'.

This version can certainly encourage an underestimation of the role that the consciousness and will of the proletariat play in this necessary development. But the new clause sins once again in the opposite direction. Zetterbaum has already justifiably pointed out, in the Vienna *Worker Times* of 10 October, how misleading is the phrase according to which the proletariat becomes conscious that the spiritual and material conditions for new forms of cooperative production and common property have yet to be created, whereas the old programme viewed them as already created, and of necessity created, at present. I can only repeat what Zetterbaum says:

> All the cooperatives, trade unions and other proletarian institutions, even the most concentrated political efforts of the proletariat in the modern state, can create these and so many important preconditions of socialist society only insofar as capitalism itself produces them daily. This is easy to confirm in reality. Incidentally, all proletarian institutions, such as cooperatives, etc., themselves emerged from the dialectical development of capitalism and emerge from it daily. While many a good comrade may like to act out a role in his vision of the future, these proletarian institutions are produced and created out of the current needs of the proletariat and not for the sake of the future socialist society. A socialist programme has to take these facts into account and not cast its demands, despite their realistic content, in utopian terms. When we draft a

municipal programme, when we demand the nationalisation of the mines, when we found a cooperative, it is less to prepare a new form of cooperative production than for the sake of today's needs and the already vital developmental interest of the proletariat. It is something else when all these demands and institutions of ours turn simultaneously by themselves into 'conditions of new forms' because the developmental interests of the proletariat coincide with the development of the socialist order.

The consciousness of the 'ultimate aim' has a big role to play in the socialist movement. But we see this role not as creating the necessary spiritual and material preconditions of the socialist production of the future, but as introducing unity into the proletariat's struggle for emancipation, in the sense in which this is discussed at the beginning of the present article.

But whereas the new draft, in striving to preclude revisionist misunderstandings, demands more of socialist consciousness than it can deliver, it opens the door to another revisionist misunderstanding. Many of our revisionist critics assume that Marx asserted that economic development and the class struggle create, not only the conditions of socialist production, but also straight away the consciousness of its necessity. And here the same critics are ready with the objection that England, the country where capitalism is most highly developed, is further from this consciousness than any other modern country.

Judging by the new draft, one might assume that this allegedly 'orthodox Marxist' standpoint, which is refuted in this manner, is shared by the Austrian Programme Committee. The draft states: 'The more the development of capitalism swells [the ranks] of the proletariat, the more is the proletariat [both] able and obliged to take up the struggle against it. It becomes conscious' of the possibility and of the necessity for socialism, etc.

In this context socialist consciousness appears as the necessary and direct result of the proletarian class struggle. But that is incorrect. Socialism as a doctrine certainly has its roots in modern economic relationships just like the class struggle of the proletariat, and just like the latter, it emerges out of the struggle against the poverty and misery of the masses that capitalism creates. But they arise simultaneously, not one out of the other, and on different conditions. Modern socialist consciousness can arise only on the basis of profound scientific knowledge. Indeed, modern economic science is as much a condition of socialist production as, say, modern technology but, with the best will in the world, the proletariat could no sooner create the former than the latter. They both arise out of the modern social process. The bearer of science is not the proletariat but the bourgeois intelligentsia; modern socialism originated with individual members of this stratum, who initially communicated it to intellectually advanced proletarians, who in turn introduce it into the proletarian class struggle where circumstances permit. Socialist consciousness is thus something introduced into the proletarian class struggle from without and not something that emerged originally within it.

Accordingly, the old Hainfield programme quite rightly stated that part of the responsibility of Social Democracy is to imbue the proletariat with the consciousness of its position and its mission. This would not be necessary if this consciousness arose of itself from the class struggle. The new draft borrowed this sentence from the old programme and hitched it up to the one mentioned above. But the train of thought is thereby completely disrupted. According to the new version, the proletariat's consciousness of its historical responsibility arises of itself from the class struggle and yet the same consciousness still has to be imported into the class struggle by Social Democracy. This does not clarify matters at all and so misunderstandings are practically invited.

The following two paragraphs do not provide very much occasion for criticism. When the next paragraph states that Social Democracy will 'energetically counteract ... the exploitation of the workers for the benefit of the ruling parties', the authors of the new draft surely do not want to say that they approve of the exploitation of the workers by bourgeois opposition parties, such as the Anti-Semites, the Peasant Alliance, the All-Germans, the Young Czechs, National Unity and the like. There might be fewer misunderstandings if one spoke of bourgeois parties.

The final sentence begins with an expression that does not appear entirely happy to us: 'It (Social Democracy) strives for legal protection of the living conditions of the working class'. One apparently meant by 'protection of the living conditions' that Social Democracy does not restrict itself to so-called workers' protection, factory and workshop legislation, but also strives to take care of the physical well-being of working people outside the production process through housing policy, state or municipal care for schoolchildren, healthcare at no charge and the like.

But it is surely the person of the worker that needs protection, not his living conditions, which are so miserable that they need, not to be protected at their current level, but to be improved. It is unusual, on the other hand, to reckon the length of labour-time among the living conditions of the worker. Perhaps it would be better to say: 'It strives for the protection of labour power and the improvement of the living conditions of the working class by governmental and municipal means'.

The last sentence concludes as follows: 'and it struggles to gain due influence for the proletariat in all areas of public life'.

This phrase provides grounds for serious misgivings. Perhaps it means simply that the proletariat must take advantage of every opportunity to strengthen its influence in public life and to that end it must make its presence felt in the most diverse areas of public life. But it says, 'in all areas'. Whether that is correct depends upon how one interprets 'public life'. It says too much if one includes therein all life that takes place in public. Then there are areas of public life that have nothing to do with class differences and just as little influence over them is due to the proletariat as a class as to any other class. Art may stand as an example. It is surely very much to be wished that proletarians take an interest, for instance in art exhibitions, concerts and theatre, but as human beings, not as proletarians. And influence in these areas of public life is due to them only insofar as they are knowledgeable, not insofar as they are proletarians.

But while the phrase grants the proletariat too much if one interprets public life in the foregoing sense, it grants it too little if public life is restricted to activity on behalf of the community or to the terrain of class struggles. The proletariat has more to demand in this area than mere 'due influence'; here it must aspire to rule, a rule that, admittedly, it can only exercise as the most downtrodden class, in order to supersede classes and therewith class rule. If, on the contrary, one restricts the responsibility of the proletariat to the acquisition of a certain influence, and thereby renounces the conquest of full power and the supersession of classes, then one contents oneself with the ideal of our bourgeois social politicians, who wish the proletariat would adapt to the existing social structure, recognise the existence of other classes as a permanent necessity and ask nothing more from them than the concession of 'due influence'.

But this interpretation is the more natural as voices have been raised among the revisionists themselves, declaring that, since the conquest of political power by the proletariat is a utopia and a dangerous utopia at that, we must aspire only to power, not to *the* power. The interpretation of the phrase in this spirit is even encouraged by the fact that the conquest of political power is not described anywhere in the programme as a responsibility of Social Democracy. This need not betoken any special intent; the old Hainfield programme doesn't speak about the conquest of political power, either. But if one only speaks about the proletariat having to gain some narrow 'due influence' in public life, one only opens the way for every revisionist misunderstanding.

Perhaps what should have been said is the following: Social Democracy maintains that it is its responsibility to take advantage of every opportunity in order to increase the influence of the proletariat in public life and so to hasten the great goal, the conquest of political power by the proletariat.

We are at the end of our critique, which has grown longer than we ourselves expected. Sharp disagreement may now and then be appropriate, but we would not want it to arouse the impression that we condemn the draft of the new programme.

Anyone who looks very closely, as we have done here and as one must do with a draft programme, will find few programmes without many a point that is open to objection. And, more often than not, what we had to uncover were merely sources of potential misunderstanding, almost nowhere simple error.

The train of thought of the new programme is scientifically well established and some of its clauses are excellent. Were the new programme adopted in its present form, it would still be numbered among the best programmes of international Social Democracy. Our comrades in Austria do not have to be ashamed of it.

But it has stiff competition: the old Hainfeld programme. When one looks at the new programme on its own, it creates a very satisfactory impression. But this impression is diminished when one compares it with its predecessor. One then finds that the best parts are borrowed directly from the latter and that the passages that arouse misgivings are just those that depart from it. One finds that, in the very attempt to preclude misunderstanding, it facilitates the appearance of new, even more serious misunderstandings; that it follows the train of thought of the old programme and reproduces its principles, but in a way that is, in some respects, more ponderous, vague, and timid. This might be an advantage in a doctoral dissertation but not in the declaration of war of a party struggling against the existing social system. And surely every Social Democratic programme is such a declaration.

When a series of party comrades as knowledgeable and canny as the members of the Austrian Programme Committee does not manage to improve the Hainfeld programme indisputably, this proves two things. First, that the time to revise the programme has not yet arrived, and secondly, that the Hainfeld programme is a work of art that may be accepted or rejected but that is tough to patch up without getting in the way of its unity and harmony and detracting from it. As already mentioned, Adler informed us that the revision of the Hainfeld programme is more a product of aesthetic than of theoretical considerations. Now, not the least important are those aesthetic considerations that allow us to experience patchwork in the programme as painful.

Recently, we read about a prudish English miss who had Apollo of Belvedere don bathing trunks in her garden, as his nudity offended her. Thus has the Programme Committee decked out Apollo of Hainfeld in bathing trunks so as to cover his Marxist nakedness that might have aroused indecent thoughts in many a chaste revisionist. No doubt, the trunks have quite a nice cut and are manufactured out of really sturdy material, but Apollo is surely more pleasing in his original nakedness.

To the pure all things are pure and whoever understands Marx properly will also understand the Hainfeld programme properly. No bathing trunks and no annotated circumlocution will help the others.

APPENDIX 2

Text and Context in the Argument of Lenin's *What Is to Be Done?*[1]

For those interested in the revaluation and reworking of the theory and practice of the classical Marxist tradition, Lars Lih's 'rediscovery' of the political context of Lenin's *What Is to Be Done?* is a work of considerable importance. Lenin's text has been a key point of reference, perhaps the key point of reference, in debates around the political function of a Marxist vanguard and the logic of political action and hence around the relation of theory and practice. According to the 'textbook interpretation', as Lih terms it, a reading that has passed into a broader conventional wisdom to the extent that it has gained the status of common sense, Lenin's scepticism as to the capacity of the working class to generate socialist consciousness spontaneously led him to assign revolutionary agency to a vanguard party of professional revolutionaries rather than to the working-class movement. The subordination of the workers to the Leninist vanguard party prescribed by Lenin thus prefigures, and thereby serves to provide the veneer of an explanation for, the authoritarian upshot of the revolutionary process. The plausibility of attributing such a blatant departure from the canons of historical materialism to a professed Marxist depends upon situating Lenin's thought in the context of the political elitism and messianic voluntarism of the pre-Marxist tradition of Russian populism. This depends in turn upon reading Marxism (or at least the Marxism with which Lenin was familiar) not as a guide to action, but, as the populist adversaries of Russian Marxism did, as a conceptual straitjacket that precluded the theorisation of effective revolutionary political action. And if this reading is to have any plausibility, it must rely upon contemporary criticism of Lenin from a few minor figures on the margins of the Russian Social Democratic movement, from the retrospective criticism of Lenin's Menshevik adversaries and from the later Leninist characterisation of Kautsky and the Mensheviks as mechanical Marxists. The textbook interpretation serves not only to sustain the legend of Lenin's populism but also to constrain debate over the logic of revolutionary political action within the narrow confines of an abstract opposition between agency and structure.

The textbook interpretation has been subjected to serious scholarly criticism before, notably in the first volume of Neil Harding's *Lenin's Political Thought*,[2] but Lih

---

[1] Originally published in 2010 in *Historical Materialism* 18, 3, pp. 75–89.
[2] See Harding 1977, chapters 6 and 7.

here lays out a much more relentlessly detailed – I am tempted to say exhaustive – refutation. The theoretical and evidentiary issues Lih addresses are complex and he combines evidence drawn from historical, literary and linguistic sources into a powerful, multifaceted argument that resists brief summary. His interpretation turns upon the meticulously argued claim that the historical narrative of the fusion of socialism and the workers' movement epitomised in Kautsky's commentary upon the German Social Democratic Party (SPD)'s Erfurt Programme and the attempt by Russian Marxists to situate their political aims and practice in the terms of this narrative constitute the context without which Lenin's text cannot be understood. The 'Erfurtian' narrative is shot through with biblical overtones – it is the 'mission' of the Social Democrats to bring to the workers the 'good news' of the world-historical 'mission' of the working-class movement to seize power and establish socialism – and so the political project of Social Democracy is not premised simply upon a dryly mechanical theory of history but resonates with activist evangelism. 'Socialist consciousness' is thus to be understood essentially in terms of the task of spreading this 'good news'; an evangelical and democratic confidence in the capacity of the workers to receive it and act upon it was essential to the Social Democratic project. This portrait of the political orientation of Kautsky's orthodox Marxism, in which confidence in the inevitable unfolding of the historical laws of capitalism, rather than excusing a political posture of passive expectation, sustains a durable will to revolutionary activism, is a crucial building block in Lih's argumentative strategy, for it is only by contrast with a fatalistic caricature of orthodox Marxism that Lenin's advocacy of the organisation of a revolutionary vanguard could appear heterodox. Once the caricature is exposed as such – and it is one of the signal contributions of this work to have done so – it is possible and necessary to measure *What Is to Be Done?* against the standard set by Kautsky's Marxism and the political project of the SPD.

How, then, does *What Is to Be Done?* measure up? The strategic perspective fashioned by Plekhanov, Lenin and their *Iskra* colleagues, the hegemony of the proletariat in the Russian bourgeois-democratic revolution, is construed by Lih in terms of the Erfurtian narrative; he accumulates a mass of evidence to demonstrate the fidelity not only of Lenin and *Iskra*, but also of the most prominent of their polemical adversaries, to its narrative structure. Indeed, he suggests that the Russians added little besides the term 'hegemony', and perhaps not even that, to the political orientation of the SPD. If anything distinguished Lenin in Russian Marxist circles, in the company both of his *Iskra* colleagues and of his polemical adversaries, it was his more unyielding attachment to the theme and the logic of the Erfurtian narrative and his correspondingly greater confidence in the political capacity of the workers to meet the demands of revolutionary political struggle: if Kautsky's rectitude in matters of Marxist theory made him, according to a witticism of the time, 'the pope of Social-Democratic ideology', then Lenin, according to Lih, 'comes off as more Social-Democratic than the pope'.[3]

Following Lenin's commentary on the 1907 edition of *What Is to Be Done?*, Lih insists that the pamphlet be read in 'connection with the concrete historical situation of a definite, and now long past, period in the development of our Party'.[4] It was widely expected around the turn of the century in revolutionary circles that the struggles of the nascent working-class movement would serve to galvanise the opposition to Tsarist rule that was welling up throughout Russian society. But early attempts to provide the movement with organised Social Democratic leadership proved abortive when police raids decimated its central organisations and reduced the fledgling party to a mere aspiration. In the resulting atmosphere of disorientation and demoralisation a tendency emerged to shrink back from the revolutionary mission of Social Democracy, to narrow its practical ambition for the working class to a kind of Gompers-style trade-unionism, pure and simple, and to cede the political struggle against the government, and consequently hegemony in the democratic revolution, to the representatives of bourgeois liberalism. Lih notes, however, that by the time *What Is to Be Done?* was written, although the Social Democratic movement remained a congeries of circles, principally those around *Iskra* and those around the journal *Rabochee delo* [Workers' Cause], loosely cooperating and at the same time contending for influence in the process of drawing together into an organised party, Lenin was able to assume opposition on the part of his readership to this 'Economist' tendency. Lih fails to note, however, that, at least according to Lenin, disagreement over how this protean tendency to Economism was to be understood – and consequently, how it was to be dealt with – played an important part in the contention among the Russian Social Democrats. As we shall see, this disagreement serves as a kind of index of tensions and ambiguities that beset the Social Democratic project of proletarian hegemony and the Marxist orthodoxy upon which it rested; it is thus an index of pervasive, if latent, differences in approach to understanding and acting within and upon the 'concrete historical situation'.

On Lih's reading, the argument of *What Is to Be Done?* was structured in two main ways by this situation. First, it was shaped by Lenin's concern to map out a plan for the construction of a party organisation through the production and distribution of a newspaper devoted largely to political agitation and thus to sustain in practical terms *Iskra*'s bid for leadership. The requisite organisation would have, under then-prevailing conditions, to be narrow rather than broad, a vanguard as distinct from a mass organisation, capable of resisting police repression and hence of growing roots in the working-class movement and focusing worker struggles on a political assault upon

---

3   Lih 2006, p. 114.
4   Lenin 1907c, p. 101.

the Tsarist regime. Thus understood, the newspaper proposal would not displace working-class activity and consciousness but rather serve to develop them and so enable Social Democratic activists to act out the Erfurtian narrative under the trying conditions of Tsarist autocracy. '[T]he vanguard outlook' not only does not contradict the Marxist assumption that 'the emancipation of the working classes must be the work of the working classes themselves' but is effectively derived from it.[5] The significance of the newspaper lies in the need for a vanguard organisation of revolutionaries, this need derives from the exigencies of political agitation under autocratic conditions, and the need for political agitation derives from the struggle for hegemony of the working class in the democratic revolution. This logic governs the last three chapters of *What Is to Be Done?*, which Lih terms its 'business part'.[6]

Second, however, the argument of *What Is to Be Done?* was subject to the political logic of the factional struggle. Lenin was obliged by this logic to respond to a virtual challenge from *Rabochee delo* to defend *Iskra* against charges of having dogmatically subordinated the spontaneous struggles of the workers to an arid theoretical purism: that is, of having abandoned the 'class point of view', which led him to introduce the 'business part' of the book with two chapters devoted, respectively, to discussions of dogmatism and freedom of criticism and of spontaneity and consciousness. But, carried away by polemical zeal, he was led to assimilate the stance of his opponents, who like *Iskra* situated themselves inside the Erfurtian narrative, to that of acknowledged Economists. In so doing, a penchant for trying to bend the rhetorical tropes of his opponent to his own purposes pushed him into a series of hasty and sometimes ill-considered and cryptic formulations, notably in his discussion of spontaneity and consciousness, that has become the focal point of subsequent political and exegetical controversy. Once Lenin's argument is read in context and its practical essence distinguished from the distortions introduced by factional polemics, Lih argues, *What Is to Be Done?* can be seen not as the site of dramatic political departures or theoretical innovations, but as nothing more nor less in substance than a reassertion and detailed application to the practical problems of Russian Social Democracy of the Erfurtian perspective of orthodox Second International Marxism. If Lih is right, the political and theoretical controversy that has swirled around *What Is to Be Done?* is simply 'much ado about nothing'.

Any reading of a text must draw some kind of distinction between what is essential to its meaning and what is merely incidental, between what is of theoretical relevance and what is merely circumstantial. This distinction corresponds, in Lih's work, to his distinction between the practical or 'business' sections and aspects of Lenin's argument, those devoted to his proposal for the appropriate tactical, organisational and

---

5 See Lih 2006, p. 556.
6 Lih 2006, 11, p. 353n.

practical arrangements to give effect to the Erfurtian perspective, itself uncontested among the Russian Marxists, and the polemical aspects of the work, dominated by the struggle as to who, which circle, would take upon itself the leadership of Russian Social Democracy within the parameters of the shared Erfurtian perspective. This distinction rests in turn upon a narrow construal of the term Lenin uses to designate the object of his criticism, 'Economism', as entailing a rejection of working-class participation in the bourgeois-democratic revolution. Thus understood, Lenin's attribution to *Rabochee delo* of an Economist perspective is a polemical distortion of little or no theoretical interest, but one that has had the unfortunate effect of fostering the impression, among those unfamiliar with the context of the debate, that the critique of Economism signified a departure from the canons of Marxist orthodoxy and hence of lending unwarranted plausibility to the textbook interpretation.

If we take Lenin at his word, however, Economism is not to be understood in such narrow terms. The term 'Economism', although entrenched by usage, did not, he acknowledged, adequately convey the character of the political trend he designated by it.[7] Understood 'in the broad sense of the word', the 'principal feature' of Economism was 'its incomprehension, even defence, of... the lagging of the conscious leaders behind the spontaneous awakening of the masses'.[8] Thus understood, the meaning of Economism is subordinate to Lenin's distinction between consciousness and spontaneity and its significance is to be sought in the relation between leadership and the masses. Not only was Economism not inconsistent with political activity, it was not inconsistent with political revolution. Thus understood, the category of Economism did indeed allow Lenin to associate *Rabochee delo* with Economism in the narrow sense, but this does not imply that he attributed the reformist views of the latter to the former – he did not. If we turn Lih's interpretive procedure around and assume that Lenin intended his category of Economism to designate some coherent referent, the question necessarily arises as to just what the coherence of its referent consists in. The coherence of Economism certainly does not consist in an agreement of ideas, but the political significance of an idea is not necessarily what its proponent professes it to be. It depends upon the context in which it is professed: different ideas may play the same or an analogous role in different contexts and even in the same context may display a convergent significance. The connection Lenin asserts between *Rabochee delo* and Economism in the narrow sense is to be understood in some such sense, not as that between different adherents of the same set of ideas, but as that between variant forms of a political tendency. Judgements in matters of this kind suppose, of course, a claim to understand, at least in its broad outline, the strategic logic of political struggles, but that Lenin was prepared to make such a claim is not, I think, a matter of debate.

---

7   Lenin 1902, pp. 386–7.
8   Lenin 1901c, p. 317.

Making sense of Lenin's notion of Economism thus requires us to grapple not only with his distinction between spontaneity and consciousness, but also with the logic of political strategy in the democratic revolution. The matter is best approached by considering the latter issue first. One of the merits of Lih's book is to have shown that working-class participation in the struggle for political freedom flows naturally from the Erfurtian perspective: according to the Erfurtian narrative, it is only in the course of the struggle for political democracy that the workers learn to wield political freedoms in their own interests and hence develop the understanding and political capacity necessary to assume political power and organise society along social-democratic lines. Since the growing political strength of the working class tempers bourgeois enthusiasm for democracy, leadership in the struggle for political democracy is increasingly incumbent upon the proletariat. This conception refers, on one hand, to the theme of proletarian self-emancipation, the idea that the working class is – in the course of its struggle becomes – capable of taking charge of its own emancipation and, on the other, to the idea that the need of the working class for democracy in its struggle for a classless society renders it the appropriate leader for the democratic aspirations and struggles of other, non-proletarian classes and strata of society. It is thus characterised by some internal complexity – it assumes that the two tasks, self-emancipation and democratic leadership, and two corresponding interests, class interest and popular-democratic interest, coincide. In Germany, where capitalism was incomparably more highly developed than in Russia and where the bourgeoisie had accordingly already been able to establish its preponderant weight in state affairs, the established role of the SPD as the pre-eminent party of opposition may have seemed, in Erfurtian eyes, to cement the conjunction of these two terms into self-evidence.

But in Russia, where this Erfurtian conception was translated into the strategic orientation of proletarian hegemony in the bourgeois-democratic revolution, the conjunction of class interest and popular-democratic interest was as yet only a strategic aspiration. Its translation into Russian political reality was conditional upon successfully coping with the challenge of rival, bourgeois projects for hegemony in the revolutionary process. And if he is to be taken at his word, Lenin took the threat of such projects seriously. It is not that he feared the spectre of some latter-day revival of the Jacobin Clubs – that prospect was, indeed, historically *dépassé*. But bourgeois hegemony could take quite different forms than this. In the important essay 'The Persecutors of the *Zemtsvo* and the Hannibals of Liberalism', written just a few months before *What Is to Be Done?* and reissued along with the latter in 1907, Lenin discerned the lineaments of such a bourgeois hegemonic project in an attempt by Peter Struve, former Social Democrat (in fact, the author of the manifesto that emerged from the abortive First Congress of the RSDLP) and future luminary of Russian liberalism, to use the threat of a revolutionary workers' movement to urge reforms upon Tsarism. This attempt presaged a scenario in which the revolutionary force of the masses played a necessary role but only as a kind of stage army with which to frighten the Tsar but which would then, when the time came for the serious business of renegotiating the redistribution of power, yield the political stage, willingly or unwillingly, to liberal specialists in constitutional politics.[9] Such a scenario did not assume workers smitten with liberal ideology; rather, it envisaged a workers' movement of militant, even revolutionary, even socialist temperament but for which revolution was a means to enforce its economic class interests, narrowly construed, rather than to transcend its interest-group limitations. Any tendency to construe the political project of the working class in restrictive terms, even one decked out, as in the case of *Rabochee delo*, in the language of revolution and claims to vanguard status, would play into such a scenario: at stake in Lenin's critique of Economism was not only the relation of politics and economics, revolution and reform, but also and perhaps more basically the relation between class interests and popular democratic interests in the project of proletarian hegemony. If, as Lih claims, there was consensus among the Russian Social Democrats over the Erfurtian narrative and the project of proletarian hegemony in the bourgeois-democratic revolution, then Lenin's critique of Economism indicates that this project was beset by internal political, and therefore perhaps also theoretical, tensions. Hegemony could not be taken as given; it would have to be constructed. This suggests, in turn, that the relation between the business and the polemical aspects of Lenin's argument is more fluid (and perhaps more productive) than Lih would have it: if we once again take Lenin at his word and assume that a tendency exists corresponding to his definition of Economism, it could reveal itself only in the course of polemics over what proletarian hegemony is, that is, how it was to be constructed. The polemical aspect plays not only a rhetorical or even political role in Lenin's argument, but also an epistemological role.

If the Economist tendency as identified by Lenin does exist, the question must arise as to how it is to be understood and, in this connection, recourse to the distinction between spontaneity and consciousness is necessary. If we retain the possibility that Lenin's polemic does play a theoretical role in his argument, then it may, conversely, help in clarifying the distinction between spontaneity and consciousness. It is a crucial weakness of Lih's reading of *What Is to Be Done?* as an exemplification of the Erfurtian narrative that it is unable to account for some of Lenin's most noteworthy (or at least most noted) formulations on the relation between spontaneity and consciousness, particularly his repeated claim that 'the task of Social-Democracy is to *combat spontaneity, to divert* the working-class movement from this spontaneous, trade-unionist striving to come under the wing of the bourgeoisie and to bring it under the wing of revolutionary Social-Democracy'.[10] The logic of the Erfurtian narrative can be stretched to accommodate a good deal of Lenin's polemic against the Economist practice of

---

9   See Lenin 1901b.
10 Lenin 1902, pp. 384–5.

subordinating consciousness to spontaneity, but it cannot contain this crucial claim; it is a tribute to Lih's intellectual honesty that he acknowledges this difficulty. And while Lih can attribute the formulations in question to a combination of polemical distortion and editorial haste, it should be noted that his procedure of determining the meaning of key terms in Lenin's text, including spontaneity and consciousness, by reference to common Russian usage of the time, while necessary and sometimes illuminating, is ill-adapted to the task of discerning their place and hence their meaning in the logic of Lenin's argument and therefore for determining whether or not they indicate an innovative movement of thought.

The role played by 'consciousness' in Lenin's text is not to be understood, Lih cautions, in abstraction from political practice; since the political practice advocated by Lenin is to be understood in terms of the Erfurtian narrative, consciousness is construed as an awareness of the task of spreading the good news of the fusion of socialism and the working-class movement. Inasmuch as historical materialism supplies the theory of the historical movement of this fusion, consciousness is to be grasped by reference to Marxist theory. The introduction of consciousness into the spontaneous working-class movement from without signifies, in terms of the Erfurtian narrative, a practice of making workers aware of a goal and a direction of their movement that is already implicit in their practice. Since the spontaneous movement and the conscious awareness of it, practice and theory, are congruent, harmonious, there is no need, and no theoretical room, for a struggle between them. This is indeed the implication of the passage by Kautsky famously cited by Lenin in his own discussion of consciousness and spontaneity in *What Is to Be Done?*[11] However, while some of Lenin's formulations can be assimilated to this logic, others, in particular those enjoining a struggle against spontaneity, suggest a different logic at work in Lenin's argument. The evidence assembled by Lih renders the 'textbook interpretation' unsustainable, yet the conceptual tensions upon which that reading feeds cannot be resolved absent an explanation of these passages.

Socialist consciousness, as it figured in Lenin's argument, certainly carried an injunction to working-class solidarity in the struggle for a socialist aim that transcended capitalism and class society, but it also assumed an awareness of 'the irreconcilable antagonism of [the workers'] interests to the whole of the modern political and social system'[12] and thus it implied attentiveness to the twists and turns in the path to the socialist end, that is, to the politico-strategic logic of the class struggle. The irreconcilability of class antagonism implied that it is built into the very foundation of the bourgeois social edifice and it enjoins systematic distrust of the class enemy;

---

11 See Shandro 1997–8.
12 Lenin 1902, p. 375.

the pervasive character of class antagonism implied that it cannot be escaped and argued that exclusion of any aspect of the socio-political totality from the purview of the socialist project might concede the strategic initiative to the adversary. Socialist consciousness could not but draw upon Marxist theory (the theorisation of the irreconcilability of class antagonism) and could not be brought to bear upon the class struggle in the absence of an organised leadership informed by that theory and able to apply it ambitiously and with confidence.

Lenin's argument distinguishes two contradictory tendencies in the spontaneous working-class movement, that is, in the working-class movement insofar as the consciousness of 'the irreconcilable antagonism of [the workers'] interests to the whole of the modern political and social system' has not been brought to bear upon it: the movement, grounded in the exploitative social relations of capitalist production that structure the workers' lives and experience, tends spontaneously through the experience of solidarity and struggle to engender a socialist consciousness (that is, the spontaneous movement is the 'embryo of consciousness'), but bourgeois ideology imposes itself spontaneously as the frame within which working-class experience and struggles are grasped, in terms that could not shake the hegemony of the adversary (that is, the spontaneous movement leads to a merely corporate or 'trade-union consciousness'). Lenin's claim is that the latter tendency 'spontaneously' predominates over the former and that it is therefore incumbent upon 'Social-Democratic consciousness' or, rather, those who have achieved this consciousness to struggle against 'spontaneity'.

To appreciate the force of this claim, we need to look at the logic of the interplay between these tendencies.[13] The workers struggle spontaneously and in the course of their struggles a combination of changed circumstances and innovative methods of struggle may result in a challenge and even, on occasion, a breach of the parameters of bourgeois hegemony. Spontaneous working-class struggles may elicit not only a reassertion of the tried-and-true themes of class rule but also sometimes innovative attempts to reformulate the parameters of bourgeois hegemony, that is, the reorganisation of bourgeois strategy and the spontaneous imposition of bourgeois ideology onto the struggle of the workers. To be effective, this kind of response must appear in forms that have some purchase upon the spontaneous proletarian experience of the class struggle; indeed, bourgeois hegemony need not depend upon denial of the class struggle and might be most effectively expressed in and through the political shape, organisation and direction of the resistance of its socialist adversary. Accommodation to bourgeois hegemony thus proceeds spontaneously, not through a failure of proletarian commitment to the struggle for socialism, which Lenin never questioned, but through failure to mount a political project of proletarian hegemony effectively: that is, to contend for, establish and maintain the strategic initiative in the struggle for hegemony in the democratic revolution. An effective project of proletarian hegemony could not

---

13   The point is more thoroughly argued in Shandro 1995.

arise simply from the workers' spontaneous experience, because that experience is structured both by the reality of class antagonism and by the bourgeois ideological construction of such antagonism as somehow reconcilable. Since each aspect of this spontaneous movement may take on novel forms beyond the current experience of the participants, the irreconcilability of their antagonism can only be grasped theoretically. Since attempts at class conciliation can draw upon ideological and political materials from anywhere in the social totality and may do so innovatively, Marxist theory must be open to the whole of the social order including the open-ended logic of the struggle for hegemony, that is to say, it must itself develop; indeed, theory and the political project grounded in it can only be vindicated through engagement with periodically renewed attempts to reconcile class antagonisms, including attempts that would instrumentalise elements of socialist theory and practice to this end.

Why could the workers themselves not grasp Marxist theory? Lenin's explicit answer was that they could do it, better in fact than the intellectuals. They would do so, however, not in the mass but as individuals, and having become conscious, they would find themselves in a position analogous to that occupied by the initial, intellectual carriers of Marxist theory, confronting the challenge of bringing consciousness to bear upon the contradictory logic of the spontaneous movement. Meeting it spontaneously, they might observe the objective logic of the class struggle and, accommodating themselves to the flow of events, no doubt participate along with their fellow workers in whatever struggles should arise, but forego any pretensions to provide leadership in the class struggle. Meeting it consciously, they would employ Marxist theory reflexively to grasp their own situation within the spontaneously given conjunctures of the class struggle and, acting from where they were, assume the burdens of leadership in the struggle for hegemony. To assume this responsibility was to take up a sophisticated political stance, sustaining the spontaneous struggles of the workers and fostering the embryonic forms of socialist consciousness thrown up in the course of them by diagnosing and combating the forms in which bourgeois ideology spontaneously imposes itself within the working-class movement. At stake in Lenin's discussion of spontaneity and consciousness was not an issue in the sociology of knowledge concerning the bearer of socialist consciousness, but the strategic – or, better, meta-strategic – issue of the terms in which Marxist political actors – intellectuals or workers – can come to grips with their own situation within the class struggle and position themselves to act effectively upon it. Indeed, that the 'profound theoretical error' of *Rabochee delo* and other economists had to do with just this issue, their inability 'to connect spontaneous evolution with conscious revolutionary activity',[14] is asserted by Lenin in a brief article he described as a 'synopsis' of *What Is to Be Done?*[15]

---

14 Lenin 1901c, p. 316.
15 Lenin 1902, p. 350.

Lenin's distinction between spontaneity and consciousness is not a transposition into political terms of an ontological distinction between matter and mind or of a social-scientific distinction between base and superstructure, or even of a sociological distinction between workers and intellectuals. It invokes, rather, the contradictory combination of a complex set of forces and tendencies in a concrete conjuncture of political struggle and implicitly, through this, the operation of a politico-strategic logic of struggle for hegemony in relation to which the Marxist political actors are invited, even required, to situate themselves. Refracted through this logic, the class struggle and, with it, working-class consciousness cannot but develop unevenly. The thesis of consciousness from without is an attempt to think through the implication of this unevenness for political action and political leadership of the working-class movement. It provides the conceptual underpinnings for the distinctive Leninist injunction to concrete analysis of the concrete situation and it mandates, accordingly, the reflexive adjustment of consciousness to the shifting lines and logic of the struggle for hegemony. Thus, paradoxically, it generates the possibility of opening Marxist theory to unexpected innovation and diversity in the spontaneous movement of the class struggle.[16] Lenin's *What Is to Be Done?* emerges from and cannot be understood without the context of orthodox Erfurtian Marxism – but it points beyond it.

If some such logic is at work in *What Is to Be Done?*, then it becomes plausible to regard *Rabochee delo* and Kuskova's *Credo* not necessarily as different expressions of the same set of political ideas, but as distinct phenomenal forms of the same underlying political tendency. On this logic political tendencies are to be identified not only by reference to the ideas expressed by political actors but essentially by reference to the role ideas and actions play in the class political struggle for hegemony. The Economism that was the target of Lenin's critique need not imply the reduction of political to economic struggle; indeed, it could be and often was articulated in quite revolutionary terms. Thus, it could assume an indefinite number of forms, leftist as well as rightist, as it did during the revolution of 1905 and again, during the First World War, when Lenin would revive the terminology of the earlier polemic to tax Bukharin and his co-thinkers with the charge of 'imperialist Economism' for their refusal to recognise a right of nations to self-determination as an essential part of a revolutionary socialist programme.[17] Thus understood, the Economist trend consisted in the effective concession to bourgeois interests of areas of political debate and activity and thereby, and to that extent, the restriction of working-class politics to narrowly corporate concerns and the accommodation of socialist politics to the spontaneous movement of the class struggle, that is, to lines, forms and trajectories of conflict prescribed by, or at least recoverable by, bourgeois hegemony. The struggle between political tendencies in the

---

16   See Shandro 2007.
17   See Lenin 1916e.

working-class movement is no longer reduced to a struggle between ideas proper to the working class itself and those proper to historically outmoded social strata intermingled with it, but is to be understood as well in terms of the logic of contemporary political struggles.

If some such logic underpins Lenin's argument, then his critique of *Rabochee delo*'s theoretical indifference in the first chapter of *What Is to Be Done?* is not, as Lih maintains, of merely polemical significance but integral to his political position, that is, to the way in which he was beginning to conceive the hegemony of the proletariat. For knowledge of Marxist theory figures there not as a rigid standard of orthodox rectitude with which to chastise his adversaries for their departures, but more importantly as a necessary condition for grappling consciously with the new and in some cases unprecedented issues posed by the struggle against the Tsarist autocracy and, consequently, for situating oneself in concrete political terrain. The importance of theory is enhanced for the Russian Marxists, Lenin writes, not only by the need to settle accounts with non-Marxist trends of revolutionary thought and the consequent necessity of a 'strict differentiation of shades of opinion', but by the need to develop 'the ability to treat [the] experiences [of other countries] critically and test them independently' and by the fact that 'the national tasks of Russian Social-Democracy are such as have never confronted any other socialist party in the world'.[18] This suggests, if it does not imply, that the defence of theory requires it to be further developed by applying it to new and as yet unresolved questions. *Rabochee delo*'s theoretical gaffes and practical blunders are to be gauged, accordingly, not only by already-established Erfurtian standards but also by the task of grappling with challenges on the frontiers of Marxist theory and practice.

Lars Lih's comprehensive demonstration that *What Is to Be Done?* cannot be understood apart from the political and discursive context of Erfurtian Marxism and its attempted translation into Russian Social Democracy provides an indispensable service to the historiography of Marxist theory and practice. But if I may borrow a Leninist metaphor, it seems that Lih has bent this particular stick too far. This is most evident in Lih's narrow construal of the pivotal concept of 'Economism' in terms of the professed positions of only *some* of the targets of Lenin's polemic, although Lenin explicitly cautions his readers against this kind of misreading. But the same sort of difficulty appears in Lih's assumptions about the status of Marxist theory in Lenin's argument. Where Lenin derived his recourse to theory from the very logic of the debate over practical proposals – 'the perplexity of the Economists over the practical application of our views in *Iskra* clearly revealed that we often speak literally in different tongues and therefore *cannot* arrive at an understanding without beginning *ab ovo*'[19] – Lih

---

18   Lenin 1902, p. 370.
19   Lenin 1902, p. 350.

subordinates the text of *What Is to Be Done?* to his distinction between its 'business' and its polemical parts, thus making it impossible to see what of theoretical significance could possibly be at stake in the controversy and reading as mere rhetoric, superfluous except for polemical purposes, the necessity Lenin asserts for recourse to Marxist theory in order to understand what is at issue in the debate over the practical project of proletarian hegemony. In these ways the necessary and proper concern with restoring the context of *What Is to Be Done?*, pushed too far, actually leads to distortions of the text itself. In effect, Lih reduces the argument of Lenin's text to its Erfurtian context and thereby misses its innovative aspect; paradoxically, this kind of procedure can occlude such a crucial contextual feature as the connection, designated by Lenin, between Economism as a political current and an emergent liberal-bourgeois bid for hegemony in the democratic revolution. Where a text challenges the terms of debate, it may illuminate unsuspected distinctions and connections in the reality it seeks to grasp, and where that reality is the political context within which it is written, it may change the terms in which its context is understood; in this – materialist – sense, a text such as Lenin's *What Is to Be Done?* may reinvent its own context.

APPENDIX 3

Lenin as a Reader of *What Is to Be Done?*

The claim that the thesis of consciousness from without, as formulated by Lenin in *What Is to Be Done?*, announces a significant theoretical innovation has been criticised on the grounds that he did not repeat it in his later writings, that he would soon repudiate it and that he would, in any case, disavow any theoretical intention in having put it forward. Robert Mayer lays out the basis for this kind of criticism by reading Lenin's thesis in terms of a definition of socialist consciousness derived from David Riazanov, a minor figure among Lenin's adversaries: 'consciousness of the necessity to struggle for a socialist alternative to capitalism'.[1] Here socialist consciousness is understood as a belief in a certain aim or goal, socialism, together with the conviction on the part of the worker that this goal must be pursued through struggle, a 'historical mission'. Mayer then goes on to attribute this understanding of socialist consciousness, which contains no reference to the shifting alignments, strategies and tactics of various class forces, social strata and political institutions, to Lenin. He thereby puts himself in a position to claim that, by denying that socialist consciousness arises spontaneously in the working-class movement, Lenin is in effect asserting that 'the proletariat is ... incapacitated [from emancipating itself] in a way that no other class is'. The thesis of consciousness from without is thus to be understood as nothing more than a theoretical rationalisation of the self-proclaimed authority of Marxist intellectuals within the working-class movement. When it is understood in this way, however, Mayer is quite right to claim that it does not appear in Lenin's later writings and right to note that Lenin repudiated it at the Second Congress of the RSDLP in 1903. Lenin was right to do so because, *understood in this way*, neither did it appear in *What Is to Be Done?*

Mayer seeks further evidence of Lenin's repudiation of the thesis of consciousness from without in his prefatory note to the 1907 republication of *What Is to Be Done?* There Lenin explains his failure to reply to the criticism Plekhanov levelled at his account of spontaneity and political consciousness (after the latter had aligned himself with the Mensheviks in 1904), finding the criticism 'obviously mere cavilling, based on phrases torn out of context, on particular expressions which I had not quite adroitly or precisely formulated. Moreover, he ignored the general spirit and the whole content of my pamphlet'.[2] Seconded by E. Haberkern,[3] Mayer somehow claims to find in this a shame-faced retraction. Since Lenin's discussion of spontaneity and consciousness

---

1 Mayer 1997, p. 371.
2 Lenin 1907c, p. 107.
3 Haberkern 1998–9.

occupies a full chapter – the second of five – in a 180-page pamphlet and spills over significantly into some of the others, one wonders just which particular expressions Lenin thinks were maladroitly or imprecisely formulated. He doesn't tell us – Plekhanov's article not having been reprinted in the latest Menshevik collection, he would not deal with its arguments at that time.[4] We find, however, that Plekhanov's polemical firepower particularly targeted the phrase, 'in Russia the theoretical doctrine of Social-Democracy arose altogether independently of the spontaneous working-class movement', the old Marxist affecting absurdly to find in the expression 'altogether independently' evidence that Lenin thought Marxist theory had arisen in the absence of a working class.[5] That Plekhanov's article was not reprinted is perhaps understandable; 'mere cavilling' seems an apt characterisation. In any case, although the second edition of *What Is to Be Done?* was somewhat abridged, the discussion of spontaneity and consciousness appeared intact. This fact and the gist of the so-called retraction cited above together suggest that the reader of *What Is to Be Done?* is being counselled (and, make no mistake, we are being counselled to read it) to pay careful attention to the historical and political context in which it was written and to assess the bearing of particular claims and the adequacy of particular expressions in light of the argument and the aim of the work as a whole.

A measure of the weight of this evidence is provided by a brief comment that appeared in the Bolshevik *Proletarii* in October 1905, more than two years after the Second Congress. The comment, written by Lenin, summarised an article by the young Joseph Stalin in the journal of the RSDLP Caucasian League, a lengthy exposition and defence of the *What Is to Be Done?* account of spontaneity and consciousness against one of the many Menshevik critiques that followed in the wake of the Plekhanov piece.[6] Lenin praised the 'splendid' way the article posed the problem of 'the introduction of consciousness from without' and qualified as 'ridiculous' the Menshevik denial of its thesis.[7]

There is, then, no evidence at all to support the claim that Lenin repudiated, however shamefacedly, the thesis of consciousness from without; what evidence there is

---

4 Lenin 1907c, p. 108.
5 See Baron 1963, pp. 248–51.
6 In view of the elaborate use made of the conventional wisdom about the thesis of consciousness from without in constructing a theoretical connection between Lenin and Stalinist authoritarianism, the virtual absence from the voluminous literature on Lenin's thesis of any reference to this article (1905b), or to another (1905a) by Stalin on the same subject, may be qualified, parenthetically, as a remarkable commentary upon the worth of scholarship in this area. To my knowledge, there is no reference to either of these texts in the English-language literature prior to Shandro 2001; the sole reference I have come across is in a footnote to the French-language translation of Lenin 1905r appended to Garaudy 1968, pp. 80–1.
7 Lenin 1905r, p. 388.

weighs against it. The idea that he denied any theoretically innovative ambition in advancing the thesis, however, deserves closer consideration. Following Plekhanov, who had addressed the question earlier at the Second Congress, Lenin suggested that criticism of his formulation of consciousness from without in the context of a discussion of the party programme confused 'an episode in the struggle against economism... with a principled presentation of a major theoretical question, namely, the formation of an ideology'.[8] When revisiting *What Is to Be Done?* in 1907, Lenin framed his remarks with the claim that '[t]he basic mistake made by those who now criticise *What Is to Be Done?* is to treat the pamphlet apart from its connection with the concrete historical situation of a definite, and now long past, period in the development of our Party'.[9] But this claim carried no implication that what had been at stake was not of theoretical significance: '[A]t that time the controversy was over the most general principles and the fundamental aims of *all* Social-Democratic policy generally'.[10] The operative distinction was not that between matters of theoretical and those of merely occasional import but that between the polemical (and therefore concrete) and the programmatic (hence general or principled) presentation of a theoretical debate. Still, he dismissed the possibility of any difference in principle between *What Is to Be Done?* and the formulation of the relation between spontaneity and consciousness in the draft party programme, agreed to by all the editors of *Iskra*, and disavowed 'any intention of elevating my own formulations, as given in *What Is to Be Done?*, to programmatic level, constituting special principles'.[11] Since the aim of these remarks was to cast doubt on Menshevik criticism by showing it to be merely *ex post facto*, Lenin had good political reason for downplaying the distinctiveness of his formulations. Although recalling[12] the warning he issued in *What Is to Be Done?* that apparently 'minor differences' between mere 'shades of opinion' could assume decisive importance[13] and characterising Menshevism with Economism as 'diverse forms of one and the same historical tendency... which *in practice subordinated the proletariat to bourgeois liberalism*',[14] Lenin did not try to connect differences in formulation concerning spontaneity and consciousness with the subsequent split between Bolsheviks and Mensheviks.

Thus, Lenin disavows any intention of introducing a theoretically significant innovation and displays no awareness of having done so. Of course, it does not follow from

---

8   RSDLP 1904, p. 168.
9   Lenin 1907c, p. 101.
10 Lenin 1907c, p. 106.
11 Lenin 1907c, p. 107.
12 Lenin 1907c, p. 106.
13 See Lenin 1902, p. 370.
14 Lenin 1907c, p. 112.

his lack of awareness that the thesis of consciousness from without does not bear significant theoretical implications. If, as Lenin implied, Marxist theory is always incomplete and if it always reflects in its development the contradictions, complexity and unevenness of political practice in the class struggle, it is implausible to suppose that the theoretical significance of a text is transparent even to its author. On the reading proposed here, the innovation of *What Is to Be Done?* lies not in any particular formulation of the thesis of consciousness from without, but in the emergence of a distinctive logic of political analysis, discernible in and through Lenin's argument. If I am right, the emergence of this logic – with its analysis of the spontaneous working-class movement and the development of working-class consciousness into contradictory proletarian-socialist and bourgeois-liberal tendencies – is a practical reflection of the struggle for hegemony in the bourgeois-democratic revolution. The presentation of Economism broadly as an expression of 'spontaneism' – a political tendency of adaptation to the influence of bourgeois hegemony in the working-class movement, capable of revealing itself in diverse forms in response to shifts in the circumstances of the struggle for hegemony and in the forms of bourgeois influence – assumes that the struggle for hegemony is a process in the course of which actors are capable of significant strategic innovation. Socialist consciousness figures, correspondingly, not only as a commitment to the struggle and an understanding of its revolutionary aims but also the ability of revolutionary political actors to orient and reorient themselves amidst the shifting currents of the struggle for hegemony. Consciousness is to be understood with reference to Marxist theory; inasmuch as Marxist political actors thus situate themselves consciously within the struggle for hegemony – endeavouring to bring to consciousness the spontaneous socialist tendency of the working-class movement, while trying to diagnose so as to be able to undo the spontaneously renewed tendency of bourgeois influence – theory is needed as a guide to action, one that would have to be developed in order to function as such on a terrain, such as the class struggle and the struggle for hegemony, that could change without warning. Since the innovative import of Lenin's thesis of consciousness from without does not consist in particular formulations, however distinctive, but in the logic of Lenin's argument, in the logic of his political analysis and of the process by which he moves from one analysis to the next, the persistence of this innovation (and hence its weight) in his thought is not to be gauged by the recurrence or disappearance of specific phrases. This is all the more so as the politico-strategic logic of the struggle for hegemony is reflexive and so open, at least in principle, to mutation. The question to be addressed is whether the logic of hegemony can illuminate movements in subsequent Leninist theory and practice that remain opaque to alternative interpretations.

Bibliography

Althusser, Louis 1970a, 'Contradiction and Overdetermination', in *For Marx*, translated by Ben Brewster, New York: Vintage Books.
—— 1970b, 'On the Materialist Dialectic', in *For Marx*, translated by Ben Brewster, New York: Vintage Books.
—— 1970c, 'The Object of *Capital*', in Althusser and Etienne Balibar, *Reading Capital*, London: New Left Books.
—— 1971a, 'Lenin and Philosophy', in *Lenin and Philosophy and Other Essays*, London: New Left Books.
—— 1971b, 'Ideology and Ideological State Apparatuses', in *Lenin and Philosophy and Other Essays*, London: New Left Books.
Anderson, Kevin 1995, *Lenin, Hegel and Western Marxism: A Critical Study*, Urbana: University of Illinois Press.
—— 2007, 'The Rediscovery and Persistence of the Dialectic in Philosophy and World Politics', in Budgen, Kouvelakis and Žižek 2007.
Anderson, Perry 1974, *Lineages of the Absolutist State*, London: New Left Books.
—— 1976, 'The Antinomies of Antonio Gramsci', *New Left Review*, I, 100: 5–78.
Angel, Pierre 1961, *Eduard Bernstein et l'évolution du socialisme allemande*, Paris: Didier.
Anweiler, Oscar 1974, *The Soviets: The Russian Workers, Peasants, and Soldiers Councils, 1905–1921*, New York: Pantheon Books.
Aristotle 1985, *Nichomachean Ethics*, Indianapolis: Hackett Publishing.
Arnold, Kathleen 2007, 'Domestic War: Locke's Concept of Prerogative and Implications for U.S. "Wars" Today', *Polity*, 39, 1: 1–28.
Ascher, Abraham 1972, *Pavel Axelrod and the Development of Menshevism*, Cambridge, MA: Harvard University Press.
Ascher, Abraham (ed.) 1976, *The Mensheviks in the Russian Revolution*, Ithaca, NY: Cornell University Press.
Axelrod, P.B. 1898 [1983], 'On the Question of the Present Tasks and Tactics of the Russian Social-Democrats', in Harding 1983.
Axelrod, Pavel 1903–4 [1976], 'The Unification of Russian Social-Democracy and Its Tasks', in Ascher 1976.
—— 1904 [1976], 'The Unification of Russian Social-Democracy and its Tasks', in Ascher 1976.
—— 1905 [1976], 'The People's Duma and the Workers' Congress', in Ascher 1976.
Bachelard, Gaston 1972, *La Formation de l'esprit scientifique*, Paris: J. Vrin.
Balibar, Etienne 1974a, 'La Rectification du "Manifeste Communist"', in *Cinq études du matérialisme historique*, Paris: Maspero.

——— 1974b, 'Matérialisme et idéalisme dans l'histoire de la théorie marxiste', in *Cinq études du matérialisme historique*, Paris: Maspero.

——— 1976, *Sur la dictature du prolétariat*, Paris: Maspero.

——— 2007, 'The Philosophical Moment in Politics Determined by War: Lenin in 1914–16', in Budgen, Kouvelakis and Žižek 2007.

Baraka, Amiri 1991, 'The Dictatorship of the Proletariat', in *The Amiri Baraka/Leroi Jones Reader*, edited by William J. Harris, New York: Thunder's Mouth Press.

Baron, Samuel H. 1963, *Plekhanov: The Father of Russian Marxism*, Stanford, CA: Stanford University Press.

——— 1976, 'Le Développement du capitalism en Russie selon Plekhanov', in Institut Giangiacomo Feltrinelli, *Histoire du marxisme contemporaine*, Tomb III, Paris: Union Générale d'Éditions.

Bartley, Kim and Donnacha Ó Briain 2003, *The Revolution Will Not Be Televised* [DVD], Galway, Ireland: Power Pictures.

Bernstein, Eduard 1898 [1961], *Evolutionary Socialism*, New York: Schoken Books.

Besançon, Alain 1981, *The Intellectual Origins of Leninism*, Oxford: Basil Blackwell.

Bettleheim, Charles 1974, *Les Luttes de classes en U.R.S.S.: prémiere période, 1917–1923*, Paris: Seuil/Maspero.

Bogdanov, Alexander 1906–24 [1977], *La Science, l'art et la classe ouvrière*, edited by Henri Deluy and Dominique Lecourt, translated by Blanche Grinbaum, Paris: Maspero.

Bolsinger, Eckard 2001, *The Autonomy of the Political: Carl Schmitt's and Lenin's Political Realism*, Westport, CT: Greenwood Press.

Bondanella, Peter and Mark Musa (eds.) 1979, *The Portable Machiavelli*, New York: Penguin.

Boulding, Kenneth E. and Tapan Mukerjee (eds.) 1972, *Economic Imperialism*, Ann Arbor: University of Michigan Press.

Brandist, Craig forthcoming, *Dimensions of Hegemony*, Leiden, Netherlands: Brill.

Brecht, Bertolt 1987a, 'In Praise of Doubt', in *Poems 1913–1956*, edited by John Willett and Ralph Manheim, New York: Routledge.

——— 1987b, 'The Truth Unites', in *Poems, 1913–1956*, edited by John Willett and Ralph Manheim, New York: Routledge.

Buci-Glucksmann, Christine 1975, *Gramsci et l'état: pour une théorie matérialiste de la philosophie*, Paris: Fayard.

Budgen, Sebastian, Stathis Kouvelakis and Slavoj Žižek (eds.) 2007, *Lenin Reloaded: Toward a Politics of Truth*, Durham, NC: Duke University Press.

Bukharin, Nicolai 1916 [1972], 'The Imperialist Robber State', in Lenin 1917a.

——— 1920 [1971], *Economics of the Transformation Period (With Lenin's Critical Remarks)*, New York: Bergman.

Bunyan, James and H.H. Fisher (eds.) 1961, *The Bolshevik Revolution, 1917–1918: Documents and Materials*, Stanford, CA: Stanford University Press.

Butler, Judith, Ernesto Laclau and Slavoj Žižek 2000, *Contingency, Hegemony, Universality: Contemporary Dialogues on the Left*, London: Verso.

Carlo, Antonio 1973, 'Lenin on the Party', *Telos*, 17, 2–40.

Carr, E.H. 1970, *Socialism in One Country*, Volume 1, Harmondsworth: Penguin Books.

Cerroni, Umberto 1978, 'Democracy and Socialism', *Economy and Society*, 7, 3: 241–83.

Chernyshevskii, Nikolai 1961, *What Is to Be Done?*, New York: Random House.

Claudin, Fernando 1977, 'Democracy and Dictatorship in Lenin and Kautsky', in *New Left Review*, I, 106: 59–78.

Claudin-Urondo, Carmen 1975, *Lénine et la révolution culturelle*, Paris: Mouton.

Cliff, Tony 1975, *Lenin: Building the Party*, London: Pluto Press.

Cohen, Stephen F. 1975, *Bukharin and the Bolshevik Revolution*, New York: Random House.

Colletti, Lucio 1972a, 'Bernstein and the Marxism of the Second International', in *From Rousseau to Lenin: Studies in Ideology and Society*, London: New Left Books.

—— 1972b, 'Lenin's *State and Revolution*', in *From Rousseau to Lenin: Studies in Ideology and Society*, London: New Left Books.

Conquest, Robert 1972, *Lenin*, London: Fontana/Collins.

Constant, Benjamin 1797 [1988], 'Des effets de la Terreur', in *De la force du gouvernement actuel de la France et de la nécessité de s'y rallier. Des reactions politiques. Des effets de la Terreur*, Paris: Flammarion.

Corrigan, Philip, Harvie Ramsay and Derek Sayer 1978, *Socialist Construction and Marxist Theory: Bolshevism and Its Critique*, New York: Monthly Review.

Crouch, Colin 1982, *Trade Unions: The Logic of Collective Action*, London: Fontana.

Dan, Theodore 1970, *The Origins of Bolshevism*, New York: Schocken Books.

Day, Richard B. and Daniel Gaido (eds.), 2011, *Witnesses to Permanent Revolution: The Documentary Record*, Chicago: Haymarket Books.

Deutscher, Isaac (ed.) 1964, *The Age of Permanent Revolution: A Trotsky Anthology*, New York: Dell.

Diderot, Denis 1782 [1983], *Le Neveu de Rameau*, Paris: Flammarion.

Donald, Moira 1993, *Marxism and Revolution: Karl Kautsky and the Russian Marxists, 1900–1924*, New Haven, CT: Yale University Press.

Draper, Hal 1996, *War and Revolution: Lenin and the Myth of Revolutionary Defeatism*, Atlantic Highlands, NJ: Humanities Press.

Duggett, Michael 1975, 'Marx on Peasants', *Journal of Peasant Studies*, 2, 2: 159–82.

Dunayevskaya, Raya 1971, *Marxism and Freedom: From 1776 to the Present*, London: Pluto Press.

Elbaum, Max and Robert Seltzer 2004, *The Labour Aristocracy: The Material Basis for Opportunism in the Labour Movement*, Chippendale, New South Wales: Resistance Books.

Elster, Jon 1983, *Sour Grapes: Studies in the Subversion of Rationality*, Cambridge: Cambridge University Press.

Evans, Richard J. 1979, '"Red Wednesday" in Hamburg: Social Democrats, Police and Lumpenproletariat in the Suffrage Disturbance of 17 January 1906', *Social History*, 4, 1: 1–31.

Fieldhouse, D.K. 1972, '"Imperialism": An Historiographical Revision', in Boulding and Mukerjee 1972.

Foster, John 1975, *Class Struggle and the Industrial Revolution*, London: Methuen.

Frankel, Jonathan 1963, 'Economism: A Heresy Exploited', *Slavic Review*, 2: 263–84.

—— 1969a, 'Lenin's Doctrinal Revolution of April 1917', *Journal of Contemporary History*, 4, 2: 117–42.

—— 1969b, 'Introduction', in Frankel (ed.) 1969, *Vladimir Akimov on the Dilemmas of Russian Marxism*, Cambridge: Cambridge University Press.

—— 1972, 'Voluntarism, Maximalism, and the Group for the Emancipation of Labor (1883–1892)', in Rabinowitch et al. (eds.) 1972.

Frankel, Jonathan (ed.), 1969, *Vladimir Akimov on the Dilemmas of Russian Marxism, 1895–1903*, Cambridge: Cambridge University Press.

Galai, Shmuel 1973, *The Liberation Movement in Russia, 1900–1905*, Cambridge: Cambridge University Press.

Garaudy, Roger 1968, *Lénine*, Paris: Presses Universitaires de France.

Garver, Eugene 1987, *Machiavelli and the History of Prudence*, Madison: University of Wisconsin Press.

Gay, Peter 1952, *The Dilemma of Democratic Socialism*, New York: Columbia University Press.

Geary, Richard J. 1976, 'Défense et déformation du marxisme chez Kautsky', in Institut Giangiacomo Feltrinelli, *Histoire du marxisme contemporaine* I, Paris: Union générale d'éditions.

Geras, Norman 1976, *The Legacy of Rosa Luxemburg*, London: New Left Books.

—— 1990, *Discourses of Extremity*, London: Verso.

Getzler, Israel 1967, *Martov: A Political Biography of a Russian Social-Democrat*, Cambridge: Cambridge University Press.

Goldman, Lucien 1970, *Marxisme et sciences humaines*, Paris: Gallimard.

Goode, Patrick (ed.) 1983, *Karl Kautsky: Selected Political Writings*, London: Macmillan.

Gorky, Maxim 1923 [1979], *My Universities*, Harmondsworth: Penguin Books.

Gramsci, Antonio 1926 [1978], 'Some Aspects of the Southern Question', in *Selections from Political Writings, 1921–26*, London: Lawrence and Wishart.

—— 1929–35 [1971], 'Prison Notebooks', in Hoare and Nowell-Smith 1971.

Gruppi, Luciano 1978, 'Lénine et la théorie du parti revolutionnaire de la classe ouvrière', in *Histoire du marxisme contemporaine* IV, Fondazione Giangiacomo Feltrinelli, Paris: Union Générale d'Éditions.

Haberkern, E. 1998–9, 'What Have They Done to *What Is to Be Done?*', *Science & Society*, 62, 4: 568–73.

Habermas, Jürgen 1984, *The Theory of Communicative Action*, Volume 1, Boston: Beacon Press.
Haimson, Leopold H. 1955, *The Russian Marxists and the Origins of Bolshevism*, Cambridge, MA: Harvard University Press.
Hamilton, Alexander, James Madison and John Jay 1787–8 [2003], *The Federalist Papers*, Cambridge: Cambridge University Press.
Hammond, Thomas Taylor 1957, *Lenin on Trade Unions and Revolution, 1893–1917*, New York: Columbia University Press.
Harcave, Sidney 1965, *First Blood: The Russian Revolution of 1905*, London: Bodley Head.
Harding, Neil 1975, 'Lenin's Early Writings – The Problem of Context', *Political Studies*, 24, 4: 442–58.
———— 1977, *Lenin's Political Thought: Theory and Practice in the Democratic Revolution*, London: Macmillan.
———— 1981, *Lenin's Political Thought: Theory and Practice in the Socialist Revolution*, London: Macmillan.
———— 1996, *Leninism*, London: Macmillan.
Harding, Neil (ed.) 1983, *Marxism in Russia: Key Documents 1879–1906*, Cambridge: Cambridge University Press.
Hardt, Michael and Antonio Negri 2000, *Empire*, Cambridge, MA: Harvard University Press.
———— 2004, *Multitude: War and Democracy in the Age of Empire*, New York: Penguin.
———— 2009, *Commonwealth*, Cambridge, MA: Harvard University Press.
Hegel, G.W.F. 1832 [1989], *Science of Logic*, Atlantic Highlands, NJ: Humanities Press.
Hilferding, Rudolf 1910 [1981], *Finance Capital*, London: Routledge & Kegan Paul.
Hill, Christopher 1971, *Lenin and the Russian Revolution*, Harmondsworth: Penguin.
Hillel-Rubin, David 1977, *Marxism and Materialism: A Study in Marxist Theory of Knowledge*, Sussex: Harvester Press.
Hirschman, Albert O. 1991, *The Rhetoric of Reaction: Perversity, Futility, Jeopardy*, Cambridge, MA: Harvard University Press.
Hoare, Quintin and Geoffrey Nowell-Smith (eds.) 1971, *Selections from the Prison Notebooks of Antonio Gramsci*, New York: International Publishers.
Hobson, J.A. 1902 [1965], *Imperialism: A Study*, Ann Arbor: University of Michigan Press.
Hourwich, Isaac 1912, *Immigration and Labor*, New York: G.P. Putnam's Sons.
Hyman, Richard 1971, *Marxism and the Sociology of Trade Unionism*, London: Pluto Press.
Joll, James 1955, *The Second International, 1889–1914*, London: Weidenfield and Nicolson.
Jones, Gareth Steadman 1975, 'Class Struggle and the Industrial Revolution', *New Left Review*, I, 90: 35–69.
Kautsky, Karl 1883 [1936], *The Economic Doctrines of Karl Marx*, London: N.C.L.C. Publishing Society.

―― 1888 [1927], *Thomas More and His Utopia*, London: A. & C. Black.
―― 1892 [1971], *The Class Struggle*, New York: W.W. Norton.
―― 1895 [1966], *Communism in Central Europe in the Time of the Reformation*, New York: Augustus M. Kelley Publishers.
―― 1898 [1900], *La Question agraire: étude sur les tendances de l'agriculture moderne*, Paris: Giard & Brière.
―― 1901–2, 'Die Revision des Programms der sozialdemokratie in Oesterreich', *Die Neue Zeit*, XX Jahrgang, I Band, Nr. 3: 68–82.
―― 1902 [1916], *The Social Revolution*, Chicago: Charles H. Kerr.
―― 1905a [2011], 'The Consequences of the Japanese Victory and Social-Democracy', in Day and Gaido 2011.
―― 1905b [2011], 'Old and New Revolution', in Day and Gaido 2011.
―― 1906a [2011], 'The American Worker', in Day and Gaido 2011.
―― 1906b [1907], *Ethics and the Materialist Conception of History*, Chicago: Charles H. Kerr.
―― 1906c [2011], 'The Driving Forces of the Russian Revolution and Its Prospects', in Day and Gaido 2011.
―― 1908a [1925], *Foundations of Christianity*, London: Orbach and Chambers.
―― 1908b [1977], *Les Trois sources du marxisme*, Paris: Spartacus.
―― 1909 [1996], *The Road to Power: Political Reflections on Growing into the Revolution*, Atlantic Highlands, NJ: Humanities Press.
―― 1914 [1983], 'Accumulation and Imperialism', in Goode 1983, 82–9.
―― 1915 [1983], 'The Social-Democracy in Wartime', in Goode 1983, 93–6.
―― 1918 [1964], *The Dictatorship of the Proletariat*, Ann Arbor: University of Michigan Press.
Keep, J.H.L. 1963, *The Rise of Social-Democracy in Russia*, Oxford: Oxford University Press.
Kemp, Tom 1967, *Theories of Imperialism*, London: Dennis Dobson.
Kingston-Mann, Esther 1979, 'Problems of Order and Revolution: Lenin and the Peasant Question in March and April, 1917', *Russian History/Histoire Russe*, 6, 1: 39–56.
Kolakowski, Leszek 1978, *Main Currents of Marxism: The Golden Age*, Volume 2, Oxford: Clarendon Press.
Korsch, Karl 1929 [1973], *L'Anti-Kautsky*, Paris: Editions champ libre.
Kouvelakis, Stathis 2007, 'Lenin as Reader of Hegel', in Budgen, Kouvelakis and Žižek 2007.
Krupskaya, Nadezhda 1930, *Memories of Lenin*, London: Martin Lawrence.
Kuskova, E.D. 1899 [1983], 'Credo', in Harding 1983.
Laclau, Ernesto 2005, *On Populist Reason*, London and New York: Verso.
Laclau, Ernesto and Chantal Mouffe 1985, *Hegemony and Socialist Strategy*, London: Verso.

Lane, David 1969, *The Roots of Russian Communism*, Assen, Netherlands: Van Gorcum.
Larsson, Reidar 1970, *Theories of Revolution from Marx to the First Russian Revolution*, Stockholm: Almqvist and Wiksell.
Lecourt, Dominique 1973, *Une Crise et son enjeu: essai sur la position de Lénine en philosophie*, Paris: Maspero.
Lefebvre, Henri 1957, *La Pensée de Lénine*, Paris: Bordas.
Lenin, Vladimir 1894a [1960], 'What the "Friends of the People" Are and How They Fight the Social-Democrats', in *Collected Works*, Volume 1, Moscow: Progress Publishers.
―― 1894b [1960], 'The Economic Content of Narodism and the Criticism of It in Mr. Struve's Book', in *Collected Works*, Volume 1, Moscow: Progress Publishers.
―― 1895–6 [1960], 'Draft and Explanation of a Programme for the Social-Democratic Party', in *Collected Works*, Volume 2, Moscow: Progress Publishers.
―― 1899a [1960], 'The Development of Capitalism in Russia', in *Collected Works*, Volume 3, Moscow: Progress Publishers.
―― 1899b [1960], 'Review of Karl Kautsky, Die Agrarfrage', in *Collected Works*, Volume 4, Moscow: Progress Publishers, 94–9.
―― 1899c [1960], 'A Protest by Russian Social-Democrats', in *Collected Works*, Volume 4, Moscow: Progress Publishers.
―― 1899d [1960], 'A Draft Programme of Our Party', in *Collected Works*, Volume 4, Moscow: Progress Publishers.
―― 1899e [1960], 'A Retrograde Trend in Russian Social-Democracy', in *Collected Works*, Volume 4, Moscow: Progress Publishers.
―― 1900 [1960], 'Declaration of the Editorial Board of *Iskra*', in *Collected Works*, Volume 4, Moscow: Progress Publishers.
―― 1901a [1960], 'The Workers' Party and the Peasantry', in *Collected Works*, Volume 4, Moscow: Progress Publishers.
―― 1901b [1961], 'The Persecutors of the *Zemstvo* and the Hannibals of Liberalism', in *Collected Works*, Volume 5, Moscow: Progress Publishers.
―― 1901c [1961], 'A Talk with Defenders of Economism', in *Collected Works*, Volume 5, Moscow: Progress Publishers.
―― 1902 [1961], 'What Is to Be Done?', in *Collected Works*, Volume 5, Moscow: Progress Publishers.
―― 1903a [1961], 'Reply to Criticism of Our Draft Programme', in *Collected Works*, Volume 6, Moscow: Progress Publishers.
―― 1903b [1961], 'An Unsubmitted Statement', in *Collected Works*, Volume 7, Moscow: Foreign Languages Publishing House.
―― 1903c [1961], 'Letter to *Iskra*', in *Collected Works*, Volume 7, Moscow: Foreign Languages Publishing House.
―― 1904a [1961], 'One Step Forward, Two Steps Back', in *Collected Works*, Volume 7, Moscow: Foreign Languages Publishing House.

—— 1904b [1961], 'One Step Forward, Two Steps Back: Reply by N. Lenin to Rosa Luxemburg', in *Collected Works*, Volume 7, Moscow: Foreign Languages Publishing House.

—— 1904c [1961], 'The *Zemstvo* Campaign and *Iskra*'s Plan', in *Collected Works*, Volume 7, Moscow: Foreign Languages Publishing House.

—— 1905a [1962], 'The Beginning of the Revolution in Russia', in *Collected Works*, Volume 8, Moscow: Progress Publishers.

—— 1905b [1962], 'Revolutionary Days', in *Collected Works*, Volume 8, Moscow: Progress Publishers.

—— 1905c [1962], 'Two Tactics', in *Collected Works*, Volume 8, Moscow: Progress Publishers.

—— 1905d [1962], 'Should We Organise the Revolution?', in *Collected Works*, Volume 8, Moscow: Progress Publishers.

—— 1905e [1962], 'New Tasks and New Forces', in *Collected Works*, Volume 8, Moscow: Progress Publishers.

—— 1905f [1962], '*Osvobozhdeniye*-ists and New-*Iskr*ists, Monarchists and Girondists', in *Collected Works*, Volume 8, Moscow: Progress Publishers.

—— 1905g [1962], 'The Proletariat and the Bourgeois Democrats', in *Collected Works*, Volume 8, Moscow: Progress Publishers.

—— 1905h [1962], 'The Proletariat and the Peasantry', in *Collected Works*, Volume 8, Moscow: Progress Publishers.

—— 1905i [1962], 'On Our Agrarian Programme', in *Collected Works*, Volume 8, Moscow: Progress Publishers.

—— 1905j [1962], 'Social-Democracy and the Provisional Revolutionary Government', in *Collected Works*, Volume 8, Moscow: Progress Publishers.

—— 1905k [1962], 'The Agrarian Programme of the Liberals', in *Collected Works*, Volume 8, Moscow: Progress Publishers.

—— 1905l [1962], 'A New Revolutionary Workers' Association', in *Collected Works*, Volume 8, Moscow: Progress Publishers.

—— 1905m [1962], 'Two Tactics of Social-Democracy in the Democratic Revolution', in *Collected Works*, Volume 9, Moscow: Progress Publishers.

—— 1905n [1962], 'Revolution Teaches', in *Collected Works*, Volume 9, Moscow: Progress Publishers.

—— 1905o [1962], 'In the Wake of the Monarchist Bourgeoisie or in the Van of the Revolutionary Proletariat and Peasantry?', in *Collected Works*, Volume 9, Moscow: Progress Publishers.

—— 1905p [1962], 'A Most Lucid Exposition of a Most Confused Plan', in *Collected Works*, Volume 9, Moscow: Progress Publishers.

—— 1905q [1962], 'Socialism and the Peasantry', in *Collected Works*, Volume 9, Moscow: Progress Publishers.

BIBLIOGRAPHY 371

—— 1905r [1962], 'The Struggle of the Proletariat', in *Collected Works*, Volume 9, Moscow: Foreign Languages Publishing House.
—— 1905s [1962], 'The First Victory of the Revolution', in *Collected Works*, Volume 9, Moscow: Progress Publishers.
—— 1905t [1962], 'Petty-Bourgeois and Proletarian Socialism', in *Collected Works*, Volume 9, Moscow: Progress Publishers.
—— 1905u [1977], 'Insertions for V. Kalinin's Article "The Peasant Congress"', in *Collected Works*, Volume 41, Moscow: Progress Publishers.
—— 1905v [1962], 'Our Tasks and the Soviet of Workers' Deputies', in *Collected Works*, Volume 10, Moscow: Progress Publishers.
—— 1905w [1962], 'The Reorganisation of the Party', in *Collected Works*, Volume 10, Moscow: Progress Publishers.
—— 1905x [1962], 'Learn From the Enemy', in *Collected Works*, Volume 10, Moscow: Progress Publishers.
—— 1905y [1962], 'Socialism and Anarchism', in *Collected Works*, Volume 10, Moscow: Progress Publishers.
—— 1905z [1962], 'The Socialist Party and Non-Party Revolutionism', in *Collected Works*, Volume 10, Moscow: Progress Publishers.
—— 1906a [1962], 'A Tactical Platform for the Unity Congress of the RSDLP', in *Collected Works*, Volume 10, Moscow: Progress Publishers.
—— 1906b [1962], 'Revision of the Agrarian Programme of the Workers' Party', in *Collected Works*, Volume 10, Moscow: Progress Publishers.
—— 1906c [1962], 'The Victory of the Cadets and the Tasks of the Workers' Party', in *Collected Works*, Volume 10, Moscow: Progress Publishers.
—— 1906d [1962], 'Speech in Reply to the Debate on the Agrarian Question', in *Collected Works*, Volume 10, Moscow: Progress Publishers.
—— 1906e [1962], 'Report on the Unity Congress of the RSDLP', in *Collected Works*, Volume 10, Moscow: Progress Publishers.
—— 1906f [1962], 'Guerrilla Warfare', in *Collected Works*, Volume 11, Moscow: Progress Publishers.
—— 1906g [1962], 'Preface to the Russian Translation of K. Kautsky's Pamphlet: *The Driving Forces and Prospects of the Russian Revolution*', in *Collected Works*, Volume 11, Moscow: Progress Publishers.
—— 1907a [1962], 'The International Socialist Congress in Stuttgart', in *Collected Works*, Volume 13, Moscow: Progress Publishers.
—— 1907b [1962], 'The International Socialist Congress in Stuttgart', in *Collected Works*, Volume 13, Moscow: Progress Publishers.
—— 1907c [1962], 'Preface to the Collection *Twelve Years*', in *Collected Works*, Volume 13, Moscow: Progress Publishers.

―――― 1907d [1962], 'The Agrarian Programme of Social-Democracy in the First Russian Revolution, 1905–1907', in *Collected Works*, Volume 13, Moscow: Progress Publishers.

―――― 1908 [1963], 'Materialism and Empirio-Criticism', in *Collected Works*, Volume 14, Moscow: Progress Publishers.

―――― 1909a [1963], 'The Aim of the Proletarian Struggle in Our Revolution', in *Collected Works*, Volume 15, Moscow: Progress Publishers.

―――― 1909b [1963], 'The "Leftward Swing" of the Bourgeoisie and the Tasks of the Proletariat', in *Collected Works*, Volume 15, Moscow: Progress Publishers.

―――― 1911 [1963], 'Old and New', in *Collected Works*, Volume 17, Moscow: Progress Publishers.

―――― 1911–12 [1963], 'Fundamental Problems of the Election Campaign', in *Collected Works*, Volume 17, Moscow: Progress Publishers.

―――― 1912a [1963], 'A Talk on "Cadet-Eating"', in *Collected Works*, Volume 18, Moscow: Progress Publishers.

―――― 1912b [1963], 'Two Utopias', in *Collected Works*, Volume 18, Moscow: Progress Publishers.

―――― 1914 [1964], 'Dead Chauvinism and Living Socialism', in *Collected Works*, Volume 21, Moscow: Progress Publishers.

―――― 1915a [1964], 'Under a False Flag', in *Collected Works*, Volume 21, Moscow: Progress Publishers.

―――― 1915b [1964], 'The Collapse of the Second International', in *Collected Works*, Volume 21, Moscow: Progress Publishers.

―――― 1915c [1964], 'The Defeat of One's Own Government in the Imperialist War', in *Collected Works*, Volume 21, Moscow: Progress Publishers.

―――― 1915d [1964], 'Socialism and War', in *Collected Works*, Volume 21, Moscow: Progress Publishers.

―――― 1915e [1963], 'On the Question of Dialectics', in *Collected Works*, Volume 38, Moscow: Foreign Languages Publishing House3.

―――― 1915–16 [1976], 'Notebooks on Imperialism', in *Collected Works*, Volume 39, Moscow: Progress Publishers.

―――― 1916a [1964], 'Opportunism, and the Collapse of the Second International', in *Collected Works*, Volume 21, Moscow: Progress Publishers.

―――― 1916b [1964], 'Imperialism, the Highest Stage of Capitalism', in *Collected Works*, Volume 22, Moscow: Progress Publishers.

―――― 1916c [1964], 'The Discussion of Self-Determination Summed Up' in *Collected Works* , Volume 22, Moscow: Progress Publishers.

―――― 1916d [1964], 'The Nascent Trend of Imperialist Economism', in *Collected Works*, Volume 23, Moscow: Progress Publishers.

―――― 1916e [1964], 'A Caricature of Marxism and Imperialist Economism,' in *Collected Works*, Volume 23, Moscow: Progress Publishers.

—— 1916f [1964], 'The Youth International', in *Collected Works*, Volume 23, Moscow: Progress Publishers.

—— 1916g [1969], 'To G.Y. Zinoviev', in *Collected Works*, Volume 43, Moscow: Progress Publishers.

—— 1917a [1972], *Marxism on the State: Preparatory Material for the Book 'State and Revolution'*, Moscow: Progress Publishers.

—— 1917b [1964], 'Letters from Afar', in *Collected Works*, Volume 23, Moscow: Progress Publishers.

—— 1917c [1971], 'Report at a Meeting of Bolshevik Delegates to the All-Russia Conference of Workers' and Soldiers' Deputies, April 4, 1917', in *Collected Works*, Volume 36, Moscow: Progress Publishers.

—— 1917d [1964], 'The Tasks of the Proletariat in the Present Revolution', in *Collected Works*, Volume 24, Moscow: Progress Publishers.

—— 1917e [1964], 'Letters on Tactics', in *Collected Works*, Volume 24, Moscow: Progress Publishers.

—— 1917f [1964], 'The Tasks of the Proletariat in Our Revolution: Draft Platform for the Proletarian Party', in *Collected Works*, Volume 24, Moscow: Progress Publishers.

—— 1917g [1964], 'Petrograd City Conference of the RSDLP (Bolsheviks)', in *Collected Works*, Volume 24, Moscow: Progress Publishers.

—— 1917h [1964], 'Seventh All-Russia Conference of the RSDLP (B)', in *Collected Works*, Volume 24, Moscow: Progress Publishers.

—— 1917i [1964], 'The State and Revolution: The Marxist Theory of the State and the Tasks of the Proletariat in the Revolution', in *Collected Works*, Volume 25, Moscow: Progress Publishers.

—— 1917j [1964], 'The Crisis Has Matured', in *Collected Works*, Volume 26, Moscow: Progress Publishers.

—— 1917k [1964], 'Can the Bolsheviks Retain State Power?', in *Collected Works*, Volume 26, Moscow: Progress Publishers.

—— 1917l [1964], 'Theses on the Constituent Assembly', in *Collected Works*, Volume 26, Moscow: Progress Publishers.

—— 1917m [1964], 'How To Organize Competition', in *Collected Works*, Volume 26, Moscow: Progress Publishers.

—— 1918a [1971] 'Original Version of the Article "Immediate Tasks of the Soviet Government", Chapters IV–X', in *Collected Works*, Volume 42, Moscow: Progress Publishers.

—— 1918b [1965] 'Original Version of the Article "Immediate Tasks of the Soviet Government", Chapters X–XIII', in *Collected Works*, Volume 27, Moscow: Progress Publishers.

—— 1918c [1965] 'The Immediate Tasks of the Soviet Government', in *Collected Works*, Volume 27, Moscow: Progress Publishers.

―――― 1918d [1965] '"Left-Wing" Childishness and the Petty-Bourgeois Mentality', in *Collected Works*, Volume 27, Moscow: Progress Publishers.

―――― 1918e [1965] 'The Proletarian Revolution and the Renegade Kautsky', in *Collected Works*, Volume 28, Moscow: Progress Publishers.

―――― 1920a [1965], 'Left-Wing Communism, an Infantile Disorder', in *Collected Works*, Volume 31, Moscow: Progress Publishers.

―――― 1920b [1966], '*Kommunismus*', in *Collected Works*, Volume 31, Moscow: Progress Publishers.

―――― 1920c [1966], 'Speech on the Role of the Communist Party', in *Collected Works*, Volume 31, Moscow: Progress Publishers.

―――― 1920d [1966], 'On Proletarian Culture', in *Collected Works*, Volume 31, Moscow: Progress Publishers.

―――― 1922–3 [1966], 'Letter to the Congress', in *Collected Works*, Volume 36, Moscow: Progress Publishers.

―――― 1923 [1965], 'Our Revolution', in *Collected Works*, Volume 33, Moscow: Progress Publishers.

Lester, Jeremy 2000, *The Dialogue of Negation: Debates on Hegemony in Russia and the West*, London: Pluto Press.

Lichtheim, George 1967, *Marxism: A Historical and Critical Study*, London: Routledge and Kegan Paul.

Lidtke, Vernon L. 1966, *The Outlawed Party: Social-Democracy in Imperial Germany, 1878–1890*, Princeton, NJ: Princeton University Press.

Liebman, Marcel 1970, 'Lenin in 1905: A Revolution That Shook a Doctrine', *Monthly Review*, 21, 11: 57–75.

―――― 1975, *Leninism under Lenin*, London: Jonathan Cape.

Lih, Lars T. 2006, *Lenin Rediscovered: 'What Is to Be Done?' in Context*, Leiden, Netherlands: Brill.

―――― 2011, 'Lenin, Kautsky and the New Era of Revolutions', *Weekly Worker*, December 22.

Linhart, Robert 1976, *Lénine, les paysans, Taylor: essai d'analyse matérialiste historique de la naissance du système productif soviétique*, Paris: Éditions du Seuil.

―――― 1978, *L'Établi*, Paris: Éditions de Minuit.

Locke, John 1690 [1980], *Second Treatise of Government*, Indianapolis: Hackett Publishing.

Looker, Robert (ed.) 1974, *Rosa Luxemburg: Selected Writings*, New York: Grove Press.

Löwy, Michael 1976, 'From the "Logic" of Hegel to the Finland Station in Petrograd', in *Critique*, 6, 1: 5–15.

Lukács, George 1922 [1971], *History and Class Consciousness*, Cambridge, MA: MIT Press.

―――― 1924 [1970], *Lenin: A Study on the Unity of His Thought*, Cambridge, MA: MIT Press.

Luxemburg, Rosa 1900 [1970], 'Social Reform or Revolution', in Waters 1970.

―――― 1903 [1970], 'Stagnation and Progress in Marxism', in Waters 1970.

―――― 1904 [1970], 'Organizational Questions of Russian Social-Democracy', in Waters 1970.

―――― 1905 [2011], 'The Russian Revolution', in Day and Gaido 2011.

―――― 1906 [1970], 'The Mass Strike, the Political Party and the Trade Unions', in Waters 1970.

―――― 1913 [1951], *The Accumulation of Capital*, London: Routledge & Kegan Paul.

―――― 1914–15 [1970], 'The Junius Pamphlet: The Crisis in German Social-Democracy', in Waters 1970.

―――― 1915 [1974], 'Rebuilding the International', in Looker 1974.

Machiavelli, Niccolo 1513 [1979], 'The Prince', in Bondanella and Musa 1979.

―――― 1517 [1970], *The Discourses*, Harmondsworth: Penguin Books.

MacIntyre, Alasdair 1984, *After Virtue*, Notre Dame, IN: University of Notre Dame Press.

Mao Tse-tung 1937 [1967], 'On Contradiction', in *Selected Works of Mao Tse-tung*, Volume 1, Beijing: Foreign Languages Press.

―――― 1957 [1977], 'On the Correct Handling of Contradictions Among the People', in *Selected Works of Mao Tse-tung*, Volume 5, Beijing: Foreign Languages Press.

Marcuse, Herbert 1961, *Soviet Marxism: A Critical Analysis*, New York: Random House.

Marx, Karl 1843–4 [1973], 'Contribution to the Critique of Hegel's Philosophy of Right. Introduction', in Marx and Friedrich Engels, *Collected Works*, Volume 3, New York: International Publishers.

―――― 1845 [1976], 'Theses on Feuerbach', in Marx and Friedrich Engels, *Collected Works*, Volume 5, New York: International Publishers.

―――― 1864 [1984], 'Provisional Rules of the International Working Men's Association', in Marx and Friedrich Engels, *Collected Works*, Volume 20, New York: International Publishers.

―――― 1867 [1967], *Capital: A Critique of Political Economy*, Volume I, New York: International Publishers.

―――― 1871 [1986], 'The Civil War in France', in Marx and Friedrich Engels, *Collected Works*, Volume 22, New York: International Publishers.

―――― 1875 [1989], 'Critique of the Gotha Programme', in Marx and Friedrich Engels, *Collected Works*, Volume 24, New York: International Publishers.

―――― 1878 [1983], 'A Letter to the Editorial Board of *Otechestvenneye Zapiski*', in Shanin 1983.

―――― 1881a [1983], 'Drafts of a Reply to Vera Zasulich', in Shanin 1983.

―――― 1881b [1983], 'The Reply to Vera Zasulich', in Shanin 1983.

—— 1885 [1967], *Capital: A Critique of Political Economy*, Volume II, New York: International Publishers.

—— 1894 [1967], *Capital: A Critique of Political Economy*, Volume III, New York: International Publishers.

—— 1968, *Theories of Surplus-Value*, Volume 2, Moscow: Progress Publishers.

Marx, Karl and Friedrich Engels 1845–6 [1975], 'The German Ideology', in *Collected Works*, Volume 5, New York: International Publishers.

—— 1848 [1976], 'Manifesto of the Communist Party', in *Collected Works*, Volume 6, New York: International Publishers.

—— 1882 [1983], 'Preface to the Second Russian Edition of the *Manifesto of the Communist Party*', in Shanin 1983.

—— 1975, *Selected Correspondence*, Moscow: Progress Publishers.

Mattick, Paul 1983, *Marxism – Last Refuge of the Bourgeoisie?*, Armonk, NY: M.E. Sharpe.

Mayer, Arno J. 2000, *The Furies: Violence and Terror in the French and Russian Revolutions*, Princeton, NJ: Princeton University Press.

Mayer, Robert 1997, 'What Is Not to Be Done: Lenin, Marxism and the Proletariat', *Science & Society*, 61, 3: 367–75.

McLennan, Gregor 1981, *Marxism and the Methodologies of History*, London: Verso.

Menashe, Louis 1975, 'The Methodology of Leninology', *Socialist Revolution*, 5, 1: 89–99.

Meyer, Alfred G. 1962, *Leninism*, New York: Praeger.

Michalet, Charles-Albert 1985, *Le Capitalisme mondial*, Paris: Presses Universitaires de France.

Michael-Matsas, Sava 2007, 'Lenin and the Path of Dialectics', in Budgen, Kouvelakis and Žižek 2007.

Miliband, Ralph 1970, 'Lenin's *The State and Revolution*', in Miliband and Saville 1970.

Miliband, Ralph and John Saville (eds.) 1970, *The Socialist Register*, London: Merlin Press.

—— 1977, *The Socialist Register*, London: Merlin Press.

Mitchell, Harvey and Peter N. Stearns 1971, *Workers and Protest: The European Labor Movement, the Working Classes and the Origins of Social-Democracy*, Itasca, IL: Peacock Press.

Moore, Barrington Jr. 1978, *Injustice: The Social Bases of Obedience and Revolt*, White Plains: M.E. Sharpe Inc.

Nabudere, Dan 1977, *The Political Economy of Imperialism*, London: Zed Press.

Nettl, J.P. 1966, *Rosa Luxemburg*, London: Oxford University Press.

Nicolaus, Martin 1970, 'The Theory of the Labor Aristocracy', *Monthly Review*, 21, 11: 90–102.

Palloix, Christian 1970, 'La Question de l'impérialisme chez V.I. Lénine et Rosa Luxemburg', *L'Homme et la société*, 15: 103–38.

Panaccione, Andrea 1976, 'L'Analyse du capitalisme chez Kautsky', in Institut Giangiacomo Feltrinelli, *Histoire du marxisme contemporaine*, Tomb 1., Paris: Union générale d'éditions.

Pannekoek, Anton 1975, *Lenin as Philosopher*, London: Merlin.

Parvus (Alexander Helfand) 1905 [2011], 'Our Tasks', in Day and Gaido 2011.

Pasquino, Pasquale 1998, 'Locke on King's Prerogative', *Political Theory*, 26, 2: 198–208.

Perrie, Maureen 1976, *The Agrarian Policy of the Russian Socialist-Revolutionary Party*, Cambridge: Cambridge University Press.

Pipes, Richard 1963, *Social-Democracy and the St. Petersburg Labor Movement, 1885–1897*, Cambridge, MA: Harvard University Press.

——— 1970, *Struve: Liberal on the Left, 1870–1905*, Cambridge, MA: Harvard University Press.

Plekhanov, Georgii 1883 [1960], 'Socialism and the Political Struggle', in *Selected Philosophical Works*, Volume 1, Moscow: Progress Publishers.

——— 1884 [1960], 'Programme of the Social-Democratic Emancipation of Labour Group', in *Selected Philosophical Works*, Volume 1, Moscow: Progress Publishers.

——— 1885 [1960], 'Our Differences', in Selected Philosophical Works, Volume 1, Moscow: Progress Publishers.

——— 1888a [1960], 'Second Draft Programme of the Russian Social-Democrats', in *Selected Philosophical Works*, Volume 1, Moscow: Progress Publishers.

——— 1888b [1960], 'A New Champion of Autocracy', in *Selected Philosophical Works*, Volume 1, Moscow: Progress Publishers.

——— 1889 [1960], 'Speech at the International Workers' Socialist Congress in Paris', in *Selected Philosophical Works*, Volume 1, Moscow: Progress Publishers.

——— 1895 [1960], 'The Development of the Monist View of History', in *Selected Philosophical Works*, Volume 1, Moscow: Progress Publishers.

——— 1896 [1976], 'A Few Words in Defence of Economic Materialism', in *Selected Philosophical Works*, Volume 2, Moscow: Progress Publishers.

——— 1898 [1976], 'On the Question of the Individual's Role in History', in *Selected Philosophical Works*, Volume 2, Moscow: Progress Publishers.

——— 1901 [1976], 'A Critique of Our Critics', in *Selected Philosophical Works*, Volume 2, Moscow: Progress Publishers.

——— 1909 [1967], *History of Russian Social Thought*, New York: Howard Fertig.

——— n. d. *Oeuvres philosophiques*, Volume 2, Moscow: Editions du progrès.

Polan, A.J. 1984, *Lenin and the End of Politics*, Los Angeles: University of California Press.

Post, Charles 2010, 'Exploring Working-Class Consciousness: A Critique of the Theory of the "Labour-Aristocracy"', *Historical Materialism*, 18, 4: 3–38.

Rabinowitch, Alexander 1968, *Prelude to Revolution: The Petrograd Bolsheviks and the July 1917 Uprising*, Bloomington: Indiana University Press.

―――― 1976, *The Bolsheviks Come to Power: The Revolution of 1917 in Petrograd*, New York: W.W. Norton.

Rabinowitch, Alexander, Janet Rabinowitch and Ladis Kristoff (eds.) 1972, *Revolution and Politics in Russia*, Bloomington: Indiana University Press.

Ralston, W.R.S. (ed.) 1883, *Krilof and His Fables*, 4th ed., London: Castle and Company.

Riazanov, David 1905 [2011], 'The Next Questions of Our Movement', in Day and Gaido 2011.

Rosenthal, John 1988, 'Who Practices Hegemony? Class Division and the Subject of Politics', *Cultural Critique*, 9: 25–52.

Rosenberg, Arthur 1962, *Imperial Germany: The Birth of the German Republic, 1871–1918*, New York: Russell and Russell.

Rotenstreich, Nathan 1965, *Basic Problems of Marx's Philosophy*, New York: Bobbs-Merrill.

Roth, Guenther 1963, *The Social-Democrats in Imperial Germany: A Study in Working-Class Isolation and National Integration*, Totowa, NJ: Bedminster Press.

Russell, Bertrand 1896 [1965], *German Social-Democracy*, London: Allen & Unwin.

Russian Social-Democratic Labour Party (RSDLP) 1904 [1978], *Second Ordinary Congress of the RSDLP: Complete Text of the Minutes*, London: New Park Publications.

Rustin, Michael 1988, 'Absolute Voluntarism: Critique of a Post-Marxist Concept of Hegemony', *New German Critique*, 43: 146–71.

Sablinsky, Walter 1976, *The Road to Bloody Sunday: Father Gapon and the St. Petersburg Massacre of 1905*, Princeton, NJ: Princeton University Press.

Salvadori, Massimo 1979, *Karl Kautsky and the Socialist Revolution, 1880–1938*, London: New Left Books.

Sawer, Marion 1977, 'The Genesis of *State and Revolution*', in Miliband and Saville 1977.

Schorske, Carl E. 1955, *German Social-Democracy, 1905–1917*, Cambridge, MA: Harvard University Press.

Schwarz, Solomon 1967, *The Russian Revolution of 1905*, Chicago: University of Chicago Press.

Service, Robert 1985, *Lenin: A Political Life*, Volume 1, London: MacMillan.

―――― 1988, 'Introduction', in Vladimir Lenin, *What Is to Be Done?* Harmondsworth: Penguin.

Shandro, Alan 1995, 'Consciousness from Without: Marxism, Lenin and the Proletariat', *Science & Society*, 59, 3: 268–97.

―――― 1997–8, 'Karl Kautsky: On the Relation of Theory and Practice', *Science & Society*, 61, 4: 474–501.

―――― 1998, 'Political Action, Context and Conjuncture: Thinking About Political Organization', *Historical Materialism*, 3: 73–84.

―――― 1998–9, 'Review of Hal Draper, *War and Revolution*', *Science & Society*, 62, 4: 592–4.

—— 2000, 'Karl Marx as a Conservative Thinker', *Historical Materialism*, 6: 3–25.
—— 2001, 'Reading Lenin: Dialectics and Eclecticism', *Science & Society*, 65, 2: 216–25.
—— 2007, 'Lenin and Hegemony: The Soviets, the Working Class, and the Party in the Revolution of 1905', in Budgen, Kouvelakis and Zizek (eds.) 2007.
—— 2010 'Text and Context in the Argument of Lenin's *What Is to Be Done?*', *Historical Materialism* 18, 3: 75–89.
Shanin, Teodor (ed.) 1983, *Late Marx and the Russian Road*, New York: Monthly Review.
Sloterdijk, Peter 1987, *Critique of Cynical Reason*, Minneapolis: University of Minnesota Press.
Sorel, Georges 1900 [1976], 'Polemics on the Interpretation of Marxism: Bernstein and Kautsky', in Stanley 1976, 148–75.
Stalin, Joseph 1905a [1952], 'Briefly About the Disagreements in the Party' in *Works*, Volume 1, Moscow: Foreign Languages Publishing House.
—— 1905b [1952], 'A Reply to *Social-Democrat*', in *Works*, Volume 1, Moscow: Foreign Languages Publishing House.
—— 1906 [1952], 'Concerning the Revision of the Agrarian Program', in *Works*, Volume 1, Moscow: Foreign Languages Publishing House.
Stanley, John L. (ed.) 1976, *From Georges Sorel: Essays in Socialism and Philosophy*, New York: Oxford University Press.
Stokes, Eric 1969, 'Late Nineteenth Century Colonial Expansion and the Attack on the Theory of Economic Imperialism: A Case of Mistaken Identity?', *Historical Journal*, 12, 2: 285–301.
Sukhanov, N.N. 1955, *The Russian Revolution of 1917: A Personal Record*, edited, abridged and translated by Joel Carmichael, London: Oxford University Press.
Sweezy, Paul 1968, *The Theory of Capitalist Development*, New York: Monthly Review.
Thomas, Peter D. 2009, *The Gramscian Moment: Philosophy, Hegemony and Marxism*, Chicago: Haymarket Books.
Timpanaro, Sebastiano 1975, *On Materialism*, London: New Left Books.
Treadgold, Donald W. 1976, *Lenin and His Rivals: The Struggle for Russia's Future, 1898–1906*, Westport, CT: Greenwood Press.
Trotsky, Leon 1904a [1970], *Nos tâches politiques*, Paris: Denoël/Gonthier.
—— 1904b [1964], 'The Proletariat and the Revolution', in Deutscher 1964.
—— 1906 [1969], 'Results and Prospects', in *The Permanent Revolution and Results and Prospects*, New York: Pathfinder Press.
—— 1908 [1974], *1905*, Harmondsworth: Penguin Books.
—— 1929 [1969], 'The Permanent Revolution', in *The Permanent Revolution and Results and Prospects*, New York: Pathfinder Press.
—— 1930 [1975], *My Life: An Attempt at an Autobiography*, Harmondsworth: Penguin.

Ulam, Adam B. 1969, *Lenin and the Bolsheviks*, London: Fontana/Collins.
Valentinov, Nikolai 1968, *Encounters with Lenin*, London: Oxford University Press.
―――― 1969, *The Early Years of Lenin*, Ann Arbor: University of Michigan Press.
Wada, Haruki 1983, 'Marx and Revolutionary Russia', in Shanin 1983.
Walicki, Andrzej 1969, *The Controversy over Capitalism*, Oxford: Clarendon Press.
Warren, Bill 1980, *Imperialism: Pioneer of Capitalism*, London: New Left Review Editions.
Waters, Mary-Alice (ed.) 1970, *Rosa Luxemburg Speaks*, New York: Pathfinder Press.
Weber, Max 1919 [1994], 'The Profession and Vocation of Politics', in *Political Writings*, edited by Peter Lassman and Ronald Speirs, Cambridge: Cambridge University Press.
Wildman, Allan 1967, *The Making of a Workers' Revolution*, Chicago: University of Chicago Press.
Wilson, Edmund 1972, *To the Finland Station*, New York: Farrar, Strauss and Giroux.
Winters, Anne 2004, 'The Displaced of Capital', in *The Displaced of Capital*, Chicago: University of Chicago Press.
Wolfe, Bertram D. 1964, *Three Who Made a Revolution*, New York: Dell.
Wood, Ellen Meiksins 1986, *The Retreat from Class*, London: Verso.
Zasulich, Vera 1881 [1983], 'A Letter to Marx', in Shanin 1983.
Zinoviev, Grigorii 1923 [1973], *History of the Bolshevik Party: A Popular Outline*, London: New Park Publications.
Žižek, Slavoj 2000a, 'Class Struggle or Postmodernism? Yes, please!', in Butler, Laclau and Žižek 2000.
―――― 2000b, 'Conference – Towards a Politics of Truth: The Retrieval of Lenin', <http://www.kwinrw.de/lenin> accessed December 15, 2000.
―――― 2002a, 'Introduction: Between the Two Revolutions', in Žižek (ed.) 2002.
―――― 2002b, 'Afterword: Lenin's Choice', in Žižek (ed.) 2002.
Žižek, Slavoj (ed.) 2002, *Revolution at the Gates: Selected Writings of Lenin from 1917*, London: Verso.

Index

absolute knowledge (or absolute truth)   12, 19, 188, 273, 314
absolute/relative   102, 138, 143, 147, 162, 188–89, 248, 256, 273, 314
absolutism (or autocracy, tsarism)   86, 90n32, 105
   capitalist authority compared to   50
   target of democratic revolution   9, 87, 92, 94–95, 103, 107–08, 168, 170, 183–84, 193, 214n52, 225
abstract/concrete   65, 70–72, 100, 107n83, 120, 146, 151, 164, 185, 188–93, 197, 248–49, 258, 270, 286, 294, 299, 303, 309, 313–14
Adler, Victor   330, 332, 333, 340, 345
Akimov, Vladimir   117, 129n33, 175, 176
Althusser, Louis   7, 16, 120n17, 248n146
anarchism   59, 68, 190, 274–75
Anderson, Kevin   253
Anderson, Perry   4, 6–7, 105n79, 255
Aristotle   206, 213, 295
autonomy/heteronomy   97, 117, 119, 166, 178, 197, 209
Axelrod, P. B. (Pavel, Paul)   141n53, 178, 184
   and the Group for the Emancipation of Labour   87
   and hegemony   94–95, 167
   and proletarian self-activity   180–82, 184
   and Menshevism   117, 167, 171–72, 173, 176, 178, 180
   critique of Lenin   117, 180–85
   and Workers' Congress   235–36

Bachelard, Gaston   71 and n
Balibar, Etienne   33 and n7, 36, 120, 276n90
base/superstructure   7, 11, 21, 136, 218, 356
Bernstein, Eduard   32, 39, 43–44, 47, 66, 72
   and Fabian Society   47
   and Kautsky   34, 37 and n19, 53–59, 65–67
   on capitalist crisis   47–49
   on liberalism/liberal democracy   49–53
   on the dictatorship of the proletariat   52–53
   on movement and end   49–52, 66
   on class polarization/working-class unity   49–50
   Marxist response to   53–59
   and Economism   146, 138–40
   and legal Marxism   158
Bernsteinism (or revisionism, opportunism)   33, 35n11, 57, 59, 68, 69–70, 146, 158, 160, 175, 187, 264–67
Bogdanov, Alexander   19, 236–37 and n127
Bolsheviks (see also RSDLP, factional struggle)   19, 34n8, 274, 282, 286, 290, 292, 298, 310, 313
bourgeois spontaneity/socialist spontaneity   133–36
bourgeoisie (or capitalist class)   40–43, 52–53, 56
   in the democratic revolution   52–53, 56, 93, 105–06, 130, 142, 185, 199, 210–12, 230–32
   liberal   96, 139, 140, 142, 193, 195, 203, 210, 211–12, 223–24, 241, 244, 247
   peasant   215, 217, 285, 287
   imperialist   260, 264, 276
   British   295–96
   in the socialist revolution   40–43, 269–70, 291, 299–302
Bukharin, Nikolai   253, 269, 274–76, 306, 310n62, 313, 356

capitalist development   28, 55, 59, 74, 82, 89, 98, 133, 205–06, 216, 217, 220, 232, 257–58, 338
   accumulation of capital   38–39, 40, 47–48, 68, 70, 77, 91, 99, 103, 261
   and division of labour   93, 102
   and nationalization of the land   208–09, 219–221, 221n75, 222–23, 342
   capitalist ground-rent   219–20, 247, 338
   American path/Prussian path of capitalist development   28, 218–20, 232 and n118
   concentration/socialization of production   40, 41, 44, 45, 46–49, 53, 54, 57, 58, 69, 91, 95, 99, 110, 231, 259, 260, 261, 278, 333, 338

capitalist development (cont.)
  class polarization   32, 44, 49, 56, 58, 69, 70, 74, 102, 215, 268
  laws of motion   51, 64–65
centrism (or Kautskyism)   33, 228, 233, 257–63, 266–67, 268
Chavez, Hugo   297
Chernyshevskii, Nikolai   118 and n14
civic virtue   324–25
class struggle
  irreconcilability of   115, 125, 131–35, 137–38, 143–46, 153, 158, 277, 290, 294, 299, 327, 354
classless society   6, 17, 23, 30, 289, 300, 302, 308, 320, 351
coercion/consent   4–8, 204–05, 246, 297, 303–14
Cohen, Stephen   275
Colletti, Lucio   37–43, 68–69
concrete analysis (of a concrete conjuncture)   86, 88, 91, 120–21, 162, 164, 248, 314, 356
community   51, 53, 62
  as a metaphor for working-class unity   16
  democratic   29–30
  of struggle   77–79, 306
  proletarian-popular   295, 309, 311, 314, 325, 327, 328
consciousness/spontaneity   2, 4, 21, 27, 78–79, 115, 117, 119–21, 123, 124, 127–28, 129–31, 133–38, 142, 143–44, 147–48, 168–69n8, 171–72, 206–07, 224, 226, 238, 239, 248, 310, 349, 351–54, 356, 359–60
  distinguished from base/superstructure   136
consciousness from without
  Kautsky on   59–72
  Lenin on   19, 31, 116, 121–23, 126–28, 132–33, 139, 144–48, 166, 200, 207, 255, 356, 359–62
  Lenin's *Iskra* colleagues on   171–73
consciousness
  and intention   23, 77, 163, 188, 247
  and reflexivity   23, 54, 77, 163, 207, 233, 247, 255, 256, 273, 308–09, 311–12, 362
  social-democratic (or socialist)   25, 26, 30, 45, 54, 59–72, 77, 81, 91, 108, 111, 115,

116, 118, 122, 124–28, 133–34, 143, 147, 171, 175, 187, 194, 312–13, 342–43, 346–47, 354–55, 359–62
  trade-union   128, 130, 354
Constituent Assembly   34n8, 184n64, 211n45, 221n75, 235, 236, 298–99
constitutional norms   27, 151, 160, 291, 294, 300
  freedom of criticism   27, 29–30, 149–60, 163, 289–90, 300, 349
  freedom of association   153–54, 160, 290
courage   283, 303, 311–14

Dan, Theodore   171, 184, 194, 227
demarcation, lines of   140, 146, 160, 167, 173, 233, 256, 255
democracy
  as an epistemological apparatus   40–41, 57, 70–71, 291–92
  democracy/dictatorship   4–8, 10, 290–93, 297–300
  liberal (or parliamentary)   20, 48, 50–52, 58, 278, 293
  bourgeois   87, 105, 209–10, 226, 278, 294, 301
  petty-bourgeois   106, 272, 283
  peasant   225
  proletarian   58, 226, 294, 301, 307–09, 311–14
  bourgeois/proletarian   226, 294, 301–02
  and socialism   51–52, 57–58, 288, 304, 306
  and populism   106–07 and n83
  democratic centralism   22, 174
dialectics   34, 78, 199–200, 313–14
  and class struggle   109, 125, 132, 134–38, 140, 249
  and transition to socialism   48, 288, 313–14
  Bernstein on   47–48, 49, 50–51
  Hegel on   51, 71, 161–62, 200, 256
  Kautsky and   37, 61, 68–69, 76–77
  Lenin on   120, 165, 189, 199–200, 253–56, 288
  of capitalist society   49, 213, 337, 341
  Plekhanov on   80, 87
  subordination of harmony to struggle   6, 171
dictatorship   290–93, 294–97

INDEX   383

of proletariat   33, 34n8, 56, 183, 226,
    275, 281, 284–85, 289, 290–93, 294–97,
    299–304, 306, 311, 314
bourgeois/proletarian   52, 296–97, 306
individual dictatorship   293, 304–08,
    311
democracy/dictatorship   4–8, 10, 290–93,
    297–300
as prerogative   296–97
Lenin's definition   295
revolutionary democratic dictatorship
    of the proletariat and the peasantry
    211–12, 219, 221n75, 228–29n104, 241–42,
    243–44, 285, 286, 311
division of labour (in politics)   139, 142, 170,
    180, 182, 186, 192, 331
divisionists   221, 222, 223, 232, 311
dogmatism   67, 112, 149–50, 158, 160, 163, 290,
    349
Dunayevskaya, Raya   273

Economism (or Russian Bernsteinism)   113,
    114, 128–29 and n33, 135–36, 139, 141–42 and
    n53, 146, 159, 165, 167–68 and n8, 176–77,
    182, 190–91, 211n45, 226, 348, 350–52,
    356–58, 361–62
    Imperialist Economism   29, 267–72, 280,
        326
    of E. D. Kuskova   138–39, 141, 202n5, 356
    of *Rabochaia mysl'*   113–14, 139
    of *Rabochee delo*   130n33, 139, 141, 157, 158,
        160–61, 189, 348–52
    revolutionary Economism   226 and n92
Elster, Jon   197
Empire/imperialism   316–322
Engels, Friedrich   25, 32, 33, 36, 38n21, 64, 66,
    99, 107, 114, 125, 126, 224, 248, 253
    and Russian revolution   25, 81, 86
    and Russian populism   224
    on the truth of illusions   224 and n83
epistemological apparatus   40–41, 72
    democracy as   40–41, 57, 70–71, 291–92
    party project as   41, 69–75, 311–13
epistemological obstacle   71–75, 310–314
equality   14, 62, 84, 202, 296, 299–301
Evans, Richard   72–74

fatalism/determinism   37n19, 38n21, 42, 77,
    228
Feuerbach, Ludwig   39, 116, 148

form/content   37, 65, 68, 76, 87, 88, 139,
    142, 181, 188, 191–92, 213, 215–16, 226, 228,
    230n106, 285, 308, 359
Frankel, Jonathan   89n29, 129n33, 287n120
freedom
    of association   153–54, 160, 290
    of criticism   27, 29–30, 149–60, 163,
        289–90, 300, 349
    of industry   152, 156
    of labour   151, 152, 156

German Social-Democratic Party (SPD)   25,
    31, 32, 36, 38, 41, 43–47, 54, 56–57, 61, 66,
    69–77, 99, 163, 225, 254, 347, 351
    and Kautsky's Marxism   38–39, 44–47,
        57–58, 69–77, 99–100, 162–63
    Erfurt Programme   31, 38, 43, 44, 60,
        332, 347
Gramsci, Antonio   1, 22–24
    and Lenin   1, 2, 3–10, 16, 23, 225
    and post-Marxism   10, 16, 316
    on coercion and consent   4–8
    on hegemony   1–10
    on passive revolution   8–10
    on permanent revolution   229–30n106
    on political party of the peasantry   225
    on the worker-peasant alliance   225
    on Machiavelli   316, 322–325
    on modern prince   30, 322–325

Haberkern, E.   359
Harding, Neil   118n14, 172n21, 179, 205–06,
    213–14, 214–15n52, 221n75, 222n76, 225n86,
    259, 275, 346
Hardt, Michael   30, 316–322
Hegel, G. W. F.   17, 161
    on refutation   39
    on dialectics   51, 71, 161–62, 200, 256
    on absolute knowledge   314
    on absolute and relative   256
    and Lenin's "epiphany"   252–255
hegemony
    as a philosophical fact   1, 2, 3, 255
    as a politico-strategic logic (or a meta-
        strategic logic)   26–30, 113, 123, 135–44,
        146, 150, 156, 161, 165–67, 175, 189,
        197–98, 206–07, 212n45, 213, 224, 233,
        237n127, 241, 243–48, 255–56, 259, 263,
        271–72, 276, 281, 285, 288, 290, 294, 298,
        300, 308, 310, 314, 316, 326, 328, 353, 356

hegemony (cont.)
　　as a strategic project　4, 9, 25, 26, 27, 81, 93, 100, 101, 104, 108, 113, 146, 161, 165–66, 167, 171, 178–79, 181, 183, 189, 193, 198–99, 202, 205, 209, 211, 212, 220, 234, 241, 244, 246, 255, 272, 284–85, 288, 298, 347, 351, 362
　　alignment of heterogeneous forces　28, 78, 205, 216, 234, 268, 272, 281
　　bourgeois　8, 13, 28, 123, 204, 232, 233, 246, 271, 354, 356, 362
　　and counter-hegemony　5, 8, 16–17
　　Gramscian　3–10
　　in economic structure　217–220
　　Mensheviks on　180–85, 187, 193–96
　　Plekhanov on　92–100
　　proletarian　9, 26, 27, 28, 29, 81, 94, 98, 104, 106, 108, 113, 122, 123, 131–33, 140, 146, 147, 160, 163, 165–67, 168n8, 171, 172, 177, 179, 181, 189, 193–94, 196, 198, 202, 205, 207, 213, 216, 217–20, 225n86, 226n92, 238, 241, 245, 247, 347, 348, 352, 354, 357, 358
　　struggle of contending hegemonic projects　232–33
Hilferding, Rudolf　251, 262
historical materialism　15, 16, 37n19, 82, 87, 101, 111, 116, 118, 124, 163, 198, 199, 216, 217–220, 297, 346, 353
Hobson, J. A.　264 and n51
Hourwich, Isaac　264n51

ideology　8, 126, 135, 168n8, 243, 264, 361
　　bourgeois (or liberal)　115, 133, 134–35, 136, 137–38, 142, 143, 168n8, 352, 354, 355
　　peasant　28, 92n42, 220–25, 232, 311
　　petty-bourgeois　107, 268, 284
　　socialist　134, 347–48
immanent/transcendent　97, 109, 110, 133, 147, 157, 213, 259, 317–19, 320, 322
imperialism　29, 35, 253, 254
　　and export of capitalist social relations　261–63, 264
　　and militarism　250–52
　　and monopoly capital　259–62
　　and finance capital　258, 260, 262–63,, 264–68
　　and labour aristocracy　29, 35, 264–65, 265n54, 266, 268

　　and parasitism　263–68
　　and self-determination of nations　269–70, 288, 356
　　and socialist revolution　255–56
　　and split in socialism　254–55
　　and Taylorism (also "scientific management")　260 and n37, 305
　　and ultra-imperialism　254–55, 257–63
　　and uneven development　29, 255–56
　　as highest stage of capitalism　257, 262–63
　　petty-bourgeois democratic opposition to　35, 75, 267, 272
intelligentsia　26, 60–61, 82, 86, 89n29, 95–98, 109, 112, 113, 114, 117, 118, 125, 126, 136, 139, 168n8, 172n21, 175, 180, 181, 182, 185, 194, 206, 224–25, 239, 342
Iskra　27, 129n33, 149, 155, 156, 160, 165–66, 167–73, 176, 181–82, 185, 189–90, 199, 208, 211, 347–49, 357, 361

Kamenev, Lev　285
Kautsky, Karl　24–26, 29–30, 32–79, 185, 251, 257–58, 290–93, 330–45
　　on dialectics　32, 61
　　as renegade　33–37, 146, 257–58, 266, 291–95, 304
　　and orthodox Marxism　33, 37–39, 53–54, 57–59, 63–72, 87, 99–100, 258, 347
　　and the political project of the SPD, 38–39, 44–47, 57–58, 69–77, 99–100, 162–63
　　on imperialism and ultra-imperialism　35, 257–58
　　and "critical Marxism", 37–43, 68–69, 79
　　and social ontology　37–39, 42–44, 68–69, 76–77
　　on the working-class movement　40–42, 55–57, 65–67, 69–72, 77–79, 99, 132
　　on working-class political agency　68–69, 75–77, 132
　　on the laws of motion of capitalism　41, 48–49, 70, 132
　　on the limits of capitalism　41–42
　　on capitalism in agriculture　44–47, 230–32
　　on peasants　44–47, 230–32
　　critic of Bernstein　37n19, 53–59, 65–67
　　strategy of attrition　42, 55–56

INDEX   385

on "consciousness from without" 59–64,
    122, 132–33, 353
on socialist consciousness 59–66, 69–72,
    79
on workers and intellectuals 66–69
on the socialist party of the working
    class 72–77
on Marxist science and the working
    class 64–66, 97, 162, 168–69n8
and political epistemology 42–43,
    64–66, 70, 168–69n8, 291–92
and leadership 70–72, 213
on theory and practice 72–79
and unilinear historical logic 59, 71, 87
on the Austrian Social-Democratic
    programme 60–61, 330–45
and the Russian revolution of 1905
    225–26, 230–32
and permanent revolution 226, 227,
    230–32
and the worker-peasant alliance 45–47,
    230–32
Lenin and 32–36, 60, 109, 114, 122, 132–33,
    230–32, 257–58, 266–68, 271, 273–75,
    290–95, 297–301, 304–06
Trotsky and 227, 228, 230–32
and the World War 251, 253, 254–55,
    257–58
critic of Lenin and the Bolsheviks
    290–95, 297–301, 304–06
on democracy and dictatorship 290–95
on individual dictatorship 304–06
Erfurt Programme 38–39, 40–41, 44, 45,
    60, 120n18, 132, 347
Agrarian Question 45–47, 53, 219n69
*Ethics and the Materialist Conception of
    History* 32, 38n20, 54
*Driving Forces of the Russian Revolution
    and Its Prospects* 230–33
Foundations of Christianity 62, 67
Three Sources of Marxism 63–64
Road to Power 35, 251, 254
Dictatorship of the Proletariat 290–95,
    297–301, 304–06
Kautskyism 33, 257, 266–68
Kolakowski, Leszek 37n18, 38n20, 38–39n21
Korsch, Karl 35n11, 37n18 and n19, 38n20
    and n21

Krishevskii, Boris 157
Krylov, Ivan 155
Kuskova, E. D. 138, 139, 141, 202n5, 356
kustarnichestvo 177

labour aristocracy 29, 264–65, 265n54, 266,
    268
Laclau, Ernesto 4, 10–17
Lassalle, Ferdinand 115, 134
Lavoisier, Antoine 248
leadership 2, 3, 9, 10, 17, 22, 25, 28, 29, 30, 66,
    76, 99–100, 104, 108, 111–12, 138, 148, 171–72,
    181, 184, 192, 194–95, 222, 225, 244, 268, 269,
    272, 279–80, 281, 307, 316, 326, 329, 356
legal Marxism 158–59
Lester, Jeremy 4–10
Lenin, V. I. 33–37, 78–79, 100–14, 115–48,
    149–63, 168–71, 187–93, 198–200, 203–05,
    207–13, 215–225, 237–49, 232–288, 294–314,
    326–329, 346–62
    Gramsci and 1–10, 16, 23–24, 225,
        229–30n106, 316, 323
    and post-Marxism 10–17, 316
    as symbol 17–22
    conventional wisdom on 5, 16, 19, 26,
        116–23, 273, 346, 360n6
    critic of Kautsky 33–37, 254–55, 257–59,
        266–68, 271, 273, 284, 293–304
    on dialectics 120, 165, 189, 199–200,
        253–56, 288
    on capitalism in Russia 100–104, 216–20
    on capitalism in agriculture 106–08,
        216–20
    on populism 106–07 and n83, 220–25
    on historical materialism and
        agency 100–03, 111–13
    on the workers as a universal class 104,
        108–09, 132
    on the fusion of Marxism and the working-
        class movement 113–14, 197–200
    on spontaneity and consciousness 115,
        117, 119–21, 123, 124, 127–28, 129–31,
        133–38, 142, 143–44, 147–48, 168–69n8,
        171–72, 206–07, 349, 351–54, 356,
        359–60
    and the logic of Marxist orthodoxy
        80–01, 101, 104, 112–13, 122–23, 171–72,
        179, 197–99, 206, 258

Lenin, V. I. (cont.)
  on "consciousness from without"   19, 31, 116, 121–23, 126–28, 132–33, 139, 144–48, 166, 200, 207, 255, 356, 359–62
  on spontaneism (or tail-ism)   142, 159, 190–91, 211–12 and n45, 328, 362
  on Economism   113–14, 128–29, 135, 139, 141 and n53, 142, 146, 159, 168–69n8, 177, 190, 211n45, 226n92, 270, 272, 348, 350–52, 356–58, 361–62
  and the politico-strategic logic of the struggle for hegemony   123, 135–46, 156, 160–63, 166, 175–76, 190, 193, 197–98, 204–07, 211–12n45, 229, 233, 236–37n127, 244–49, 256, 259,263, 271–72, 276, 285, 303, 308–10, 316, 326, 355–56, 362
  on economic and political struggle   128–30
  on liberalism   140–42, 159, 193, 245, 351–52, 361
  on freedom of criticism   149–60, 290, 300
  on freedom of association   153–54, 160, 290
  on independent organization of the working class   154–56
  on Bernsteinism   157–58
  on legal Marxism   158–59
  on lines of demarcation   140, 146, 160, 167, 173, 233, 256, 255
  on politics as pedagogy   166, 179, 180–82, 195, 243–44, 261–62, 291–92
  on party organization   168–71, 175–77, 188–93
  and centralism   170, 174, 176–77, 190
  on abstract and concrete   107n83, 120, 164, 188–89, 248
  on form and content   191
  on centrism (or Kautskyism)   33, 228, 233, 258, 266–68
  on the peasantry as a social force   28, 106, 205, 207–09, 212, 215, 217–19, 285, 286–87
  on two paths of revolution   28, 217–19, 232–33, 241
  on the soviets   147, 205, 228–29n104, 237–46, 248, 281–86, 288, 298, 306, 309, 312
  on the worker-peasant alliance   6, 9, 28, 205–16, 224–25, 232, 247–48
  on two paths of capitalist development   218–20, 232
  on the nationalisation of the land   208–09, 219–23
  and a political party of the peasantry   28, 225 and n86, 228–29n104
  on peasant ideology   220–25, 232, 312
  and permanent revolution   228–29n104, 229–30n106, 232–33
  on imperialism   29, 35, 75, 254–72, 280, 285
  and Hegel   161–62, 200, 252–56, 314
  on the split in socialism (or in the working-class movement)   29, 254–56, 271
  on monopoly capital   258–62, 264–65, 278
  on the export of capital   261–64
  on uneven development   261, 263, 266, 270
  on parasitism   263–67
  on the labour aristocracy   264–66, 268, 272
  on Imperialist Economism   29, 267–72, 280, 326, 356
  on the self-determination of nations   269–70, 288, 326, 256
  on proletarian internationalism   270–72, 326–27
  on the state   243, 272–79, 281–84, 301
  on dictatorship and democracy   211–12, 219, 221n75, 228–29n104, 241, 285–86, 294–304, 306–07, 311–14
  on the Constituent Assembly   211, 221, 298–99
  on relative and absolute   188, 256, 314
  on the transition to classless society   29–30, 260, 275–77, 284, 289–90, 293, 304–14
  on petty-bourgeois democracy   106, 107 and n83, 268, 272, 281, 286
  What the "Friends of the People" Are and How They Fight the Social Democrats   100–03, 105–08, 110–12, 223
  The Economic Content of Narodism and the Criticism of It in Mr. Struve's Book   102, 103, 105, 110
  Draft and Explanation of a Programme for the Social-Democratic Party   109, 110, 132

INDEX   387

*The Development of Capitalism in
  Russia*   83, 218
*The Workers' Party and the
  Peasantry*   207–08
*The Persecutors of the Zemstvo and the
  Hannibals of Liberalism*   140, 141, 352
A Talk With Defenders of Economism   136,
  350, 355
What Is To Be Done?   26–27, 60, 113,
  115–48, 149–63, 165–68, 171–72, 179,
  182n58, 192, 199–200, 203–04, 226, 248,
  253–54, 271, 290–91, 346–58, 359–62
One Step Forward, Two Steps Back   164,
  189–92, 200
*Two Tactics of Social-Democracy in the
  Democratic Revolution*   201, 204,
  209–12, 214–15n52
*The Victory of the Cadets and the Tasks of
  the Workers' Party*   242–43
*The Agrarian Programme of Social-
  Democracy in the First Russian
  Revolution 1905–07*, 218–220, 222 and
  n76, 228–29n104
Materialism and Empirio-Criticism   14,
  18, 23
Philosophical Notebooks   256
*Imperialism, the Highest Stage of
  Capitalism*   35, 257, 259–60, 262–67
*The Discussion of Self-Determination
  Summed Up*   78, 254, 262, 268–69,
  280, 327
*A Caricature of Marxism and Imperialist
  Economism*   270–71, 327, 356
The State and Revolution   34n8, 35,
  273–79, 281–82, 284, 288, 293n18, 303
Can the Bolsheviks Retain State Power?
  283–84
*The Immediate Tasks of the Soviet
  Government*   302, 304–09
*The Proletarian Revolution and the
  Renegade Kautsky*   33, 35, 293 and n18,
  294–95, 300–02
*Left-Wing Communism, An Infantile
  Disorder*   36, 146
liberal opposition   9, 140, 184, 193, 195, 299
  Kadets   195, 299
  Osvobozhdenie   140, 193, 210, 211, 223
  Zemstvo   140–41, 183, 193, 221

Lichtheim, Georg   38–39n21
Liebman, Marcel   206–07
Lih, Lars   31, 119n14, 120n18, 130n33, 150, 254,
  346–358
Linhart, Robert   260n37, 305n48 and n50, 315
Locke, John   296–97
Lukács, Georg   177–79
lumpen-proletariat   73–74, 280
Luxemburg, Rosa   76, 157, 178, 196
  response to Bernstein   48, 54
  on economic and political struggle   74
  on mass strikes   74, 75, 76, 227
  on Marxist theory and practice   148, 187
  critique of Lenin's *One Step Forward, Two
    Steps Back*   167, 185–87, 196
  on self-activity   148, 185–86, 188
  and hegemony   187
  and Menshevism   167, 185–87
  and permanent revolution   225–27
  and Russian revolution of 1905, 225–27
  on imperialist war   32, 252

Machiavelli, Niccolo   30, 316, 322–26
Makhnovets, Lydia   174
MacIntyre, Alasdair   117, 144
Mao Ze-dong   311n62
Martov, Julius   185, 187
  on socialist consciousness   167–68,
    171–72
  and Menshevism   176–78
  and party membership   173–75, 179, 190,
    192
  on self-activity   203–04
Martynov, Alexander   117, 171, 176, 211n45,
  214n52, 226–27
Marx, Karl   39, 58–59, 61, 81–87, 125, 337,
  342, 345
  on practice   10–11
  on the wage relation   15–16
  on capitalism and Russia   25–26
  and Russian populism   81–86
  and *mir* (Russian village
    commune)   83–86
  and revolution in Russia   81–82, 86
  and historical materialism   38–39n21,
    82–83, 86, 87
  on working-class self-emancipation   61,
    116

Marx, Karl (cont.)
   on bourgeois ideologists   99
   on petty-bourgeois strata   107–08
   on the proletariat as a universal class   109–11, 132
   on capitalist ground rent   119–20
   on the Paris Commune   33, 278, 281, 312
   on the form of universal bookkeeping   260
   on joint-stock companies   261
   on parasitism   263
   on modern industry and the transition to classless society   320
   Contribution to the Critique of Hegel's Philosophy of Right. Introduction   109–11, 132
   Theses on Feuerbach   39, 116–17
   German Ideology   10–11
   Communist Manifesto   81, 99, 107–08, 263
   Provisional Rules of the International Working Men's Association   61
   Capital   38–39n21, 68, 83n6, 119n69, 248n146, 260, 261, 320
   Civil War in France   278, 281, 312, 325
Marxist political party   4, 12, 19, 43
   class character   19, 25, 27, 49, 59, 70–71, 96, 162, 180–81, 183, 186–88, 240, 255, 308, 329
   party and movement   171, 191–92, 206, 234, 236–39, 272–288
   programme   66–69, 109, 330–45, 361–62
   organisation   22, 70, 119, 123, 145–46, 157–59, 165, 173–76, 180, 185–88, 195, 247, 348
   membership   157–59, 173–79, 186, 190–92, 203
   inner-party struggles   115, 154–57, 167, 173–77, 187–94
   and political will   75–77, 161, 198, 323
   theory of the party (see also theory and practice)   77–79, 161, 162, 196–98, 255–56, 272, 351–57, 360–62
Marxist theory   146, 156–63, 248, 255, 354–58
   primordial authentic Marxism   33–36
   "critical" Marxism   37–43
   as theorisation of the irreconcilability of class antagonism   146, 156–63
   and the logic of political struggle   248, 255, 354–58
   as a guide to action   26–27, 36, 146, 150, 156–63, 189, 197, 255, 346, 354–58, 362
   as the standpoint of the proletariat   59–69, 96–97, 107–08, 127
   fusion with the working-class movement   59–69, 98–99, 112–14, 127, 133, 148, 162, 179, 197–200, 347, 353
   orthodox Marxism (or unilinear historical logic)   25, 26, 37–40, 52, 54–57, 69–72, 75, 78–81, 87, 94–96, 98–104, 112–14, 118n14, 123, 132, 162, 171, 179, 195–96, 197–98, 206, 216, 228, 254, 326
Mayer, Arno   300n35
Mayer, Robert   359
Mensheviks (see also RSDLP, factional struggle)   27, 146, 184, 196, 204, 243, 247–48, 285–86, 302
Mikhailovskii, N. K.   82, 111
modern prince   10, 323–29
More, Thomas   62–63
Mouffe, Chantal   4, 10–18
multitude/people   317–22
Münzer, Thomas   62–63

nationalization of the land   208, 209, 219–23, 342
Negri, Antonio   30, 316–22

Paris Commune   33, 251, 276n90, 219–223, 342
parliamentarism   58, 278
Parvus (Alexander Helphand)   225–26, 230n106
peasantry   44–47, 215
   petty-bourgeois peasantry   106, 213, 214n52, 215, 229, 286, 287
   poor peasantry   110, 133, 214, 287
   rural proletariat (also agricultural labourers)   106, 207, 213, 287
   peasant bourgeoisie   106, 208, 215, 285, 287
   peasant committees   208, 221 and n75, 222, 228–29n104
   peasant ideology   220–25
   struggle against landlords   215, 219, 220, 228–29, 287
   political agency   46–47, 82, 85, 89–90, 92, 106–07, 205, 208, 215–17, 223–25, 228–29, 304

peasant political party 28, 225 and n86, 228–29n104, 298
worker-peasant alliance 205–06, 213, 214–15n52, 215–16, 220, 228–29n104, 231–32, 233–34, 244, 247, 281
the people 51, 222–23, 229, 242–43, 279–85, 285–89, 295–96, 303, 322–26
petty bourgeoisie 29, 36, 107–08, 120, 214n52, 225, 230, 232, 242, 266, 268–69, 280, 286, 301, 304, 308
   and populism 92, 100, 106–07
   and soviets 242, 282, 286
   petty-bourgeois democratic opposition 35, 75, 267–68, 272, 281, 299–300
Plekhanov, Georgi 4, 54, 87, 126, 141, 165, 214n52
   critic of Bolshevik strategy 4
   response to Bernstein 54
   on dialectics 80, 87–88
   and *Chernyi peredel* 87
   and the Group for the Emancipation of Labour 87
   and Marxist orthodoxy 26, 80–81, 87, 94–95, 98–100, 101
   on capitalism in Russia 88, 93–95, 105–07
   on concrete and abstract 88
   on form and content 87–88
   on peasant lack of political agency 89–90 and n32, 92
   critic of populism 9, 87, 92n42, 100
   on proletarian political agency (also self-emancipation) 91, 93–94, 96–98
   on proletarian hegemony 26, 81, 93–95, 99–100, 108, 111
   on oriental despotism (also patriarchy, absolutism) 89–90 and n32
   on the Russian bourgeoisie 92–93, 105–06
   on the intelligentsia 95–99
   on Marxist theory and the working-class movement 96–99
   on socialist consciousness 96–99, 108, 171–72 and n21
   on science and the producers 87
   and *Iskra* 165, 175–76, 347
   at the Second Congress of the RSDLP, 165, 175–76, 361

   on nationalization of the land 220–21
   and Kautsky 230
   critic of Lenin's *What Is To Be Done?* 172, 359–60
   and the World War 252, 257
Polan, A. J. 272–73
political agency 3, 21, 23, 54, 77–78, 81, 254n18, 271, 281, 294, 316, 319, 321–22
   and leadership 3, 17, 30, 111–12, 174, 328
   and social structure 21, 25, 26, 54, 82, 110–12, 135–36, 216–18, 327
   and reflexivity 54, 77–78, 204–05, 232–33, 254–56, 271
   of prince/of citizen 324–25
   expressive conception/strategic conception 23, 28, 165–67, 174, 179, 197, 321–22, 326
   mechanistic conception 216–218
   Kautsky and 37–44, 75–77, 232–33, 254–55
   Lenin and 135–48, 232–33, 254–56, 271, 311–14, 356
   Trotsky and 227–29
politics as pedagogy 28, 166, 179, 180–82, 195, 243–44, 261–62, 291–92
populism 83n6, 87, 92n42, 100–01, 106–07, 111–12, 118, 123, 158, 207, 222–25
   Chernyi peredel 83
   legal populism 100, 106–07, 107n83
   Narodnaia volia 84, 173, 220
   Narodnoe pravo 107n83, 223
   Zemlia i volia 173
post-Marxism 10–17, 18, 19, 47–53, 59, 158, 316
Potresov, A. N. 171–72, 176, 185
practical wisdom 3, 162
prerogative 296–97
Priestley Joseph 247–48
professional revolutionaries 119, 146, 168, 170, 171, 173, 206, 346
Proudhon, Pierre-Joseph 59, 126

Red Wednesday (or Hamburg suffrage disturbances) 72–76
republic (or rule of law) 291–97, 318, 322–25
representation/direct action 74, 296, 316, 322–25

revolution   57–58, 200–04, 208, 236, 251, 256, 272–75, 295, 310, 312
   and counter-revolution   9, 30, 210, 211–12n45, 221, 245, 274, 282, 289–90, 291, 298–99, 300n35, 302–03, 325
   reform/revolution   43, 45, 50–53, 56–58, 134, 140–41, 151, 210, 240, 265–66, 269–70, 351–52
   as transfer of power/as social transformation   55–56 and n82, 292, 302
   from above/from below   56
   bourgeois (and/or democratic)   29, 92–95, 103–06, 130, 199, 209–10, 215–16, 217–20, 222
   passive   8–10
   people's   285–88
   permanent   184n64, 225–33
   socialist (and/or proletarian)   29, 91, 55–56 and n82, 100, 268–72, 276–77, 279–85, 288, 292, 302–03, 327
   bourgeois/proletarian (also democratic/socialist)   4, 81, 86, 107, 108, 178, 214n52, 225–29, 230–33, 255–56, 298
revolutionary defeatism   271
Riazanov, David   226–27, 359
Russian Social-Democratic Labour Party (RSDLP)   167, 181, 193–94, 196, 234
   First Congress   164, 351
   Second Congress   165, 172–78, 218n63, 359
   Fourth Congress   178, 217, 242
   membership   173–78
   factional struggle (or Mensheviks and Bolsheviks)   9–10, 27, 165–67, 173–85, 187–97, 209–13, 228, 231–40
   agrarian policy   208–09, 217–225, 234, 311
Russian village commune (or *mir*)   82–86, 88, 222n76

Salvadori, Massimo   34n8
Sawer, Marion   274, 275
Scheele, Carl Wilhelm   247–48
Schmitt, Carl   306n54
science/producers   60–61, 64–65, 68, 99, 112–13, 168–69n8, 342–43
self-emancipation
   proletarian   9–10, 26, 28, 61, 64, 68, 91, 95, 96–100, 110, 116–24, 127–28, 147–48, 166, 351

   of the peasants   222
   and self-activity   166, 194–96
   and self-arming   203–04
   and revolutionary self-government   234–35, 239, 243–44, 248
   as strategic independence   138–44, 196–97
social whole   37n19, 64–65, 131–36, 143–44, 178–79, 290, 354–55
socialism
   as a doctrine (or scientific)   60–69, 97, 124–28, 144–45, 156–63, 274–75, 342–43
   bourgeois   63
   petty-bourgeois   106–07, 219
   authoritarian   292
   state (or police)   96, 201
   Christian   62–63, 67
   democratic   50–52, 55, 57, 151, 266, 292
   utopian (or peasant)   62–63, 64, 89, 92, 100, 106–07, 223–24, 225
   proletarian   50, 57, 62, 63, 64, 67, 97, 108–09, 113–14, 134, 162, 194, 236n27, 240, 300, 347, 354
   objective and subjective conditions of   26, 40–41, 47, 59, 60, 80–81, 98–99, 261
   transition from capitalism to   38n21, 48, 259, 275, 284, 304–10, 312–14
solidarity   68–70, 104, 108–09, 233–34, 237–38, 245–46, 247–48
Sorel, Georges   59
soviets
   in 1905   205, 206, 225, 233–37, 244–46, 282, 284–85
   in 1917   274, 281–85, 306, 309, 312
   and the Constituent Assembly   294–302
   and hegemony   28–29 and n104, 244–46, 285–88
   Lenin on   237–40, 242–43, 248, 304–312
   Mensheviks on   9–10, 234–36, 243–44, 247–48
   Petersburg Bolsheviks on   236–37
spontaneism (or tail-ism)   142, 159, 190–91, 211–12 and n45, 328, 362
Stalin, J. V.   119, 314
   on consciousness   360 and n6
   and divisionists   222, 311
   and peasants   222

and "consciousness from without", 360 and n6
the state   5–14, 34n8, 243–44, 272–79
   as a strategic nodal point in the class struggle   55–56, 140, 198
   withering away   279–85
state form/government form   243–44, 293–94
state power/state apparatus   5–7, 55–56, 105, 276–77, 282–84, 319
Struve, Peter   140–41, 193, 199, 210, 211, 223, 351
Sukhanov, N. N.   284n115

terror   73, 82, 129, 296n25, 299, 328
theory and practice   1–3, 22–24, 35–37, 39, 43–44, 51–52, 64–66, 69, 70–77, 79, 81, 156–63, 188–89, 213–16, 246–49, 255–56, 361–62
Timpanaro, Sebastiano   38n20
transition from capitalism to classless society   6, 8, 29–30, 38n21, 40, 42, 48, 58, 85, 257–61, 273, 275, 276n90, 277–78, 284, 289–93, 304–10, 312–13, 320
Trotsky, Leon (or Bronstein)   4, 178, 184n64, 187
   on "political substitutionism"   119, 182
   critic of Lenin   181–84
   and Plekhanov   90n32
   on self-activity   167
   on party and class/party membership   175
   on permanent revolution   227–30
   and Kautsky   230–31
   centrism of   227–28, 233
   Our Political Tasks   119, 181–84
   Results and Prospects   227–30
Tugan-Baranovski, Mikhail   37n19

universality/particularity   13, 51, 64–66, 71–72, 109, 132, 152, 162, 168–69n8, 299, 321

vanguard (of the proletariat)   22, 26, 71, 104, 110, 128, 132, 136, 144–45, 161–62, 165, 168–69n8, 174–75, 178–79, 188–89, 195–97, 199, 239, 245, 268, 272, 280–83, 288, 308–13, 323, 346–49

Warren, Bill   258–59
Weber, Max   300n35
Wildman, Allan   129–30n33
workers and intellectuals   5, 17, 25, 64, 66–69, 95–100, 115, 116, 119, 126, 137, 139–42, 146, 164, 168–69 and n8, 172n21, 175, 182, 192, 194–95, 238, 355–56, 359
working class
   as "subject position" (or identity)   11, 14–17, 253, 319
   and political agency   45, 54, 57, 69, 70, 75, 81, 87, 93–94, 103–04, 166, 173–74, 227–28, 247, 300, 348–49
   and consciousness   19, 20, 40–41, 45, 69, 91, 95–98, 110, 116–35, 137–38, 181, 184–85, 308–14, 348–49, 356
   unity/disunity of   25, 26, 49–50, 54, 67–68, 69, 70–71, 72, 73, 74, 76, 77–79, 194–95, 228, 265, 268–69, 270–71, 308–314
   as universal class   71–72, 109, 132
   as ruling class   277–84, 303–04
   and Marxism   59–72, 75, 77–79, 99–100, 113–14, 144–45, 146–48, 162–63, 171–72, 200, 237, 353
working-class movement
   political independence   81, 87, 96, 116, 138, 142–44, 145–46, 153, 156, 178, 185–86, 197, 209–12, 241, 244–45, 286, 291
   split in   233, 250–52, 254–55, 266, 271, 275, 289

Zazulich, Vera   83, 87, 176
Zinoviev, Grigorii   4
Žižek, Slavoj   17–22, 253–54

www.ingramcontent.com/pod-product-compliance
Lightning Source LLC
Chambersburg PA
CBHW071145070526
44584CB00019B/2666